Cases in Human Resource Management in Hospitality

Cases in Human Resource Management in Hospitality

Shirley A. Gilmore

Upper Saddle River, New Jersey 07458

Library of Congress Cataloging-in-Publication Data

Gilmore, Shirley.
   Cases in human resource management in hospitality / Shirley A. Gilmore.
  p. cm.
     ISBN 0-13-111983-4
   1. Hospitality industry--Personnel management--Case studies. I. Title.

TX911.3.P4G55 2005
647.94'0683—dc22   2003068923

Executive Editor: Vernon R. Anthony
Executive Assistant: Nancy Kesterson
Editorial Assistant: Beth Dyke
Director of Manufacturing and Production: Bruce Johnson
Managing Editor: Mary Carnis
Creative Director: Cheryl Asherman
Interior Design: Pine Tree Composition, Inc.
Manufacturing Buyer: Cathleen Petersen
Full-Service Project Management: Ann Mohan, Word Crafters Editorial Services, Inc.
Senior Production Editor: Adele M. Kupchik
Senior Marketing Coordinator: Elizabeth Farrell
Senior Marketing Manager: Ryan DeGrote
Marketing Assistant: Les Roberts
Composition: Pine Tree Composition, Inc.
Printer/Binder: Phoenix Book Tech
Cover Design: Jill Little
Cover Printer: Phoenix Book Tech

Pearson Education LTD.
Pearson Education Singapore, Pte. Ltd
Pearson Education, Canada, Ltd
Pearson Education-Japan
Pearson Education Australia PTY, Limited
Pearson Education North Asia Ltd
Pearson Educación de Mexico, S.A. de C.V.
Pearson Education Malaysia, Pte. Ltd

To my husband John,
my daughters Sarah, Gretchen, and Rachel,
my parents,
and my sister Sharon,
who have encouraged me to pursue my professional goals.

Contents

For information about all Prentice Hall Hospitality Management and Culinary Arts titles visit: www.prenhall.com/pineapple

Part 2 Hotels

General

Full Service

Rooms

Preface

Cases in Human Resource Management in Hospitality is designed to provide interactive discussion among class members and the instructor as they discuss problems, risks, opportunities, and alternatives related to each case study. The cases are real-life stories of positive and negative situations that managers have experienced in relating to their employees within the hospitality arena. They are designed to help students develop professional characteristics that can be inherent in their futures as hospitality managers.

The cases are organized by segment and include situations in restaurants, hotels, country clubs, business and industry, healthcare, university/college/public school food services, and other facilities. The cases include both domestic and global hospitality operations with opportunities to explore a diverse workforce.

The textbook provides meaningful case studies on which to center application-level learning in active class participation. Students are required to move from basic understanding to analysis, synthesis, and evaluation of what is presented within each case. Each case includes discussion questions to facilitate discussion. The cases are designed to require critical thinking skills that will prepare students for management careers and allow for incorporating various teaching strategies such as debates, role plays, small- and large-group discussions, written assignments, and presentations. Students are provided the opportunity to grow in depth and understanding as they interrelate their working experiences with analysis of each case.

An outstanding feature of this book is that it is very flexible; educators can pick and choose cases they would like to discuss. Students have an opportunity (if given by the instructor) to peruse the cases and select the ones they feel would be most beneficial to them. Another feature is case studies within the global arena that give students an opportunity to recognize the cultural differences in various countries and how working with individuals in a global setting brings many challenges.

All names and places within the case studies have been changed to protect the confidentiality. Any similarity in name and place is coincidental.

Key concepts include the following:

Leadership problems/absent owners	Managing problematic operations
Communication/non-English-speaking employees	Incompetent managers
	Orientation/training/evaluation/compensation
Selecting employees/managers	
Low employee morale	Insubordination
Turnover/employee productivity	Terminating employees
Empowerment/delegation	Employee/management conflict
Employee treatment (unfair, inconsistent)	Downsizing labor force
	Employment laws, EEOC
Disciplining employees/grievances	Illegal employees
Ethics	Working with employees who are challenged
Cultural/ethnic diversity	
Discrimination charges/sexual harassment	Unionized operations

The cases vary in length as well as in the depth of discussion required by students. Depending on course objectives, these cases can be used with students at various educational levels and within courses related to human resources, management, and strategic management or as part of a comprehensive course that relates the functional areas of the industry. The cases lend themselves for use within the industry by managers and human resources personnel. Students in an advanced human resources management course have pretested and evaluated each case. Responses from students were very positive.

Acknowledgments

I wish to acknowledge Iowa State University, which provided a grant that allowed me to take professional leave to develop a prospectus for the book. I thank Doris Andera, Jamie Courtney, Joan Dolezal, Dan Fuhrman, Sandra Hunter, David Kinney, Bill McFadden, Ilene Thorman, and Frank Tupy for their assistance in developing the case studies. A thank-you also goes to Kathy Killorn and Vickie VanVoorhis, who provided typing assistance. A special thank-you is given to my husband, John, who provided endless support and limitless time in reviewing and editing many cases. Finally, I wish to thank the many students who provided me with real-life situations to enable me to bring each case to life.

Shirley A. Gilmore

INTRODUCTION
How to Prepare for Case Study Discussion

A case study is a written record of a *real-life* situation encountered by practitioners in the course of performing their duties. Unlike other types of stories, a case study does not include analysis or conclusions, but only story facts. The reader is expected to read the story and identify decisions that need to be made or problems that must be solved. The decision maker must consider surrounding facts, opinions, and prejudices that affect decisions. The reader must distinguish between pertinent and peripheral facts, identify plausible alternatives among several issues competing for attention, and formulate strategies and policy recommendations. Analyzing cases provides an opportunity to sharpen problem-solving skills and to improve the ability to think and reason rigorously.

Case studies provide the reader with the following opportunities:

- Develop a variety of ideas to avoid tunnel vision
- Develop skills in analyzing factors, appraising alternatives, reaching sensible decisions, and planning the implementation of the decision
- Enhance verbal and written communication skills
- Develop team skills that reduce judgmental behaviors
- Apply theory to real-life situations
- Be responsible for his or her own learning

The focus of each case study is on the main protagonist, the individual who needs to make a major decision. Typically, the information presented is only what was available to the protagonist in the real situation on which the case is based. Thus, as in real life, important information often is unavailable or incomplete. Because a case study describes reality, it may be frustrating. "Real-life" encounters are ambiguous, and cases reflect that reality. A right answer or correct solution is rarely apparent, and in many instances, there is more than one.

In this textbook, each case study tells a story that unfolds into issues with a human resources management plot. Through active involvement in the case, the reader must assume the role of a working manager to identify problems and develop solutions.

An opportunity to experience the intellectual adventure of risk taking comes to life as the decision maker works with the "as is," not the "might be." A tolerance for incompleteness of information and ambiguity of situations is necessary. There are no real-life consequences for a decision other than from peers and/or the instructor.

Conceptual, theoretical, and analytical skills will be needed in preparation for case study discussion. Information may be obtained from textbooks, outside readings, or personal experiences. To better understand multidimensional issues, case study problems may be broken into understandable parts. Case study analysis provides an opportunity to reinforce theory and help the reader develop critical-thinking skills. During case study discussions, the analysis is presented or communicated to others in a manner that would be used by a real-world manager.

In preparation for class, the student should step into the decision maker's position as he or she:

- Skims the case study quickly to determine the issues and types of information available for analysis
- Rereads the case study very carefully, underlining key facts
- Identifies the goals and objectives of the main decision maker
- Identifies the goals and objectives of other decision makers
- Notes key problems
- Rereads the case study and sorts out the relevant information
- Determines decisions that need to be answered
- Identifies problems, opportunities, and/or risks that the decision makers face
- Prioritizes problems
- Determines alternative courses of action for solving problems
- Evaluates alternatives by assessing the consequences of each
- Selects and supports an appropriate course of action
- Considers appropriate strategies for achieving the desired outcome
- Develops strategies for convincing others of the legitimacy of the action taken

During class discussion, the reader must be able to:

- Make required decisions related to the case study
- Demonstrate the ability to think logically, clearly, and consciously, showing knowledge of appropriate facts, assumptions, and realities

- Present ideas in a convincing manner within a supportive framework
- Demonstrate common sense in selecting relevant information for use in supporting decisions
- Get beyond the basic, concrete facts and view the case study from different perspectives
- Form a well-supported plan of action to use in making major decisions
- Apply analytical and conceptual reasoning to human resources management decisions
- Listen to other class members and critique their positions
- Examine critically other class members' analyses
- Keep an open mind and be willing to change recommendations/decisions
- Identify human resources concepts that will help in preparation for a hospitality management position
- Enjoy the discussion

Cases in Human Resource Management in Hospitality

PART 1
Restaurants

FINE DINING
Actuall
The Dynasty Inn
The Italiano
Le Talbooth
Michelangelo's

CASUAL
Antonio's Bar and Restaurant
The Cardinal Grill
Central City Burgers
CLG Management
The Copperfield Corporation
Deno's Restaurant Chain
El Chico's House
Fish N More
Garden View
Julio's Mexican Restaurant
The Sheffield Diner
The South-40 Family Restaurant
The Uptown Grille

QUICK SERVICE
Chow's Express
House of Fine Pizza
Rockin' Robbins

Actuall

Over the last two months something has begun to change with **Steve Hinge,** Actuall's sous-chef. Steve's relationships with other employees are suffering. His enthusiasm for flawless food seems lost, and his punctuality has even declined (**Fritz Hofbrau,** the executive chef, believes strongly that if an employee is not early, then he or she is late). Now employees are complaining about Steve's behavior. At first, Fritz could hardly believe that the complaints were true and wanted to dismiss them as misunderstandings. Further, these behaviors are puzzling to him because they happen only when Fritz is gone.

Background

Actuall, a fine dining restaurant, opened in Johnstown four years ago. The name Actuall represents the restaurant's dedication to contemporary cuisine. No restaurant like Actuall had ever been introduced into the Johnstown area. Despite Johnstown's having a large state university that accounts for an affluent community, most of the area's "fine dining" restaurants have much to be desired. Actuall can seat 155 guests throughout its three dining rooms, as well as accommodate up to 200 guests in its banquet room.

    Upon entering Actuall, customers are engulfed in the aromas that emanate from the centrally located open kitchen. A white grand piano, located left of the main entry, typically is played throughout the evening by one of the area's many accomplished pianists. On occasion, a cellist or harpist will join the pianist. Due to the owner's love for fine arts, a variety of unique, contemporary artwork hangs on the walls. Actuall serves an average of 150 customers on weeknights and up to 350 on some weekends. Reservations are not required; however, they are strongly recommended. Although no dress code is enforced, it is not unusual for customers to dress in tuxedos and evening gowns, especially those who come directly from the theater or symphony. This elegant restaurant is a delightful surprise to a community that has always longed for a true fine dining restaurant.

During the first six months of business, Actuall was doing very well, and had received tremendous reviews from the various local media. Fritz, the executive chef, had trained at a famous chef school in Europe and worked under several certified master chefs prior to opening Actuall. One thing that Fritz wanted to do differently in his kitchen was to eliminate the "military-like" atmosphere that was so prevalent in his own past. Fritz felt that a kitchen could run efficiently without yelling or instilling fear into employees, as had been the situation he had found himself in throughout most of his career. Fritz made every effort to be approachable and maintain a professional disposition, even in the busiest of times.

The other chefs and cooks are a sous-chef, banquet chef, saucier, garde manger, entrée chef, vegetable chef, and three prep cooks (see the Actuall kitchen hierarchical structure and job summary sheet). All of these people except for one of the prep cooks, have been with Fritz since Actuall's opening and have undergone extensive training in preparation to execute the responsibilities involved in their positions. A well-trained, committed staff resulted.

Training the Staff

When Fritz was approached about opening Actuall, he was concerned about finding enough qualified chefs and cooks to make his menu concept a reality. Some thought was given to bringing in a few key individuals from outside the Johnstown area to ensure success, although this idea was eventually dismissed due to excessive costs. Fritz interviewed twenty people to fill the nine positions that would make up his brigade de cuisine (kitchen staff). The whole process was long and tedious, but it resulted in what Fritz felt could become an excellent staff. Prior to opening Actuall, Fritz worked extensively with each person, taking close note of the person's strengths and weaknesses. After Fritz had finally determined each person's kitchen position, work began on producing each specific menu item. For three long days, refinements of production techniques and menu modifications were made. Finally, Actuall was ready to open its doors.

After the Opening

Rather than opening Actuall to the public, for the first two days each guest was personally invited and was not charged for the meals. These guests were asked to fill out a questionnaire and offer comments based on their dining experiences.

Despite an occasional conflict, the kitchen staff got along very well. They were even known to have a few beers together after work on special occasions (such as on days that had vowels in them). A strong believer in providing good opportunities for communication among his staff, Fritz held kitchen staff meetings.

Actuall's Kitchen Hierarchical Structure and Job Summary

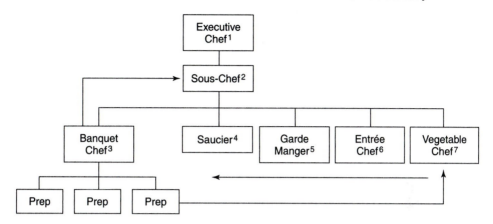

[1]Responsible for staffing, training, scheduling, production, procurement, recipe and menu development, and maintaining profitability of kitchen.
[2]Second in command to the executive chef. Pronounced *soo chef.*
[3]Supervisory position.
[4]Responsible for the preparation of all sauces and stocks. Pronounced *saw-see-AY.*
[5]Responsible for all cold food preparations and all garnishes. Also responsible for service during dinner hours. Pronounced *gar muh-ZHAY.*
[6]Responsible for the preparation of all main course items. Also prepares items during service hours, assisted by the saucier.
[7]Responsible for the preparation of all vegetable items. Also involved with service of vegetables and plate setups during service.

During the first month, Fritz held meetings each week, but as daily routines became more established, meetings became less frequent. Fritz was very pleased to have been able to put together such a committed and professional staff in such a short time. Everything had gone so well to that point that Fritz was beginning to take a few days off, entrusting his reputation as a chef to his staff in absentia.

Most of the credit for trusting the staff's ability to maintain a high level of food quality in the executive chef's absence belongs to Steve, the sous-chef. Steve started with Actuall as the saucier and displayed a real mastery for culinary arts. After Fritz's former sous-chef, Michael, quit due to an irreconcilable dispute with the owner, Fritz decided to promote Steve into the sous-chef's position, rather than bringing in a chef from the outside.

Steve had never attended college nor received any formal education in culinary arts, although he had more than four years of previous cooking experience. Fritz's main concern in promoting Steve rather than the banquet chef (the normal order of promotion) was Steve's lack of experience in managing other employees. Fritz felt confident that Steve could handle the production requirements, but knew that Steve was inexperienced in ordering food and supplies, scheduling employees, and managing crises. Fritz was aware that Steve had insulin-dependent diabetes, but after discussion, they both were confident that this would not affect Steve's ability to do his job. Despite the fact that Steve was admittedly in poor control of his diabetes, Fritz never regretted promoting Steve. All the cooks and chefs held Steve in high regard. Fritz was very grateful for Steve's abilities and played an important role in obtaining a large pay raise for Steve.

Conflicts

Everything continued to go very well at Actuall, and the restaurant rapidly increased its popularity. However, Fritz was becoming aware of conflicts which he needed to handle.

Conflict One

Because Actuall was a seven-day operation, Fritz had begun to take Sundays and Mondays off each week. Fritz has a wife and two children and enjoys being able to spend time with his family. Steve then has Tuesdays and Wednesdays off, allowing for both the executive chef and sous-chef to be at the restaurant on the busiest days of the week. This system worked very well for six weeks; then, bit by bit, a problem began to surface.

Upon returning to the restaurant one Tuesday, Fritz was confronted by **Jay Popp,** a server, with a complaint about Steve. Jay explained to Fritz that on Monday evening about 6:30 he asked Steve to redo a sauce painting for an appetizer he had touched accidentally with the cuff of his shirt. Instead of simply redoing the plate, Steve called Jay an idiot and told him to take it out to the customer. Jay admitted that the damage to the painting was minimal but, being aware of the high standards at Actuall, Jay thought it necessary to point out the problem to the chef in charge. The following Thursday Fritz spoke with Steve about the incident, and they agreed it simply must have been a lack of communication.

Conflicts Two and Three

On the following Tuesday, after returning from a short fishing trip with his spouse and children, Fritz was asked by **Shelly Hsu,** the maître d', if she could discuss a problem that occurred during Sunday brunch. Shelly, who had been working at Actuall for only one month, had been in charge of the dining room during that Sunday afternoon. She explained that Steve had been very rude to her in front of a group of customers. "I simply told Steve that we were running low on salmon, and he nearly bit my head off," reported Shelly. "And then, what made matters worse, when he finally did bring out the salmon, it was a mess. The mirror was dirty, and, well, it just didn't look like it usually does." Fritz was very disturbed by news of this nature, and told her he appreciated knowing about this.

As Fritz was showing Shelly out of the office, he noticed two prep cooks standing outside the door. Fritz greeted both cooks and asked how things were going for them. "Not too good, Chef," replied **Nick Peters.** "May **Jim Meeks** and

I come in?" They told Fritz that Steve had been fifteen minutes late for work on Sunday morning. "It wasn't just being late that bothered us, Chef. It was how Steve treated us the rest of the day. He did nothing but yell and scream all day," said Nick. "We were hoping to get an early start on things, so we were here twenty minutes before our shifts. Nick and I ended up waiting for more than half an hour before we could even get in," added Jim. Fritz was beside himself! He could hardly believe they were talking about Steve.

Confrontation

Fritz had had total confidence in Steve up to this point, but these types of situations went on for four consecutive weeks. Finally, after no longer being able to dismiss the issues as petty or simple misunderstandings, Fritz decided to investigate each incident fully. At the end of the fourth week, he held a meeting with employees involved in the situations. Because Fritz had documented most of the complaints filed against Steve, he was able to recall exact dates and times of the alleged incidents. Fritz addressed each issue by stating the alleged problem, then allowed each involved employee to express his or her interpretation of the problem. By the end of the meeting, Steve had accumulated five official warnings for various types of misconduct. Included in the five warnings were four for failing to meet minimum food standards set by Actuall, and one warning for failing to report to work on time.

Chef's Decision

After the meeting concluded, Steve and Fritz met in the chef's office. Fritz decided to suspend Steve for three days without pay. Fritz also asked that Steve use the time off to decide whether he was still interested in being the sous-chef. Fritz told Steve that if he returned he would need to apologize formally to the employees who were affected by Steve's unprofessional acts.

Discussion Questions

1. Should Fritz have promoted Steve into the sous-chef's position from the saucier's position? Justify your answer based on Steve's work background and other characteristics of the case.
2. If you were Fritz, would you suspend Steve for three days without pay? Justify your answer. If not, suggest alternative methods for addressing the five official warnings.

3. Should Fritz call Steve in on his day off to discuss the problems rather than wait until Steve's next day (Thursday) on the job? What precedents will be established by your answer?
4. If Steve chooses to return to Actuall, what special conditions, if any, should Steve be under? Justify your answer.
5. Do you feel that the meeting held to establish the facts was fair to Steve? Why or why not? Was it necessary? Why? Is there a better way to handle the situation? Suggest alternative solutions.

The Dynasty Inn

Background

The Dynasty Inn is located on the Fox River in the small town of Geneva. The Dynasty Inn is known for its four-diamond, AAA rating for the last eight years, and for its four-diamond restaurant, Atwater's. Eighteen months ago, the hotel opened a new banquet facility with a kitchen and three separate rooms that open into one large room. The three rooms are known as The Creamery, The River Room, and The Rock Springs. The banquet facility can hold up to 150 people comfortably for a plated dinner.

The hotel consists of forty rooms, with seven different room types. At the end of the year, twenty-three additional rooms will open that are featured for the business traveler with boardroom tables, Internet connection, presentation equipment, and suites. Each room is uniquely decorated in a European theme.

Guests who stay at the Dynasty Inn receive the comfort of a cozy hotel along with a fireplace, whirlpool, and minibar in the privacy of their own rooms. The hotel offers a turndown service every night that includes chilled milk and warmed cookies delivered to each room, and in the morning a paper of the guest's choice, along with a continental breakfast in the hotel's lobby.

The hotel's largest moneymaker is the banquet facility, with weddings bringing in the most revenue. The Dynasty Inn hosts ceremonies in its courtyard, which is surrounded by the hotel on three sides and the Fox River on the fourth side. Weddings and other banquet events are new to the Dynasty Inn, and every day is spent improving service and operations.

Management Staff

Paul Peng is the general manager of the Dynasty Inn. He has a bachelor's degree in hotel and restaurant management. His wife works full-time, and they have two children. Paul believes in being at the Dynasty Inn in order to handle day-to-day interactions with his employees and his guests. He prides himself and the hotel on winning the four-diamond AAA award eight years in a row. Paul believes in a participatory management style, and empowers his management team to make executive decisions. This style allows Paul to take off at least one day a week, and also allows his management staff to take possibly two consecutive days off a week. Each morning and night there is a manager on duty, with a rotating weekly schedule. Paul constantly finds himself in the middle of two managers, and deals with it in a subtle way that only seems to cover the problem, not resolve it.

Nicole Landon has a bachelor's degree in marketing and is the director of marketing for the Dynasty Inn. She has been with the Dynasty Inn for the past seven months and came from a great hotel in Chicago, where she was also in charge of the marketing department. Nicole recently married, and her husband works full-time. Nicole takes on the role of head manager when Paul is absent. She feels that it is her role to take care of situations that occur in the hotel, and is often found in Paul's office complaining about other managers and their actions. Nicole's job consists of booking corporate business and room blocks. In order to do this, she designs all marketing material and makes sales calls to potential and current clients to sell the hotel.

Deanne Epstein is the director of catering. She recently was promoted from catering manager. Her new title came with new business cards, but not a pay raise. Deanne has an associate degree in hospitality, and has worked in the industry for thirteen years. Deanne has been with the Dynasty Inn for the last six months; she worked for an independent catering company for ten years before coming to the Dynasty Inn. Deanne's job consists of booking social events and weddings. For the current year, every Friday, Saturday, and Sunday are booked with a wedding, and the weekends for next year are quickly being booked. Deanne spends the majority of her day dealing with brides and their upcoming weddings. A typical wedding consists of the initial consultation, the contract, setting up a date and time to do a meal tasting, finalizing details and head counts, setting up the room(s) the day of the wedding, and managing the wedding. Deanne also is responsible for tracking payments made to the hotel and collecting the balance one week before the event.

Tom Walstad is the executive chef at the Dynasty Inn. He is in charge of Atwater's, the hotel's four-diamond restaurant, along with the banquet kitchen. Tom is married, with no children. He has worked his way up in the restaurant industry, and does not hold any degrees. His job consists of designing seasonal menus for Atwater's and the banquets. He works closely with Deanne and Nicole in selling and marketing the banquet facility. Tom also is in charge of hiring kitchen staff, along with ordering, preparing, and approving food while meeting sanitation codes. He has been with the hotel for two years, and has been noted in several local papers for his uniqueness as a new and up-and-coming chef.

Natalie Mong was hired as the summer intern for the Dynasty Inn. Her job was to work at the front desk a couple of days a week, and in catering and sales the rest of the week. On Natalie's first day, she found herself permanently moved to the catering and sales department. Her job consisted of filing, typing contracts, going on sales calls, and sitting in with brides during their consultations.

The Situation

During Natalie's internship, she found herself in a whirlwind of problems. There were days when the hotel seemed like a soap opera instead of a business. It took time, but as each day passed, Natalie became closer to the food and beverage, catering, and sales staff. Natalie found herself going out for drinks and shopping sprees with managers during work hours. Soon managers confided in her with their feelings and aggravations. Natalie often found herself stuck in the middle of a "he said/she said" conflict.

The goal of the Dynasty Inn was to promote the new banquet facility. Since the opening of the banquet facility a year and a half ago, the management staff had each gone a different way, deviating from the original goal. With each of them going in a different direction and failing to find common ground, service and quality offered at the Dynasty Inn no longer meets the AAA four-diamond standard.

Natalie noted several incidents that occurred during the last few banquet events. With her relationships, she also has become aware of each manager's views.

Incidents

- Recently, a wedding couple requested no nuts in their dinner because of guest allergies. This request was noted on the banquet event order, and was highlighted and mentioned to the chefs. During the night of the dinner, nuts were added to two of the courses, and were discovered, not by the chef or wait staff, but by the bride. The executive chef had already gone home for the night, and the situation was left to Deanne to handle.
- In preparation for the upcoming holiday season, new menus were created for wedding and corporate events. Items for corporate events included executive breaks and gourmet lunches, along with plated dinners. Nicole's job was to sell the food when corporate events were held in the hotel. Lately there have been guest complaints that the food received was not what was ordered.

Nicole decided to investigate the situation, and after she talked to Deanne, Deanne broke down and admitted that for the past several months Chef Tom had not been completely fulfilling the banquet event orders. Deanne mentioned that customer complaints were not as frequent because most of the corporate clients were there for business meetings, and the meeting planner who ordered the food was not one of the attendees. Meeting planners were blinded to the fact that their original contracts were not being followed.

Deanne noted all these problems and tried to handle the situations by having meetings with Chef Tom, but she heard one excuse after another from him. When confronted by Nicole, she summed up the problems and mentioned that either the kitchen staff was replacing food items on the menu or the selections were not offered at all to the guests. Nicole approached Tom in an aggressive manner, and the situation escalated into a heated debate in Paul's office.

Natalie thought each problem was easy to fix. But soon, through her private meetings with each manager, she started to see the hotel unravel.

Management's View

The following are the managers' views on the situation, and their contribution to the problem:

Paul finds himself stuck in the middle of the staff and, while trying to remain neutral, finds most of his days in private meetings with managers. Paul does not seem to approach any of the problems with intentions to solve them. He is constantly calming people and reassuring that the hotel is fine and that there is nothing wrong.

Nicole lately has been absent from the hotel. The entire summer, she spent half of her time in the office talking on the telephone with friends and family, and the other half running personal errands on company time. Nicole views herself as second-in-command, and feels that Deanne needs to tell her everything that happens in the hotel. Nicole works only during the week, and has Deanne manage weekends and events. Nicole mentions situations that happen between Deanne and the management staff that have already been resolved, and causes the situation to arise once again. Nicole, unaware, causes tension between the management staff because of her lack of knowledge on how the banquets and sales offices operate, and her persistent attitude about being involved in every situation.

Deanne found herself in a mess of paperwork when she came to the Dynasty Inn. Jill, the former catering manager, was not organized, and did not have a concept of the banquet business. Contracts that did not cover food costs were being promised to clients. The hotel was losing money on many weddings because the client was quoted the wrong price. Deanne found herself losing money by honoring the signed contracts and trying to figure out a new system to keep new contracts in order. Deanne also found herself in a tough position working in the same office as Nicole. It bothered Deanne that Nicole took off all the time, and she resented Nicole when she acted as if she knew what was going on and stepped on Deanne's toes. Management staff secretly disliked Nicole, but only talked behind her back, as she talked behind their backs to Natalie and Deanne.

Lately, Nicole seemed to be in the office less and started to take more personal days without telling any of the management staff, including Paul. Due to her absence, Deanne was left with handling both the wedding and corporate events, doubling her work and her time spent at the hotel each week. When Deanne signed her contract with the Dynasty Inn, the agreement was for a set pay and a percentage of all events booked. Her contract stated:

- Two days off per week
- Set pay with a percentage of all events booked
- In charge of social events
- Promotion to include an increase in pay

The stated terms currently are not being honored. Deanne finds herself carrying the work of two people while acting as a counselor between the managers and as a personal secretary for Nicole.

Tom prides himself on his culinary ability. With the holiday season approaching, new menus needed to be designed and sent to corporate clients to book holiday parties. Deadlines were made for the menus to be done, but Chef Tom failed to meet the goals of having the new menus designed. Deanne and Nicole found themselves creating the menus and designing the layout to meet Dynasty standards.

A review of comment cards indicated concerns about the quality of the food and service. After further investigation, it was discovered that most items in the kitchen were ordered through a distributor. Standard items, such as soups, breads, desserts, and sauces, were all premade, heated and served to the customer as four-diamond quality. Chef Tom rarely made the food from scratch, and not he but his kitchen staff created the specialty recipes. Chef Tom has also been accused of leaving the hotel early in the afternoon, relying on the kitchen staff to run the restaurant and prep for the upcoming banquet events.

Last week the health inspector made a surprise visit to the hotel, and was preoccupied with Tom and a tour of the hotel while the kitchen staff brought the kitchen up to code. Tom had a taste of how stressful every day is for Deanne with the pressure of the surprise inspection. He found himself scrambling to get the place fixed up, the same thing Deanne found herself doing each day, scrambling to find what the client ordered when Chef Tom was nowhere to be found. Tom did take shortcuts, but viewed them as time savers. There was always an excuse why something was not done, and he failed to step up and admit he was wrong.

Natalie, at the end of her internship, had learned more about how to manage people and problems than about the hotel business. Natalie realized that her summer experience was not uncommon in the hospitality industry, and that it was common to find small problems escalating into large problems. Future employment opportunities are available for her, but Natalie questions her ability to work with friends and the effect it will have on her friendships. To this day, Natalie keeps in contact with the management staff at the hotel, and the problems from the summer still persist.

Discussion Questions

1. Describe the main issues at the Dynasty Inn.
2. What, if any, are the problems with the way Paul is handling the issues with his managers? What would you do differently? Why?
3. How can Natalie avoid being the mediator for the management staff? What is Natalie's role as the intern?
4. As an HR consultant, what suggestions would you have to solve these problems? Describe how you would implement your suggestions.
5. Would you promote socializing between the management staff outside work? Why or why not?
6. If you were Deanne, explain what issues you would take to Paul. Justify the importance of the issues.

The Italiano

As **Gary Adair** walked out of the coffee shop, he was still in a daze after hearing from his former co-worker about the situation at the Italiano restaurant. He hadn't expected that the recent incident he had experienced at the restaurant would make a significant impact on employees and customers.

Mitch Benson had called Gary and wanted to meet for coffee to discuss recent changes at the Italiano. He told Gary that the business had suffered more than a 50 percent turnover because the employees who shared Gary's feelings of betrayal had all resigned. Customers who once dined at the Italiano regularly are not remaining loyal because they do not feel comfortable with the new staff. The "family atmosphere" of which the Martinez family was so proud was being seen as a fluke. Employees also believed that talk of "family" was a front for the Martinezes' true concern—money—and they had left to find employment in one of the three new Italian restaurants that had opened nearby.

Little Italy and Ricardo's are upscale and elegant restaurants like the Italiano and have a similar price range. The third new Italian restaurant is two miles away and has a casual atmosphere. These restaurants have had a significant impact on the Italiano's net revenue. In addition, the Italiano offers classical Italian cuisine with rich ingredients, which are considered high in fat, whereas the competitors have adapted the trend of lighter recipes, which has taken some business away from the Italiano. The owner advertises that the Italiano is committed to bringing the true taste of southern Italy to America.

Background

The Italiano, a ninety-five-seat elegant Italian restaurant, is located in a metropolitan city near the Rocky Mountains. The restaurant's interior, with its polished oak wainscoting, warm colors, linen tablecloths, and fresh flowers, encourages guests to mingle over food with family and friends.

Guido Martinez, the owner, was raised in Los Angeles and opened his first restaurant thirty-five years ago. His work ethic, built as he started at the bottom and worked his way up, helped Guido become a well-known, financially successful restaurant manager. He worked only in what he considered the finest restaurants. Five years ago, he decided to move on to greater and greener pastures and open his own restaurant. The Italiano is open every day of the year except Christmas.

Guido; his wife, **Gina;** their 24-year-old daughter, **Margaret;** and her husband, **Dino Romen,** moved to the Rocky Mountain area when Guido bought the Italiano with his savings. His goal was to staff the restaurant with the best employees. Although Guido had hoped to entice a couple of his excellent cooks to move with him, only **Riley Leno,** who was considered an average cook, moved his family to work with Guido.

The Italiano had a good reputation for its outstanding food and service. An average lunch costs $15 to $20, and an average dinner between $30 and $40 per person. It was the only Italian restaurant within several blocks of the downtown area. The Italiano was known for its low employee turnover. Guido considered himself lucky to be able to retain the seven part-time servers. Expecting business to increase, he added eight part-time servers. The retained servers all had more than two years of experience in fine continental dining room service, so he made that a requirement for new employees. The part-time servers held full-time jobs, and the full-time servers were part-time students at a local community college.

Guido kept two current employees and hired two additional people from the area as kitchen staff who would work with him in food preparation and cleanup. Guido did the early-morning preparation and prepared most dishes from fresh foods he purchased daily. He enjoyed making homemade pastas and sauces. Guido's wife and daughter worked well with him in the preparation of signature dishes.

Guido's son-in-law, Dino, oversaw final preparation and presentation of all food served to customers. Guido was in the dining room seating guests. At first, kitchen employees didn't say much to Dino, but they were frustrated with his lack of knowledge and skills.

Conflicts

Front of the House versus Back of the House

There was a fair amount of tension between the front and back of the house. Within a relatively short time, what began as sharp comments between the two groups of employees became heated nightly conflicts. Much of the tension was related to differences in compensation between the two areas. Back-of-the-house employees believed servers were able to make lots of money because the kitchen staff prepared excellent food to be served to customers. Servers discussed the size of their tips in front of the kitchen staff, sending the kitchen staff into a rage. When the kitchen staff tried to take credit for the servers' successes, the reaction was that anyone can cook and wash dishes. The conflict grew into outright battles with sharp words and loud attacks on each other. When one side attacked the other, the other side would counterattack with more abusive language.

Full-time servers felt far superior, both personally and professionally, to the kitchen staff and in some instances even to the part-time servers. Part-time employees didn't get involved because they knew their job was temporary, and they lacked real commitment to Guido.

Guido was not distressed because he had seen this behavior in his earlier jobs. While living in Los Angeles, he often discussed this behavior with other managers. Even so, Guido wanted all conflict to be brought to him so he could help settle the issues. After a few attempts by employees to discuss compensation issues with him, the employees became disillusioned. Each side of the house felt he favored the other. They maintained he was looking out for himself and the profit that he was expecting to make.

Guido's background had instilled in him the importance of treating his employees like family. Because the atmosphere of the dining room demanded attention to detail, Guido insisted that servers arrive one and a half hours prior to opening to prepare for the evening. He wanted his servers to share in an evening meal with the kitchen staff in a family-type atmosphere. Preparation of this meal was an additional responsibility of the kitchen staff, and as the conflict between the two groups escalated, little attention was paid to how the meal was prepared. In addition, conflict carried over from the day before, and the two groups separated themselves from each other while they ate.

Conflict among Servers

Conflict sometimes occurred within the two groups. Employees often were upset with **Michael Law,** the dining room manager, who had been retained by Guido. However, with direction from Guido, Michael changed his procedures for seating guests, making the servers upset. Part-timers would get upset if they thought Michael was seating large parties with full-time servers. The single men would get upset when they felt Michael was seating more parties with servers who had families. Eventually, the servers held a meeting with Guido and Michael to discuss their frustrations. Although Guido rationalized Michael's method of seating guests, during the meeting all agreed that the seating should be done on a rotating basis. Guido suggested that Michael might pay attention to servers who were busy and those who were not. In the past, when Michael had noticed that a server was not busy, he asked that person to help the busy servers. However, in the end there was no sharing of tips.

Although problems between the front and the back of the house and between server teams continued, the turnover rate remained low. Employees that Guido had retained were still there, and most full-time employees remained because they were still in school. Employees had come to believe that conflicts between and among employees were normal in most restaurants, so it was not perceived as a good reason to quit. However, two full-time students who were majoring in hospitality management quit because they felt that what Guido stood for was against what they were studying in their management courses.

Conflict with Dino

When Michael quit, Guido made Dino the dining room manager. He realized that Dino didn't have the skills needed in the kitchen, so this was an opportunity to move Dino and keep his daughter happy. This decision frustrated many servers because they knew that Dino had no experience in the dining room. This meant that Dino would recruit, hire, train, schedule, and evaluate dining room employees.

After four months as dining room manager, the servers felt that Dino was covering his lack of experience with arrogant comments to the employees. They felt that Dino got the promotion only because his in-laws owned the Italiano and not through demonstration of knowledge. They noticed that Dino lacked commitment to his job. When asked a question, he often ignored it. However, if he noticed some detail out of order, he ranted and raved at the responsible employee all evening. Servers often made comments in earshot of Guido and Gina, hoping it would do some good. Fortunately, customer satisfaction remained high, the result of experienced servers. The servers resigned themselves to dealing with Dino.

Conflict among Kitchen Staff

Besides the dislike for the front-of-the-house employees, the kitchen staff felt frustrated when they had to deal with Guido and his demands. Sometimes he took shortcuts with meals, and what was printed on the menu was not always what was served. It appeared that Guido felt that most customers couldn't tell the difference between different cuts of meat, so if the kitchen ran short of one cut, he would substitute another cut without adjusting the bill. Some employees were affected by this unethical behavior.

Riley also is a bone of contention in the kitchen. Riley has been very loyal and works hard at the Italiano. Because he believes he owes Guido for the favor of making him head chef, he takes pride in his job. Riley doesn't have a culinary degree but has been in the restaurant business for many years. While at the Italiano, he has developed a few recipes with Guido. One specialty, seafood pasta with dill alfredo sauce, has been a hit among customers. The Italiano has received high accolades in several local papers. When Guido suggested to Riley that he felt they should make some changes to the menu to include lighter menu items, Riley's temper flared. He said Italian food is better when it is made with traditional recipes. He told Guido that if the menu changed, he would continue to use his ways to prepare food.

Kitchen employees don't understand why Guido doesn't force Riley to make changes. Employees think business could increase. Often they have heard Guido say, "Being best is not enough; standards must increase to outdo the competition." They wonder why Guido appears to be afraid that Riley might quit.

The Conflict Comes to a Head

It was a very busy night. Both the kitchen staff and dining room servers were extremely busy. Tempers were getting hot. The longest-tenured waiter, Gary, was feeling the pressure when two of his large parties had been waiting too long for their food. When Gary went to the kitchen to ask about his food, Riley overheard his requests. Riley, who caused the most tension with the servers, got extremely agitated and started yelling at Gary. Although Gary had not made his initial comments to Riley, he retaliated with harsh words. He knew it was best to bring Guido in on the kitchen activity. He quickly looked around the kitchen to see if Guido was available and did not see him. Riley mouthed back at Gary, making a comment that suggested Gary was trying to hide under Guido's authority. Gary responded, and the next thing out of Riley's mouth was a threat of physical harm. Gary turned his back to Riley, so he was completely surprised when he was hit in the face by brass knuckles. His face was bleeding and there was a gash above Gary's eye. It appeared to be swelling quickly.

The explosive screams of other employees brought Guido to the kitchen. He asked another server to take Gary to the emergency room. Guido then demanded that everyone, including Riley, return to work.

Gary had several stitches, and was told by the emergency room doctor that he would be fortunate if he did not lose his eye. Gary returned to discuss the incident with Guido. After a lengthy discussion on how Guido would discipline Riley, Gary decided not to press charges. Gary was told that in the meantime he would not have to work with Riley. Gary assumed that Riley would be terminated for this uncalled-for behavior. Gary took several weeks off work, and Guido agreed to pay him for part of the time off as compensation for what happened to him.

Upon returning to work, the kitchen staff told Gary that Riley was still working. Gary approached Guido and was told that no replacement could be found. Gary knew that Alex was capable of being promoted. Gary also knew that there was a high unemployment rate in the area, and that finding additional cooks would not be that difficult. When Gary investigated more thoroughly, he found that Guido had not even advertised the position.

Gary began to question the sincerity of Guido's promise to fire Riley. Guido told him he had not promised he would fire Riley. He said he and Gina had talked and felt responsible for Riley's relocating to work at the Italiano. Gary asked Guido if it was true that Riley had borrowed money from Guido to pay for his moving costs. Guido didn't respond.

The next day Gary turned in his resignation. When Gina read the short letter, she asked him to understand why they had trouble firing Riley. She reminded Gary that he would not have to work with Riley. She also asked Gary to speak to Guido before he left. Gary threw up his hands and walked out of the Italiano.

Gary thought about pressing charges, but decided to get on with his life and forget the legal battle that could go on for some time.

Discussion Questions

1. Describe what could have been done to limit the conflicts between the front- and back-of-the-house employees. Why do you think these ideas would work?
2. Respond to Guido's saying that being the best is not enough, and yet not forcing a change to lighter menus to keep up with trends. Why do you think Guido says one thing and does another? Justify your response.
3. Should employees be treated like family members? Explain.
4. Does the fact that the incident between Riley and Gary occurred in a small restaurant have an impact on how it was handled as compared to a larger organization? Why or why not?
5. Do you think Guido would have handled the incident differently if Riley had attacked a family member? Why or why not?
6. Why do you think Guido decided to keep Riley? Explain.
7. Was Gary's decision to not file a lawsuit a good one? Why or why not?
8. As a consultant, how would you work with Guido to improve employee morale (be sure to recognize that Guido is a proud family man)?

Le Talbooth

Background

Le Talbooth is an original timber-framed house built in 1520 and named for the original tollhouse that stood on the border of Essex and Suffolk. Over the years, it has been enlarged and restored to its present premier dining status. Only changes that are in complete accordance with the historic building codes are executed, thus maintaining a feeling, both inside and out, of "old-world charm."

The timbered exterior hides fully functioning facilities that include a modern and well-equipped kitchen. The restaurant space is divided into the Old Room and the River Room, accommodating seventy-five guests total. A private dining room located on the first floor seats twenty-five guests and is used regularly for meetings and dining. Overlooking the river is a small cocktail bar where guests take appetizers and order their meals. Adjacent to the cocktail bar is a large paved terrace that greatly increases the bar's capacity when the weather is nice.

The building also houses the main offices that oversee the operation of "The Empire" (see the Le Talbooth Group organization chart). It also is the marketing and coordinating center for a newly formed, exclusive referral group of the privately owned country house hotel, The Pride of Britain. In addition to the building, there are four acres of landscaped grounds with terraced lawns that border the river. The grounds are used regularly in the summer for weddings by individuals lacking sufficient space in their own gardens. The river also allows for a unique sendoff for wedding parties, with the groom rowing his bride away. Once the couple goes around the first bend, a staff member from the Dedham Vale Hotel meets the boat and escorts the couple to their car or hotel room.

Le Talbooth Group Organization Chart

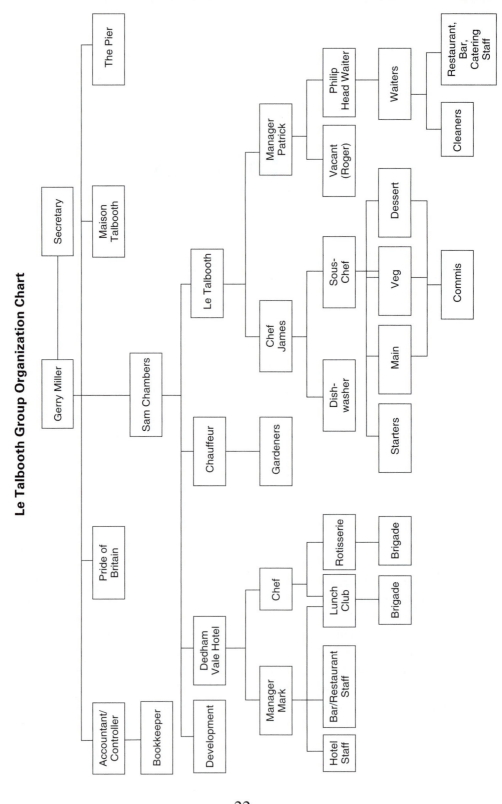

The Le Talbooth Group

Three of four properties in the Le Talbooth group are situated in and around picturesque Dedham in Essex, which was made famous by the painter John Constable. The restaurant, Le Talbooth, provides luncheons and dinners. The ten-bedroom, all-suite hotel, Maison Talbooth, is one mile away. The only food service available at the hotel consists of breakfasts and light meals.

Between these two properties lies the third, the Dedham Vale Hotel. The operation's main feature is its 120-seat restaurant, The Terrace, which is totally different in style and concept from Le Talbooth and is modeled after an ornate Victorian conservatory. The restaurant features the largest indoor rotisserie in England. Sleeping accommodations include six comfortable suites. Guests from both Maison Talbooth and the Dedham Vale Hotel can eat at either restaurant. They are given preferential booking rights, which can occasionally cause problems due to hotel or restaurant front desk oversights or late arrivals on full nights.

The fourth property is a specialty fish restaurant. The Pier is located on the harbor side of a fishing port some fifteen miles away. The restaurant has upper and lower levels; the former, with its superior view, is upscale, while the latter serves more modest meals primarily to family diners.

Personalities

Gerry Miller, owner, patriarch, and mastermind of The Empire, has run the business for thirty years. He is regarded highly by his peers and respected throughout the industry. He has been honored by the queen with the Order of the British Empire, the second-highest honor to a knighthood, for his services to British tourism.

Gerry runs a tight ship and is frustrated easily by staff who can't answer his frequent questions or do not pay enough attention to detail. Due to the high quality and reputation of his products, many prominent businesspeople (and his friends) from a city five miles away are regular customers. He likes to keep a close eye on his business and is involved at all levels in the decision-making process. He is known to reward loyalty, hard work, and honesty, not necessarily in terms of pay, but with respect, trust, and standing.

Gerry and his second wife recently purchased a vacation home on a beach in South Africa. They eventually intend to spend six months of each year there. It is well known that his two sons are earmarked for positions and leadership within the organization. One is still working on a bachelor's degree at a prominent university, and the other works in marketing for a major hotel corporation. However, Gerry very fairly states that they both must earn the respect of his peers (employees) before he will hire them.

Sam Chambers has worked with Gerry for fourteen years. He started as a chef and is now Gerry's right-hand man. Sam maintains very close ties with the kitchen staff, and his uniform still consists of chef's whites over a shirt and tie, even though for the past four years most of his day is spent in the front of the house or his office. He likes to return to the kitchen at service times to run the hot plate. The restaurant has Michelin Star status, a recognition given to exceptional restaurants in Europe. This award was given for Sam's menu and cooking. However, he rarely becomes very involved anymore, preferring to bask in the past and reflect on the glory.

Sam is a Scot with a hot temper and a short fuse. He does not have a college background and likes nothing more than to make a fool of the "educated" restaurant management team in front of the kitchen staff. He consistently is biased toward the kitchen side in any disagreement even though he needs the support of the full restaurant staff.

Often, "just for fun," he will incite the kitchen staff against specific servers and enjoy a laugh at their expense. These incidents often result in tears and service time lost in consoling the injured party. The chip on his shoulder in regard to those with a college education is becoming a problem. Nothing that goes wrong in the course of service is ever the fault of the kitchen staff, and the restaurant manager often publicly eats 'humble pie' simply to appease him.

Sam's wife, a former manager at the Maison, is known for her manipulative character. She always is pushing Sam to make sure he gets his fair share and more of any rewards or honors.

James Heydon, the head chef, has been at the restaurant for three years. He is aware that Sam likes to take credit for the cooking and to a large extent he lets him do so. However, James has a price. Sam's siding with the kitchen in a dispute, free drinks twice a night for kitchen staff, better meals, and more than generous salaries are just some of the items on his list.

Out of the kitchen, James is an amiable person who often socializes with the restaurant staff. However, once in his whites and behind the hot plate, he takes on a more unpleasant manner. Taking orders on a busy night is very trying. The orders are too fast, too slow, too special, and just plain wrong, or for items they have run out of . . . and so it goes. James is a good chef and rightly takes pride in his young, talented employees and their efforts. If only his ego didn't get in the way.

Patrick Smith, the restaurant manager; his assistant, **Mark Davies;** and the head waiter, **Philip Doran,** constitute the upper-level staff in the dining room. It is a known fact that Mark, in Gerry's eyes at least, did not go to the "right" school and does not have the "right" accent. Mark is sure he will never get any further within the company. It is somewhat of a surprise to all when, after the sudden departure of the number one and two people at the Dedham Vale Hotel, Gerry offers the top position to Mark.

Behind-the-scenes talk, however, reveals that the promotion is in fact only one step up from being fired. The Dedham Vale has a reputation as a management graveyard. Mark decides to accept the position anyway, as it will ultimately do his résumé more good.

Mark's departure leaves Patrick and Philip at Le Talbooth. Both have good industry background and went to the "right" schools. They are fair with the restaurant staff and work hard. Patrick has been with the company for eighteen months and Philip for one year. They have a good working relationship, and things are working well, at least for the time being. Normal problems such as a lack of available quality staff in a rural location, the kitchen disputes, and not enough hours in the day are dealt with, but gradually take their tolls.

The Month of May

Le Talbooth has been steadily building clientele and an excellent reputation as a caterer. The catering business peaks in the summer months, especially on weekends, when weddings and parties are most popular. This, in addition to running the restaurant at 80 percent capacity seven days a week, means a full schedule for all. Days off accrue, and everyone is expected to pull their weight and more.

Gerry has heard from his wife that Patrick and Philip are becoming weighed down by all the extra work since Mark was transferred, so Gerry has contacted a former summer intern, **Roger Starling.** Roger is now working in London as a restaurant manager but is looking for a change. Sam does not approve of Roger's hiring because he feels that the new threesome with their academic advantages will make his life harder. Roger is hired by Gerry anyway and will start at the beginning of June.

Sam always acts as the figurehead in all events and parties once Gerry has made initial contact. Sam then delegates everything, except the credit, to Patrick and Philip. Sam lacks tact and diplomacy, and he leaves much to be desired in terms of organizing. However, he is a good chef, clients regard him as second-in-command, and he has been at Le Talbooth for some time.

In fact, it is Philip and two dedicated full-time waiters who enjoy a challenge and do all the planning, ground work, and moving of heavy equipment. Many nights, after the restaurant has slowed down, Philip and one waiter will be found in the office preparing for an upcoming event. Still later in the evening, former teammates Philip and Mark will be found in the restaurant manager's apartment, discussing the latest events and crises. They also try to solve some of the logistic headaches of staffing and catering.

Luckily, there always has remained a close rapport between Le Talbooth and the Dedham Vale staff. The Dedham Vale staff is thankful that the Le Talbooth staff has to deal with Sam and Gerry most of the time. This factor alone helps make the Le Talbooth staff turnover the highest of the four properties. Other contributory factors such as the higher level of business, more exacting guests, and more stressful conditions play their parts, too.

Although Patrick and Philip enjoy their work and will give 120 percent effort and time, they feel it is unfair that the kitchen staff still gets two days off each week. Sam always delegates the cooking side of the catering to the Dedham Vale and Pier restaurant kitchens because James, the head chef, refuses to become involved in this side of the business, another part of their bargain. The only involvement James allows is for one sous-chef to coordinate the food and make the centerpiece item or a specialty dish that will receive more notice and credit.

There are several big parties in the next few weeks, some in the Le Talbooth gardens, but the majority of the parties are at private homes. It is very crucial that everyone work together to succeed.

By chance, while walking in the village one afternoon, Philip sees a planning application on display, which is a legal requirement. Closer inspection shows that the application is for a new restaurant in a converted schoolhouse approximately a five-minute walk from Le Talbooth. He strolls down and investigates further. Imagine his surprise when he finds that the names behind the application are none other than Sam and his wife.

Discussion Questions

1. How should the situation of unfairness among restaurant employees be treated? Why?
2. Evaluate Mark's transfer. Was it the right decision? Justify your answer.
3. If you were Philip, what would you do, knowing that you have stumbled on an obviously secret plan of Sam's to set up in direct competition? Defend your actions.
4. If you were Gerry, what would you do if you found out about Sam's plan? Justify your actions.
5. How would it affect your decision making if you knew that James, a sous-chef, two other key members of the kitchen staff, and two wine stewards were planning to leave with Sam?
6. Describe threats, opportunities, and problems that face the restaurant. How would you take advantage of the opportunities? How would you handle the threats and problems?

Michelangelo's

Background

Bob Dansbury is a recent graduate of a hospitality management program at a state university. He has eleven years' experience in the restaurant business. During eight of these years, Bob served as a cook; he recently gained chef status by completing the chef standardization exam. He spent two years working as a bartender and one year as a server. Throughout his career, Bob has been included in management decisions and served as an interim manager in both the front and back of the house when permanent managers were away or ill. Bob was interested in the challenges of front-of-the-house work and getting away from back-of-the-house operations. Bob's research to advance his career consisted of numerous newspaper classifieds, friendly suggestions, and career day for employment. The advertisement most appealing to Bob appeared in the Sunday classified ads:

Front-of-the-House Manager
Michelangelo's

Position available for a front-of-the-house manager in independently owned restaurant. Must have excellent customer/employee relations skills, strong leadership qualities, and a positive attitude. Cost control is necessary. Résumé required. Call (123) 555-1234.

Bob contacted the owners, filled out the application, and was asked by **Jack Whitmore** (co-owner) to interview one week later. **Thomas Burch** (co-owner), who held the first interview, was quite short with Bob, holding mostly to experience and ability. The second interview was with Jack. Jack asked similar questions

27

to those of Thomas, with some mention of personal aspirations and goals, and he showed great interest in Bob's college degree.

During both interviews, Bob asked questions related to topics such as employee satisfaction with Michelangelo's, customer expectations, frequency of menu changes, the executive chef, and the mission for the restaurant. The two owner/interviewers gave similar answers except for the mission. Jack spoke of the "independently owned Michelangelo's," while Thomas spoke of the "multi-unit Michelangelo's." Bob took the reference to type of ownership as a grammatical error on the part of the two managers. Two weeks following the interview, Bob received a call from Jack saying he had been accepted at Michelangelo's. Bob was ecstatic about the opportunity and quickly accepted the position. Bob has been the front-of-the-house manager for the last two months.

The Restaurant

Michelangelo's is an independently owned restaurant located along a major river in the eastern part of the state. The restaurant is a contemporary-themed fine dining establishment. Michelangelo's seats sixty people at capacity and is open from 5:00 P.M. to 10:00 P.M. Monday through Thursday, and 5:00 P.M. to 10:30 P.M. Friday and Saturday. Sales have been around $1,200,000–$1,300,000 per year, with approximately 70 percent of sales from food and 30 percent from liquor. Sales traditionally have remained high due to low turnover and inelastic price points on menu items. The business has shown minimal gains in sales, check contribution margin, and nightly volume.

The Owners

The two owners, Jack Whitmore and Thomas Burch, were longtime college friends who wanted to go into business together. They are both graduates of the same university; Jack from the hotel, restaurant, and institution management (HRIM) program and Thomas from the college of business. They developed the classy, casual, fine dining restaurant with each owner supplying equal capital to the business. In the past two years, they have developed separate business philosophies and beliefs on how the business should be run. The differences in opinion have transcended business relations into personal perceptions about each man.

Before Bob's arrival, the two rarely were seen together at the restaurant on the same evening. They contacted each other at the beginning of the week to discuss who would run the restaurant for each evening and who would carry on with peripheral management duties (marketing, purveyor selection, new site selection possibilities, and so on). However, they couldn't agree on the quality of each other's work. Jack would manage operations and Thomas would call three purveyors for new linens. Thomas would manage operations the next evening, and Jack was to follow up on Thomas's work. Unfortunately, Jack wouldn't agree with the choice of purveyors Thomas had selected and called new purveyors. Interestingly, both owners used a participatory management style of leadership and engaged employees rather than telling them how to do a task.

The owners decided to hire a front-of-the-house manager to relieve them of operation responsibilities so they could concentrate on expansion of future Michelangelo's units in the surrounding areas. Bob was hired for this position.

New Management

Jack introduced Bob as front-of-the-house manager to employees at the first meeting after his hire. He announced that the position was created to relieve the owners of that responsibility. Thomas wasn't around for Bob's introduction. Those employees who favored Jack picked up on Bob as "another Jack" and seemed relieved; those who were for Thomas reacted negatively. Bob briefly noticed several negative looks from employees and regarded those looks as being common reactions to "the new face in management."

Unfortunately, Bob's first two months of work have been a continual downward spiral. The two managers refuse to relinquish any hold on operations to Bob. Thomas shows up and provides constructive criticism and insight into how *he* would handle situations. The next day, Jack arrives and provides more on-the-job training and some insight on how *he* would handle the situation. Unfortunately, the two often contradict each other in practice. Bob wonders how the restaurant stayed organized at all.

Bob began to see problems unfold before his eyes as to why the restaurant had reached a plateau in business and was now inevitably failing. The current employees seem normally competent and reasonably good at their respective positions. Half of the employees are "better off" in their socioeconomic standing in the community. Both their aesthetic beauty and personal material goods are at a higher level than those of the other half of the employees.

Thomas's personal belief is that aesthetic beauty and the quality of material goods people surround themselves with transcends into work habits and ability. Thus, Thomas indirectly favors those employees who were more beautiful and had nicer things. The other half of the employees, seemingly not in Thomas's favor, ran to Jack for approval. Jack immediately embraced those employees without knowing their apprehensions about Thomas's philosophy. The subject was never made public and soon forgotten.

Employees would go only to the owner in whose camp they felt they belonged. For example, a server who couldn't get the section he or she wanted from Jack would wait for the next evening when Thomas would manage. If a cook wanted an employee-discounted drink after the shift and Thomas wouldn't uphold the policy, that employee would ask Jack the next day for the drink. Inevitably two factions developed in the employee ranks. When Jack works, the Thomas-bound employees are upset and their service efforts diminish, while the employees who favor Jack and his management style are generally happy and give good service. The following day, the employees who favor Thomas put forth quality, efficient service, which seems to contradict their efforts from the previous evening, while employees in Jack's camp work less efficiently and do not care about their rapport with guests.

Soon Bob began adapting a "balance between the owners" methodology at the restaurant. He took good ideas he found from each owner and applied them to work. Each owner became very upset when Bob ignored his ideas though they obviously contradicted those of the other owner. An example of when they contradicted each other is related to closing time. Jack believed in closing the restaurant early, for variable cost purposes, if no additional guests showed up within thirty minutes following the last guests' arrival. Thomas believed in following the hours printed on the door, so that the restaurant stayed open until the very end.

Bob was unsure of his future with Michelangelo's. He could quit, but he feared the negative effects on his brief résumé. He could stay and grind through contradictory managerial styles and two factions of employees with whom he had little or no credibility. Finally Bob worked out a list of weaknesses he had observed to give to Thomas and Jack; he wanted to tell them about his observations about the restaurant, but he didn't quite know which owner to approach. Bob's list was as follows:

- Micromanagement by the owners
- Lack of formal training for new employees
- Lack of identification of a standard mission for employees and management
- Lack of identification of business policy/rules/procedures to govern day-to-day operations
- Employees going over Bob's head to Thomas or Jack, following a request by Bob when the employees do not agree
- Favoritism by the owners toward individual employees, causing a division among employees
- Continual and progressive customer dissatisfaction
- Continual and progressive product deterioration
- Employee theft
- Lack of teamwork as a result of owner favoritism toward a "type" of employee

Discussion Questions

1. What criteria should be used for preparing a job advertisement? Why would they be important?
2. Evaluate the operation of Michelangelo's under Jack and Thomas. What changes would you suggest? Describe how you would implement these changes.
3. Identify any forms of bias in the case. Describe the impact.
4. Whom should Bob approach with his list, Jack or Thomas? Why?
5. How would you, as the new front-of-the-house manager, remedy the problems? Be specific.
6. Can Michelangelo's succeed? Why or why not? What must happen to improve employee morale? Explain.

Antonio's Bar and Restaurant

Background

Antonio's is a fifty-year-old prestigious and popular bar and restaurant located downtown in a large midwestern city. **Pete Espinosa,** the owner and executive chef, inherited Antonio's ten years ago from his late father, Antonio Espinosa. Pete grew up in Antonio's and after his father died, he worked extremely hard for the next two years to keep Antonio's reputation; this schedule eventually contributed to his divorce.

For the past eight years, Pete has become more of an absentee owner, although still retaining the title of executive chef. Pete is somewhat of a playboy, hanging around with his buddies in the limousine business, and is seldom at the restaurant, keeping both infrequent and irregular hours. Antonio's has many long-term "family" employees, with very low turnover, and many regular customers. The restaurant has consistently made a profit through fifty years of economic boom-and-bust cycles, all restaurant equipment is paid for, and the building's landlord is a cousin of Pete.

The Staff

Carl Rodriques, the sous-chef, has been employed at Antonio's for more than eight years. Carl is Pete's right-hand man and is well paid for the work that he performs. Carl holds an associate degree in culinary arts, which he earned while working at Antonio's, and is qualified and authorized to run the kitchen as he sees fit. He is somewhat arrogant, however, and continually boasts (when Pete isn't around) that *he* should be executive chef, or at least have his name mentioned on Antonio's menu. Pete holds great admiration for Carl and the kitchen crew.

Carl is an overgrown kid, but nevertheless is an excellent worker, and is highly respected by all Antonio's employees for his ability to get orders filled quickly and correctly. Carl does have a wild side to his personality and has been known on occasion to exhibit a bad temper. This often happens when food is brought back to him or when he is confronted by servers, especially new trainees. Carl has been known to intentionally "heat up" those very servers' plates for them, thus "reinforcing" his authority as commander-in-chief of Antonio's kitchen.

Carl is well known for his never-ending, long-winded stories of partying at the local nightclub with his fellow workers, **Don Kelly** and **Leo Martinez,** the two A.M./P.M. cooks. Don and Leo are basically Carl's fan club and personal cheering section. They will do anything that Carl asks them to do at and outside work. In turn, Carl sticks up for his kitchen crew. Due to his tenure, he believes he has free access to the bar, especially after busy nights. Carl has an agreement with the bartender, Isaac, that he will trade the kitchen's "mistakes" (many times more than one) for the bartenders' "mistakes" (again, usually more than one per night). Carl will then drink some of the "mistakes" and give the extras to Don and Leo, getting them primed up for the later evening's debauchery out together down at the local headbanger's club.

As the person in charge of purchasing, Carl has been known (and seen) to take restaurant food and purveyors' samples home. However, because of his position, temper, and colossal ego; everyone turns a blind eye to his follies.

A few part-time kitchen prep/pantry employees assist with production and dishwashing. Because they are immigrants and don't know much English, they remain quiet and keep to themselves. Each one works very hard, and all are very grateful for having gainful employment in such a well-known restaurant.

Todd Martinez, the full-time night dishwasher, rounds out this cast of kitchen employees in his own unique way. Todd is Leo's older brother and a Vietnam veteran. Todd was involved in plenty of combat during the war, and suffers from shell shock. His wages are subsidized by the government, much to Pete's liking, and he fulfills an EOE clause as well. Todd is a fast worker, but he has a rather standoffish attitude that can devolve quickly into a rage when confronted or corrected. Loud noises also can set Todd off, so most folks from the front of the house tend to avoid him at all costs. Todd is also a drug dealer. Carl, Don, and Leo all partake of Todd's "services" and admire his rogue attitude and military stories.

On any given evening, many of Todd's friends (non-employees) will come in and out of the back door at will, which is located right next to the dishwashing area. Todd will then take the trash out, which he does several times a night, many times taking several 30-minute breaks, leaving a good share of the work for his part-time helpers, who again, keep quiet and work hard. After his break, Todd comes back and proceeds to wash the dishes at an extremely fast pace, often accidentally dropping silverware and occasionally breaking glasses. Although nobody would ever dare bring it up, it is rumored that Todd and Carl swap food and liquor for drugs and/or cash.

Isaac Cruse, the head bartender, has worked at the restaurant for almost eight years, and is in charge of the bar's upkeep, promotions, and all the ordering of beer/wine/liquor for the restaurant. Isaac has a B.S. degree in hotel and restaurant management (HRM) and has had experience bartending both in the hotel industry and on a cruise ship. Isaac receives kickbacks from his vendors through promotional beer/wine/liquor items. He now has more than sixty-seven bottles of assorted cordials, thirteen cases of beer, seven cases of wine, and six cases of liquor at home in his basement.

Isaac also receives kickbacks from Lucy, the head cocktail server, by giving her up to fifteen free drinks a night without ringing up the charges. Lucy, in turn, pays Isaac an additional 15 percent tip out at the end of the night, on top of his usual 5 percent, for a total of 20 percent. Isaac also receives monthly kickbacks from the sous-chef, Carl, in the form of three beef tenderloins in exchange for two bottles of Carl's favorite Scotch. Isaac also has a taste for drugs, which the kitchen helps out with as well. Isaac makes up to $200 an evening from wait staff tip-out as well as skimming from the cash drawer at the bar. He often gives his regulars at the bar a few drinks for free, and they, in turn, give Isaac larger cash tips.

Lucy Silvermen is the head cocktail server and has worked at Antonio's for more than five years. She has a B.A. degree in marketing and is dating Isaac. Lucy is well-liked by the bar patrons, but some front of-the-house staff members are quietly suspicious why Lucy always seems to make the most money each night, averaging $50 or more than other servers. Lucy occasionally "covers" for servers who have too many tables, those who want to take the night off, or those who call in sick. Some of her former customers still ask for her to wait on them.

Lucy got her start at Antonio's as a server, at which she was very successful, eventually working her way into the bar about two and a half years ago. Due to lucrative pay and the bar atmosphere, which she prefers, she has more or less assumed the role of the only "official" cocktail server at Antonio's, although she requests help on busy nights. Lucy also covers as bartender for Isaac on his days off, knows how to do both the ordering and purchasing for all bar items, and regularly does the bar staff scheduling. Other servers are scheduled in as relief or second cocktail servers/bartenders on a part-time basis.

Susan Petri was the assistant manager for more than four and a half years. She just finished her master's degree in HRM and is excited about her future. She was hired seven years ago as a server, and quickly worked her way into the assistant manager's position. When B.J., the former restaurant manager, left abruptly one month ago to take a maitre d'hotel position in a downtown Chicago restaurant, Susan was promoted to manager due to her hard work and longevity with Antonio's. She is now under pressure from Pete to fill the vacant assistant manager's position within two weeks, preferably from within Antonio's.

The assistant manager's position is really nothing more than a glorified server position; responsibilities include closing duties (keys issued) and dropping the night deposit at the bank, one block away. A nominal hourly pay increase is included for the individual promoted to assistant manager; however, he or she can still wait tables and earn tips.

Susan's responsibilities include scheduling, table assignments, ordering for the front of the house, and overall accountability for servers. Pete comes in midway through lunch and midway through the evening to "z-out" the servers and pay them their charge tips. After the last server is "z'ed out," Pete leaves, never staying around for very long. Pete never stays until closing, leaving closing tasks to the restaurant manager or the assistant manager. Susan has been extremely busy with learning the ropes of her new position. Therefore, one week has slipped by, and she has not done anything about hiring an assistant manager.

Before Susan became restaurant manager, she considered herself "one of the family." Not a "party animal," she would, however, discreetly hang out and have one or two drinks with the restaurant crew after hours at Antonio's bar. Susan and Lucy are good friends within the work setting, and Susan is acutely aware of some of the goings-on between Isaac and Carl, as well as Todd's little circus. Susan does not participate in any of the theft or corruption at Antonio's, nor has she had any reason (until now) to be concerned about it. In fact, she often has thought of the "goings-on" as hearsay.

Jill Whitmore has been working at Antonio's for almost five years as a server. She is number two in seniority of servers behind an elderly woman, **Flo Ray,** who is now only working part-time. Flo is semiretired, and her feet give her problems from her many years as a server.

Jill is currently working on her master's degree in HRM, so therefore she looks up to Susan (who has a master's degree in HRM) and always gives her best effort at work, constantly exceeding employee expectations. Jill is recently married, with no children, and always leaves work promptly after each shift, never staying around to "have one" with the crew at the bar.

Jill gets along fine with everyone at Antonio's, but she believes in keeping work and play separate, which everyone understands and respects. Jill, an "up-and-comer," consistently performs as the top server. She has successfully implemented many procedures and ideas she has learned along the way from her continuing schooling. Jill prefers to stay clear from the restaurant gossip, and is very "by-the-book" and businesslike, never bad-mouthing anyone, but instead maintaining a firm but friendly countenance. She seldom talks about her personal life and keeps herself busy during her entire shift. She really can turn on her charm for Antonio's patrons, and has many customer requests for her service when reservations are taken. When it comes to the pecking order with her fellow servers, she is the informal leader due to her strong work ethic, helpfulness, and quiet but firm leadership style. Although she has taken both wine and purchasing classes, she doesn't have any real bartending experience.

Hiring the Assistant Manager

Both Jill and Lucy, who are friends, have applied and interviewed for the assistant manager's position, and are equally capable of "holding their own" with other employees. Jill remarked in her interview with Susan that the assistant manager's position would really help her with her master's degree and that, if she was hired, the experience would be "just like you did it, Susan" (referring to Susan's past experience both in graduate school and as assistant manager). Susan respects Jill's educational aspirations.

Since *her* interview, Lucy has been hinting to Susan that she will do a good job "when she is hired," and that she will "make things run smoothly" for Susan. Lucy is aware of Jill's interest in the assistant manager's position, and feels that because of her own bartending experience and her slight tenure (two months) over Jill that she is the most qualified person for the position, and makes her opinion publicly known to other restaurant employees. There is a general feeling among Antonio's employees that either Lucy or Jill will get the assistant manager's position, and this has become a hot topic going through the restaurant's rumor mill.

Employees are beginning to take sides and becoming polarized by choosing either Jill or Lucy as *their* vote for assistant manager. Each side have said they will quit if "their candidate" is not selected. Jill and Lucy haven't had any personality conflicts in the past, but this situation has definitely brought out Lucy's aggressive, competitive side. Jill has remained discreetly quiet about her opinions on the matter, even when pressed by her co-workers, changing the subject quickly or finding "busy work" to do.

After careful consideration, Susan has determined that from the pool of applicants and subsequent interviews, Jill and Lucy are the two finalists most qualified for Antonio's assistant manager's position. No one from the outside ever applied or interviewed for this position; in fact it wasn't even advertised, by Pete's request.

Discussion Questions

1. What is the major problem of this case? Defend your answer.
2. Would you hire Lucy or Jill? Justify your decision. What about hiring someone from the outside? Justify your answer. Should Susan have placed an advertisement anyway, against Pete's wishes? Explain.
3. What are the pros and cons of hiring Lucy or Jill? Are any problems associated with hiring Lucy? How about Jill? Justify your response.
4. How does Susan's promotion affect her management decisions that she will have to make in her new job? Justify your response.

5. Evaluate the assistant manager's responsibilities. What would you change, if anything? Why?
6. If you were Susan, how would you handle the overall situation at the restaurant? Explain.
7. If you were Carl or Isaac, would you fear any repercussions of Susan's promotion? Why or why not?

The Cardinal Grill

The Cardinal Grill is located within the Outback Club, a very popular local health club located in a suburb of Phoenix, Arizona. The suburb has a population of 30,000, with 90 per cent retirees.

The Cardinal is a full-service restaurant and lounge specializing in southwestern cuisine, but with a variety of menu selections. In addition to the restaurant, employees are involved in catering parties, hosting receptions, and working with the club management to provide food and beverages for various club functions. A newer sister restaurant located thirty miles away (about an hour's drive) in another suburb is under the same general manager (GM).

A major goal of the restaurant is to provide quality products with superior service at a price the average customer can afford. The philosophy is to go beyond what the customer expects. If possible, the staff will do anything, within reason, to make customers' dining experiences truly memorable.

The Cardinal has a staff of thirty-eight people, including ten floor and twenty-one kitchen employees, two bartenders, a kitchen manager, a floor manager, two assistant managers, and one GM. During the slower summer months, all employees' hours are drastically reduced, causing a great deal of tension between managers and employees. The tourist season begins in October and business increases drastically, as do employee hours, thus eliminating most tension between staff and management.

The Staff

Barb Anderson, the current GM, has worked at the Cardinal for the past seven years. She was an assistant manager for three years before becoming GM for the first Cardinal. Most recently, she was named GM for both operations. Lately, she has been spending much of her time at the newer location, so the assistant managers are covering most of her responsibilities. Barb doesn't have any problem with this arrangement, as she believes in participative management and likes to give her assistants the added responsibilities. She is well liked by her assistants and the hourly employees as well, and she trusts them to uphold the work ethic of fairness and honesty.

That is why Barb is confused about the theft of money from the safe on New Year's Eve. It was a busy night and the revenue should have been large. Was the money misplaced? Who would have taken it? These questions were on Barb's mind as she tried to put together the pieces of the missing money.

Donna Smith has been an assistant manager for three years. Before coming to the Cardinal, she was a bartender at another restaurant. Her management style is different from Barb's style, and she often doesn't implement Barb's decisions because she likes things done her way. However, she does have a fairly good relationship with the other employees. She encourages employees when they do a good job by complimenting them in front of others. She also takes time to point out problems by talking to employees privately and helping them establish goals to correct the problem.

Donna received one month of training and is the one who assists Barb with the financial reports. She has been involved in hiring and firing employees. There have been rumors that Donna uses drugs on occasion. Donna is being transferred to the new Cardinal to assist with the restaurant.

Richard Edwards has worked at the Cardinal for five years as assistant manager. He is not very popular among hourly employees because he often passes his responsibilities onto them. He usually goes along with Donna's decisions. He was fired at his previous job for theft and was unemployed for four months. Barb is not aware that Richard was fired from his last job. She gets along well with Richard, and Barb has no problems with Richard's work.

Curtis Tyler has been the kitchen manager for the past two years, having been promoted from cook, a position he held for four years. Curtis is very efficient and sometimes intimidates the kitchen staff. As long as they follow his orders, everything seems to run smoothly. Three years ago, the company paid for Curtis to enter a drug rehabilitation center, where he stayed for two months during the summer. Barb welcomed him back because she trusts him as an employee, and customers give many compliments about the food and beverages served at the Cardinal. He has stayed clean for the past three years, but rumors are circulating that he has started again. Barb is unaware of any drug use, because it doesn't take place on the premises and doesn't seem to be affecting Curtis's work performance. Curtis also is being transferred to the new Cardinal. Curtis has been dating Donna for about one year.

Sarah Utoff, the floor manager, graduated from a four-year college with a degree in hospitality management. She gained many management skills during a six-month internship at the corporate office of a restaurant chain during her junior year. Sarah worked at various positions in the restaurant chain and worked as a supervisor for three months. She understands the jobs and challenges of employees she supervises. She has been at the restaurant only three months. After one month of training, she was placed in charge of the front of the house. She is involved in hiring and firing wait staff, hosts, and bussers. She has seen low productivity in the wait staff and other kitchen employees. She has heard employee complaints abut Bill Buchman, the executive chef. Employees respect and work well with Sarah.

Bill Buchman has been the executive chef at the Cardinal for six months. He graduated from a well-known culinary school and was hired for his excellent culinary talents. He was a sous-chef before coming to the Cardinal. He won many awards during school and as a chef, which attracted the owners to him. Bill has made the restaurant very profitable; however, he has a reputation for being verbally abusive, arrogant, and demeaning to Curtis and the rest of the employees. He is not open to any suggestions.

Lora Brody has been the sous-chef for about three months. She graduated at the top of her class from a local cooking school, but has very little work experience. She came with strong recommendations from her instructors. She has become a favorite at the Cardinal because she has a very positive attitude. Barb sees one problem with Lora. She does very well with familiar tasks but falters when presented with new tasks. This upsets her greatly and her work performance suffers. It becomes obvious that her motivation decreases also.

Investigating the Theft

As the four managers left Barb's office, Barb tried to piece things together. Neither Donna nor Richard had checked the safe that morning, and neither Curtis nor Sarah had any reason to enter the office. However, because the door was unlocked, anyone could have entered the office. The office was across the hall from the restrooms that employees and customers use.

Barb had so much faith in her employees that she couldn't imagine any of them taking the money. It would almost be better to think that a customer had taken it. Barb would feel better, but it was also unlikely. She knew she had to question her employees, but she didn't know where to start.

Last night Barb was overseeing a large party at the newer Cardinal, but felt comfortable with her managers running the evening at the older Cardinal. The restaurant was only open until 10:30 P.M., a common closing time for a restaurant serving retired customers. Almost all employees were scheduled to work that evening, with some leaving before closing. Employees who stayed to clean up celebrated in the bar after the work was done. Both assistant managers were there, and everyone had left by 1 A.M.

On New Year's Day, the Cardinal was open at 7:30 A.M. for breakfast. Two cooks arrived at 6 A.M., each having a key to the restaurant. As the morning employees arrived, the cooks let them in because the assistant manager on duty wasn't coming in until 8 A.M.

Barb showed up at the Cardinal shortly after lunch, and went directly to the office safe to check the night deposit. When she reached the safe, she found it unlocked, which wasn't unusual. The door to the office had a broken doorknob, so it had not been closed lately. Upon opening the safe, she was surprised to discover that the nightly deposit was not there. According to the receipts, there was approximately $12,000 in sales from the night before. When Barb called the assistant manager and kitchen manager into the office, they were equally shocked to learn that the deposit was gone. Together they had placed the deposit in the safe before they left but had not checked it that day. Then Barb called the other two managers into her office.

Discussion Questions

1. How would you handle the complaints about Bill's personality flaws? Defend your response.
2. What steps would you use to help Lora with her lack of experience and decreased motivation and productivity? Does lack of experience affect decreased motivation and productivity? Why or why not? Are decreased motivation and productivity related? Explain.
3. What steps should be taken during the job search to ensure that the best person is being hired for the job? Would these steps have changed your decision to hire Bill? Why or why not?
4. How should the scheduling problems (busy versus slow seasons) be handled to avoid conflict? Why do you think this will work?
5. What options does Barb have concerning the missing deposit? What are the pros and cons of these options? If you were Barb, what would you do? Why?
6. What security measures should Barb implement to prevent theft? Defend your response. How should she implement them?
7. What changes should Barb make in decreasing these types of problems in the new Cardinal? Why do you think these changes will work?
8. How should Barb deal with workplace rumors regarding employees' personal lives? Why did you suggest these actions?
9. Should all managers use the same management styles? Why or why not?

Central City Burgers

Central City (CC) Burgers is one of five restaurants owned by Camelback Corporation. Camelback also owns Camelstop, a large chain of restaurants in a four-state area of the Midwest. Due to the success of the Burgers theme, Camelback is in the process of expanding by remodeling and converting the Camelstop restaurants into Burgers restaurants. The original CC Burgers is located in a midwestern college town, while the other four Burgers restaurants are located in a neighboring state.

The management team at CC Burgers consists of a manager, an assistant manager, and a shift supervisor who is able to work approximately forty hours a week. In most Burgers restaurants, there are two part-time shift supervisors who each work approximately twenty hours a week. The chain of command goes from manager to assistant manager to shift supervisor. The manager reports to an area supervisor who is in charge of all five Burgers restaurants.

Each member of the management team has scheduled shifts when he or she works without other management present. A typical shift for management team members would be for one management person to open the restaurant around 10:00 A.M. and work until after the early evening rush. The other management person would come in a little before 5:00 P.M. and stay through closing. This type of schedule enables two management personnel to always be working over the busiest time, 5:30 P.M. to 7:00 P.M.

CC Burgers is a family restaurant with a seating capacity of ninety-eight guests. The restaurant is open seven days a week: Sunday through Thursday from 11:00 A.M. to 11:00 P.M. and Friday and Saturday until 1:00 A.M. The restaurant is seldom completely full unless there is a community activity such as a sporting event or a concert, when there is usually a long waiting list of customers to be seated.

CC Burgers employs almost all part-time help. Once in a while, a full-time server will work during the day shift. Of the part-time help, there are fifteen to twenty servers, five to seven cooks, and two to three dishwashers. Many employees are college students, several attend high school, and occasionally an older adult will be a part-time employee working for a little extra income.

The Staff

Larry Sullivan, the area supervisor, has been with CC Burgers since it opened fourteen years ago. He started as a cook, worked his way up to management, and eventually was promoted to area supervisor. Larry has an HRIM degree from a four-year university that he attended while working at CC Burgers. He is very efficient, and he knows what he is doing. All employees like him because he is easy to get along with, and he shows that he cares about them. Larry is far from a pushover, however. He knows what he wants done and what goals he wants the restaurant to accomplish. He visits CC Burgers only once or twice a month because he seems to spend most of his time at the other four Burgers restaurants that are in the same area of a neighboring state. When Larry visits a restaurant, he carries around a pad on which he makes notes related to how each situation is being handled. Before Larry leaves the restaurant, he talks to the management staff and lets them know what he has seen and how he thinks things can be improved.

Devin Kraminer is the manager of CC Burgers. He has held this position for almost seven years. Devin has a high school education. Previous to his employment at CC Burgers, Devin worked for a quick-service national burger chain for over eight years. A well-kept rumor is that he was fired from this previous job for sexual harassment. There are many reasons Devin is not liked by most of his employees. He has a very abrasive personality and is very stuck in his old ways. He does not like the idea of changing procedures, even if the change would be beneficial to the restaurant. Devin also has a bad attitude toward customers and most female employees. There have been many instances where he has yelled at a female server and brought her to tears. It is not unusual for Devin to talk poorly about an employee to one of the "regulars" or in front of other employees.

There also have been several instances when Devin has been in the back of the house talking poorly about some customers who are in the restaurant. He usually comments or makes gestures about some physical characteristic of the customer. These comments have been quiet enough so customers aren't aware of what Devin is saying or doing.

Because Central City is a college town, many different groups visit the town and use the college facilities. On many of these occasions, the groups come to CC

Burgers to eat. Devin gets very upset because the restaurant will be full, and everything is hectic for a while. At these times, he has been known to complain and talk badly about these situations and the customers. Devin probably believes he is talking quietly enough so he cannot be heard. But in reality, some customers have heard him.

Devin is in charge of making the schedule, so he takes advantage of these hectic times by not scheduling himself to close at night or work late on weekends. Devin works only day shifts, and most of the time during the day he can be found sitting and talking to regular customers who come in for coffee. If he is not talking to anyone, he sits and reads the newspaper, getting up only when the phone rings or when he has to greet a customer at the door. Devin is not worthless, though. He does some ordering, and the people in the corporate office do read a profit on the bottom line every year. He also is well known in the community for his involvement in using the restaurant for charitable functions. For the past seven years, Devin has been very involved with a group of hobbyists who meet in the restaurant and support the restaurant's theme. Devin's public relations skills have proven to be very beneficial to CC Burgers.

Will Stuart is the assistant manager. He is a very hard worker and is well liked by most of the employees. Will also has only a high school diploma, but he wants to further his education someday. He previously worked at Burgers in another state for about three years before quitting to move to the East Coast. After a couple of years on the East Coast, he came back to the Midwest and was rehired at his old job. He was working as a shift supervisor when he was asked if he would be interested in relocating as assistant manager at CC Burgers. Will took the job and has been the assistant manager for over a year. He is very energetic and has lots of enthusiasm for improving CC Burgers. He cares about his job and the employees who work for him.

Will and Devin clashed from the start because of their opposite attitudes. Devin does not care for his job and does not like change at all, and Will is all for change if it is going to improve things. Because of his dedication to his job, it is not unusual for Will to be at the restaurant for many more hours than he was scheduled to work during the week.

Don Paulson, the shift supervisor, has a college degree from a four-year university in an unrelated field. While attending college, Don worked in the residence hall foodservice department. Previous to his job as shift supervisor at Burgers, Don was a cook for a national hotel chain. He and Will are close in age and believe in the same management style. Don is a hard worker and expects his employees to be hard workers as well. He believes there is room for fun in the workplace, but only if the work is being completed in an acceptable manner. Just like Will, Don is well liked by the rest of the employees. In the time Don has worked for CC Burgers, the assistant manager job has been offered to him twice, but he turned it down both times. Don has no intention of working for CC Burgers for a long period of time.

The Problem

Don had been at CC Burgers for almost a year when Will was hired as the assistant manager. Will was taking the place of an assistant manager who was promoted within the company. Right from the start, Will and Don got along, and Will and Devin did not. Further, Will and Don had the same ideas. They wanted to make CC Burgers the best it could be. They had many ideas on ways to improve and increase business, but whenever they brought them to Devin's attention, nothing happened. The three would have weekly management meetings where all ideas, problems, and solutions would be discussed. But the next day, when it was time to implement the solutions or new ideas, Devin would not change anything. Devin went so far as to cancel weekly meetings and have only one or two meetings a month.

One situation that showed Devin's resistance to change was when Don told Devin it would be a good idea to change an abbreviation used on guest checks. Two abbreviations the servers were writing looked very similar to each other. Many times there would be confusion in the kitchen when the cooks read the guest check. Because they could not decipher which abbreviation was being used, they did not know which item to prepare. Sometimes cooks would guess and prepare the wrong item, thus wasting food. Other cooks would wait to catch the server to confirm the food item to be prepared; this resulted in decreased productivity. On many occasions, this led to an argument between cooks and servers. Don went to Devin with an idea to change one of the abbreviations, but Devin did not give the idea a chance.

Will and Don were getting very frustrated with Devin because he did not want to make any changes. CC Burgers is well known for its ice cream desserts and drinks. Although there are many different flavors on the menu, occasionally a customer would ask for a flavor that was not available, such as cinnamon or marshmallow. The server would always have to tell the customer that CC Burgers did not offer that flavor. The servers would repeatedly tell Devin that some customers were requesting these flavors, but Devin would do nothing. Some customers even went so far as to bring their own cinnamon to the restaurant to be used to flavor their malts. Still Devin did nothing about ordering cinnamon or any other new flavors.

What really frustrated Don and Will was how Devin would act when Larry would stop in to check how things were running. Every time Larry was present, Devin was a different person. His whole attitude would change, and he would try to be the best manager possible. He would treat employees nicely and act professionally with the guests. Employees started joking that they knew when the corporate people were here, because Devin was a totally different person. Then as soon as Larry would leave, Devin would be back to his normal self. On Larry's next visit to check on the restaurant, Don and Will would tell him that Devin was being impossible and had a bad attitude. But whenever Larry was present, Devin would put on his act and fool Larry. The result was always the same; Larry would never do anything about Devin.

Many times Don and Will would discuss what they could do about Devin. They were really getting fed up with the situation. By now Don had been at CC Burgers for well over a year, but had received a total raise of only forty-five cents per hour. Every time he talked to Devin about getting a raise, he was told that someone from the corporate office would have to approve it, and that the raise could only come in a maximum of twenty-cent increments. None of this was true; it was just the way Devin had done it for the past seven years. In fact, Don had gotten twenty- and twenty-five-cent raises.

Another thing that bothered Don and Will was that they always had to work the closing shifts. Devin only worked day shifts, and he scheduled Don or Will to work all closing shifts. To make the situation worse, Devin would not put deliveries away the day they were delivered. He would leave everything stacked in dry storage and say that he did not have time to put it away. As a result, Don or Will would have to find the time to put deliveries away at night. Not only did Devin not work the night shifts, he scheduled himself to work when he knew the restaurant was not going to be busy. He avoided shifts when he knew there were major events at the university. He also would understaff the restaurant when he was not working. His theory for doing the schedule this way was that he had put his time in at CC Burgers for the past seven years, and now it was time for him to take it easy.

Devin was taking everything a little too easy. Recently there was a fire at CC Burgers. The restaurant had to shut down for over a week to clean up from the fire and do extensive remodeling. The fire occurred when Devin was on vacation. During the cleanup, Devin stopped in a couple of times and snickered at the fact that he was on vacation and did not have to help. Not only did the employees resent the way Devin acted, but many corporate people who were overseeing the remodeling thought poorly of Devin's actions. Larry even asked where Devin was during a visit to see how cleanup was progressing.

Another incident that upset some employees happened several years ago. No current employees at CC Burgers witnessed the incident or even worked when the incident took place, but the employees have heard the story from previous workers. **Teresa Smith,** a shift supervisor who had worked for CC Burgers some time ago, filed a sexual harassment complaint against **Brad Sheldahl,** a fellow shift supervisor. Devin did nothing about this complaint except to question Brad. Devin then refused to believe Teresa and denied that Brad had done anything wrong. When Larry investigated, however, he found out what really happened, and Brad was terminated immediately. Teresa was awarded a $10,000 settlement, and Devin received no reprimand.

Discussion Questions

1. What would you do if you were in Don's position? In Will's position? In Larry's position?
2. Should Devin be allowed only to work day shifts? Explain. If not, who should ensure that he is scheduled for other shifts? How should the changes be implemented?
3. Do you think that Devin is just "burned out" from his job? Explain. Is there any way to keep a manager from becoming like Devin? How? If not, why?
4. Did Devin handle the sexual harassment complaint properly? Explain. What should Devin have done about the complaint? What is a manager's responsibility when dealing with a sexual harassment complaint?

CLG Management

Background

Partners of CLG Management Inc. own and operate two restaurants in a popular midwestern tourist area, The Rothenberg (RB) Restaurant and Stonebrook (SB) Restaurant. CLG Management Inc. was formed in 1980 with **Cliff Thompson, John Pierson,** and **Grace Koehn** as partners. In the agreement, Grace was named president of the company and general manager (GM) of The RB; Cliff was named vice president of the company and GM of SB; and John was designated treasurer, in charge of some management at RB and all company benefits, and would oversee the search for further development opportunities (see the CLG Management Organization Chart).

Four years ago, after a series of lengthy disagreements among the partners, Grace and John bought out Cliff's shares. Because John was busy with his duties and Grace had her hands full operating The RB, **James Mills,** who had been with the company for twenty years, was named GM of SB. James had started as a grill cook at SB; after graduating five years later from a community college with a two-year degree in hospitality management, he was hired as manager.

The Rothenberg Restaurant

The RB is part of Vacationer's Inn and was built in 1971. It has won numerous awards, including awards from RGH Hotels and Resorts (Vacationer's Inn's parent company) for the highest food-to-room sales ratio in the Midwest and the nation. It has a very loyal following of local customers. The RB consists of four different operations: Kaffee Haus, a family-style dining room, banquet facilities, and the Village Pump Lounge.

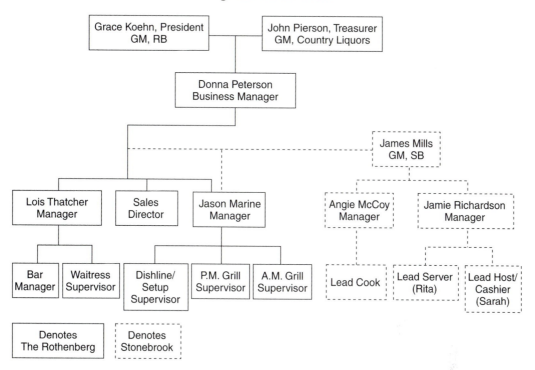

**CLG Management, Inc.
Organizational Chart**

The Kaffee Haus, open from 6:00 A.M. to 10:00 P.M., can seat up to 125 people with a menu of plated dinners, soups, sandwiches, and à la carte items. The family-style dining room, open from 5:00 P.M. to 10:00 P.M., seats up to 135 people and has a family-style menu where guests choose the meat entrée and are served the seven all-you-can-eat side dishes. The banquet facilities for 450 people consist of four rooms on the main floor and meeting space on the second floor for 230 people. The Village Pump Lounge opens at 5:00 P.M. daily and closes around 11:00 P.M., but the hours depend on the amount of expected business for that night.

The RB management structure consists of four managers: Grace (the GM), John, Lois Thatcher, and Jason Marine, who rotate shifts throughout the week. Grace also tends to all the food procurement for The RB. In addition, John continues to manage benefits for the company and is GM of Country Liquors, a liquor store purchased by Grace and John three years ago.

Lois Thatcher handles all front-of-the-house scheduling, including bar tenders, wait staff, and cashiers. She has been with the company since the mid-1970s and is very close to retirement age. Employees find her very hard to please. She is very curt in how she asks for things to be done and is seen, most of the time, as a "slave driver." She seems to have the attitude that an employee gets paid for the work done, so saying thank you is not necessary. On the other hand, she knows what needs to be done to make the company succeed and will stop at nothing to achieve that goal. She is a very dedicated, loyal company employee who always is looking for ways to improve the establishment.

Jason Marine was hired as a manager three years ago after graduating with a B.S. degree in hospitality management. He started with the company seven years ago as a prep cook at SB and eventually worked in all the positions there. After doing an internship at The RB, he was hired as a full-time manager upon graduation. Jason is responsible for all back-of-the-house scheduling, including prep, salad, and grill cooks for both dining rooms; dishwashers; and banquet setup crews. He also is responsible for sanitation and administers the ServSafe® exam to eligible employees. In addition to his manager's duties at RB, he runs a shift at SB about once a week to cover days off, vacations, and so on. Most employees see Jason as one of them, so they feel comfortable talking with him about their problems with the company and know that he will try to get something done about it. However, he is relatively new to management and is a "greenhorn" as far as other managers are concerned.

Stonebrook Restaurant

SB was built forty years ago in a growing town of two thousand people. SB is located right off the interstate five miles from The RB. While it has always relied on interstate traffic as a major part of its customer base, it also has a very loyal following of local customers. To this day, between 9:00 A.M. and 10:00 A.M. or 3:00 P.M. and 4:00 P.M. the coffee shop will be filled with farmers and retirees discussing the day's news and gossip. SB is open daily from 6:00 A.M. to 10:00 P.M.

About ten years ago, SB and the surrounding area got a major economic boost when an outlet center located right across from SB. This was good news and bad news for the restaurant. Not only did it bring with it hundreds of thousands of tourists every year, it also brought two major fast-food concepts. The mall offered hundreds of jobs, creating a labor crisis in the area and one of the lowest county-wide unemployment rates in the nation. Yet SB remained the only full-service family restaurant in the immediate area.

One thing very distinctive about SB is that the employees are very close-knit, almost like a family. This is good in most instances, but can be bad. For instance, four years ago a waitress was hired whom the employees did not consider part of "the family." Consequently, they banded together against her to make conditions so unbearable that she eventually quit.

The management structure of SB is much the same as The RB. In addition, the managers consist of James Mills as GM and Angie McCoy and Jamie Richardson as assistant managers. Also, Sarah Weiss, a full-time host/cashier, sometimes covers a shift as manager in an extreme emergency. John and Grace do not really care for this idea, but realize that there are times when she is needed.

James acts as SB's liaison to Grace and John. When the partnership was formed, Grace and John decided they would use a "hands-off" approach with SB and allow Cliff full control over the establishment. They continued the approach when James became the GM.

Angie McCoy has been with the company for nearly twenty years. She worked her way through college by working at SB, and after graduating with a political science and history degree, she was hired as an assistant manager. Angie was a fairly effective manager and, for the most part, had good rapport with employees. She knew the company like the back of her hand. However, some employees felt that she was lazy and did little to help them. For example, unlike all other managers, she would do little to help clean and reset tables during busy spells. Angie also has a very temperamental personality; one minute she jokes around with employees, and the next minute she is their worst enemy.

Angie also had great respect for Cliff and was very unhappy about his buy-out. She rallied a number of SB employees against John and Grace. When the partnership was formed, Angie spread lots of propaganda about The RB employees and management, causing SB employees to be resentful about RB employees. So when she needed their support, she had it because her employees disliked RB employees and management.

Another example of Angie's disloyalty happened three years ago when Grace and John hired a consulting firm. Angie went against any programs that were implemented as a result of the consultants' suggestions. The consultants suggested that Grace and John have management meetings for the entire management team. During a meeting, it was decided to put in another line of supervisors who would report to the managers. It was hoped that this would take some of the burden off the main managers. These supervisors would be on an incentive-based program and would not be given hourly raises, a fact that was repeatedly discussed and agreed on by all managers. Yet when the positions were put in place, Angie took it upon herself to give all employees who were in these head positions a raise to $11/hour. In some cases, employees received at least a $2/hour raise. This created a mess, not only for John and Grace, but also for employees who were put in the middle.

Angie also had a problem keeping company information confidential. There were times when company issues were the talk of the coffee shop customers, especially when Angie was working. She also had a tendency to tell customers, if they stepped on her toes, what was on her mind. Often these customers complained to John and Grace about her behavior.

Jamie Richardson has been with the company for about fifteen years. She had no formal education, but worked her way up to assistant manager. She started out as a waitress and proved to be one of the best. Upon returning from a maternity leave, she was offered a management position, which she accepted with enthusiasm. James considered her his "right arm," often commenting that he didn't know what he would do without her. She was just as likely to be found in the office working on her schedules as she was helping the dishwashers get caught up, and she even attempted to fix the dishwasher when it broke down. Employees respected her for that and recognized that she was a major part to the success of the restaurant.

Some employees felt that Jamie favored certain employees who worked under her, such as her two college-aged children and her sister, Sarah. Jamie occasionally was wrapped up in company bashing with Angie. She usually came in on the tail end of it and followed, never leading the pack like Angie did.

The Problem—Part I

Two years ago, James made it known to Grace and John that he would be leaving the company in two months. John and Grace had approximately one month to find his replacement. To add fuel to the fire, speculation around The RB was that Jason would soon be leaving the company to go back to school to get a master's degree, yet John and Grace knew nothing for sure at this point. They wanted to move fast, as they wanted the new manager or GM to train with James as long as possible. Besides James, Grace, and John, Jason was the only one who knew about James's leaving, and they wanted to keep it that way until a formal announcement was made. Jason was told of James's leaving as an enticement to keep him. John and Grace appreciated his longevity with the company, educational background, and loyalty to them.

John and Grace thought that because the SB staff was so close-knit, they would have to promote from within the company. They feared that SB employees, unhappy about them selecting an outside person, would quit. In this difficult time and tough labor market, a company of this size in this type of community would be hard pressed to find new employees. They decided to continue in much the same management fashion after James left; it was not an option for one of them to take over SB. They were highly committed to The RB and Country Liquors. It might be possible that Grace could offer assistance from off premise, but she could not manage regular shifts there.

The owners discussed moving Jamie, Angie, Jason, or Lois into the GM spot. They questioned whether that was a good decision. Who would it be, if any? If they moved a current manager into the GM spot, they would have to hire another manager, whether from within or outside the company. If they didn't promote someone, then they would need to bring in a manager who might be able to take the GM spot in time, after earning the SB employees' respect.

Three employees being considered for the manager's job (not the GM) are Sarah Weiss, Rita Kahler, and Paul Marine.

Sarah Weiss is currently the host/cashier coordinator at SB. She is Jamie's younger sister. She started as a cook while in high school and is skilled in all aspects of SB. Recently, she has been having problems at home, and it is speculated that she is considering moving to a town forty miles away to be with her husband, from whom she had been separated for three months. She has been known to do what Angie tells her and is very biased against The RB.

Rita Kahler is the server coordinator at SB. She started at SB right out of high school and worked there before moving away. She has been at SB since returning ten years later. She always is willing to help out and work extra hours to get the job done. She has never cooked, and often has stated that she wasn't really interested in learning the job. She too has the SB mentality about The RB and tends to back Angie.

Paul Marine started working at SB when he was 15 and worked through every position, except for manager. After high school he earned a two-year degree in small-business management from a local business school. After his marriage, he moved away and was forced to quit at SB. He worked as a kitchen manager in a small café in the northeastern part of the state before becoming a manager for a pizza chain. Two years later, he and his wife moved back to the area, and he went to work for Lancaster Inn as a dining room manager. Lancaster Inn has a good reputation as a family-style restaurant and is The RB's only major competitor. Two years ago, he became the human resources manager for Lancaster Inn, the position he currently holds. Grace and John considered calling the Lancasters for a reference, but they knew that the owner was quick to jump to conclusions and would rather fire someone before he or she had the opportunity to quit. They didn't want to place Paul in that position. If hired, Paul would have his work cut out for him because he was no longer considered part of the "SB gang." Paul is Jason's older brother. However, the two would not be working together on a day-to-day basis.

Discussion Questions

1. If you were Grace or John, what is the first thing that you would try to do? Explain.
2. If you were Grace or John, what options would you be willing to consider? Support your answers.
3. What is your opinion about family members working together? Are there any dangers when this happens? Explain. Are there advantages? Explain.
4. What additional information would aid you in making a decision about whom to hire as the GM or as a manager? Explain why this information is important and/or necessary.
5. What is your decision on personnel changes? Explain. Describe how you would implement your decision.

The Problem—Part II

The first thing John and Grace wanted to find out before making any decisions was whether Jason was going back to school. As they had discussed, they approached him about possibly becoming the new GM of SB. After much thought, Jason decided that he was going to pursue his master's degree.

Grace and John then decided that the only person to whom they could conceivably offer the GM position was Jamie. They considered Angie, but decided that given her track record, they would not feel comfortable at all offering her the GM position. Grace and John wanted to keep the offer quiet until Jamie made a decision. They were afraid that Angie would be mad about the offer to Jamie and quit.

Grace and John met with Jamie and offered her the position on Thursday afternoon. Jamie decided she wanted the weekend to think about it. Grace and John agreed, telling her that Angie did not know anything about the job being offered to Jamie and they would rather keep it that way. Later that afternoon Angie called **Donna Peterson,** CLG Management's business manager, and asked what the vacation policy was and how much they would pay a manager if he or she quit with several unused vacation days. Angie had accumulated vacation days from previous years and did not want to lose them. Donna explained that according to the manager's contract he or she would be paid for only fifteen days. Approximately ten minutes later, Angie called back and gave Donna a list of twenty-two days on which she wanted to take vacation, mostly during October, leaving her with fifteen remaining vacation days for which she would receive pay if she left.

Later that day, James informed Grace and John that a notation on the calendar for October 4 read "Angie—give 30-day notice." This, of course, had Grace and John very concerned. They later found out that when Jamie returned to SB, she cornered Angie and told her that she was offered the job. However, Jamie later turned down the job, citing personal reasons. Grace and John realized that Jamie had not kept their request to tell no one of the offer. In hindsight, Grace and John thought that Jamie's decision was probably for the best.

Discussion Questions

1. Should Grace and John even consider going with no GM? Why or why not?
2. Evaluate the idea of using three managers, who are all on the same level, with Grace overseeing them and directing the restaurant from afar? Justify your answer. If you do not like the idea, whom should they hire to fill the vacant GM's position? Why? If you like the idea, whom should they hire to fill the vacant manager's position? Why?
3. Should the "hints" that Angie is giving be considered? If so, what should Grace and John do about it? If not, qualify your answer.
4. If you were one of the owners, what would you do? Explain.

The Copperfield Corporation

The Copperfield Corporation began operating twenty years ago as a single restaurant, but has since opened up two other properties (Baron's and CJ's) within the same community and currently is working on a new project. Throughout the history of the corporation, there has always been the same philosophy and attitude: "Everyone is family, both customers and employees." All employees are treated with respect and are provided with a great place to work. The management teams work hard to provide a fun and friendly place in which to work. Employees at Baron's and CJ's have become friends and hang out with each other outside work.

Ryan Edwards

Ryan Edwards, a bartender, has worked at Baron's for more than two years. Although he had never worked in the hospitality industry before, he was hired as a bartender and received the proper training. He soon became the best bartender at Baron's and was well liked by all employees, managers, and owners. Ryan is very opinionated, and it has been rumored that he can have a very bad temper if provoked. However, it is obvious that he genuinely likes his job and is dedicated to the company.

    Julie Keller has worked at Baron's longer than all other servers. She began hosting at age 16 and eventually became one of the top servers. After four years, she still enjoys her job and her relationships with other employees. Julie has been Ryan's friend since he began working at Baron's; they clicked at the start.

The Door Incident

Ryan had been working at Baron's about six months when he decided to spend his day off drinking with his girlfriend. They started drinking around 5 P.M. and continued throughout the evening. After hitting a few bars, Ryan and his friend decided to visit CJ's. Upon their arrival, **Dan Cjaikowski,** the manager on duty, immediately noticed that Ryan was drunk. Dan instructed the bartenders not to serve Ryan any drinks. When Ryan tried to order a drink and was refused, he began to yell at the bartender, saying it was "bogus" that he couldn't get served. Immediately, Dan got involved and asked Ryan to leave. Ryan became irritated, pushed Dan, and told him he couldn't believe that he was being treated like this, because they both worked for Copperfield.

Finally, Dan talked Ryan into leaving by suggesting that he try another bar. Ryan left through the front door, but half a block away he snapped and became outraged. He turned around, walked back to CJ's, and kicked the front door as hard as he could, shattering the stained-glass window. **George Conrad,** the sous-chef, went outside to talk with Ryan and determine what was happening. Ryan didn't appreciate George's concern and punched him. They wrestled around the front of the building and into the street for about five minutes. Ryan left when they were told the police had been called.

The next day Ryan was called into the office of the two owners. They conveyed their anger about his actions, explained that this behavior was unacceptable, and fired him.

A Few Months Later

Ryan had another talk with the owner and the general manager at Baron's. After an hour of talking, the owners decided to rehire Ryan as long as he promised that his previous unacceptable behavior would not be repeated. The owners cautioned Ryan that if he did anything remotely out of line, he would be fired on the spot. Ryan paid for the door repairs.

The owners rationalized that Ryan was their best bartender; he had apologized to them and all others who had been involved in the "door incident" for his behavior. Of course, everyone had heard about the incident and was genuinely curious about the situation. It eventually blew over and basically was forgotten.

A Friday Night at Baron's

It had been a hectic evening. Around 10 P.M. when it began to quiet down, everyone started to relax and mess around. Julie and **Nick Reis,** one of the cooks, were talking. Nick was showing her how to snap a towel, a popular game among kitchen staff. Julie had never been able to do it quite right, so she was asking for instructions on what she was doing wrong. Nick politely obliged and showed her the proper way.

Ryan had been bartending that night and was getting off work while the others were playing around. He sat at the bar and had some dinner. He walked into the kitchen to drop off his dishes and was on his way out the back door when the other bartender asked him to stick around for another thirty minutes because it had suddenly gotten busy. Ryan agreed and was headed back to the bar when Julie decided to try her towel-snapping skills on the back of Ryan's head. For the first time ever, Julie did it right. The towel got him dead center on the back of the head. This irritated Ryan, more so because he had not expected it. He went off on Julie, saying that she was wrong in what she had done, and began to snap his towel at her. He got her about three times in the stomach and walked toward the bar. As he was almost to the door, Julie hollered a derogatory name at him. This provoked Ryan. He came back to the kitchen and an intense argument ensued in front of all of the servers and kitchen staff. At first everyone thought it was just a joke because their friendship seemed strong. It didn't take long for everyone to figure out that it was no joke and Ryan was mad. He was calling Julie all sorts of names, and she replied with the same sort of language. Ryan got even madder and left Baron's. The other bartender was left with no help.

All the servers reported that they didn't want to work with Ryan anymore. Some were worried about his temper and didn't want to have to worry about him snapping on them. Julie had bruises on her stomach and was quite upset by the situation. Ryan was very bothered by the whole situation. He knew that after the "door incident," management could review this seriously. He stood by his work. He felt he had done nothing wrong and reacted in a manner that he would have toward anyone in the place. He claimed that he didn't like to mess around at work, and that the fact that Julie had started the whole thing was not his fault.

The situation got worse when the thought of a lawsuit came around. Ryan's temper was a major concern, and no one really knew what to do.

Discussion Questions

1. Describe your views on friendships within the workplace. Are there disadvantages to having close relationships among employees? Defend your answer.
2. After the door incident, would you have rehired Ryan? Why or why not?
3. Were the other employees justified in getting involved when it really had nothing to do with them? Why or why not?
4. Describe how you would have handled both situations in which Ryan was involved. Why would you take these actions?

Brett Hensley

Brett Hensley was promoted to assistant manager of CJ's less than a year ago. At the time of his promotion, some managers were outspoken about his lack of experience; he had been with the restaurant only two years. But Brett, appearing eager to learn, applied considerable energy to the job and took instructions and directions well. He seemed to be making progress in the job and obtaining good results.

Recently, some disturbing symptoms began to appear. The first sign was his appearance. Gradually, he seemed to be adopting some disturbing modern trends in dress and grooming. While his departure from acceptable norms did not seem to be dramatic, it finally became obvious to **Dan Ramsey,** Brett's boss. The owner, **Bill Temple,** asked Dan what kind of impression Brett made outside the restaurant. Later, some managers commented on Brett's increasing tendency toward spending his coffee breaks with some female employees, a situation they felt was not exactly appropriate of an assistant manager. Dan also received criticism of Brett's habit of whistling on the job.

As time went on, Brett seemed to become less willing to understand why tasks should be done in a standardized way. He constantly bombarded management with ideas and suggestions—first verbally, then in lengthy, detailed written form. Once he suggested that a new plan be developed for the restaurant to improve efficiency. The idea was tried but failed. A short time later, Brett was overheard complaining that the idea had been dropped before it was given a fair chance of succeeding.

It soon became obvious that Brett did not have the necessary loyalty to the organization. He seemed to live for the weekend, when he would dash off in his little sports car for a skiing junket with a group of wild friends. He was reported to be very active in outside activities, and it was even rumored that he was involved in some "way-out peace group." Then one day, without consulting anyone, he suddenly enrolled in night school. It wasn't only the time he devoted to his studies that concerned Dan; it was the embarrassment Brett caused when he suggested highly theoretical ideas as solutions to organizational problems. Many solutions emphasized the "social responsibilities of management."

Dan seemed to spend more time reacting to all of Brett's ideas than performing his management/supervision responsibilities. Dan didn't want to complain to Bill because Dan was the one who had encouraged Brett's promotion. It had been a year, but Dan was not sure he could continue dealing with Brett much longer. When Brett had an idea, he didn't seem to want to drop it.

It wasn't very long before Brett started complaining more about his job. In one conversation, it was reported that he openly stated that his talents were not being used, and his job was really not challenging. On another occasion, he mentioned that he was supposed to be in a development program but nothing different seemed to be happening to him than was happening to anyone else. He wanted to know what specific plans there were for him "in the very near future."

Bill began to take notice of Brett's behavior and conversation when visiting CJ's. He finally asked Dan how he had selected Brett. Dan replied that when he interviewed him for the position, he made a very solid impression, and Brett's credentials also seemed very substantial. He had graduated from a well-known university, where he had been active in several student associations. He had a wide range of interests and had held a number of interesting previous jobs in foodservice operations. After Dan had finished his explanation, Bill mentioned that some of the new student interns were developing similar attitudes, and he wondered if Brett might be influencing others.

Dan is trying to figure out what to do about Brett's situation.

Discussion Questions

1. Is spending breaks with employees of the opposite sex appropriate for an assistant manager? Defend your response.
2. When employees have disturbing "habits" on the job, should the manager do anything about it? Why or why not?
3. If you were Dan, what would you do? Defend your answer. How should Dan implement his solutions?
4. Is Brett's behavior appropriate? Why or why not? Should it be tolerated? Discuss.
5. Should Dan have done anything differently during the interview process? Explain.

Deno's Restaurant Chain

It is February 28 and **John Deno** just received a call from his lawyer, **Jack Keene,** who told him that **Sue McHall** had filed a discrimination suit against Deno's Restaurant Chain. John was surprised. Furthermore, he couldn't remember Sue McHall. John made an appointment to visit with his lawyer the next morning, but he knew he first had to do some research.

During the visit with Jack, John was informed that Sue McHall had charged that she was qualified for but did not receive the district human resources manager position with Deno's Restaurant Chain because she was female and had children. She claimed that the company judged that she should not be away from her family and that she was not able to travel by herself. Her suit charged that these assumptions by Deno's managers were not true, and she should receive the position based on her activities as a manager and qualifications for the job.

Jack explained that he, representing Deno's; a government official; and Sue's attorney would attend the hearing. There would be questions from both attorneys and the government official concerning the recruiting and selecting practices of Deno's Restaurant Chain. The advertisement for the district human resources manager position would be reviewed.

Background: Sue McHall

Sue McHall was eager to make a change in her hospitality career. She has been an assistant manager at the Town Center Restaurant for four years. Sue had received an associate degree in restaurant management three years ago. Prior to taking classes, she and her manager agreed that he would allow some flexibility in her work schedule if she would work at the restaurant for two years after completing school. She also has completed two additional short-term courses in managing employees this past year. More than two years has passed. She has fulfilled her obligation.

The Town Center Restaurant is a family restaurant whose customers are from the local and surrounding communities. Gross income for the last three years was between $565,000 and $600,000 per year. As assistant manager, Sue supervised eight full-time and six part-time employees.

Before holding the assistant manager position, Sue had worked in all positions at Town Center Restaurant: production and cleanup, table service, hosting, and cashiering. She had been responsible for employee scheduling, customer relations, and bookkeeping. She was sure there were no possibilities of future promotions because the manager was also the owner. She had supervised all the front-of-the-house employees and had some back-of-the-house management. She was ready for a change. It was time to move on and get more management opportunities.

Sue noticed the following ad in the local paper for the district human resources (HR) manager position in Deno's Restaurant Chain.

District Human Resources Manager
Deno's Restaurant Chain

Position available for district human resources manager in locally owned chain. Must have excellent communication skills, strong leadership qualities, and good people relations. Restaurant management experience helpful. Background in training employees, cost control, and quality control necessary. Will provide some training. Must travel. Good benefits.

One of her close friends, an assistant manager at Deno's, told Sue that it would be a very good place to work. Employee benefits also were better than at Town Center Restaurant. It seemed like the ideal situation. Her friend thought there also might be an opportunity for advancement within the organization. Sue knew she had the drive and family support to move to the top of the right organization.

Background: Deno's Restaurant Chain

Deno's Restaurant Chain has three properties in southern Kansas and three in northern Oklahoma. The largest property, in Osage City, Oklahoma, employs sixty-two full-time equivalents (FTEs); the smallest property, in Skatesville, Kansas, employs thirty-eight FTEs.

The district HR manager position would involve responsibilities related to quality and cost control, including visiting each property at least once a month. The person hired would be involved in hiring, terminating, and other employee changes in status. In addition, the job would include planning and conducting in-service training for management, and developing and/or revising training materials for all employee levels.

The First Interview

Sue called about the position and received an appointment with two managers for the following Monday. Upon arrival at the main office of Deno's Restaurant Chain, she received a warm welcome from the secretary. He offered her coffee and asked her to complete the application form. She was told that Mr. Becker would be with her shortly.

Sue found **Bill Becker** to be a friendly, laid-back individual who was able to put her at ease immediately. He began by asking her questions about her outside interests. Next he concentrated on her work experiences and told her about the chain. He highlighted the main responsibilities as HR manager of six restaurants within a two-state area. It would not be unusual, she was told, for the HR person to spend three or more days at a time at one restaurant, requiring some overnight travel.

Bill was the type of manager who believed he could find out more about applicants through follow-up questions to their responses. He felt he did a good job of developing additional questions as the interview progressed. In reviewing his previous interviewing experiences, Bill determined that his success rate at hiring the right person for the right job was pretty good. He believed that by showing individuals he was interested in all aspects of their lives, he portrayed a good public relations image for the company.

Bill seemed interested in Sue's previous experiences managing employees, preparing reports, and analyzing problems. His questions about previous work experience emphasized her responsibilities as assistant manager. They discussed in detail her relationship with other employees and the style of leadership/management she used.

Sue said that she felt it was important to be in control. Rather than taking risks, she liked to supervise employees closely. She also indicated that if she supervised closely, employees would have less failure, and therefore they would feel more successful in their jobs. Success should increase morale and job satisfaction, she explained. She stated that she wanted to be ready to answer their questions and check carefully on their work.

Sue did not feel that employees were lazy, but if the job was to be done correctly, she needed to be in charge. She explained that she did not feel her current employees have the time or experience to make decisions, so she did not give them the opportunity.

Bill closed the interview by asking Sue if she had children who would need to be cared for while she was away. He then asked her to think about how she would manage being away from home and her children for three or more days at a time. He was concerned about her safety as she traveled alone and spent evenings alone in strange cities. He asked Sue to discuss the situation with her husband.

Sue told Bill that she had great family support. She had already checked with her parents, and they were more than willing to help with the children.

After Sue left his office, Bill made some notes about the interview. He completed the job specification chart with information about her experiences, including supervisory experiences. He made comments about her management style and interaction with employees.

The Second Interview

Next, **Robert Moss,** who appeared very straightforward, interviewed Sue. He did not establish rapport as easily as Bill. He asked her to tell him why she was interested in the job and about her previous work experience and her goals for the next five years. He asked Sue how she could be of benefit to the company. When asked to tell of a situation that showed her management style, Sue talked about how she had one person in a lead position who did not seem to work unless she was checking on him. Therefore, to treat all employees equally, Sue kept a constant check on production and service activities of all employees.

Robert asked questions from Sue's application form and stuck to those questions. He believed it was important to be consistent in questioning applicants, so he followed a written set of questions he had prepared before the interview.

The Follow-Up Interviews

Sue left the interviews with a very positive feeling and was sure she would be considered for the job. She had been told that the hiring decision would take place in two to four weeks. When she had not heard from Deno's in two weeks, she phoned Bill and was told to come back for a second interview with both him and Robert.

The format of the second interviews puzzled Sue. Some of the good qualities she felt were important to her getting the job were not discussed. Bill seemed concerned about her ability to handle the job and balance the care of her three young children with overnight travel. The relaxed, comfortable feeling she had had with Bill seemed to disappear. Sue assured Bill that all arrangements for her family could be made when she officially was selected for the position. The second interview with Robert seemed to concentrate more on her leadership style. He presented her with hypothetical situations and asked her to explain how she would handle them. He asked for more examples of actual situations she had experienced when she was assistant manager at Town Center. He quizzed her about courses she had taken in human resources management.

Because John Deno was out of town, Sue did not have an opportunity to interview with him. It was known in the company that John usually went along with the recommendation of his two right-hand people, Bill and Robert. He prided himself on the fact that he believed in participative management and by accepting the recommendation of Bill and Robert, he showed them how important they were to his chain.

After the second interview, Bill and Robert discussed the possibility of Sue McHall for the new district HR manager. After an hour of discussion, both agreed that this was probably not the time to hire Sue. As they analyzed the managers and assistant managers in each of the properties, they felt that Sue would have trouble relating to many of them with her leadership style. It appeared from all the discussion they had with her that she might not be able to change her management style. The company could not afford to have managers in their properties upset. Their recommendation to John was to not hire Sue McHall.

One week after the interview, Sue received a letter from John Deno stating that she had not been selected for the position of district human resources manager. He indicated that he would keep her application on file for any future positions in his chain. Sue's immediate reaction was to file a discrimination charge against Deno's Restaurant Chain, Bill Becker, and Robert Moss.

Discussion Questions

1. What was Sue's main objective? Support your response. What were the interviewers' objectives? Support your response.
2. What documents should be used in the interview process? Why?
3. Should Sue McHall have been hired? Why or why not?
4. If you were John Deno, how would you handle the lawsuit? Be specific.
5. What records would you gather to prepare for the defense of this discrimination charge? Why?
6. Discuss the positive and negative aspects of each interview. Be specific.
7. List (a) three problems, (b) three opportunities, and (c) three risks that Deno's faces.
8. Suggest ways to improve Robert's interview. Why are these important? Suggest ways to improve Bill's interview. Why are these important?
9. What types of questions cannot be asked in an interview? Give examples.
10. Sue's attorney wants Robert and Bill to testify at the hearing. Should John Deno's attorney encourage this request? Why or why not?

El Chico's House

Dan Knutson's partners have just finished a conference phone call. They are perplexed to think that problems at El Chico's House had escalated to the point that they had. Why hadn't Dan shared any of the problems with them earlier? Did he think they would go away? Why did he decide to hire Loren and not advertise for the job? Did he trust Ross's opinion to that extent?

Background

Dan Knutson is one of four owners of El Chico's House, a 140-seat restaurant with a limited bar. El Chico's House is located in a college town in central Oklahoma and relies on students as its main source of labor. He also served as the general manager (GM) when it opened.

Dan had no GM experience before opening El Chico's House. He had been an assistant manager in a smaller restaurant for five years prior to opening El Chico's House. His dream had been to own several restaurants, but he didn't have the financial means to get started on his own. He talked with **John Sturgis** and **Tim Gregory,** two friends who had the same interest. They decided to approach **Steve Waters** to help with the financial aspect. Steve agreed to put up 40 percent of the cost needed to get four restaurants started, but wanted to remain a silent partner.

Dan, John, and Tim knew they could contribute 20 percent each, so they decided to become partners and open four restaurants that were bought at the same time. The three active partners each selected the restaurant they wanted to manage and then worked on finding a manager for the fourth restaurant. Dan became the manager of El Chico's House. The two restaurants in Colorado are managed by the other two partners, and the one in Utah is managed by Dan's nephew, Ross Troy.

Ross Troy is a recent graduate of a hospitality program and had not even considered managing his own restaurant upon graduation. When his uncle approached him with an opportunity, Ross thought it was to be an assistant manager under him. When he learned it was to manage his own restaurant, he immediately grabbed at the chance. He was not excited about moving to Utah, but felt this was his golden opportunity. He had never considered a business venture with his uncle, but with his education background, Uncle Dan had encouraged him to come with the company.

Dan was excited to get El Chico's House up and running under his management. He recruited **Peter Coleman** to be his assistant manager, acting as the maitre d' and managing the bar. The two were good friends and Peter had worked under Dan when Dan was an assistant manager. To persuade Peter to join him, Dan provided him with both a higher position (assistant manager) and a $5,000 raise. Business was steady, in line with Dan's projections. The restaurant was a success, and Dan was eager to expand his management team. He promoted **Paul Nelson,** who had worked as head cook for two years, and **Fred Clark,** who had worked as a bartender for two years. This decision allowed Peter to become the GM and continue as maitre d'. Paul, the new kitchen manager, was responsible for kitchen activities, purchasing, and inventory control. Fred became the bar manager, controlling all bar functions, including liquor inventory and control (see the El Chico's House organization chart #1).

Expanding the Business

Dan was eager to expand, and business at El Chico's House was growing faster than he had expected. He talked with his partners and they supported his desire to purchase another restaurant on his own. The partners were confident that Peter

El Chico's House Organization Chart #1

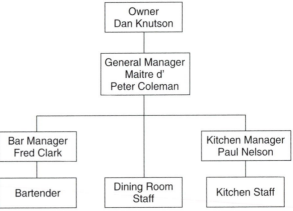

could manage El Chico's House while Dan was busy with his new restaurant. Dan pointed out how well Ross was doing with his restaurant, suggesting that an owner does not need to be on premise to have a successful business. Dan increased Peter's salary by $15,000, plus bonuses, and gave him the responsibility and authority to do what needed to be done. Dan agreed to spend three months helping Peter adjust to his new position. Feeling that Peter was doing a good job after two months, Dan began looking for another restaurant. His visits to El Chico's House became more infrequent, sometimes only once a week.

Peter was very competent in his job and built close relationships with customers. He knew how to communicate well with the back of the house, even though he had primarily been responsible for the front of the house. Employees were happy to work with him and he had their respect. Employees could count on his help and mediation when inevitable conflicts between the two sides of the house arose. He was perceived as being fair to everybody most of the time. Turnover was very low and new hires were the result of increased business. Business at El Chico's House was booming and sales were increasing. When Dan reported this to the other owners, they were ecstatic. Steve was pleased with the return on his investment.

On one of his infrequent visits, Dan was pleased to see how the restaurant was performing. The situation was much better at El Chico's House than at any of the other restaurants. With the other restaurant and some of the problems Dan was facing, he basically quit coming to El Chico's House. Peter was sending reports to Dan electronically, but Dan was not paying close attention to them.

The Problem

One day, Fred called Dan and asked him if he had been reviewing the reports. When Dan analyzed them, he found that costs had increased drastically. He wasn't sure why. Maybe it was carelessness with food in the kitchen or an increase in the labor hired to keep up with the business. When the situation continued for several months, Dan felt that something was wrong, and he scheduled himself to be at the restaurant more often. He observed what was happening in the kitchen. He checked inventories to determine whether employees were stealing food. After several days, Dan discovered that the high costs were due to theft of money by Peter.

Dan unraveled the mystery and learned that while he was involved with the new restaurant, Peter had agreed to be responsible for accounting and checking to see that sales corresponded to the cashier receipts. Peter had been falsifying figures on the bank slips before making deposits. Dan examined the cashier slips and found that the cash amounts listed on the slips were not what had been deposited.

Dan found a difference of $4,000 and confronted Peter. Peter indicated that he had had a recent gambling problem and needed a few dollars to take care of his debt. He said he had planned to pay the money back as soon as possible. Because Dan wasn't checking records, he felt that he could return the money before Dan noticed it was missing. Dan was irate. Although he took some of the blame because he gave the accounting responsibility to Peter, Dan asked Peter to return the money immediately. Peter said he could borrow the money from a brother, and Dan agreed to give Peter the time to get the cash. One week later, Peter handed Dan a check for the stolen money, and Dan handed Peter a pink slip because he could no longer be trusted.

Dan decided not to press charges because the two had been working together for a long time. Instead of telling the employees that Peter had stolen money and had been fired, Dan told them that Peter had found another job and resigned.

The New Manager

Now Dan had to find a new manager to replace Peter. Dan decided to try to promote again from within, because he believed it would increase employee morale. At first, Dan considered promoting Fred or Paul, but they had asked to move to the new restaurant. Dan wasn't sure what he should do. Maybe he should advertise in the local media.

After much thought, he agreed to transfer Ross's assistant manager, **Loren Roberts,** as a potential for the GM position. When Dan discussed the GM opening with Ross, immediately Ross suggested that Dan hire Loren. Ross gave him an excellent recommendation. After a second conversation with Ross, it was decided that instead of making Loren GM, he would work only as maitre d' because Dan did not want to give him too many responsibilities at one time (see the El Chico's House organization chart #2). Dan increased Loren's salary by $5,000 over what Ross was paying him. After a three-month probationary period, Dan agreed to review Loren's progress and decide whether to promote him to GM. At that time Loren would receive a significant increase in pay. Dan would spend lots of time at the restaurant training Loren.

El Chico's House Organization Chart #2

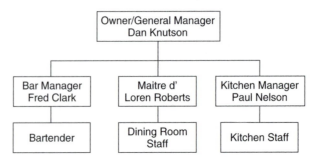

When Fred and Paul heard what was going on, they were disappointed that Dan had not contacted them about the possibility of the GM position at El Chico's House. However, they did not say anything to Dan.

Loren had an undergraduate degree in hotel and restaurant management. Dan hoped that Loren would work out well and that he would continue at El Chico's House. He noticed that Loren had some unusual behaviors that bothered some of the employees.

Loren's probationary period ended with an excellent review and a promotion to GM. Two weeks later, Dan left for a short vacation. Within a week, El Chico's House employees' tempers started flaring. The cooks, **Craig Rosin** and **Phil Dimetreus,** challenged Loren's decisions because they did not believe he had the needed experience to be a GM. The new kitchen manager, **Shaun Wendt,** who was promoted after Paul transferred, began to undermine Loren.

Servers compared Loren to Peter and discussed how Peter was superior to Loren. Some employees were disrespectful to him. As employees began to find excuses to be absent or late for work, production decreased. Loren starting using discipline techniques to prove he was manager. The relationship between Loren and the employees became strained.

Two months after Loren was promoted to GM, Dan heard through the grapevine that many employees were planning to work at another Mexican restaurant. This restaurant was only two blocks away from El Chico's House. Dan was stunned to learn that the manager there was Peter.

Dan called his partners a few days later to ask for their help in solving his problems. His partners were shocked because Dan had not kept them up to date on the situation.

Discussion Questions

1. If you were Dan, would you have fired Peter because he stole $4,000 from your restaurant? Why or why not? Would you have pressed charges? Defend your answer.
2. Would the amount of money Peter stole make a difference in how you handled the situation? Why?
3. Should Dan have told his employees originally that Peter had stolen the money? Why or why not? Why do you think he didn't?
4. After finding out that several employees are planning to work for Peter, would you tell them about the theft of money? Explain.
5. Did Dan use an appropriate process to hire Loren? Support your answer. Would you have done something different? Why or why not? How would you feel if you were Fred or Paul?
6. If you were Dan, could you have done anything to help Loren win the respect of his employees?

7. At this point, should Dan consider either hiring a new manager or selling El Chico's House? Describe other options Dan has. What should he do?

8. If Dan decides to hire a new GM, what qualifications should he require? Why would these be important?

9. What kind of help, if any, should Dan expect from his partners? If you were a partner, what would you do to help? Why do you suggest these actions?

Fish N More

Emma Lloyd had mixed emotions about her future. Due to major frustrations, she had quit on the spot last Wednesday. She had been with Fish N More for more than one year when she came to the end of her rope. She felt she had no other alternative but to quit. She wasn't sure she ever wanted to work in the hospitality industry after this experience. She knew she wanted a career that she enjoyed and not one that brought new frustrations each day. She had also learned the value of a good training program. She had looked forward to the training program that had been described to her during the interview. In fact, that was one of the perks that had helped her decide to go with Fish N More.

Emma can't believe that a company with a reputation for having an excellent training program did not come through for her. Was this just a coincidence or was the training program overrated? Emma didn't know what the reason was for her lack of training, so decided to take a few days to think about the past year.

Emma had tried to tell **Tyler Williams** several times that she never received the effective training she was promised. She frequently asked for his help on what to do, but didn't pursue the issue beyond asking because she wanted to be considered for employment at the end of the training period. It appeared that Tyler thought the problem would take care of itself.

The final straw was last Tuesday, when Tyler and **Kevin Montes** formally evaluated Emma's performance as if she had received proper training. She couldn't understand how she could be held accountable for job responsibilities for which she had never been trained. She fretted over the less-than-satisfactory evaluation all night and the next day, without a prior decision, told Tyler she was done.

71

Background

Fish N More is a casual 350-restaurant franchise that is known for its quality food and service. Most of the restaurant's business is during the evening, with a steady flow for the seafood buffet that is offered at lunch.

Each restaurant is provided with well-developed training videos and handbooks for use with employees. There is an extensive checklist that the trainers review with trainees to ensure that all aspects of the restaurant are covered. Extensive training materials have been developed specifically for use with up-and-coming managers.

Each Fish N More property has a general manager (GM), associate manager, assistant manager, and dining room manager (see the Fish N More organization chart). A district supervisor oversees five restaurants and, on average, visits each restaurant two or three times a month. The supervisor's main responsibility is to help solve problems within the restaurant. In addition, the district supervisor evaluates all components of each restaurant, such as financial, sanitation, service, and labor turnover. There may be times that the district supervisor helps with employee problems, but that is not a key responsibility. Together with the GM, the supervisor is involved in evaluating the entry-level managers at the end of their training. This process allows the supervisor to spot potential managers and get them on the fast track to management. The company is planning to open several hundred properties in the next couple of years, so developing strong managers is important. Area recruiters visit college campuses to select outstanding hospitality students for entry-level positions.

The GM is responsible to the district supervisor for all aspects of the operation. The other managers report to the GM. When the GM is out of the restaurant, the associate manager is in charge. Because the dining room manager receives little training beyond the front of the house, that manager is seldom in charge of the operation.

On average, each Fish N More restaurant employs about equal numbers of full-time and part-time employees. Fish N More is reputed to be a good place to work, so there is a constant pool of applicants.

Recruiting Emma

In late February, **Peter Waddel,** a recruiter for several districts, visited three campuses to interview several hotel and restaurant management (HRM) majors who were graduating that spring. He was very impressed with Emma's foodservice experiences during college, where she had some management experiences during her final year. She had completed two internships. One internship was at a camp for physically challenged campers, where Emma managed a kitchen staff that served three meals a day to about fifty campers plus thirty leaders. Her six-month internship with Disney World was in a theme restaurant where she was provided various management opportunities.

Fish N More Organization Chart

```
                              District Supervisor
                                      │
  ┌───────────┬──────────────┬────────┴────────┬──────────────┬───────────┐
  │           │              │                 │              │           │
Saylorville  Water's View   Harbor Inn       Unit 4         Unit 5
General      General        General          General        General
Manager      Manager        Manager          Manager        Manager
  │           │              │                 │              │
┌─┴─┬──┐    ┌─┴─┬──┐      ┌──┼──┬──┐       ┌──┼──┬──┐     ┌──┼──┬──┐
Assoc. Asst. DR  Assoc. Asst. DR  Assoc. Asst. DR   Assoc. Asst. DR   Assoc. Asst. DR
Mgr.  Mgr. Mgr.  Mgr.  Mgr. Mgr.  Mgr.  Mgr. Mgr.   Mgr.  Mgr. Mgr.   Mgr.  Mgr. Mgr.
```

During the interview, Peter noted Emma's positive attitude toward work. He also documented her leadership experiences. Emma had served as treasurer and president of the HRM Club. She co-chaired a department open house during the university's three-day celebration. Faculty members often looked to Emma for her organizational skills. As a junior she was selected by faculty to attend a weeklong leadership conference, and she spent her senior year mentoring potential leaders. Her references were very positive and comments were made about her attention to detail, friendliness, and strong work ethic. One reference noted that Emma worked hard to please everyone. Emma also had been involved in community and church activities during college.

Emma felt honored when she was one of five applicants selected for a second interview that would be done at a company property. During this visit, Emma met with **Matt Carlson,** the district supervisor at that time, and GMs at two restaurants, Saylorville and Water's View. Emma was told she could have a position at Saylorville. She also had a chance to talk with several employees, including **Greta Stiles,** the dining room manager at that restaurant. It was from Greta that she found out she was the third person to visit the restaurant within two weeks.

Emma felt confident it would be a good training opportunity, and when Matt offered her the position, she accepted it. Emma was excited and full of anticipation for learning as much as she could to help her climb the corporate ladder as fast as possible. Emma was eager to begin the training program as an assistant manager.

The training program is an intensive thirteen weeks covering both the front and the back of the house. All the training is done by the GM. During this period, the assistant manager is responsible for cooks and dishwashers and often has closing responsibilities. Emma was happy to be at Saylorville because the restaurant had a record for training new managers who were promoted to GM positions in a short time frame. Emma also learned that **Carla Jones,** GM at Saylorville, was the best manager under whom to learn management techniques.

Saylorville

Emma started her training at Saylorville under Carla's direction. Emma found that she was very conscientious about Emma's training and gave her lots of attention. She lived up to the accolades of her employees when it came to training.

In the fourth week of training, Carla was fired. The reason was never disclosed. Emma wondered whether Carla's business philosophy didn't match Matt's. She was shocked, especially when Carla had such a good reputation among her employees. It was evident that this firing put a burden on the restaurant.

For the next few weeks, Emma desperately tried to learn what she should have learned from Carla. **Derik Hanson,** the associate manager, was doing his and the GM's jobs and had very little time to spend with Emma. Derik was being groomed for a GM position. He knew what it took to be promoted and he gave 150 percent, and training Emma would not count toward this promotion. Derik had been with the company for eight years and was considered a valuable employee. He hoped that being the interim GM would lead to a promotion. He gave it his best shot but was fighting low employee morale after Carla left. In the end, Matt decided that Derik was not ready for the GM position, and **Jason Keller** was hired. Emma quietly wondered whether Derik was overlooked because he had been hired and trained by Carla. Derik was a very quiet individual who did more than was expected of him without telling others. He expected to be rewarded for what he did, not what he told others he did. Emma wondered if that was the way to get ahead in management.

When Derik learned that he would not be promoted, his initiative declined. The next time Matt was in the restaurant, Emma spoke to him about her lack of training. Matt assured her that he understood her situation and would see what he could do. Specifically, she had requested a move to another property, and Matt promised to discuss this with corporate management. Time passed and Emma seemed to be relying on the training manuals to learn what she should be learning during training. When Emma did not receive any answer to her request from Matt, she sought out Greta.

Greta had limited knowledge of the operation. The front of the house was the only experience she had in the restaurant business. Although Greta told Emma as much as she could about supervising the front of the house, Greta couldn't provide much other training. Emma later learned through the grapevine that Matt had not talked to corporate about her situation. During the time the restaurant did not have a GM, Matt visited the store three to four times a month. He seemed more interested in the restaurant operation than in Emma's training. In fact, Emma thought Matt went out of his way to avoid her.

As Emma's training period was ending, Emma learned that Matt had taken a job with another company, a promotion. Tyler replaced Matt as new district supervisor two weeks before Emma's required evaluation, which was scheduled at the end of her training. Tyler conferred with Greta and Derik concerning Emma's potential, including her customer and employee relations and technical and conceptual skills.

Emma's evaluation showed that she had good customer and employee relations but was weak in the technical and conceptual skills. Tyler told her that he had based the evaluation on the reviews he received from Derik and Greta. Emma was disappointed both in the evaluation and in Tyler's lack of consideration that she had never received the promised training in addition to having had several changes in superiors.

Kayla Fury, the new GM, came to the restaurant the last week of Emma's training period. Because she was being relocated to Water's View at the end of the week, she communicated very little with Kayla. Emma looked forward to a new start.

Water's View

Emma hoped to get more training at Water's View so she could meet Fish N More's expectations. Unfortunately, the GM at the new restaurant resigned two weeks after she began. Rumor was that he was dating one of the employees, which was frowned on by management. It appeared that it was in the GM's best interest to resign rather than risk the possibility of being terminated. Emma couldn't believe that she had to experience another change in manager. A new GM, **Kevin Wyatt,** was quickly assigned because the associate manager, **Tricia Heandon,** was not capable of being the interim GM. Emma later learned that Derik didn't express interest in the Water's View job. She expected that he was frustrated with Fish N More and was looking for a management job with another company. She wasn't sure she could blame him, because in her eyes he should have been promoted to manager.

One day Emma learned that the next week that she would be transferred to Harbor Inn because Kevin had not been a GM and Tyler didn't want Kevin to have such a new assistant manager. Emma felt that her poor evaluation played a part in the decision.

Harbor Inn

Emma didn't know what to think, but she hoped the next GM could fill in the gaps that training had not provided. When she met **Lance Andrews,** she thought he seemed arrogant with his know-it-all attitude. She noted that Lance would do or say anything that made him look good. He was very inconsistent with his behavior. What he might say or do one day could be entirely different the next day. It was obvious that Lance did not have a good understanding of the policy and procedure manual. As manager, Emma expected that Lance would be a "walking" manual. However, Emma recalled hearing that Harbor Inn was not considered a good place to train.

Lance did not have any patience or understanding about Emma's lack of training. He expected that Emma already had a full understanding of operational procedures. Emma talked with him about her lack of training due to changes in personnel at Saylorville and Water's View, but Lance did not seem interested in her situation. He suggested that she view two or three videos that were informative on management techniques that she wanted to learn. Emma took a videotape home, but thought it was too time-consuming for what she was learning.

Tom Tricia, the associate manager, had been at Harbor Inn for six months. He had crossed the line with employee relations by constantly going out with servers. It was common knowledge that he considered himself a ladies' man. It wasn't unusual for him to come to work with a hangover. Rumors suggested that he might even be using hard drugs. However, he was the only one at Harbor Inn who seemed interested in Emma's training. She was suspicious that it could be related to his interest in women.

Lisa Woods, the Harbor Inn dining room manager, was somewhat helpful to Emma about front-of-the-house operations, but Emma still lacked a full understanding of the entire operation. As with Greta, Emma didn't receive much insight and training from Lisa. Her knowledge of the entire operation was too limited.

Finally Emma assessed the situation. She was not getting the training she was promised. Tyler was not interested in Emma's situation and showed no interest in Emma's attempts to seek help from him. Her informal, frequent reviews by Lance and Tom were getting worse because her performance was being compared to the performance of someone who had received the training she never received. She realized that the evaluations were judgmental and looked at her past performance rather than being proactive and planning what she could do to improve. The discussion never centered on Emma's goals and developing as a manager.

After trying to get help, she often sat in the office wondering what to do to improve her performance. She was very frustrated and felt defeated, especially after yesterday's performance review. Emma wondered if she could go on and decided there was no way to meet her goals, so she turned in her resignation.

Discussion Questions

1. Describe the human resources issues present in these restaurants. Why are these issues?
2. What would you have done if you were Emma? Why would you choose that action?
3. What would you have done about Emma's situation if you were Matt? Derik? Tyler? Explain your reasoning behind your actions in each case.
4. Is there impact if different managers are involved in informal performance appraisals rather than formal appraisals? Explain.
5. Describe your suggestions for Tyler as he relates to Emma's performance. Why do you think these will work?
6. What were the reasons Emma quit? Was she justified in quitting? Why or why not? What remedies are there to prevent this kind of turnover? Justify your remedies.
7. What was Matt's responsibility to Emma when Carla was fired? Justify your answer.
8. Evaluate the decision to move Emma to Harbor Inn. Support your evaluation.
9. Did Lance reach a level of incompetence? Describe.
10. If you were in management, what would be your policy about managers dating employees within the company? Support your answer.

Garden View

Garden View, one of two successful restaurants owned by **Garth Youngberg,** is a casual 250-seat restaurant in downtown Ocean City. The restaurant, which welcomes families, is open from 10:30 A.M. to 12:00 A.M. Monday through Saturday and from 10:00 A.M. to 7:30 P.M. on Sunday. There is a brisk bar business at night. A loyal local customer base and a constant supply of tourist and convention customers provides a nice business for Garden View. Garden View is known for its unusual food items that are served daily in addition to its regular menu. Tourists enjoy experiencing an evening at Garden View that they can share with their friends back home. Garden View is located within walking distance of a new, multimillion-dollar convention center, which has brought an increase in business during the past years.

Garth graduated with a degree in hospitality management and began working in fine restaurants. A few years later he aspired to open his own restaurant, so he returned to school to get a minor in entrepreneurship. He wanted a restaurant that was a low-cost provider while simultaneously providing a high level of exceptional personal service.

Garden View was his first restaurant, and after he got the operation at the level he wanted, he opened Ocean View fifteen miles away on the East Coast, where communities are booming. Both restaurants were doing well until the economy took a downward swing, and customers were being more conservative with the dollars they spent on food eaten away from home.

The Past

Five years ago, Garth found himself with the same problems many other businesses were experiencing—declining income, growing expenses, and operating losses. Food costs were rising, and labor costs increased markedly when the state raised the minimum wage and increased tip credits to offset wage expenses. Expenses were not managed in a way that brought dollars to the bottom line. Garth estimated that waste and theft were costing him up to 10 percent of gross revenues.

Garth knew that he needed to cut costs drastically rather than be forced out of business. After reviewing the situation further, he chose to reduce costs by downsizing. He was aware that the conventional approach to downsizing was to eliminate frills and peripherals and decrease waste. Outside of waste, there were no peripherals. Garth accomplished his downsizing effort by letting some middle managers go. He remembered hearing about empowerment during recent conferences he had attended, but he wasn't sure what was involved. He vaguely recalled something about giving more power to make decisions to lower-level employees. So he did just that. He gave more responsibilities to hourly employees and provided them with excellent training and continuing-education programs. He made quality customer service a top priority. Garth believed that providing excellent customer service went hand in hand with a well-trained staff. He wanted his restaurants to be the restaurant of choice for those who were eating away from home. He hoped that the quality service he was establishing would provide word-of-mouth advertising for the restaurants. Garth recognized that to ensure employee loyalty, employees needed to feel good about their jobs. Thus, he implemented a well-designed training program.

For years, Garth had not seen the value of training. He didn't want to put money into training employees, but rather wanted their services as quickly as possible once they agreed to work for him. He believed that training was a cost that he seldom recovered. Often employees left after six months, and he thought that he would not get the value back from the cost of training. What he didn't realize is that the cost of training often is not seen for a period of time, and that with a good training program employees stay. When dollars aren't being spent for recruiting and hiring employees, profits should increase.

Initially, empowering some employees brought rewards to Garth. He saw that when employees were given some decision-making power, a team approach to customer service was promoted. When customers are happy, tips increase and employees are more committed. He found that empowered employees were more likely to be flexible about job assignments and help where needed.

Garth empowered servers by giving them authority and power to make immediate amends to customers for such things as slow service, confused orders, and overcooked meat. They were allowed to give away food or drinks or even pick up a check. He found that empowerment had done wonders to increase repeat business and employee commitment. Customers were pleased when staff were proactive in identifying problems before customers even had a chance to complain about them, and to correct causes of each system failure. He had not given this same empowerment to his managers because he wanted more control. Garth decided to let his general managers make some decisions about marketing, hiring, training, and general operating decisions.

Management

Scott Thomas was the general manager (GM) when Garth began giving managers more power. Scott had extensive management and supervisory experience. He also had an intense task-oriented management style and allowed for very little delegation of authority. Although he liked having the additional responsibilities, he had trouble empowering others. Scott practiced a more inflexible, autocratic leadership style. He tended to keep to himself and preferred to make decisions on his own without consulting his staff.

Under Scott's control, Garden View had a terrible reputation for employee treatment within each operation. Employees who were empowered earlier by Garth had some of the flexibility stripped from them. Turnover was twice the average for similar businesses in the area. Employees who had not bought into empowerment were happy. Those who enjoyed the extra "power" were frustrated. Employees started to complain about the workload, stress, poor management, and pay. Eventually, turnover and employee dissatisfaction at Garden View became so costly in terms of recruiting and hiring employees that these problems had to be addressed formally. Garth hired **Kirby King,** a consultant, to work with Scott and his staff on numerous problems.

Kirby's report to Garth suggested that Scott be asked to resign. He wrote that employees blamed Scott's task-oriented management style for their dissatisfaction. Kirby stated that in his interviews with and survey of employees he was certain that Scott could not regain credibility and was not capable of repairing the morale problem.

The Present

Richard Jobe became the new GM with the restaurant a little over six months ago. When he interviewed for the GM position, he left the interview believing that the previous GM left for another business opportunity. After receiving his undergraduate degrees in business administration and hospitality management, Richard spent four years as an assistant manager in a large national restaurant chain. This is his first GM position.

Richard believes that he practices a participatory management style. In an effort to make equitable decisions, he solicits information and opinions from those people affected by the decision. He has an open-door policy and is available to help wherever and whenever he is needed.

Richard took a very conservative approach when he began his new position. He knew that he needed to improve the overall quality of the operation and increase revenue. He also knew that if he acted too quickly and made a lot of changes early on, his staff and customers might be resentful and resist the changes.

The first item on Richard's agenda was to get a sense of the restaurant's operating procedures and general work climate. He worked directly with the kitchen and wait staffs to evaluate firsthand current operating procedures. He developed a computer program with which he could keep track of customer and staff comments, interactions among staff and customers, sales and revenue figures, and any information he could use to gain a comprehensive understanding of current working conditions to make changes. After a couple of months, Richard was surprised at the length of the compiled list.

As the new manager, Richard believed that the company's two primary goals—to be a low-cost provider while simultaneously providing a high level of exceptional customer service—were inherently in conflict with each other. To satisfy the former goal, the staff needed to work as quickly and efficiently as possible to serve large quantities of required food. To satisfy the latter, employees were expected to take time to meet customers' needs both in preparation of unusual products and in preserving the atmosphere for which the restaurant was known.

Richard observed that employees did not trust him, nor did they trust each other. When visiting with key employees, he was informed about problems the restaurant had had under Scott's leadership. He was told that some tasks delegated to employees were never-ending and afforded no sense of closure. Being assigned leadership of a whole project was a reward in itself, and employees competed for such assignments. However, employees had experienced little appreciation for their efforts. What started out as empowerment and team building ended with distrust and competition, both interpersonally and between departments.

Richard was surprised at how few personal friendships there were among employees. The only encouragement employees received from each other was when they shared mutual tales of being mistreated. In reviewing the results of Kirby's employee survey, Richard noted that only 42 percent of employees surveyed felt that Garden View was a good place to work.

Not surprisingly, employees felt overworked and underpaid. However, the pay structure was in line with similar area restaurants, considering the tenure of Garden View employees. This issue appeared to be a question of perception rather than a problem with absolute levels of pay.

Richard's Dilemma

Richard is frustrated that he was not made aware of the problems earlier, but he is determined to get the job done. He knows he has to build employee trust. Richard is confident in his ability as a manager and believes he can solve Garden View's problems. However, he is worried about Garth's intent to close Garden View if conditions do not improve. Richard suspects that increasing employee morale appears to be part of the expected results.

Richard has become enamored with the idea of empowerment. He has read articles on empowerment and talks about it frequently to Garth, who tells him about his previous experience with empowering employees a few years ago. Garth didn't feel that the program was a success, although he wouldn't be totally opposed to Richard's setting up a procedure in which it could be done.

On his day off, Richard is sitting on his couch thinking about Garden View and possible approaches he could take to turning it into a stable, happy, and profitable restaurant. Should he reestablish the empowerment program? Despite Richard's noble intentions, he knows he may have difficulty letting his management team make decisions. How can he let his assistant managers have more power to make decisions?

Discussion Questions

1. Evaluate Garden View's operation under Scott. What impact did Scott's leadership style have on Garden View? Explain.
2. Explain why a manager would behave like Scott.
3. What potential is untapped within employees under Scott's management? Aside from quitting or seeking a transfer, what are other employee options?
4. Will empowerment help employee morale and job satisfaction at Garden View? Explain.
5. What conditions are necessary for empowerment? Why?
6. If Richard decides to implement empowerment, how should he proceed? Justify your recommendations. Would you use the same approach? Why or why not?
7. What barriers to empowerment does Richard need to overcome? Why do they affect the success of empowerment?
8. Should Garth allow Richard to make changes? Why or why not?
9. Do you think Garth should allow Richard to empower all levels of employees? If yes, why? If no, where should Richard start the process? Why?

Julio's Mexican Restaurant

The Situation

John Day, general manager (GM) of Julio's Mexican Restaurant, received a phone call from the clergy of a local church requesting a meeting. When the two met, the cleric informed John that Jane Hansen, a member of his church and a hostess at Julio's, had confided in the him that she had been sexually harassed by Wes Smith, an assistant GM at Julio's, while she was hosting.

John was taken back. Wes was a loyal, committed employee whom he had observed as hardworking. John's evaluation of Wes supported his feelings that Wes had high standards and played an important part in the success of Julio's.

The Operation and Staffing

Julio's, a full-service Mexican restaurant, has a seating capacity of 175. The restaurant features a full Mexican-fare menu and full bar, including margaritas as a house specialty. The restaurant is located in a midwestern town with a population of about 30,000 and a nearby air force base of 10,000. Annual revenue averages more than $1,200,000 in food and beverage sales.

There is a staff of fifteen full-time and about thirty part-time employees. The part-time staff is made up of approximately two-thirds college students and one-third high school students. The management staff includes a GM and two assistant GMs, one in charge of the kitchen operation and the other in charge of the dining room and bar. The GM reports to the vice president of operations, who reports to the company president.

Julio's had been open just six months when John was hired as the GM. **Nick Johnson,** the assistant GM in charge of the kitchen and employed since opening day, has worked his way up from a waiter position to assistant GM one month ago. Nick was excited to begin his job in a management position.

Karen Kellerson, the assistant GM in charge of the front of the house, started as a waitress and became an assistant manager at the time John was hired. Six months after John started, Karen decided to move out of state, leaving an unfilled management position. After conducting several interviews with people from within and outside of the company, John decided to promote **Wes Smith** to assistant GM in charge of the dining room and bar.

Wes originally was hired by John as a bartender and had been with the restaurant only a few months. He had a few months of supervisory experience at another local restaurant and bar. The decision to promote Wes upset several internal people who were considered for the position.

After only a few weeks, it was obvious to John that Wes had problems with several employees. One waiter told John he was going to quit because Wes was constantly nitpicking about his performance. A waitress complained that Wes was changing standard operating procedures when John was not working. Some employees reported to John that Wes had a problem with his newfound power and was abusing his authority by threatening to fire them for any reason he could find. John dismissed it as animosity between Wes and a few employees with whom he probably had a personality clash.

The Problem

Two weeks after being promoted, Wes hired **Jane Hansen,** a high school senior with no related work experience, as a part-time evening hostess. Although John thought Jane seemed rather quiet and shy, attributes not ideal for a hostess who has significant interaction with the customers, he allowed Wes to hire her. After a few days, John thought Jane was doing an adequate job, considering her shyness. Two weeks later, the sexual harassment complaint surfaced. At the time of the sexual harassment complaint, Wes had been an assistant GM for one month.

Now that John was aware of Jane's complaint, he had to do something about it. This was a situation he had never experienced. He had not known sexual harassment to be a major problem in the workplace in this rural setting. In fact, Julio's, like many other small corporations, did not have a policy that dealt with sexual harassment. John decided that he would first talk to Jane so he could get her side of the story.

Jane contended that one evening while working at the hostess station, Wes was talking with her. Business was rather slow, and so the two talked quite a while. Wes began to complain of a sore neck and moved his head about in an attempt to stretch while rubbing his neck. He asked Jane if she would give him a neck rub. She refused, and contends that Wes threatened to fire her. She said, "He told me that if I refused to rub his neck, I should be reminded that my job rests in his hands, and he has the power and authority to fire me for any reason."

Before questioning Wes about the incident, John decided to talk to a couple of other hostesses to determine whether any other employees had had a similar experience but had not come forward. Two other female employees did say that Wes had requested a neck rub, but neither agreed to fulfill the request. By the same token, neither one was threatened with losing her job for refusing. When John asked Wes about the situation, he emphatically denied ever asking any employee to rub his neck and wanted to know who had brought such charges against him. After further discussion, Wes did say that he might have made comments to some people about a sore neck, but he had never asked any employee to rub his neck, and he had certainly never threatened to fire anyone.

Discussion Questions

1. Why has the sexual harassment problem evolved? Could it have been prevented? Why or why not?
2. Does Jane's description of the situation with Wes fall under the EEOC definition of sexual harassment (see the nearby document)? Why or why not?

EEOC Definition of Sexual Harassment

The EEOC has set forth specific guidelines regarding sexual harassment in the workplace. (The principles announced in these guidelines apply equally to harassment based on race, color, religion, age, handicap, veteran status, or national origin.)

Sexual harassment includes any unwelcome sexual advances, requests for sexual favors, and other sexually related comments and conduct when (1) submission to such conduct explicitly or implicitly is made a term or condition of the employee's employment; (2) submission to or rejection of such conduct is used as a basis for an employment decision; or (3) such conduct unreasonably interferes with the employee's performance or creates an intimidating, hostile, or offensive work environment.

The EEOC's guidelines state that employers will be liable for sexual harassment by supervisors under all circumstances and will be liable for sexual harassment by fellow employees where the employer knew or should have known of the conduct, unless it can be shown that appropriate action was taken promptly. In addition, under some circumstances, the employer may be liable for sexual harassment of employees by non-employees (such as customers) where the employer knew or should have known of the conduct and failed to take prompt correction measures.

3. If Jane is telling the truth, should Wes be punished? Why or why not? If so, to what degree (reprimand, suspension, termination)?
4. Describe John's responsibility in this case. Describe the responsibility of the owners of the corporation.
5. Describe John's options. If you were John, what would you do? Why?
6. What measures can be taken to prevent future occurrences? Why do you think these measures would work? How would you implement these measures?

The Sheffield Diner

Jill Kolbe, a recent graduate of an accredited hospitality program, has been hired to co-manage the Sheffield Diner, a midsize, successful restaurant in a large midwestern city. Jill is 24 and highly skilled and knowledgeable. The absentee owner of the restaurant, **Steve Watson,** was very impressed with Jill's grade point average, civic involvement, and college activities. During the previous year, Jill had worked in a similar-size restaurant during her summer intern experience. Both Jill and Steve have discussed their mutual expectations and a few anticipated difficulties with Jill's co-manager, Bill. **Bill Kriner,** 28, has worked at the restaurant for eight years and has performed every job with a fair degree of success. Bill's "can-do" attitude and loyalty were reasons that Steve promoted him to manager six months ago when the position opened. However, the restaurant has recently become more popular, and Steve desires a more polished and technically competent individual to ensure the operation's long-term viability and profitability. Steve has discussed his business intentions with Bill and has informed him of Jill's position and his expectations of her contributions. Bill is excited about the opportunity to learn from Jill, and he envisions no difficulty in getting the management team formed quickly.

The first few weeks of the management relationship appeared to work well. Jill's quiet confidence and administrative abilities impressed Bill. Jill was likewise impressed with Bill's thorough knowledge of each position in the restaurant. It appeared that each of the co-managers' areas of expertise provided a complementary balance. Employees and guests alike were pleased at the new, improved operation. Steve was pleased with the results of the "shared duties" arrangement and was especially pleased that he did not have to visit the restaurant as frequently as previously required.

At the end of the third month, Jill discovered that the delivery receipts did not match the inventories. Apparently, someone was taking items from the restaurant, although not a huge amount and not any specific type of product. Jill was perplexed. The meat and seafood showed only slight sporadic losses and the liquor order was almost always correct. Jill asked herself: Could it be different employees, each taking what they desire? Or was it a single employee taking just a little to augment his or her take-home pay? Or could it be a series of shortages from the various vendors who deliver to the restaurant? What should she tell Bill? *Should* she tell Bill? What if it was Bill? What about sharing all of this with Steve? What if Steve suspected that *she* was responsible? After all, she was responsible for keeping the books.

Ultimately, Jill decided to tell Bill about her findings regarding the shortages, thinking he might know how to resolve this problem quickly. After all, Bill had been there eight years and had considerably more experience.

Bill became quiet as Jill began to explain her findings. Jill sensed that Bill was uneasy and wanted the discussion to end. Jill asked Bill if they should inform Steve now, or wait until they had solved the question about the shortages. Bill suggested that they wait until he had made some preliminary observations. He also suggested that they change the locks as a precautionary measure. Bill assured Jill he would get to the bottom of this situation in a week or so. He said he had some hunches.

During the next few nights Jill evaluated all of the evidence she had collected. She firmly believed, but could not prove, that Bill was responsible for the shortages.

The next week, Bill approached Jill with an offer: Stop the investigation, and he would make it financially advantageous for her. After all, he said, Jill must have some college loans to repay; why make it tough on herself? The restaurant was doing well. Steve was happy, the guests were happy, and the employees were happy. What was the problem? The shrinkage was not large, and no one else, including the assistant managers, even suspected there was any difficulty with the inventory.

Discussion Questions

1. What part does Jill play regarding the theft that is occurring? Does any responsibility lie with her? Why or why not?
2. How would *you* respond to Bill's offer? Why?
3. Describe potential ramifications of your decision. Explain why you think these ramifications might happen.
4. How would you respond to each ramification you identified in question 3?
5. What further action would you take? Why? Describe how you would implement your action.

Two Weeks Later

Jill decided to talk to Steve about the shortages. Although she was very careful with what she said, she sensed that Steve thought that she was implicating Bill. Steve said he would see what he could do about the situation. He told her he would get back to her within the next couple of weeks.

During this time, **Andrew Kuhn,** a 20-year-old student who had been studying hospitality management at a local university, joined the staff as a full-time waiter. Andrew had decided to take a year off to earn some needed money to continue his education. He had worked at the Sheffield Diner prior to beginning college; he had left because he had a disagreement with one of the former assistant managers. Bill had thought Andrew had potential, but didn't try to keep him from quitting. He felt that the conflict might continue if Andrew stayed. Besides, Andrew was going to college and probably wouldn't have time to commit to the restaurant. Bill was glad to have Andrew back.

Andrew and Bill became good friends, and soon they were seen visiting during Andrew's break. Over the next few weeks, Bill convinced Steve that Andrew should be given extensive training in all areas of the restaurant. Steve agreed, and Andrew became a half-time waiter and spent the rest of his time learning the other areas of the restaurant. Although Bill didn't tell Steve, he had discussed the possibility of Andrew becoming an assistant manager. He had heard that **Ellen Fox,** a female assistant manager, might be leaving because her husband had received a promotion and was to be transferred.

Steve was pleased with what Bill was telling him about Andrew's performance and, in the next few months, agreed that Bill should give Andrew more responsibility. Andrew was soon supervising the restaurant when Bill was not managing, even though there had been no change in management staff. Ellen had asked to have her hours cut, so in reality Andrew was picking up some of her management hours.

Andrew brought new ideas on how the restaurant should be operated, ideas he took the liberty of implementing on the days he supervised. This caused confusion in the normally smooth-running restaurant. Over the next few weeks, several servers became upset, but never voiced their opinions to management.

Finally, following one very chaotic and harrowing night under Andrew's supervision, **Peter Martin,** a headwaiter, decided to visit with Jill the next time she was supervising. Peter approached Jill about problems when Andrew was in charge. He said he was representing many of the other servers. However, Jill knew that Andrew and Bill were good friends, and Steve liked what he saw or heard from Bill. Jill decided to take no action, but suggested that Peter approach Bill with the servers' concerns. Peter took her advice.

The next day, Jill noticed that Andrew began taking a dislike toward Peter, giving him undesirable tasks to do. Andrew and Bill frequently contradicted Peter in front of the other employees and criticized his work. Over the next couple of weeks, tension increased between Andrew and Peter, especially when they both were assigned to be servers. Despite these heated arguments, Bill and Steve didn't take any action. Jill sensed that they thought the tension was just a short-term problem.

However, the arguments continued. When Andrew was supervising, even the most trivial occurrence would spark another disagreement with Peter. Bill told Jill that he thought the best action in this situation was no action. He stated that he thought sooner or later the arguments would just blow themselves out.

Two months later, Peter quit his position, citing financial reasons for his departure. Two days later, three of Peter's colleagues (and better servers) resigned, indicating personal reasons for their moving to another operation. This left the restaurant short-staffed for the busy summer months. In addition, there would be the costs of recruiting and training additional servers.

Jill, once again, was frustrated with Steve. After the four waiters departed, Jill realized that in the hectic activities of the Andrew-Peter conflicts, Steve had never gotten back to her about the theft problem. She wondered what she should do.

Discussion Questions

1. If you were Jill, what action would you take regarding the theft issue? Why?
2. Should Jill have gotten more involved in the Andrew-Peter conflicts? Why or why not?
3. Could the conflict between Andrew and the servers been avoided? Why or why not?
4. Should Jill have done more when Peter approached her about the servers' concerns? Why or why not?
5. Identify some pros and cons of the present management styles. Support your answers.
6. Discuss your thoughts about Bill's statements: (a) that he believed no action was the best action. Do you agree with this statement? Why or why not? (b) that these arguments would just "blow themselves out." Do you agree with this statement? Why or why not?
7. Discuss Steve's actions throughout this case. What should he have done? Why?

The South-40 Family Restaurant

The South-40 Family Restaurant is a single-unit operation located in a midwestern college community of about 30,000 people. The population during the school year is over 50,000. Because of the style of foodservice, it is not unusual for a table to turn every twenty to thirty minutes. On a busy weekend, more than 1,000 people can be served each day. The quick service and good food have made the South-40 a very popular place. The restaurant is famous for barbecued ribs and a variety of sandwiches. Customers come from a fifty-mile radius on a regular schedule to eat at the South-40. It is not unusual for out-of-town individuals who visit the city on an infrequent basis to put the South-40 on their itinerary to visit during their stay.

The Staff

Dana Stidwell, the owner, started the restaurant about twelve years ago. She frequently can be found helping in the kitchen or observing the dining room. Even though she spends a great deal of time in the restaurant, she lets the manager and assistant manager make all decisions for the front of the house. She expects to be informed of everything, but she doesn't get involved in the decisions.

The dining room management team consists of the manager, **Terri Williams;** the assistant manager, **Shelly Forth;** and four supervisors. Terri is responsible for the day-to-day dining room operating decisions. She also handles payroll and oversees staffing. Shelly does the ordering for the bar, which carries only beer and wine coolers. In addition, she is in charge of hiring, training, and firing servers and hosts. When Terri is not in, Shelly makes the decisions. This is an aspect of the job Shelly has really come to enjoy, although she does not always handle things the way Terri would like. On a typical night, the manager, the assistant manager, and one supervisor are on duty. The supervisor helps out wherever he or she is needed during the shift.

The dining room managers are responsible for a staff that includes servers, hosts, ice cream fountain workers, bartenders, an order-entry keypuncher, and dishwashers. In all, there are sixty employees; however, a normal shift includes twelve servers, four hosts, two fountain workers, a bartender, a keypuncher, and three dishwashers.

Terri has been with South-40 for more than ten years. She did not attend college, but has progressed from host to manager because she has an outstanding work ethic and a high degree of loyalty for the restaurant. The employees like Terri and respect her authority. Although she makes some unpopular decisions, Terri is seen as fair and consistent in dealing with employees. She also has a very good rapport with a number of regular customers. Terri expects that everyone can and will do their jobs, and she keeps out of their way if they perform to her expectations. When problems arise, she keeps a cool head and talks the problem out with the involved employees, leading them toward finding their own solutions. This approach helps employees feel that they can talk to Terri about problems and concerns they have at work. Although she oversees all staffing decisions, Terri allows Shelly to assume the responsibility for serving staff decisions.

Because South-40 is in a college town, 75 percent of the servers are college students working part-time. This makes scheduling more difficult because students have night classes, tests, breaks, and other college activities. The other 25 percent are slightly older than the college servers and work most of the day hours. Many older employees have small children and work so they have a second source of income. Their hours and quality of shifts are very important to them.

The higher rate of turnover means that servers are being trained frequently, usually four to five each month. When someone is hired, he or she is given a packet of guidelines concerning uniform, tardiness, and sick day policies. There is nothing written concerning discipline. After passing a written test on the menu, new servers follow an experienced server for at least three shifts. Following that, they serve guest tables by themselves with a more experienced server checking their tickets before they are sent to the kitchen. Shelly usually schedules training on Monday night, when she does not work.

Shelly was taking some general business courses at a community college when she was hired as a host. During the year she was a host, she took one class per semester. Shortly after she had been at the restaurant for one year, the assistant manager left to open a new restaurant. Although Shelly was only 19, she was promoted to assistant manager. She spent two months training for her new position before she was left on her own. Once she was promoted to assistant manager, she quit taking classes.

The Problem

From the start there has been trouble. Whereas Terri remains calm in the face of trouble, Shelly panics and begins shouting at employees. Terri allows things to go on as long as everything is getting done, but Shelly feels that she has to tell everyone what they should be doing at all times. If anyone questions Shelly's commands, she gets defensive. It seems that she enjoys telling people what to do and being in control at all times.

After a few servers complained to Terri about Shelly's behavior, Terri discussed these concerns with Shelly. Shelly indicated that she feels everyone is trying to undermine her authority. Terri tried to convince her that she should have more confidence in employees and let them do their jobs. Terri explained that at any one time, there is more than one thing servers should be doing. She pointed out that Shelly seems to notice whatever is not being done, and has servers drop what they are doing to follow her orders. When she stops them as they are getting drinks, it causes frustration and a great deal of waste. The servers leave the drinks half done and eventually another employee dumps them.

After the talk, Shelly seemed to be trying to use some of Terri's advice, and things were running smoothly. This lasted only a few weeks before Shelly slipped back into the same style she had before Terri talked to her.

Shelly is known for being concerned about too much talking among employees, especially when things are slow. She deals with this by threatening to cut their hours or scheduling them for undesirable shifts. On the other hand, Shelly often follows her reprimands by pulling a couple of servers aside to ask them what she should wear on a date or what is happening on a soap opera—chatter that the employees see as idle and unproductive. They question, among themselves, the inconsistency of Shelly's actions and directives.

Terri is nearing the due date for her third child, and Shelly is organizing a baby pool. During slow time on a Sunday afternoon, two servers, **Pam Watson** and **Jess Muller,** were checking the calendar and talking about what date they would pick for the baby's birth. Shelly yelled at them in front of several customers as well as other employees. She was upset because they were nearing the end of their shifts and still on the clock. As they were leaving fifteen minutes later, they saw Shelly talking with a group of servers who had just punched in for the night shift. She was trying to get them to buy guesses in the baby pool right in the middle of the restaurant and in front of some customers.

One week after the yelling incident, Shelly stopped Pam in the employee lounge as she came in for her shift. She yelled at her about what she had done the week before as well as some other unimportant things. She made statements such as, "You didn't seem to be yourself last Friday," and "Sometimes you are not as productive as other servers in your room." In addition, she asked Pam if her schedule was affecting her mood and commented about how she had noticed Pam's negative attitude. Pam told Shelly she was unhappy last week because she was scheduled to come in last every shift, which meant the other servers got the first tables in the room. Shelly became very defensive and began yelling about how difficult it was to schedule around everyone's special needs. She told Pam to do the schedule if she thought she could do a better job. She also asked her why she hadn't said anything earlier. Pam told her she was afraid if she had, it would have seemed like she was complaining and her hours would get cut further. This time Shelly really blew up, stating that she did not understand why everyone thinks she is so unreasonable. By this time, Pam was in tears and Shelly had to do something because the restaurant was getting busy. She left Pam in the employee lounge and returned to her duties. About thirty minutes later, she returned and told Pam to do cleanup duty before going home, not allowing her to wait on any tables.

News of the incident spread fast. When other servers, including Jess, asked what was wrong with Pam, Shelly told them Pam didn't feel well and wanted to go home. The other servers knew better, and that day tension began to show in everyone. Customers seemed to sense the tension and it affected service.

That night Pam told Terri about what had happened that day. Pam had talked to Jess and learned how Shelly had described the reason for Pam leaving early and not working that day. She decided it was time to explain the inconsistency between Shelly's talk and actions. Terri asked Pam what precipitated the confrontation, and Pam shared about the episode regarding the baby pool.

Pam also told Terri she did not want to quit because she enjoys working in a restaurant where the guests are happy with the food. Pam also knows that happy customers usually leave excellent tips, and Pam is a college student who is funding some of her education.

Terri was concerned because she is nearing her maternity leave, and Shelly would be acting manager in her absence. She wanted the restaurant employees to be there when she returned from her leave.

Discussion Questions

1. If you were Terri, describe how you would conduct the conference with Shelly. Why do you think this method would work?
2. What do you think are some reasons for Shelly's behavior? Be specific.
3. As Shelly, how would you handle discipline problems with servers? Develop a specific plan. Why would you use this plan?
4. What tactics, if any, would you use to help the servers change?

5. What, if anything, do you think could have been done at the beginning to avoid the friction between Shelly and the servers? Explain.
6. What effects can Shelly's behavior have on the overall operation? Support your response. How can her behavior affect service? Support your response.
7. Does Terri have any other options for her replacement during her maternity leave? Why or why not?
8. Evaluate Dana's decision to let the manager and assistant manager make all decisions for the front of the house.

The Uptown Grille

The Uptown Grille, located on the far north side of a large midwestern city, has been a popular dining establishment for years. **Wes** and **Sarah Walton** opened the Uptown Grille in 1970. Through hard work and skill, they built the restaurant into a thriving business. Within fifteen years, the Uptown Grille was doing almost $1,000,000 per year in sales, with 75 percent of sales from food and 25 percent from liquor. Food costs averaged 34 percent of food sales; beverage costs, 24 percent of beverage sales; and labor costs, 28 percent of total sales during the last few years. The Uptown Grille serves lunch and dinner six days per week, Monday through Saturday. Almost 60 percent of the Uptown Grille's customers are regulars, many visiting the restaurant at least twice each month.

Wes and Sarah, like many independent restaurateurs, encourage a family atmosphere among their employees. Many employees have been with the Waltons five years or more, and turnover has been less than 40 percent (mostly dishwashers and bussers). Under the Waltons' management there were no written policies, procedures, or rules, so problems were settled on a case-by-case basis. The Waltons counted on the respect and affection of their employees to keep the operation running smoothly. Despite their upbeat management style, the Waltons were not pushovers. Wes had fired a few employees, and was not afraid to discipline employees when necessary. In general, the system worked well. The Uptown Grille was considered a pleasant place to work.

After thirty years in the business, Wes and Sarah decided they would like to step out of the Uptown Grille's day-to-day management. They wanted to travel and visit their widely scattered children and grandchildren. Both Waltons were tired of their required seventy- to eighty-hour workweeks. With pretax earnings over $125,000 per year, they decided to hire a manager for the Uptown Grille while retaining ownership. This arrangement would assure them of a comfortable retirement income. After interviewing several candidates, the Waltons decided to hire Russ Braun.

Russ Braun, age 42, had recently retired from the U.S. Army after twenty years of active service. Russ had worked his way up from kitchen patrol as a private to general manager of the officers' club on several military bases. Russ developed strong technical skills in the kitchen and service areas as well as expertise in cost control and purchasing. He was known as a stern, no-nonsense manager who ran operations "by the book." Despite his toughness and rather authoritarian management style, Russ's former employees (mostly lower-level enlisted personnel and army spouses) felt he was fair. Employees knew where they stood with Russ, generally respected him, and performed well for him.

Upon retiring, Russ returned to his hometown and sought work as a restaurant manager. Prior to his interview with the Waltons, several establishments had turned Russ down. The Waltons thought Russ Braun was a "dream come true." Wes had served in the Korean War and had great affection and respect for the military. Even more important, Russ had an excellent pension and was willing to work for only $40,000 per year. The Waltons hired Russ and agreed to train him for four weeks.

The Braun Regime

During the first month of the joint Braun-Walton management, the Uptown Grille seemed to be running smoothly. Due to the presence of Wes and Sarah, Russ's personality was relatively low-key. However, three weeks after the Waltons left, tempers were flaring. The Waltons had been easygoing about lateness and absences; Russ laid down the law. The Waltons managed employees on an individual basis with few rules or written standards; Russ developed policies, procedures, and rules and strictly enforced them. Perhaps the final blow came when Russ banned the employees from the Uptown Grille's bar. The Waltons had allowed employees to go to the bar after work and purchase drinks for half-price. They believed that this encouraged good relations among employees and good will toward the Waltons.

A core group of employees (approximately half) rebelled. Two long-term employees—**Molly Mason,** a waitress, and **Greg Hunter,** the head cook—spearheaded the revolt. After a very distressing Saturday night, the unhappy employees met at a local lodge to discuss their complaints. Within an hour, they prepared a petition calling for Russ's termination and everyone signed it. On Monday morning, Molly and Greg met with the Waltons, who had just returned to town the previous Thursday, to discuss the employees' complaints.

The Waltons were outraged and sympathetic: outraged at Russ's authoritarian ways, and sympathetic with the plight of the employees. That evening, they met with Russ and demanded that he relax the many restrictions. Russ flatly refused. He threw his keys on the table and launched into a heated defense of his previous management record and his current actions at the Uptown Grille. Finally, Russ offered to quit, if the Waltons wanted him to do so.

The Waltons were impressed by Russ's defense of his actions and were reluctant to take over the management of the Uptown Grille again. Also, they were leaving the next day for a six-week trip to Arizona. For these reasons, the Waltons decided to keep Russ as manager. They urged him to "lighten up" a bit and expressed their faith in his ability to manage the Uptown Grille. Russ stayed on as manager, and the Waltons headed southwest in their motorhome.

As one might expect, Russ was irritated with what he termed employee insubordination and proceeded to crack down even harder on the Uptown Grille's employees. Three employees quit and one more was fired for "insubordination." Several customers even picked up on the problems and sided with the employees.

On Friday, when the Waltons returned from Arizona, they were greeted by calls and visits from disgruntled employees. The pleasant retirement to which they had looked forward was turning into a nightmare, and the Uptown Grille was sinking fast. On Monday, the Waltons had a meeting with Russ. They insisted on his rehiring the fired employee and relaxing most of the new rules. After an hour of bitter discussion, Russ quit.

For the next six months, the Waltons managed the Uptown Grille, reinstating their management philosophy and getting everything back to normal. Within three months, they felt that conditions were reasonably stable at the Uptown Grille. Again, Wes and Sarah started seeking another manager. They were determined to avoid making the same mistake. After interviewing several different candidates, they hired Fred Rogers.

Fred Rogers was a recent graduate of Independence State University (ISU) with a degree in secondary education. He had played baseball at ISU and had hoped to coach at the high school level. However, no teaching/coaching jobs were available in his hometown, forcing Fred to look for other types of work.

At ISU, Fred had worked as a waiter and bartender to help defray his college expenses. By the end of his senior year, Fred was a bar manager. Upon graduating and moving home, Fred found a job as assistant manager of a local restaurant. One year later, after moderate success, Fred read about the manager position opening at the Uptown Grille.

In the initial interview with the Waltons, Fred was told about the problems Russ Braun had encountered. Wes stressed the importance of treating employees like family and warned against the authoritarian, by-the-book approach of Russ Braun. To the Waltons, Fred seemed to be the perfect choice. He was personable, had some good restaurant/bar experience, and appeared to be a relaxed, low-key sort of manager. Fred was offered the position, and he accepted it.

The Rogers Regime

The Waltons worked side-by-side with Fred for six weeks, hoping to ease Fred's transition to general manager. Despite some slight concern over Fred's deferring to the Waltons on many decisions, the Waltons felt Fred could manage the Uptown Grille effectively.

Fred's management style was the opposite of Russ Braun's approach. Where Russ was intense, Fred was extremely laid back. Where Russ had ruled "by the book," Fred dealt with situations as they arose, often negotiating a solution to problems. Fred believed that if all the employees liked him, productivity would increase. Soon Fred began socializing with the employees, and most of the Uptown Grille staff could be found drinking with Fred after work every night. Morale seemed very high; everybody liked Fred and his easygoing ways.

However, the "sweet life" at the Uptown Grille started turning sour within a few weeks of the Waltons' departure. Little by little, Fred began to delegate most of the power and decision-making authority to various employees. If employees came in late, Fred ignored the problem. Operational problems were handed back to employees: "Why don't you check with Greg or Molly to see what he or she wants you to do?" Or "What do *you* think we should do?" Servers dealt with customer complaints, often with expensive, inappropriate solutions. Scheduling and purchasing fell to Molly in the dining room and Greg in the kitchen. Soon Fred became little more than a figurehead.

If Molly and Greg had been good managers, this arrangement might not have caused major problems. However, Greg's priorities were (1) looking out for Greg and (2) making the cooks' lives as easy as possible. Greg would give the best hours and shifts to his friends. He consistently overstaffed the kitchen and caused overtime to accrue. No attention was given to arrangement and garnishing of food before it was sent to the dining room. Perhaps most serious of all, no recipes or procedures were followed, ordering was haphazard, and leftovers were improperly handled. Food quality declined as food costs increased.

Molly's priorities were similar to those of Greg. She looked out for herself and tried to make the servers' lives easy and profitable. Her friends also were given the best shifts and sections. Side work started to slip because no one checked it. Free food and drinks were given to customers in hopes of bigger tips. Insufficient numbers of servers were scheduled to cover the business, because Molly and her friends believed they could make more money with bigger stations.

Within nine months of Fred's arrival, the Uptown Grille was in an uproar. Employees were mad about preferential schedules, and servers were concerned about poor food quality, increased complaints, and declining customer counts. Regular customers, in particular, complained about poor food quality and service and the dirty, rundown appearance of the dining room. Server tips and customer numbers both declined.

Of greater concern to the Waltons was the poor financial performance of the Uptown Grille. Food costs had jumped to 42 percent (from 34 percent under the Waltons), liquor costs rose to 31 percent (from 24 percent), and labor costs climbed to 36 percent (from 28 percent). The Uptown Grille was now losing money in a big way! The Waltons had met with Fred twice during this period of decline to discuss problems, but Fred always seemed to have good excuses. Importantly, employees strongly supported Fred for the first few months, although that support seemed to be dropping. Also, the Waltons' youngest daughter had recently given birth to their first grandson, and they were often in Texas helping her.

During a dismal two-week period in late January, several events occurred that forced the Waltons to make a change. Two long-term purveyors threatened to put the Uptown Grille on C.O.D. due to unpaid bills, and the county health inspector gave the Uptown Grille a failing score on its annual inspection. Finally, several senior employees called Wes to discuss problems at the Uptown Grille, and two valued customers called Wes to complain.

Wes and Sarah returned home quickly and summoned Fred for a serious conference. Fred showed up for the meeting with liquor on his breath and appeared to be disoriented. After failing to get any intelligent responses from him, Wes fired Fred. Wearily, the Waltons contemplated stepping back into managing the Uptown Grille.

The Tragedy

The Waltons, now two years older, again worked feverishly to get the Uptown Grille back on track. After two weeks of fourteen-hour days, tragedy struck. On a busy Saturday night, when the kitchen staff and servers were both backed up and screaming at each other, customers were complaining, and the air conditioner was out of service, Wes suffered a serious heart attack and collapsed in the kitchen. One customer, a physician, administered CPR while waiting for the ambulance to arrive. Wes was admitted to intensive care, where he remained for the next forty-eight hours. Sarah was at his side.

Following triple bypass surgery, Wes began a slow recovery. His doctor told him and Sarah they had to get out of the restaurant—either sell it or hire a competent manager. Because the Uptown Grille had severely declined in recent months, the Waltons feared they couldn't get a decent price for it. After much discussion, they decided to hire an employment agency to find a competent manager, and agreed to pay top dollar for an experienced, proven individual. If things didn't work out this time, they would close the Uptown Grille, sell the building, equipment, and liquor license; and lower their expectation of a comfortable retirement.

Within a month, the agency had recruited five different candidates. Sarah tried to run the Uptown Grille while Wes carefully interviewed candidates. After thorough interviews, background checks, and discussion, the Waltons decided to hire Jane Robson.

Jane Robson, age 28, was divorced with no children. She had graduated from a highly respected local university's hotel and restaurant management program six years earlier, and had built a successful career as a manager with two well-known full-service restaurant chains. Her credentials showed that she was competent in both the kitchen and the front of the house, and she had been involved in two turnaround situations. The challenge of turning around the seriously troubled Uptown Grille was appealing to Jane. She was offered $25,000 more than she currently was making plus a bonus. After much soul searching, Jane accepted the position.

Sarah and Wes introduced Jane to the Uptown Grille employees and asked them to give Jane their support. During this introduction, Jane noticed Molly roll her eyes in exasperation, and heard Greg mutter expletives. Other employees obviously were less than thrilled at the prospect of a third manager in less than three years. In many ways, Jane felt like a substitute teacher in a tough high school. She wondered how she would manage this turnaround.

Jane's Dilemma

Sarah was totally exhausted from six weeks as solo manager and couldn't assist in the transfer of management. Wes was forbidden to work by his doctor. As a result, Jane was forced to begin managing the first day.

Jane's plan of attack, which had served her well in her previous positions, was to tread lightly her first two or three weeks. She held one-on-one meetings with each employee, as well as various work groups. These meetings helped her understand past problems. Jane also talked with various customers. She observed and recorded the many problems, large and small. From big problems, such as high food and labor costs, to small problems, such as frequent personal phone calls to and from employees, Jane's list of "opportunities" seemed endless.

Jane was confident in her abilities as a manager and believed she could solve the Uptown Grille's problems. However, she was very worried about the Waltons' intent to close the Uptown Grille if conditions (including employee morale) did not improve. She also was quite concerned about the personnel-related problems of her predecessors, Russ and Fred, and the power of Molly and Greg. Jane had her work cut out for her, and she needed to consider how to go about it.

On her day off, she lay on her sofa, thinking about the Uptown Grille and possible approaches to turning it into a stable, happy and profitable restaurant. She asked herself, "What tactics would produce the needed results?"

Discussion Questions

1. Evaluate the operation of the Uptown Grille under the Waltons. What are the main issues? Why are do you consider these issues?

2. What caused Russ Braun's problems? Support your answer. Could Russ have succeeded at the Uptown Grille? Support your answer. Why was he hired? Be specific. Was he a good choice? Why or why not? Who is to blame for the problems under Russ? Explain your answers.

3. What caused Fred Rogers's problems? Support your answer. Could Fred have succeeded at the Uptown Grille? Support your answer. Why was he hired? Be specific. Was he a good choice? Why or why not? Who is to blame for the problems under Fred? Explain your answers.

4. How would you handle employees like Greg and Molly? Defend your plan.

5. If you were Jane, what would you do about the Uptown Grille's problems? Develop a possible strategic plan to pursue in turning around the Uptown Grille, both short term and long term. Identify goals. Determine alternatives to evaluate. Discuss the strengths and weaknesses of your plan. How would you evaluate your success? What would your evaluation provide?

Chow's Express

Joan Chung is a junior in the business college majoring in management at a midwestern university. She is from an Asian country and has had little working experience before and during her first two years at the university. During the summer prior to her junior year, she decided to find an off-campus job, hoping to enhance what she had learned in class with real industry experience. Many of her friends recommended that she apply for a job at Chow's Express—an Asian-style quick-service restaurant owned by an Asian couple. She was told the business was very successful and the Chows were looking for a cashier for the dinner shift. Even though she has never been a cashier, she was hired. She is fluent in English, which is not common among representative employees in ethnic restaurants but often is important for businesses to run smoothly. Joan was excited and looked forward to meeting new people and learning new things.

Background

Chow's Express has been in business for twenty years and is one of the half-dozen Asian restaurants in the community. Both lunch and dinner are served seven days a week with about forty menu items from which to choose. Its dining area, which can seat seventy, is always full during rush hours. Most customers are students at the university. Chow's Express has been a famous Asian quick-service business for several years and has been more successful than all competing restaurants.

Chow's success can be attributed to good location, reasonable meal prices, consistent food quality, and quick service. It is located near both campus and student apartment complexes and has convenient parking nearby, an advantage compared to several similar restaurants in town. Meal prices have risen very little since last year, although according to some old customers portion sizes have become

103

smaller. Customers can count on consistent food quality for the price. Their expectations will be met every time they eat at Chow's Restaurant. Whether the order is dine-in or takeout, customers wait a maximum of six to seven minutes.

As with typical small Asian restaurants, Chow's Express is owned by a couple, **Mr.** and **Mrs. Chow,** with the husband taking care of the cooking and the wife running the day-to-day business in both the back and the front of the house. In addition to Mr. Chow, there are three kitchen employees; **Aren Lee,** an assistant cook; and two prep workers. Mr. Chow is a very skillful chef who does most of the cooking. Because the food has been consistent and distinct, most regular customers develop their own "favorites" from the menu and order them on a regular basis.

Mr. Chow has begun to train Aren to be a cook through very intensive on-the-job sessions. He is pleased with how well she is doing.

Jina Huang, the dining room supervisor, oversees four servers and two cashiers for lunch and dinner shifts. Except for Jina, who works full-time, all the other employees are part-timers, and most of them are students at the university. In order to preserve the Oriental style and ambience, all employees either are from Asian countries or are Asian Americans.

On the Job

During the first week, Joan was very excited about her new job—learning cashiering skills, learning more about food, and talking to customers. She was a fast learner and in a short amount of time her cashiering job was going well. As time passed, she got to see, know, and experience more of what was happening at the restaurant, which resulted in Joan's feeling more uncomfortable working there.

The Chows are both owners and managers of this typical small ethnic restaurant. Mrs. Chow is very authoritative and controlling and she must make every decision, big or small. Even her chef husband has little to say most of the time. She has little respect toward her employees and words like *lazy* and *stupid* are frequently yelled at employees whose work is not up to her standard of speed and efficiency. Mrs. Chow does not hire enough servers, so there are only two servers even at the busiest hours. Her rationale is that with customers picking up their own food, cleaning and resetting tables should be pretty easy and fast. But for each server taking care of ten to twelve tables during the whole shift, the workload is quite physically challenging. Due to the nature of service, no tip is involved. Everybody in Chow's Express, except Aren and Jina, gets minimum wage. To date there has never been a raise. Performance and seniority are not factors in Mrs. Chow's decisions about wages. No job description or specification is available, and no formal, consistent training procedure is provided to new employees, because as Mrs. Chow puts it, "If you are smart enough to go to college, you should also be smart enough to do the job here."

Jina, the dining room supervisor, is almost a replica of Mrs. Chow—controlling, hot-tempered, and often nasty toward the servers. She is pushy like Mrs. Chow but seldom gives servers a hand no matter how busy they are. Whenever servers complain to Mrs. Chow about the way Jina treats them, Mrs. Chow always supports Jina and blames servers for not being fast or efficient enough. Working in such a negative environment, employees are not happy and turnover is very high. Students come and go. Mr. and Mrs. Chow do not care or worry too much about the availability of their labor sources.

Besides the management style, Joan can't accept several customer-related issues either. Almost every day at lunch and dinner times, a long line extends all the way out the door. In order to get guests seated and served faster, Mrs. Chow and Jina push customers out by walking back and forth among customers who are almost finished. As soon as a guest puts the last spoonful to his or her mouth, they collect the guest's plate, so others at the table feel the pressure to eat faster. If they catch customers enjoying conversation after they finish eating, they never hesitate to go to their tables and ask them to leave. As guests keep coming, the dining room is always crowded at the two meal times. Joan asked Mrs. Chow why she didn't consider expansion because business is so good. The answer was, "There's no better location in town than here and expansion here is impossible."

The dining room is not only crowded but also eroding, the carpet is old and greasy, chairs are uncomfortably hard with worn fabric, and the few posters and decorations on the wall are faded. The biggest problem is the cooking odor from the kitchen. The restaurant's ventilation system always has problems, and sometimes the dining room smells as if Mr. Chow were doing the frying right at the table. Joan has overheard servers and some customers complain about it, but it seems the Chows don't mind the odor themselves. Another thing that is unacceptable to Joan is that when she helps prepare take-out orders, she frequently finds that the amount in the "to-go" boxes is noticeably less than the amount on plates. She has never said anything to anybody, but it's not hard for her to figure out why.

In spite of all these problems, the business is good, with customers lining up every day waiting to be served. Several Asian restaurants tried to compete with Chow's Express, offering a more spacious and better-decorated dining area, more meal choices, and even lower prices and numerous promotions. But strangely enough, people still keep coming to Chow's Express, and Chow's Express is still number one.

Joan once heard Mrs. Chow say, "As long as you have good food and low prices, people will always come back no matter what." Joan is pondering whether that statement is really or always true. Recently, something new happened to Chow's Express. They plan to open a new unit very soon in another college community 300 miles away. The Chows plan to transfer Jina and Aren there and promote Aren to chef and Jina to manager. Joan has been cashier for several months and also is fairly familiar with the dining room routine by observing and sometimes helping serve. She does a good job and is friendly to customers and other employees. Because of the nature of her job, she is relatively less involved in other employee work. Therefore, she has had no major conflicts with anybody. Mrs. Chow asked Joan if she would be interested in being promoted to dining room supervisor and hinted that there might be a small increase in her hourly wage.

Joan can't make up her mind. She believes that Chow's Express has the potential to serve its customers better and provide a more positive working environment for employees, even though the improvements may not necessarily correlate with a further increase in profit. Joan thinks that to run or manage a business, there are more things to be considered than merely making more and more money. If she holds a managerial position, she would want to keep employees longer and increase their job satisfaction. She would want to gradually systematize hiring, training, and performance appraisal procedures, and establish a wage scale. She would want to determine better ways to provide customers a more welcoming and relaxing dining atmosphere. But on the other hand, she can foresee inevitable conflicts with the Chows if she accepts the promotion and suggests any changes in the restaurant operation. Considering their differences in management style and philosophy of doing business, Joan doesn't think the Chows will buy any of her ideas.

Discussion Questions

1. In your opinion, what are the major problems in Chow's Express? Elaborate on your answer.
2. Are there any positive aspects about Chow's Express? Support your response.
3. Considering the situation of the business and customer composition, is there any reason to make any changes in the restaurant operation? Why or why not?
4. What do you think are the chances of TQM principles being adopted in Chow's Express, considering the nature of the business and the owners? Defend your answer.
5. Should Joan accept the promotion? Give reasons for your answer.
6. If you were Joan and decided to accept the promotion, what changes or improvements would you set forth? Why?
7. How would you persuade the Chows to accept your ideas on changes or improvement? Explain why you chose this approach and why it is appropriate.
8. If you were a consultant for small business, would your suggestion for changes be different than your response to question 6? If so, what would be your top three recommendations for the Chows to improve their business? If not, why?
9. If you were Joan, what advice would you give Jina? Explain.

House of Fine Pizza

House of Fine Pizza (HFP) is a nationwide pizza restaurant chain with stores in forty states. Each area manager supervises about twelve stores, and each store has a store manager, an assistant manager (if volume permits), and two shift managers.

The Elm Street Store

Jeff Carson, manager of the Elm Street store, is reflecting on the meeting he just finished with most of the store's employees. He informed them that he will be conducting performance appraisals and making decisions about raises at the end of the month. While the form for employees to sign for a thirty-minute evaluation time was being circulated, he heard many employees grumbling about the changes that were taking place. They didn't like how he was on them about things that Holly Steltz, the previous manager, didn't think were important. They openly discussed that if they didn't get a good evaluation with a raise, they would request a transfer to Pilot Mound, where Holly had become manager. Jeff recently hired enough employees to handle the amount of business that the store does, and he doesn't want to spend time recruiting new employees. Yet he doesn't want the labor problem to overshadow his objective evaluations.

Jeff is contemplating the past few months. While visiting with two other store managers, he learned some of the history of the Elm Street store. Now he is trying to piece the bits of information together.

The Staff

Holly Steltz was previously the store manager for a delivery/carryout-only store, where she didn't think the opportunities were as good, in Clarksdale, a large metro area. Holly met an HFP manager at a party and, after hearing about the opportunities the company provided, she made her wishes known that if there was an opportunity for a management position she would be interested. Holly had worked for HFP four years when she became the West store manager two years ago. When the Elm Street manager resigned suddenly, **Erika Bergan,** the area manager, needed someone to move quickly. Holly volunteered, and Erika was pleased because an experienced assistant manager was ready for promotion and could replace Holly at the West store. Erika had a strong philosophy about promoting from within, and always looked for that opportunity when a position opened.

Holly supervised three shift managers, which was different from the previous stores. She had always been at stores that had an assistant manager. Together the three shift managers had about eighteen months of management experience. However, Holly was very flexible and enjoyed challenges such as the one that an inexperienced management team could bring. She looked at this as an opportunity to make an impression on Erika.

Lori Williams, a shift manager for the past nine months, had been a shift manager at a store in Rock City for two years before Elm Street. She began her career with HFP as a part-time employee while she was a high school student. After graduating from high school, she began work as a cook for three years before being promoted to a shift manager position at Rock City.

Brad Thompson was hired as a cook at Elm Street when he graduated from high school. He performed so well that he was promoted to shift manager just six months later. Brad was attending night school to get a two-year degree in business. Brad and Lori became very close friends, both in and out of the store. Brad often went to Lori with problems about his new job. He recognized Lori's experience and didn't feel intimidated by her. He knew he could trust her not to tell Holly about the work problems. Holly didn't seem to mind that Brad didn't discuss work-related problems with her.

Jackie Bryan was hired as shift manager at Elm Street two weeks before Holly arrived. She had worked at another HFP store as a cook and was promoted to shift manager. She worked with HFP for four years while working on a degree in hospitality management. Jackie liked the Clarksdale area and was happy to be hired as a shift manager. She anticipated that with her degree she had an opportunity to advance within the company. Jeff liked the skills Jackie brought to the job.

One manager who talks to Jeff often had told him that Jackie had had aspirations to become a manager of a larger store before pursing an area manager position. He suggested that Jeff might consider relying on her for assistance in making necessary changes. However, last week as Jeff was scheduling her performance review, she told Jeff she wasn't sure that she wanted to be an area manager. Jeff noted that Jackie wasn't included in the Lori-Brad twosome, and that pleased him.

Recent History

The store had run fairly well under Holly's leadership. It was a definite "gold mine." Gross revenue for an average evening was $3,000, and up to $6,000 on Friday and Saturday. It was recognized as the highest-profit delivery and carryout store in the region. Employees were happy. Everyone seemed to get along with each other. It was obvious they liked Holly's lenient style. Turnover was relatively low. Deliveries were getting to customers on time, and complaints were few.

Jeff learned that Holly had let other factors, such as costs of sales and labor and store cleanliness, slip below company standards so that high performance could be achieved in delivery. Shortly before Holly transferred, a health inspector made a store visit; the store barely passed. The health inspector told Holly he would return in a few weeks for a follow-up inspection. Holly was not there for the follow-up, so Jeff had to take the brunt of what the inspector had to say. He felt fortunate that he could persuade the inspector to give him additional time to bring the store up to standard. The inspector told Jeff he would give him three weeks. Jeff was amazed that Erika was not on top of the store's condition. When Jeff told Erika about the inspection, she replied that Jeff knew what to do, and the store needed to be brought to the inspector's standards at the return visit. To have the store closed would not make the company happy, and Jeff would mostly likely lose his career with the company.

Looking back to his notes on Elm Street history, Jeff recalled that his friends had told him that in early fall Holly was told that she would be transferred to the Pilot Mound store, which had major management problems. The manager had been terminated, and the assistant manager was not ready to take over the store. It would be unusual for an assistant to move to manager of such a large store. Erika's mode of operation was to move the assistant to a smaller store and move a more experienced manager to the large store. Erika was certain Holly could bring the store into compliance.

Erika had considered several people for store manager, but Holly had impressed Erika with her strengths related to highly visible performance factors such as delivery percentages, employee relations, and customer complaints. Assuming that other performance factors also were satisfactory, Erika saw no reason not to transfer Holly. Erika liked Holly's willingness to move and considered it when making the decision.

Holly was excited to get the promotion and challenge. She could use the extra salary to pay off her new car and possibly move to a larger apartment. The promotion would be one step closer to area manager. She was ready to work hard, and she knew Erika would be supportive.

Holly and Erika had gotten along very well. Although Erika did not visit Holly's store very often, they talked on the telephone and e-mailed each other. Several times lately, they had gone out for dinner. Erika hoped that Holly's promotion would boost their friendship. Erika liked doing things socially with Holly and felt that this move could secure their relationship. She assumed Holly would feel that she owed Erika for the promotion. Holly enjoyed Erika's company and the opportunity to share her successes with Erika.

Holly completed the move within the week. Erika asked Jeff to take over as the Elm Street store manager as soon as possible. Jeff knew there would be no overlap in managers because it would be a couple of weeks before his replacement would be available. In the meantime, Erika served as interim manager, which meant that the three shift managers were in charge.

Jeff had been an assistant manager for two years at a smaller HFP store before becoming an assistant manager at a somewhat larger store. He moved to the Clarksdale area in April to work as an assistant manager for a much larger store. He accepted the store manager position at Elm Street immediately because he needed to further his career with the company, and this was the first opportunity offered him. He neglected to visit the store, but with the report from Erika and his experience at the current store, he didn't have any concerns.

After reviewing the store's history prior to his taking over as manager, Jeff reflected on his first day at the store. When Jeff arrived at the Elm Street store, he immediately noticed that store records were unorganized, the store was not very clean, and employees were not following policies. He noticed they often were a few minutes late to work and took breaks on the clock, and many of them never wore their hats and nametags.

HFP has standard specifications for all its food products that are measured by different size cups and certain number requirements. Food-quality managers at corporate determine these specifications for a reason, and there is a need for each store to follow them to ensure consistency within the chain. Jeff noticed that cooks rarely used measuring cups; they told him him that they had made enough pizzas to know by instinct how much of each topping and how many toppings to use. He immediately stated that all pizzas were to be made according to the specifications, something the cooks were not pleased to hear. Food costs also were higher because of rejects on the carryout orders. Approximately one out of every twenty pizzas had some mistake, whether it was supposed to have mushrooms and didn't or was to be pan crust and not thin and crispy. Jeff also noted that discounts were given on delivered pizzas for some of the same reasons. And many drivers did not use the sign in their vehicles while delivering pizza.

The Meeting

Jeff determined that Holly and the shift managers had been very lenient in enforcing these policies, and employees rarely followed them. He held an employee meeting to discuss the situation and his plans for change.

Jeff was surprised to learn that employees weren't aware of the policies and that there was an employee handbook. Jeff told employees that shift managers would enforce policies that were being ignored. If employees forgot their nametags or hats, they were given replacements for that shift. The next time they forgot their hats and nametags, a small fine was assessed. Employees were told to clock out anytime they were being nonproductive, such as for taking cigarette breaks, making personal phone calls, and using the restroom. Cleaning schedules were to be developed, and employees would be given certain items/areas to clean every night. Drivers were told that failure to use the signs in their vehicles would be documented. After three documentations, they would be terminated. Jeff told them that he personally would be checking the vehicles every hour.

Because rules were enforced, several employees requested a transfer to Holly's store. Those who were not transferred to Pilot Mound requested transfers to other stores or quit. Many employees, including Brad, reminded Jeff that he had never worked at a delivery/carryout-only store, and therefore did not know how to manage Elm Street.

Most employees who remained resisted changes, and many of them, including Lori and Brad, voiced their resistance openly in Jeff's absence. Jeff frequently noticed that Brad and Lori still were very lenient with enforcing policies. Jackie tended to be less lenient and to give Jeff more support than the other two shift managers.

Another problem that Jeff encountered was the number of employees who were calling in on a regular basis with excuses for not coming to work. The day-time drivers and cooks seemed more loyal than the nighttime employees. Between 3:30 P.M. and 5:00 P.M., at least three drivers and one cook called with either car problems or sickness. This caused extreme trouble for the dinner and mid-evening rushes that occurred nightly. It also caused distress for the closing shift manager because chances were that at least one or two of these employees were scheduled to close. This left at least some of the nightly cleaning and stocking tasks for the next day.

Jeff knew it would take time to make significant changes. During the first month, his main concern was not to get shut down by the inspector. He avoided talking with Erika because he wanted to make the changes on his own. He wanted her to be impressed with his ability, and maybe some day an area management position would be offered to him.

Discussion Questions

1. What are the major problems in the store? How should they be handled? Justify your response.
2. Did Jeff make a mistake in not visiting the store before he accepted the manager position? Defend your response.
3. Was Jeff too strict with enforcing policy and procedures? Why or why not? Are there any policies that Jeff could have ignored? Why or why not?
4. If you were Jeff, would you have conducted an employee meeting to discuss the situation at the store? Why or why not? If so, what major points would be on the agenda?
5. Is there anything that Jeff could do initially to remedy this situation? Support your answer. Why do you think your ideas would work?
6. Compare and contrast Holly and Jeff's management styles. Which person would you want to work for you, if either? Support your answer.
7. Describe Erika's management style. Would you want her to be one of your employees? Why or why not?
8. What action would you take when you heard employees' comments during the employee meeting? Why would you take these actions?
9. How should Jeff tackle the task of performance appraisals? Be specific and justify your suggestions.

Four Months Later

Jeff has completed all performance reviews and did not feel good about giving raises. He felt that the employees were not doing their jobs, and didn't deserve much of a raise. He gave a minimal cost-of-living increase to most employees. Some got less. He was surprised that employees felt their performances were much better than what he noticed. For most criteria, his evaluation was lower than employees' self-evaluations.

However, costs of sales and labor at the Elm Street store were within acceptable limits. On the other hand, the percentage of pizzas getting to customers on time dropped drastically, and customer complaints subsequently increased. Jeff knows that the delivery time has increased because his drivers are not taking direct routes and are wasting time leaving the store after their orders are ready. In some instances, drivers are intentionally leaving the vehicle signs in the store and having to return to get them. They make sure that Jeff is aware that this procedure is delaying deliveries.

The store as a whole is 100 percent cleaner than when Jeff started, and the health inspector is very pleased. In fact, at the three-week visit, the health inspector told Jeff he had never seen a food operation make such significant changes in a short time. Jeff remembers many late evenings at the store making changes and cleaning walk-ins, scrubbing equipment, and improving the grounds.

A major concern is low employee morale. Lori transferred out of the store two months ago, leaving Brad and Jackie. Brad openly criticizes Jeff's style of leadership in front of employees. He has made his wish to transfer from the Elm Street store known to anyone who will listen. He has e-mailed Erika about his desire to move up in the company by becoming an assistant manager. Jeff is sure that Brad's frustration with Jeff's management style has played a significant role in his wanting to leave the store.

Jackie has been less vocal about Jeff's management style, but Jeff senses that she really would like a promotion and wants to leave. He knows that she doesn't like the conflict that seems to be constant among employees.

Discussion Questions

1. What problems does Jeff now face? Describe.
2. How should Jeff deal with the employee morale problem? Be specific and explain why this process would work. How should Jeff implement these suggestions?
3. How would you conduct a meeting with Brad and Jackie? Be specific. What would you put on the agenda? Why?
4. How would you proceed with hiring another shift manager? When would you do this? Support your responses.
5. How would you deal with Brad? Support your response. Compare Brad and Jackie's behavior.

Two Weeks Later

Jeff has just learned that Jackie will be promoted to assistant manager within two months at another HFP store. Rumor continues that Brad is checking with other stores for the possibility of transferring. He continues to e-mail Erika and has been in communication with Holly. Jeff assumes that Brad will either transfer shortly or leave the company. Jeff is sure that as soon as Jackie leaves, Brad will also leave.

Discussion Questions

1. Describe the opportunities that face Jeff. How would you make the most of them?
2. Describe the problems that Jeff faces. How would you handle them?
3. What risks does Jeff face? Would they concern you? Why or why not?
4. If you were Jeff, what would you do now? Why?

Rockin' Robbins

A disturbing problem recently has been brought to the attention of Peter Vess. Maggie Smith, swing manager at the northside Rockin' Robbins, is accusing the company and a northside manager of sexual harassment. She believes that the restaurant's head manager has discriminated against her through third-party sexual harassment.

Background

Rockin' Robbins is a quick-service restaurant with a limited menu of hamburgers, French fries, and milkshakes. The restaurants all have a dining room and drive-through service. Rockin' Robbins is owned and operated by Nelson Enterprises. There are six Rockin' Robbins restaurants located in a large metro area with a variety of quick-service restaurants. Rockin' Robbins has been in the area for seven years, and all restaurants are open seven days a week, from 10:30 A.M. to midnight. Nelson Enterprises has had great success in this area and is planning to build two additional restaurants. The northside restaurant has the highest volume, with $50,000 in product sales a week.

Each restaurant has a head manager, a first assistant manager, and a second assistant manager who are full-time and required to work forty-five scheduled hours a week. There are four to six part-time swing managers, with variable hours, at each restaurant. Peter supervises all six Rockin' Robbins restaurants. The majority of the fifty to sixty hourly employees consist of high school students from the surrounding community who work an average of fifteen to twenty hours per week.

Peter Vess has been with Nelson Enterprises for the past five years. He has a four-year degree in hotel and restaurant management and extensive management and supervisory experiences. He managed a family-style restaurant for four years before joining Nelson Enterprises.

Peter spends most of his time in his office completing the large amount of required paperwork. On average, Peter spends one full day per month at each restaurant to ensure that it is running smoothly and that all policies and procedures are being followed. Recently, Peter has spent less time in the restaurants because he is involved in planning a new restaurant.

The problem with sexual harassment that was brought to Peter's attention came from the restaurant located on the north side. This was a surprise to Peter, because the northside restaurant always has been the most productive, receiving the number one award for several consecutive years. The store has the best food and labor costs and quality control records.

Sue King, who manages the northside store, has worked at Rockin' Robbins for the past five years. She began working at Nelson Enterprises following completion of her associate degree in hotel and restaurant management. Before that, Sue worked part-time at a local quick-service restaurant for three years. She has had great success with the restaurant by decreasing labor costs while increasing sales. Sue has attended several management seminars that focus on customer satisfaction and human resources management. She tends to be a delegating-type manager and delegates small management projects and decisions to lower-level managers. They perceive this as "passing the buck," but Sue thinks this makes the management team stronger as a whole. Peter recently decided to let Sue handle most supervisory decisions within the restaurant because he is very busy with plans for the new restaurant. The hourly employees do not have much contact with Sue, who does not like to socialize with them.

Maggie Smith has worked at the northside Rockin' Robbins for the past three years. She started as a cashier and has progressed to the part-time position of swing manager. Maggie hopes to be offered a full-time management position in the near future. She is not attending college because she believes that the job experience surpasses a book-learning education.

Maggie's personnel record shows that she has never missed a shift, although she has been late several times. She has a positive attitude toward customers and usually is friendly with fellow employees. Peter isn't sure that Maggie has the strong leadership skills needed to be a manager. In stressful situations, she loses control, and has broken into tears. Maggie becomes defensive when confronted with a complaint. She shifts the blame to members of the general staff.

Brad Ross is also a swing manager on the north side. He has been with the company for six months. He started as an hourly employee and has worked his way to swing manager. Brad has no previous experience in the foodservice business. Prior to this job, he worked in a retail clothing store at the local mall. He is attending night school studying business and plans to leave Rockin' Robbins in two years, after he completes his degree. Brad is an efficient manager and has increased employee morale by emphasizing the importance of their positions.

He likes to play jokes on employees at work, and Maggie is often the target of his jokes.

Brad assists full-time managers with their duties. Sue has delegated the inventory to Brad, so he forecasts and orders products for the restaurant. He does not mind the extra duties because when he does the purchasing he does not have to work on weekends, which allows him time to catch up on his studies. Brad recently has been offered a full-time management position. He is uncertain whether he wants the position with the extra responsibilities because it will require him to cut back his class load.

The Complaint

The sexual harassment complaint from Maggie says that Sue has discriminated against her. Maggie says that Sue deliberately offered the full-time position to Brad because she has been dating him for about a month. They have the same days off and often spend them together. Sue will talk about her relationship with Brad with the restaurant's general staff.

Maggie accused Sue of giving Brad other special attention. For example, he never has to work on weekends. It always has been required that swing managers work at least one weekend shift per month. Maggie would like to have the weekends off to visit her family. Maggie also points out that Sue allows Brad to leave early for his night class but never requires him to make up the time he misses. Maggie would like Peter to see her side of the story and consider her for the full-time position. If he does not, she is threatening to file a formal sexual harassment complaint.

Peter decided to look into the sexual harassment case himself. He began by reviewing the company's policy. He found a policy but recognized that it is not being enforced. The policy is not even presented in the employee handbook. According to the policy, socializing with employees whom you supervise is discouraged and sexual harassment of any kind is not tolerated. Next, Peter decided to read more about sexual harassment and how it is defined. He was very surprised to read about third-party sexual harassment:

> Although a consensual relationship *per se* does not necessarily constitute sexual harassment, such relationship may give rise to claims of sexual harassment where (1) third parties are affected adversely in employment matters because of a consensual relationship between others, or (2) where the consensual relationship creates a hostile and intimidating work environment for third parties.

This creates a different view for Peter toward the relationship Sue and Brad are sharing. Peter would like to address the issue, but fears that he may disturb the emotional climate of the restaurant. He also knows he can't ignore the problem that Maggie has brought to his attention.

Discussion Questions

1. How should Peter handle the sexual harassment situation? Why? Describe how you think this action will affect the company.
2. What are Maggie's options for dealing with this problem? If you were Maggie, what would you do? Why?
3. If you were Peter, what actions, if any, would you take against Sue King? Be specific.
4. Describe specifically how the sexual harassment policy should be presented to employees so they understand it. Why is this necessary?
5. How could this problem be prevented in the future? Justify your answer.

PART 2
Hotels

GENERAL
The Caribbean Executive Inn
The Dream Hotel
Home Place
The Kenyatta Hotel
The Powers Hotel
Redfield Hotels Worldwide
The Viking Hotel

FULL SERVICE
The Gabon Inn
The Harrington Hotel
The Lakeside Inn

ROOMS
The Bridgeport Inn
The Fairfax Hotel
The Riverfront Inn and Convention Center
The Suite Hotel

FOOD AND BEVERAGE
The Bern Hotel
The Britton Hotel
The Embassy Hotel
The Oak Tree Hotel
The Palm View Hotel

The Caribbean Executive Inn

Alexis is waiting for a call from the Department of Labor. As the time goes by, she is more and more convinced that she did the right thing in filing a lawsuit against the Caribbean Executive Inn. If Paul had not been involved in trying to turn her employees against her, she might have just parted ways and gone on with her life. She was interested to learn that several lawsuits had been filed for unjust firings. She supported any co-workers who called her to discuss the process.

Why had a property like the inn, which had been such a great place to work when it opened, become one with so much turmoil? Alexis still can't understand why Marty was terminated. She had so much respect for him, but Paul was another case.

Background

The Caribbean Executive Inn was an old, out-of-commission property that had great potential. The inn was located on a tropical island and overlooked the Atlantic Ocean. A group of investors (shareholders) became interested in doing some renovations and opening the inn for business as soon as possible. The group entered into a joint venture and obtained permission from the local government, after receiving permits, releases, and other necessary documents, to run an inn. The investors formed a board of directors, composed of shareholders, to oversee the management of the inn.

Two years later the new inn was opened for business. The inn's stated purpose was to target businesspeople and specialize in conferences, meetings, and elegant banquets.

An open house was held to show the inn to potential guests. Several travel agents from the United States were invited to spend a weekend with all expenses except air travel paid. The new inn includes 185 rooms and fifteen executive suites. There are two restaurants, one casual and one high-level fine dining, and a bar that surrounds the lobby with piano music from late afternoon until 9 P.M.

Monday through Saturday and on Sundays from 11 A.M. to 3 P.M. The main lobby is magnificent, with a gallery including artwork by local artists. An upscale gift shop also includes artwork that can be purchased. An upper floor has five banquet facilities and five conference rooms. The inn also has a state-of-the-art fitness room and an Olympic-size pool. Another pool, eight tennis courts, and a private beach are available for guest enjoyment. A contract with a country club that has an eighteen-hole golf course is available for a fee.

The board of directors (shareholders) hired **Marty Coffman** as general manager (GM). He managed a multinational inn chain for twenty years and currently owns the consulting/management firm of Coffman, Inc. The contract with Coffman's firm gave him total control of the inn. The three-year contract had a clause stating that if either party broke the contract, the party breaking the contract would have to pay a $100,000 penalty to the other party. Marty's salary was $90,000 plus medical and life insurance benefits. Coffman, Inc. would provide janitorial services, parking system management, and audiovisual equipment for meetings, conferences, and shows.

Marty was responsible for hiring all management employees, many of whom spoke Spanish as their first language. These positions included a food and beverage director, an executive chef, and managers for the banquet, catering, room service, engineering, and security departments. Hourly employees were recruited and recommended by the managers, but Marty made the final decision. At Marty's recommendation, the inn became associated with the multinational chain Pierre Inc. Pierre Inc.'s strong reputation in the business world, with more than 300 inns, would benefit the inn. Additionally, Pierre would provide free advertising and large kitchen equipment for a reduced price.

The Conflict

After one and a half years of operation, the board of directors held a meeting to discuss a change in the inn's purpose. They wanted to increase their occupancy rate and assumed that they could do so if they changed to a more modest property. Marty opposed the proposal and argued that it would affect their image and reputation. Although the board directed Marty to begin making plans to move ahead with their idea, he refused to work on the changes. The board became irritated and discussed firing Marty so they could hire someone who would be able to make drastic changes in the operation.

The shareholders held several secret meetings over three weeks to discuss their next moves. Marty was not invited to these meetings. In fact, he was unaware of them. He believed that the board had decided to remain with the status quo because he had not heard from them for several weeks. After a month of silence, the board president called a meeting, and the topic of change was not on the agenda.

However, at that meeting the resignation of the board president was accepted, and he immediately sold his stock.

Marty felt encouraged when the board urged him to take a much deserved two-week vacation. Marty and his family decided to go to an exclusive resort. Marty told few people about his plans. He truly wanted to have a relaxing vacation and think about what was happening at the inn. During that time, the shareholders hired an auditor to investigate the financial records. They wanted an excuse to fire Marty. No material discrepancies were discovered.

Nick Patterson, a middle-level manager, heard about what was happening in the inn and contacted Marty while he was vacationing. Nick and Marty had become close friends even to the point of dining out together with their wives. Nick thought Marty ran a good operation and that the board was treating him unethically. Nick realized that his e-mailing Marty about what he had heard could hurt his tenure with the inn. If Marty was dismissed, Nick would surely be terminated. His respect for Marty influenced his decision to write the e-mail. Nick was one of the few people who knew where Marty was vacationing.

Upon learning of the board's activities, Marty canceled the rest of his vacation and returned to the inn to negotiate his departure from the company. He came to grips with the fact that if the board wanted him out, he needed to depart. After a four-hour meeting, the company gave Marty the remainder of his contract (slightly more than one year's salary), the $100,000 penalty because the board broke the contract, and benefits throughout the contract period or until other arrangements were made. Marty could not "double-dip" benefits. The board agreed that Coffman, Inc. would continue to provide services to the inn for the near future.

A New Manager

The board hired a new GM, **Paul Walker.** They were pleased with Paul's willingness to make drastic changes. The only reservation the board had about Paul was his inability to speak Spanish. Paul's first order of business was to eliminate all management personnel hired by Marty. Nick was the first to go.

Next Paul combined the banquet kitchen with the restaurant kitchen. After the change in kitchens, Paul hired **Eric Stowell** as the new food and beverage director. Eric replaced the former director, who had left immediately upon learning that Marty's contract was terminated. Eric was to fire all middle managers in his area but retain hourly employees and service staff.

The pressure and stress placed on the employees who remained led to some quitting. Those who stayed were unhappy with the working environment. Fear of losing their jobs resulted in competition among employees, which resulted in personal conflicts. Employees became distrustful of each other.

Alexis Kramer, banquet manager, had been hired by Marty when the inn opened. She had a four-year degree in hospitality management with seven years of supervisory experience in catering and managing a hotel restaurant. She was a hard worker and attended to details. Her evaluations were excellent. She realized that her time might be limited with a new GM and a new food and beverage director.

Shortly after Eric was hired he told Alexis that he was trying to keep her, but Paul wanted her fired. He told her that Paul had received complaints from **Adam Small,** a male server, that Alexis favored female servers. Adam later told **Darin Stahl,** the head server, that Alexis wanted to fire him. The lies Adam was circulating affected the confidence that Alexis's employees had in her. Soon everyone was complaining about her treatment of employees. The tense situation was affecting the performance of the employees and the quality of service was deteriorating.

Alexis began to talk with key employees and discovered that Paul was using Adam to create an atmosphere that would cause Alexis to leave. Alexis requested a meeting with Paul to discuss her findings. Paul openly admitted that he was looking for a way to terminate her.

The next day Alexis sent a letter to Paul agreeing to leave the company if they provided her with a letter regarding her excellent work and a monetary compensation. Paul asked her to sign a form letter of resignation with the following statement written in Spanish at the bottom: "If you have any complaints or concerns, contact your lawyer." When Paul told Eric about the agreement he had made with Alexis, Eric asked to see the form. Eric was shocked when he read the bottom line. He interpreted the message for Paul, who was dumbfounded and had to react quickly. He ordered Alexis to return the letter to him. At first she refused, but later consented on the condition that he would give her a copy. After much discussion they agreed. She left the office and filed a lawsuit against the inn with the Department of Labor.

The occupancy in the inn and the number of banquets fell drastically, as did the overall service, because a tense, unstable atmosphere resulted in low employee morale. Six months after the start of these changes, the company again has a vacant GM position. Paul was let go last week when he was unable to reunite the employees into a workable team.

Most managers who were terminated have filed lawsuits against the board of directors for unjustified firings. The board is perplexed about all that has taken place. One of them suggested that they contact Marty to see if he would return to the inn on a temporary basis with a better compensation package.

Discussion Questions

1. Describe the legal grounds on which Alexis can base her lawsuit.
2. Did the board of directors conduct the internal changes wisely? Defend your response.
3. Describe potential problems, in addition to the lawsuits, that the company may face with decisions they have made. Suggest a better method to achieve desired changes. Why would your suggestions work?

4. If you were Paul, explain how you would handle the mandate to fire all managers who were hired by Marty.

5. As a consultant, what would you recommend to the board of directors when they came to you about their desires to change their customer base? Justify your response. If shareholders do not have knowledge about the hospitality industry, but their main objective is profit, would your alternatives be different? Why or why not?

6. If you were Marty, would you accept the board's offer to return to the inn on a temporary but well-compensated basis? Why or why not? Assume that you are not employed.

The Dream Hotel

The Dream Hotel is only one of four five-star hotels located in the Chitou, which is the largest forest recreation area in the center of Taiwan. The Chitou has an average of one million visitors annually, making it one of the country's most popular attractions. The Dream Hotel is also the only hotel that provides an open-air heated swimming pool, table tennis, and a health club in the area.

The Dream Hotel has 250 rooms, with both Chinese and Western-style restaurants. The Chinese restaurant has a good reputation for its excellent food prepared by a well-known executive chef. Local people also like the unique European-style pub, a facility that cannot be found anywhere else within the community.

Background

Linda and **Steve Chang** built the Dream Hotel and retain ownership. They started their careers thirty years ago by running a construction company. The economic growth and strong demand for construction brought a lot of business to their construction company, and it became one of the top twenty construction companies in Taiwan.

Linda had often dreamed of owning an elegant, European-style hotel, so the Changs built the Dream Hotel seven years ago. They fashioned the hotel after what they saw in hotel properties while traveling throughout Europe as well as ideas from their twenty years of experience in construction. The terrain on which the Dream Hotel was built allowed for the use of most of the construction stones and furnishings they brought from Europe, and thus had the highest construction cost ($3,700,000) in Taiwan's hospitality industry. The Changs hoped that the Dream Hotel could cover its construction costs within ten years.

Although Linda now had her "dream hotel," the Changs continued to focus on their construction company. Moreover, without any hotel operation experience and with the five-hour driving distance from the construction company to the Dream Hotel, they were forced to hire a general manager (GM) to manage the Dream Hotel (see the Dream Hotel organization chart). At first the Changs attempted to visit the hotel about twice a month. In actuality, Steve had little interest in the hotel's operation and left all the supervision for Linda. With Steve's lack of interest, Linda visits the Dream Hotel several times per month. Many visits are unannounced.

The Dream Hotel's three sales offices are located in northern, middle, and southern Taiwan. The northern office is the largest and is located next door to the Changs' construction company. Therefore, Linda supervises this office instead of the GM. One of the other two offices managed by the GM is on the Dream Hotel's property. The other is a distance from the hotel. Therefore, the GM must take a full day to go to the southern office, leaving the management of the Dream Hotel to a senior employee. Often on the day he is gone, Linda shows up and acts as manager. She ignores the few policies and procedures and shoots directions "from the hip." This frustrates the employees more than ever. When the GM returns, they complain to him, but his hands are tied because Linda is the boss.

Although the GM manages the operation, Linda has a strong personality and often overrules the GM's decisions. This has resulted in seven GMs within the first five years that the Dream Hotel was open. In the sixth year there was no GM, so Linda promoted Harris Donner, the director of northern sales office, to assistant GM and gave him management responsibilities for the Dream Hotel. She also increased his salary by $7,500.

The Dream Hotel
Organization Chart—Front of the House

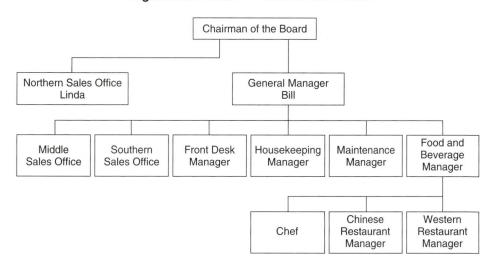

Harris Donner

Harris Donner was 40 years old and had worked at the Dream Hotel for one year. He came to the Dream Hotel from a midprice hotel where he had been a food and beverage manager for five years and restaurant manager for five years. He did not have any experience in the rooms division.

After Harris had spent a few months as assistant GM, it was obvious that he was not well liked by employees. The front office staff complained that he tended to show up in the front desk area, not to help, but to annoy them during the busiest check-in and check-out times. The front desk manager complained that she did not have the power to handle customers' complaints. The salespeople felt that Harris did not understand the sales office work at all, and sometimes without any reason he would take charge of transactions that were being handled by the salespeople. However, Linda liked Harris a lot because she felt he supported her, and he made decisions based on Linda's ideas.

After six years, the Dream Hotel's profits had not covered even half of its construction costs. In addition, they had to shut down the Western-style restaurant because the food was not of high quality, and there were no quality chefs who could be hired. The occupancy rate also was lower than expected.

Linda began to worry about whether the Dream Hotel could reach its goal of covering construction costs at the end of ten years, a little more than three years from now. She also doubted Harris's management ability and decided to replace him with Bill Morgan, who would become the GM.

Bill Morgan

Bill Morgan was the assistant GM of a well-known upscale chain hotel, and he was good at handling various management problems. Linda talked with Bill about the goals she had regarding the Dream Hotel's profit. Because she believed in Bill's ability, she gave him $15,000 more than his current salary. She also promised him that she would support his decisions totally as long as the Dream Hotel's profits increased.

Bill had worked in the hospitality industry for twenty years. He started as a management trainee after he graduated from a hospitality program and moved up to assistant GM. He was seeking more challenges in his career, so he accepted Linda's offer. He had heard about some of the problems at the Dream Hotel, and he thought that this would be an opportunity to demonstrate his management ability, especially if he met Linda's profit goals.

During Bill's first month at the Dream Hotel, he observed the work being done in each division and met with each manager. All managers mentioned that Linda likes to disturb the management process and change procedures whenever she wants. Generally, Bill found that employees didn't seem to have confidence in the GM. They believed that with the Dream Hotel's history, Bill would be gone at the end of the year. When they were out of his sight, they joked about changes that he wanted to make, and wondered why they should change their ways only to have new GM within a short while who would have new ways to do things.

Bill found that the Dream Hotel had a 40 percent employee turnover rate. The workload for employees in food and beverage was heavy and many staff quit as soon as they found something else. There also were problems finding qualified employees. More disturbingly, Bill learned that the executive chef of the Chinese restaurant had been offered $10,000 more per year by another restaurant, and planned to leave within the next two weeks.

During a conversation with **Cathy Landis,** the front desk manager, Bill found that she did not have authority to handle guest complaints, so when there are complaints, employees had to find the GM. He wondered why there hadn't been some use of empowerment. It appeared that the manager would be very interested in Cathy's handling guest complaints.

A benefit for the 40 percent of employees who came from other states was provision of very low-cost housing. This recently had been terminated because of high maintenance costs. These employees now had to find their own apartments, and the costs were much higher than the original employee housing. Bill wondered if this change in benefit had some impact on local employees' morale. They had told him that they were ignored because promotions seemed to go to employees from other states. Bill was not sure if or why this happened, and realized he needed to do some investigating. Did the promotions come so those from other states could make more money to compensate for the more expensive housing? How could all employees be treated fairly? Bill learned that there were no training programs in place for employees, and even the employee orientation was hit-or-miss, depending on who was in charge of completing the orientation. Nothing was in writing.

As Bill walked through the hotel, he noticed the light-colored carpets that seemed to need cleaning. He knew that his costs in maintaining them would be high and thought about the difficulty in keeping them clean. Why would someone purchase this color, he wondered.

With so many problems, Bill thought about how he would reach Linda's goal to cover construction costs within three to four years. He wondered whether Linda would keep her promise to support his management decisions fully or, as it appeared she had done, disrupt his actions?

Discussion Questions

1. What do you think the Dream Hotel manager should do to cover its construction costs by the end of ten years? Why? Should covering costs continue to be a top priority? Why or why not?

2. If you were Bill, what would be your priorities? Why?
3. What solutions would you offer for your top three priorities identified in question 3? Explain.
4. What role should Linda play in managing the Dream Hotel? Why?
5. Should the front desk manager be empowered? Justify your response. How would you go about empowering her?

Home Place

Background

Home Place, the former home of Lord and Lady Rydal, was purchased by a Canadian company, Canfelt Plc (public limited company). The estate included the house, with permission to convert it into a hotel, as well as the gardens and adjoining meadow. The hotel would have twenty-five suites, several public rooms that could be used for executive board meetings and private dining parties, and a dining room that seats seventy-five people. One of the most splendid rooms that would be available to guests was the library, complete with a secret door. Facilities include an indoor swimming pool, an all-weather tennis court, a clay pigeon shooting range, and large beautiful gardens.

The Staff

The managing director, **Rupert Carter,** (see the Canfelt Plc organization chart) formerly owned a successful independent hotel approximately 300 miles from Home Place. It had been in the family for many years, and he reaped a good life from the hotel. Rupert knew that buying into this Canadian company was a good business proposition. He became a part of Canfelt when he sold his property to the company.

Matthew Bates was lured away from a famous hotel in the heart of London to become the general manager (GM) of Home Place. He was young and enthusiastic. This was his first position as a hotel GM and certainly would be a challenge for him. Matthew had been a successful food and beverage manager in his previous employment. He started in January just six months before the scheduled opening date of June 1.

Canfelt, Plc Organization Chart

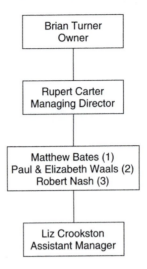

Liz Crookston was currently employed in the front office of a renowned hotel about half an hour's drive from Home Place. She had attended college with Matthew, but had lost touch with him. Now working in the vicinity, he contacted her unexpectedly and invited her out for a drink. Over drinks in the pub, she and Matthew discussed his new venture, and Liz showed great interest in the project.

A second meeting was arranged so Liz could tour Home Place and meet Rupert Carter. Liz was offered the position of assistant GM. She was very tempted by the offer. She had been at her current employment for four years and was held in high esteem by the proprietor, **Simon Klein.** Liz worked hard and continually gave great input to improve the front office, but she had itchy feet for a career move. She could not see any promotion opportunities with her current employer because her immediate superior was not about to leave.

Liz had attended a hotel and catering college for two years and landed a two-year management trainee position in a large, privately owned hotel. After training, she worked at the hotel for three more years. At that time, the hotel's management encouraged Liz to continue her education and earn a hotel management degree. After college, she returned to the industry and gained extensive experience in both the food and beverage and rooms divisions. She particularly enjoyed working in the front office.

Liz accepted the position of assistant manager at Home Place. Her job description was setting up the rooms side of the business, training the front office personnel, overseeing the housekeeping department, and training all employees in service standards related to guest satisfaction. Although Liz needed to give only a month's notice to her current employer, she gave six weeks because she felt she owed it to Simon to give him extra time to find a replacement.

A few days after giving her notice, Liz received a private and confidential letter from Simon. The letter addressed Liz's departure and stated that Rupert also would be receiving a letter saying that if his company headhunted any more of Simon's employees, Simon would take the matter up with his own lawyer.

The hotel opened, as scheduled, on June 1 with rave reviews. Business was sporadic over the next two years, as for any new business. Liz ran the operation when Matthew was off for the day or gone on vacation. Their styles complemented each other. Matthew's strength was in the food and beverage area, and Liz concentrated on the rooms side. Matthew would put off until tomorrow what he could, whereas Liz was methodical and did tasks in a timely manner.

Two Years Later and a Departure

Matthew was offered a position within his old hotel in London as assistant to the managing director. It was highly likely that in a short while he could be transferred with the company to open a new hotel in America. The temptation this opportunity provided was too great. He also realized that he desperately missed the London scene. His decision was made. Matthew owed it to Liz to share his intentions, but he did not want the staff to know, as it might interfere with the busy upcoming Christmas period.

At the annual staff party, he announced that he was leaving in the new year, and that the new manager would be a husband-and-wife team, **Paul** and **Elizabeth Waals,** who had run a hotel in Scotland. It was common knowledge in the business that "their services were no longer required" in the Scottish hotel. Two staff members announced their apprehension at the choice of managers, because they had worked under the Waalses during an internship and had vowed that they would not work for the Waalses again. They handed in their resignations.

The New Year

Paul and Elizabeth Waals arrived on January 2. Within two weeks, they quickly made it known to the employees that the operation of the property would change. Paul met with all employees on an individual basis to discuss their new roles in the operation. Liz was one of the last to be called in for this meeting. She realized that in reorganizations, positions change, people are reassigned, and not all employees are asked to remain with the company. Liz also wondered whether her position would be eliminated with a husband-and-wife team taking over the management. During the meeting, she felt that her days were numbered as an assistant manager.

The environment at Home Place declined within one month of the Waalses' arrival. The hotel's reputation for having a young, enthusiastic team was changing for the worse. Regular clients noticed the change and indicated that they were not in favor of the new managers. The owner and Rupert, the managing director of the company, were very worried with the situation. They interviewed members of the staff to get feedback about the Waalses and their management style.

Two Months Later and the Second Departure

After two months, all staff were summoned to a mandatory meeting in the library. Paul announced that the move from Scotland to Home Place had not been as he and Elizabeth had planned, and they would be leaving the position.

Home Place was now without a GM. Rupert decided that Liz would run the hotel until a new GM was found. She would report directly to Rupert. Also, if she had any operational difficulties, she could consult **Robert Nash,** GM of the sister hotel 300 miles away. Liz knew that Robert loved Home Place and had made it known to Rupert that he would like to transfer to Home Place if the opportunity arose.

Because Rupert now spent most of his time at the sister hotel, Robert's availability increased. Rupert knew that Liz would be a valuable asset to Robert, as she knew all the clients and vendors and had a good working relationship with all the local businesses. Rupert offered the GM position to Robert, who accepted and assumed his duties in early May.

Robert's wife was expecting their first baby and decided not to move until after the baby's birth. The baby was due within two weeks. Liz was on her day off when she received a message that Robert had returned to be with his wife at the birth of their first child. He would be gone for the next three weeks.

Before Robert's departure, Liz had felt that she and Robert worked very well together. Liz appreciated the comments Robert made about her insight in running the rooms side. She was eager to do as well as possible because she thought Robert would give her the credit she was due.

During this time, Liz again assumed total responsibility for the hotel. She had no time off during the three-week period, but snatched a few longer afternoons before coming back to the hotel for the evening shift. If things were very quiet, she left the hotel in the capable hands of the restaurant manager, but was always on call if needed. She slept in the hotel every night. Liz also used the time on quiet evenings to catch up with the hotel's ever-increasing paperwork.

When Robert returned, he turned very hostile toward Liz for no apparent reason. They no longer had their daily meetings. Three weeks later, at the end of an exhausting day, Robert called Liz to the office and told her that she was no longer needed at the hotel. The reason he gave was that while he was away she had not always been at the hotel. He stated she would be paid one month's salary and all vacation pay due her. She was to collect her belongings the next day.

Discussion Questions

1. Why did Simon Klein react the way he did when Liz handed in her notice? Was he justified in the two letters he sent? Why or why not?
2. What would you have done if you were Liz when you received the letter from Simon? Be able to support your answer.
3. How would you have handled Liz's departure if you were Simon? Explain.
4. Why were Paul and Elizabeth Waals unsuccessful in the position of joint managers at Home Place? What factors contributed to their failure? Explain.
5. Was Liz a valued employee? Give reasons for your answer.
6. Why do you think Liz was dismissed? Justify your answer.
7. If you were Liz, what would you have done in the two interim periods when Home Place was without a GM? Why? Would you have handled the situation differently? Give reasons for your answer.

The Kenyatta Hotel

The Kenyatta Hotel is located on the Mombasa coral island and overlooks the Indian Ocean. Although the hotel is part of an international chain, it is allowed to make many of its own operating decisions. All promotional materials must be approved by the parent company. Suggestions for policies and procedures are provided, but the human resources department is given authority to modify them to meet the needs of specific hotels.

Mombasa is a major sea gateway for eastern Africa and is Kenya's oldest and second-largest city. A spectacular coral reef runs along the coastline. The beaches of Kenya have become one of the world's greatest attractions with plenty of opportunities for water sports. More than half of the country's international hotels are based along the coast and boast warm sandy beaches. Mombasa, a popular tourist town along the coast of Kenya, hosts numerous worldwide business travelers and tourists. The coastal climate is hot and humid with temperatures averaging 70 degrees Fahrenheit. There are many international hotels on this coastal strip. Some hotels are franchises with the parent company situated in rich industrialized countries, while most are owned privately by foreigners. The hospitality industry is welcomed by the Mombasa citizens because it boosts their economy.

The Kenyatta Hotel is a four-star hotel that has 200 double rooms and twenty-five suites. Each room has individual climate control, direct-dial phone service, a color television, a balcony, and a safe-deposit box. Many rooms have microwaves and small refrigerators. The hotel is a main conference and meeting center for the area, with a capacity of 550 guests. The hotel generates more than 80 percent of its income from guest rooms and food and beverage, and about 20 percent from meetings and conferences.

The Organization

James Thomas has been the general manager (GM) for three years. He holds an MBA from a British university. He was GM at a three-star hotel before coming to the Kenyatta Hotel. James is in charge of ten department heads who oversee 150 operative employees who work as room attendants, porters, housekeepers, security assistants, maintenance assistants, cooks, and front office assistants. They work forty-eight hours per week and get overtime pay after forty-eight hours. They receive medical benefits for all immediate family members and retirement benefits. The employees are represented by the Kenya Hotel Workers Union.

All but two of the department mangers are from other countries. **John Green,** the finance manager, came from Australia and holds a B.S. degree in financial accounting. He worked for three years at an accounting firm in Australia before joining the Kenyatta Hotel three years ago. Finance serves John well because he likes to work alone. Although he is polite to co-workers, he dislikes people who talk too much.

The food and beverage manager, **Anthony Textor,** came from Britain two years ago. He received his master's degree in hospitality management from a U.S. university and returned to Britain to manage an upscale restaurant before joining the Kenyatta Hotel. He has a warm, friendly attitude.

Owen Andera, the human resources manager, is from Kenya and has a B.S. degree in business administration. After graduation, he was the human resources manager for Wimpy, a quick-service restaurant. The Wimpy franchise had twenty-five stores throughout areas of Kenya. He then worked for two years as the human resources manager at Sun Beach Hotel in Mombasa before joining the Kenyatta Hotel four years ago.

Omari Koch has been the head cook and kitchen supervisor for eight years. He has extensive experience working for the Lion Tourist Hotel. Former residents of Mombasa who now reside in America own the Lion Tourist Hotel. They were passive managers and left much of the management responsibilities to Omari, as they seldom visited the hotel. Omari has a one-year culinary diploma and learned all his management skills on the job. He is an excellent cook and has a good rapport with people, both employees and guests. He tends to be shy when it comes to his creative endeavors. He doesn't speak English well and is concerned that he might not explain the ideas clearly. He also believes that Anthony would regard his ideas as insignificant, so he keeps quiet.

More than 80 percent of operative employees come from various parts of Mombasa or live within the vicinity. Most of them come from the Swahili ethnic group and speak Swahili, Kenya's national language. Most employees can understand English, but few are fluent in spoken English. Most employees have a high school education and many years of work experience.

Work Relationships

About 60 percent of hotel guests are business travelers or tourists from English-speaking countries. James has stated that consistent high-quality products and outstanding services are necessary in order for the Kenyatta Hotel to maintain a competitive advantage in the coastal hospitality industry. When it comes to poor quality of products and services, James is very impatient. He rules with an authoritative style. He argues that any communication barriers might interfere with meeting guests' needs. He therefore imposed an English-only communication policy at the Kenyatta Hotel. This policy required all workers to communicate with each other and guests in English only. He rationalized that, if the employees accepted work at the Kenyatta Hotel, they should adjust to the organization's culture. He saw no need to learn the language and customs of the Swahili people. Since the new policy has been implemented, a few department managers have noted that employees are reluctant to discuss job-related issues or provide suggestions. Employees are hesitant to try to speak English correctly because it might shame them in the presence of superiors and peers.

The managers have expressed their concerns to James. However, Anthony told James that he disagreed with the others. He stated that he visits daily with Omari and, though he is never sure whether Omari understands him or not, he is impressed by Omari's exceptional work. By nature, the Swahili people prefer to perform tasks at a steady and slow pace. This behavior disturbs James, who values speed and efficiency in work performance. He noticed what he terms "sluggishness" and wonders how much money is lost in unproductive time. He is frustrated that employees never seem to be in a hurry to accomplish any task, and that on arrival they take almost five minutes greeting each other and inquiring on the welfare of the whole family, instead of getting to work immediately. He concluded that they were just a bunch of lazy people and discussed his observations with Owen.

Owen alerted department managers to James's concern. The supervisors told him that usually all tasks are completed by the expected time, and no work is left pending without due cause. Owen knew that, but he had to find a way of assuring James that work gets done. It seemed to Owen that James overlooked performance and was concentrating on behavior.

Amina Aerol is the housekeeping supervisor, a position she has held for ten years. She holds a high school certificate and acquired all her housekeeping skills on the job. She believes in training new employees through demonstration because they master required skills very quickly and that makes her work easier. In addition, she does not speak English very fluently, so demonstrating tasks decreases the amount of speaking she needs to do. Amina likes her work and knows that her manager is satisfied with her performance.

One Thursday morning, Amina was showing a new employee the proper procedure to clean the elevators. She noticed John rushing to his office and moved aside to let him pass as she loudly said, "Good morning, sir." John did not respond or even look in her direction, but it was obvious to her that he heard her. Amina was confused. Did she make an error? Should she have pretended not to have seen him and just let him pass? Unknown to Amina, John had a very important call to make in just ten minutes, and he had to get some final figures together. As he sat down at his desk to make some notes, he wondered whether Amina was actually greeting him or someone else. He knew that Amina shows respect to many people. He decided he would find that out later.

Later that day, Amina was called to the office of the executive housekeeper, **Paul Halland,** to discuss a problem with one of her employees. As Paul, who is known to all as a friendly, kindhearted person, began to speak, Amina dropped her eyes and kept them down during the entire conversation. Paul assumed that avoiding eye contact meant that she was not interested in what was being said or felt guilty about a problem employee. He did not know that Amina's culture dictates that to look at someone, particularly a superior, directly in the eye is to be rude, intrusive, and disrespectful. By looking away, she was communicating respect and compliance to her boss. She believed she was behaving properly as an employee. Paul talked with Owen about the situation.

Managers from foreign countries often don't understand the culture in which they are working. The Kenyatta Hotel management did not realize that some employees need to be careful not to display the foreign culture they are exposed to at work to the local community. To do so might breed certain misunderstandings. These employees gain identity and become respected figures in their society from family and other communal achievements, not from individual advancements at their work. The local people expect them to engage in cooperative activities in the community such as soil conservation, building schools, and building roads. Failure to do so would be seen as self-seeking, which would not be tolerated.

Owen finally convinced James that there should be in-service workshops for management staff to discuss some of the observed behaviors and how to talk with employees. During one in-service, Owen informed the senior managers of the dangers of cultural misinterpretations. Cultures are different, not better. He asked the managers to be aware of their workers' perspectives and feelings. Failure to understand cultural variances has caused managers to react inappropriately to people from other countries. He gave instances of how some corporations had erred by not considering cultural differences. He told them how Nike had to discontinue a line of shoes whose logo looked very similar to the Arabic script for the word "Allah"; in Middle Eastern cultures the sole of the foot is considered a "dirty" body part, and so putting the highly revered name of the Islamic deity on the sides and bottom of a shoe was highly offensive to Muslims. Nike apologized to the Islamic community and ceased production of the shoes. Owen concluded by saying that cultural misunderstandings can encourage feelings of inadequacy, frustration, and aggression, and even disrupt productivity.

Discussion Questions

1. What is culture shock? What employees are experiencing it in this case? Give specific examples.
2. Identify cultural differences between operative employees and department managers. Why do these happen?
3. Think about a time when you felt left out, different, or in the minority. Discuss how you felt and/or reacted. What methods did you use to cope with the situation?
4. What can you do to overcome fears of humiliation and to encourage speaking English in the Kenyatta Hotel workplace? Explain.
5. How would you facilitate a conversation with a non-English-speaking employee who has a fair grasp of English? Why do you think your ideas would work?
6. You have received a job offer to be the managing director for a large modern tourist hotel in a country less industrialized than yours. Describe the kinds of preparation you would make in anticipation of joining the management team should you decide to take the job.

The Powers Hotel

Ted Powers is a very successful businessman in the Midwest. He owns his own chain of hotels that consists of two large conference centers and three rooms-only properties that have an average of eighty rooms. Each of these properties is located in one of five separate cities. The two closest properties are three hours apart. Eight years after he built and began managing his first hotel, Ted promoted his assistant general manager (GM) to the GM position so that he could serve as the GM of a similar hotel that he had recently purchased. He managed the second hotel for nine years; then he promoted that assistant GM and moved on to a new venture as the owner and GM of the first of the two large conference centers. Eventually he turned over the daily management of the conference centers to two separate management companies; he had spent eighteen years managing the conference centers before realizing that he wanted to spend more time with his wife and family. Ted is now semiretired.

An Opportunity

During Ted's last year as GM of his second conference center, he stumbled across a deal that he was having a hard time dismissing, being the great businessman that he was. The situation involved a small seventy-room hotel that was being sold at quite a bargain but needed a good management team to improve. In other words, the property and location were just great, but the better managers were leaving one by one to take better jobs. The ones who were sticking around were not able to keep the hotel in the black. The owners were losing money on the deal and were willing to sell the property cheap to cut their losses and get out of the business.

Enter Ted Powers. The uniqueness of Ted's situation was what made the situation so attractive to him. He had personal experiences in running such an operation.

He also had the collateral to finance a purchase at a time when others in the industry were trying to retain their current holdings and were not looking for growth opportunities. What made him hesitant about the purchase was his strong desire to spend more time with his wife and family. It turns out that he could not pass up the offer.

Caroline Turner

After buying the hotel, Ted Powers hired an old friend, **Caroline Turner,** as the hotel's new GM (see the Powers Hotel organization chart). She had been an assistant GM at a similar property many years ago, although she had never worked for Ted. She had gotten out of the business to raise a family but always thought about returning to work. Caroline's husband had passed away about four years ago, leaving her with no reason not to work. She was given complete control over the management of the Powers Hotel, including the hiring of almost a completely new staff. The seventy-room property employed roughly a dozen people. Caroline had two department managers, one in housekeeping and one in maintenance. She also had an assistant front office manager. The rest of the staff was mainly front desk help or housekeepers. Almost half of the employees were part-time. As agreed to by Ted, Caroline put her house up for sale and moved into a converted two-bedroom suite near the front office. This arrangement allowed her to be on call twenty-four hours a day while minimizing the inconvenience of returning to work.

Ted spent the next two years traveling the globe with his wife and visiting his children in different parts of the United States. Mr. Powers was confident that Caroline would do a great job and checked in with her only about once a month. He would actually visit the property five or six times a year. The property was bought

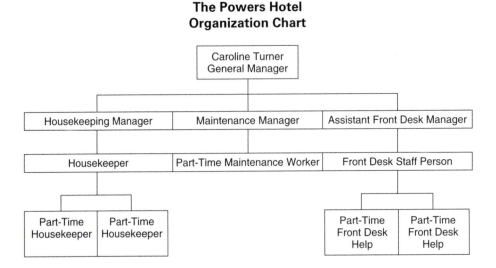

**The Powers Hotel
Organization Chart**

at such a price that a 35 percent occupancy rate was all that was needed to keep the operation in the black. Ted was not worried.

Kris Powers

Ted's children had spread themselves across the country and in several different fields, including medicine, law, and business. Only his oldest daughter had followed in her father's footsteps and entered the hotel business. **Kris Powers** had worked her way up into a very nice position in the corporate offices of a large international hotel company. While on a visit out east to see Kris and her family, Ted talked with Kris about how things were going with the hotel. Very interested in seeing the hotel, Kris decided to accompany her father on his next visit to the property. Kris loved the property. The staff was very friendly, and everything about her stay was great. On their way back to Ted's home, Ted gave Kris, at her request, some reports and financial statements of the hotel. In these reports, Kris found disturbing news.

Ted had not been paying much attention to his new property, and occupancy was just above the break-even level for the year when other hotels in the area were doing much, much better. During some months, there was actually a loss for the hotel. Kris asked if she could help change things to get the hotel operating at the level of other hotels in the area. Ted was all for Kris helping out at the property. He had a high respect for his daughter's business decision-making skills. The next day, the two went back to the hotel and met with Caroline to discuss Kris's involvement in the hotel operations. Ted decided that Kris was to have a great deal of involvement in all decisions in order to get things on track. Once things were running smoothly, Caroline would be solely in control of daily operations.

Changes

Over the next two weeks, things went very smoothly between Caroline and Kris. Caroline seemed receptive to Kris's suggestions and agreed on their implementation. Kris returned to her corporate office for several weeks before taking a four-month leave of absence to return to help at her father's hotel. Caroline had made some of the agreed-upon changes, but many had not been implemented. When pressed, Caroline came up with several reasons for why changes were taking place at a much slower pace than Kris desired, but Kris gave none of these excuses much weight. She sensed that Caroline was fighting the changes without openly admitting it to Kris. Luckily Kris was going to be present for quite a while to make sure that necessary changes were being made.

Over the next few months, business was beginning to increase. Repeat customers had never been a problem. It was mainly a matter of bringing people in for the first time. Once they had stayed at the hotel, a large majority of guests became repeat customers. Occupancy continued to rise, and Caroline started to work more with Kris on remodeling projects and outside sales efforts.

After four months, occupancy had more than doubled. Business was as good as it had ever been in the history of the property. The hotel was doing as good as or better than the other hotels in the area, partly because of Kris's efforts to attract a lot of new business and partly because of the staff's established practices of guest satisfaction. Ted thanked Kris for all of her help before Kris went back east to her corporate office.

Things went very well for another month or two; business remained high and even picked up a little. Then Ted got a letter in the mail. Caroline was quitting and planned to move out of the hotel by the end of the week. She gave no reason for her leaving. Ted had not sensed anything wrong a week ago on a trip to visit the hotel. What had gone wrong?

Discussion Questions

1. What is the major problem in this case? Defend your response.
2. What do you think was Caroline's reason for leaving? Why didn't she want to tell anyone her reason for leaving?
3. What would you do before the end of the week if you were Ted? Why would you take this action?
4. Do you think Caroline should stay? What are the pros and cons of her staying with the hotel?
5. What things would you have done differently if you were Ted? If you were Caroline? If you were Kris? Defend your responses.

Redfield Hotels Worldwide

It is May 15 and **Jake Harding,** vice president of Redfield Hotels, wonders what to do regarding **Jason Smith,** his manager of the northeast district properties in the United States. Jason received an offer from another large hotel chain with an annual increase of $20,000 plus bonuses. Jake understands that Jason must decide by June 1 whether he will accept the offer. However, Jake can't wait until Jason decides before finding a replacement. Once Jason decides, Jake wants to be ready to make some moves. Further, Jake has an upcoming trip to Japan to visit some properties, so he needs to get started with the hiring process.

Redfield Hotels has several properties worldwide with fifty-five properties in nine districts in the United States, twenty-five properties in three districts in Canada, seventeen properties in two districts in Mexico, and ten properties in one district in Japan. A district manager of operations oversees each district and reports to Jake, which currently means that he oversees fifteen managers.

It has been a while since Jake has had to replace a district manager, and he realizes that he will need to brush up on his hiring skills. Jake has three applicants for Jason's job. Each has strengths and weaknesses, making it a difficult decision. Adding to Jake's consideration is the knowledge that Jason was well liked by his employees, although he wasn't the most dynamic manager under Jake's supervision. The three candidates to consider are Bill Stoehr, Brenda Kelson, and Keith Burns.

The Candidates

Bill Stoehr, well known for his technical ability and efficiency in operations, had been a successful district manager in Mexico. He had left the position under frustration. Because of a lack of general managers, he had felt compelled to spend lots of overtime working with and in various properties. He has been working for another highly respected hotel chain and would be able to bring a new perspective to Redfield Hotels.

There is a good chance that Bill could make some excellent improvements in the northeast district (better than any other district manager). Jake knows that Bill could add much to the district managers' meetings, which are held twice a year.

Bill is very arrogant and has an abrasive personality. Jake worries that employees and managers of properties within the northeast district might be antagonized to the point of a decrease in productivity and even some resignations. However, Jake is considering taking the chance. He realizes that if there is friction between Bill and the GMs he supervises, he could replace Bill with another district manager. To move Bill to this position would take an extra $25,000 over Jason's current salary. Jake needs to look at some financial records before he decides.

Brenda Kelson has been the GM of the largest Canadian property for the past three years. She gets along well with others. In fact, Jake cannot recall a time when Brenda hasn't worked well with Redfield's internal and external customers. The greatest concern with Brenda is that she doesn't possess the conceptual skills needed for a district manager. Because Brenda is a quick learner, Jake believes that within a year Brenda could have the experience needed to be an effective district manager.

Jake likes some of Brenda's creativity and her ability to think out of the box. **Sharon Kopple,** Brenda's district manager, often has remarked to Jake on the excellent technical and human relations skills Brenda possesses. Sharon believes that Brenda can do anything almost as fast and accurate as her average employees. Brenda takes time to care about her employees and treats them more fairly than any other GM Sharon has ever seen in her twenty-five years with Redfield Hotels.

Jake is giving strong consideration to Brenda because he could offer $10,000 less than Jason's current salary. He wonders if the GMs in the northeast district would be frustrated by Brenda's lack of conceptual skills. He knows they would enjoy working with her and thinks they might overlook her weaknesses in light of her pleasant personality.

Keith Burns is a likable person who tries to be a participatory manager but frequently falls into an autocratic type of leadership. He doesn't have as much confidence in his GMs and sometimes gets involved in micromanaging properties. This behavior irritates those GMs, but they don't complain to Jake because they like Keith. They are not willing to risk having a new district manager. They realize that things could be worse if Keith is replaced.

For the last five years, Keith has been the district manager of the south-central district, a smaller district with only five properties that are farther apart than properties in other districts. The properties in this district are doing better than properties in seven other districts. For this reason, Keith has gotten some good bonuses that Jake believes would mean a higher salary offer, probably $10,000 above Jason's current salary.

Properties in the northeast district function fairly independently. Some GMs have time-management problems. This usually means that they stay at work more hours than others. Harding doesn't think he should blame those problems on Jason, but he thinks that Keith may take the problem "under his wing" and work with the GMs to be more productive and better organized. Keith isn't afraid to make changes.

Discussion Questions

1. What hiring skills does Jake need to consider as he prepares to hire a new district manager? Support your answer.
2. If you were Jake Harding, what alternatives would you be willing to consider? (Think outside the case.) Why? Evaluate the options that you believe you would have in making this decision. Why do you think these are options?
3. What criteria should be considered in making a decision? Why did you select those criteria?
4. What additional information would you want in order to make a good decision? Explain why you would want this information. How important would this information be (that is, would you make the decision without this information)? Support your answer?
5. If you were Jake, who would be your choice for the northeast district manager? Explain your decision.

The Viking Hotel

The Viking Hotel, located in the Midwest, opened fifteen years ago and was an instant success. It was built to meet the needs of an expanding metropolitan area; it quickly became a leader in the area market and has retained that position. The public view of the Viking Hotel is that of an upscale hotel and conference center.

Background

The Viking Hotel is a franchised hotel and pays Dart Hotels Inc., the franchisor, for the right to use its name; it also agrees to do business according to the standards of the parent company. The Viking Hotel is owned and managed by Landmark Inc., which owns and manages more than fifty hotels across the country including both franchised and independent properties. Landmark hotels are located mostly in medium-sized cities that include at least one university/college. Landmark hotels are recognized for their architectural designs but do not have a standard design for all hotels. The Viking Hotel has 288 rooms, including 62 suites, within its ten-story structure.

Approximately half of the suites have a refrigerator and microwave, and the other half are extended rooms with a seating area. The hotel does a high volume of business-type meetings during the week and its guests are mostly business people. On the weekend, there are more family-type guests enjoying the local and area attractions.

Many business-type services, including fax, photocopying, computer access, notary service, and access to a business center, are offered to guests at the hotel. Other services include a fitness center for $5/day, washer and dryer, complimentary personal items, check cashing, and a swimming pool/health center/sauna. There is also a complimentary shuttle to and from the airport and within a three-mile radius of the hotel.

148

The convention center has 15,000 square feet of meeting space. The main ballroom can be divided into eight different meeting rooms in addition to seven individual meeting rooms. There also is an atrium that often is used for lunches and can seat a maximum of 198 guests.

One restaurant, Scandia Place, offers breakfast every morning (including a children's menu) from 6 A.M. to 11 A.M. with a seating capacity of 165. The lounge (nearby) can be used for lunches of up to 65 guests; otherwise it opens at 3 P.M. Monday through Saturday. David's is open from 11 A.M. to 11 P.M. Monday through Thursday and from 11 A.M. to midnight on Friday and Saturday. Although it features an extensive menu of steaks, burgers, chicken, and seafood, David's is famous for its barbecued ribs and prime rib. It features sports excitement with four large-screen televisions that have individual tabletop speakers.

Hotel employees, known as associates, receive several benefits. Full-time employees receive life, health, dental, and disability insurance that begins the month following the ninety-day probationary period. In addition, all employees receive discounted room rates at all Landmark hotels, a 20 percent discount at the gift shop, and $150 for referrals of potential employees who stay at least ninety days. An incentive program is offered to increase employee commitment. Hotel management offers "reward bucks" for perfect attendance, above-average performance, and meeting personal and department goals. Reward rallies are held each month so associates can purchase merchandise, free rooms, free meals, and so on with their reward bucks. The rallies are centered on a theme meal, and each department takes a turn planning the event, including buying gifts for associates to purchase.

The Staff

Jason Parks, the general manager (GM), has an administrative assistant, **Beth Carlson,** who works under his direction. **Peter Jones,** the assistant GM, is also the director of food and beverage. Peter has an executive chef, two restaurant managers, and a banquet manager who report directly to him. The directors of engineering, human resources, and sales; the controller; the front office manager; and the executive housekeeper report directly to Jason.

The front desk team includes the guest service representatives, who check guests in and out and meet their various needs during the stay. Also under the direction of the front desk manager are the night auditors, the bellhops, and the hotel operator. The reservations office works closely with the front desk for groups and individuals coming into the hotel.

Nancy Watts is the banquet manager and has one assistant, **Jack Lenning.** Last year, the Viking Hotel showed slightly more than $3 million in revenues from banquets, with $1.7 million coming from food, $240,000 from beverages, $380,000 from room rental, $220,000 from audiovisual rental, and $500,000 from service charges.

There are two job categories in the banquet department: the convention center housemen and the convention center service area. The housemen set up and break down tables, chairs, and other nonfood items used for meetings, breaks and meal functions in accordance with hotel standards and guest banquet event orders. The service-area employees are responsible for setup and breakdown of food and beverages for meals and snack breaks, and for clearing dishes and table linens in a professional manner.

Nancy's department works very closely with the director of sales, **Janice Carson.** Janice supervises the sales manager, **Karen Jensen,** and the director of catering, **Mark Murdock.** Karen oversees the work of **Dawn Hedman,** an assistant manager of sales, and Mark has direct supervision of the three sales and catering representatives (SCRs). The hotel policies stipulate that all managers/directors must have a college degree. The SCRs are not required to have a college degree because this job is seen as entry level. However, the current SCRs all have four-year degrees.

The sales and catering offices are located next to each other to facilitate much of the activity in the sales area. Company policy states that the GM's office must be located in the sales areas.

The Sales and Catering Department

Mark Murdock, director of catering, grew up in the food and beverage industry. His career in restaurants began in high school, when he spent many summers working as a busboy and later as a waiter at a resort near his home. Although he liked the atmosphere of the hotel, he pursued a degree in business management from a state university and eventually became the GM at a chain seafood restaurant. He thought the seafood restaurant was a good operation, but his friends lured him back to the resort area when they hired him as a banquet manager. Mark eventually was promoted to the event services department, where he realized the hours were not as long as working in banquets. He discovered that he really enjoyed the selling side of the business.

After five years, the owner (a utility company) sold the resort, and the new owners replaced the current employees. The previous owner felt guilty when it realized that all employees would be dismissed. Because it could afford to do so, the utility company offered the resort's former management employees a nice severance package.

Mark's next job was director of catering for a chain hotel that was opening 400 miles away. He began working at that property six months before it opened. He developed policies and procedures and hired all his employees. Three years later, he moved to the Viking Hotel when the director of catering position opened. He has been the catering director for four years. When the opportunity to become the director of sales opened a year ago, Mark was not interested due to family medical problems. He did not want to take on the extra responsibilities.

Mark is the only male employee in the sales and catering department. He oversees the catering sales effort of the hotel, including meetings, conventions/conferences, wedding receptions, and local business dinners. He is involved in seeking groups to use the hotel for meetings. His position actually is above Karen; however, they often work so closely together that it is not noticeable. When Karen is absent from the hotel, Mark fills in for her. He feels that he and Karen have a very positive working relationship. He doesn't hesitate at all to make room sales in her absence.

The director of sales, Janice Carson, has been with the hotel three and a half years and in her position for one year. She is mainly involved with the rooms division and selling of rooms. However, Mark works extensively with her because the two areas are intertwined. The two sales managers (Karen and Dawn) are responsible for getting business from the outside and are expected to spend much of their time out of the office. The three SCRs, who report to Mark, are involved with internal sales and work with the food and beverage details of groups that have been booked. Karen leads the one-hour weekly sales meetings that include Jason (GM), Mark, and the SCRs. A policy identifies which area is responsible for selling rooms to certain groups. If the sale of rooms is forty or more, then Karen or Dawn is responsible for selling; less than forty and it is the SCRs' responsibility.

SCRs are nonexempt salaried employees who are scheduled to work forty-five hours per week. A company-wide policy states that if they work over forty-five hours, they are paid overtime; if they work less than forty-five hours they lose pay. During their first year, SCRs get no leave, so if they miss a day of work they lose pay. They may make up the time lost if the work is available. The current GM at the Viking Hotel is pretty lenient about letting them have overtime.

Although the SCRs usually work forty-eight to forty-nine hours per week, they find the compensation policy disturbing because they see that sales managers get paid even if they are not at work. SCRs can handle accounts as large as those of the sales manager and don't understand why they are treated differently. Mark quietly agrees with them on this policy and would like to see it changed.

All SCRs have been at the hotel for at least a year and a half. However, the turnover rate of this position is a little higher than that of others because of the high stress level, which seems to be the main reason SCRs leave. An SCR must be able to handle multiple group accounts at one time and keep the details straight. He or she must be able to shift between accounts quickly and balance many activities at one time. During interviews Mark tries to determine whether the applicant is able to handle the stress levels related to the job responsibilities. Most applicants for SCR positions are in their lower to mid-20s, and this position is usually their first or second job.

Communication within the department and with other departments in the hotel is very important to Mark. He expects excellent communication between his employees and himself, between and among employees, and between employees and clients or guests. He insists that employees show respect to each other by communicating on the same level and not talking down to each other. He has trained the SCRs to show respect when talking with potential, current, or past clients.

Mark stresses two-way communication and helps his employees see that all questions are important. When employees ask him questions, he responds in a manner that respects the employee and increases the chances of that employee asking other questions.

Mark works hard to keep employees abreast of their standing in relation to their job expectations and consequently, evaluations. Through his continual discussion with employees, he expects no surprises during performance appraisals. Mark does expect the SCRs to come to him before they go to Karen with problems or concerns, but he does not get upset if they go to her first.

Mark emphasizes that communication among employees is very important because they work with many departments within the hotel to ensure that promises are fulfilled. He stresses that it is important to let others know what is happening and what is expected of them so that guest needs are satisfied. He believes that there is enough stress in dealing with clients; employees don't need added stress due to inadequate or nonexistent communication.

Mark considers himself an employee who wears several hats within the hotel. However, he is very concerned about his integrity as a salesperson because he encourages clients to come to the Viking Hotel. When the client is not satisfied with his or her experience, Mark receives the call. Service recovery is on his shoulders and his credibility is on the line. If the front desk employee is grouchy, the projector is not set up, or the food isn't up to expectations, Mark hears about it. When guests are dissatisfied, Mark tries to resolve the situation so they will give the Viking Hotel another chance. Mark follows up on each dissatisfied client's call. After visiting with the client, he meets with the department manager and maybe other department employees to discuss the concern. He knows that he needs to include the GM in each of these meetings because Jason wants to be very engaged in the happenings at the hotel. For example, if there is a problem with the food, Mark meets with the food and beverage director, the chef, and the GM.

Mark describes himself as a participative-type leader. He is not as structured as some of the SCRs would like him to be, but he thinks the SCRs should run the show. He explains to them what needs to be done, provides the information they need to get their jobs done, and lets them go. His goal is to hire smart people so there is no need for him to look over the SCRs' backs.

Problem Employee—Kathy Robb

Mark is not sure what to do about **Kathy Robb,** an SCR who has been employed at the Viking Hotel for about nine months. She seems to need more guidance than most SCRs have needed. She likes things more structured and would be happy with a checklist to use when working with clients, so that when she has completed the checklist she knows she has done a good job. Kathy would like a manual with a list of dos and don'ts that would help her handle all situations. However, Mark believes that in the SCR job, much is learned by doing. He stresses to Kathy that most clients are satisfied with waiting for an answer. However, Kathy wants to have the answers when they ask her. Clients who can make others feel stupid intimidate Kathy.

Mark has talked with Kathy periodically as well as at her six-month review about her behavior. Because Mark and the SCRs are located close to each other, it is not uncommon for Mark to hear phone conversations. Whenever he notices that Kathy's behavior needs to be checked, he quietly reminds her to keep a calm demeanor. If he hears Kathy talking quickly, he approaches her after the phone call and reminds her to slow down. He encourages her to listen to herself and recognize how the client is hearing her. His approach is accompanied with a dash of humor. During the six-month review, Mark asked her if she was happy with the job. Although she didn't seem to respond directly, there was no indication that she would rather be working another job.

Problem Employee—Jane Coy

Training is another important aspect of helping SCRs do a good job. Because a background in hospitality is not a qualification for an SCR, it is important that during training the job content is not taken for granted. He realizes that it is easy to forget to do a good job of training for someone who is totally foreign to the industry. **Jane Coy** is a case in point.

Jane was hired as an SCR because of her extensive background in planning weddings. She had no idea that the sales and catering department worked extensively with other departments. Because she would be the liaison between the client and operations, she needed to know the right questions to ask and the importance of accurately communicating information to the other departments. She didn't seem to realize how important it was to provide correct, timely information to banquets and other departments so they could do an effective job. Previously, she had been in charge of helping others plan weddings and making the calls to arrange for facilities and services. Being on the other side of the working relationship was very different for her. Mark realizes now that he may not have spent enough time working with her on how her job relates to so many others, and showing her that they can't do their jobs right if she does not provide the necessary information.

As part of her training, Jane observed every department including front desk, kitchen, reservations, banquet, and engineering. With her lack of understanding and communication problems that are arising, it seems that Jane needs to spend more time with each department beyond what is normally done. She seems to think this is a failure to learn on her part and has been resistant to supplement her training.

Mark is perplexed because he has been getting calls from other key personnel complaining about Jane. Just yesterday **Brett Rosin,** the assistant banquet manager, was paged several times within thirty minutes. Three pages were housemen inquiring about details regarding the room setup for two meetings and about the audiovisual request for a third meeting. Brett has told Mark that this is not unusual, but it has become a typical pattern for each day when Jane is involved in the plans. Usually the housemen pick up the work order for room setup on their way to the room, and they realize that the information is incomplete when they begin setting up the room. Often the audiovisual equipment requested is not listed on the work order.

This morning **Trevor Boots,** the food and beverage manager, called and was very frustrated with Jane. Mark realizes that Jane is a very sensitive person and Trevor is not as considerate of her feelings, which often results in tears after she talks with him. Trevor is irritated because he thinks Jane is making his job harder than necessary. It seems obvious to him that she lacks the background necessary to do the job, and he has told Mark this several times within the last month. In fact, Trevor has all but told Mark that he thinks Jane should be fired. However, it's the time of year when business at the Viking Hotel is increasing, and Mark does not want to start looking for Jane's replacement.

Discussion Questions

1. The Viking GM seems more lenient than previous ones. What problems might arise if he leaves? Explain.
2. What suggestions would you have for Mark in the recruiting of SCRs? In the training of SCRs? Why would your suggestions work? Does Mark need to accommodate different learning styles? Explain.
3. Did Mark make good choices when hiring Kathy? When hiring Jane? Defend your answers.
4. Should Jane be retained as an employee? Why or why not? If so, how would you work with her? If not, how would you terminate her?
5. If you decided to keep Jane, how would you respond to Trevor about your decision? Support your response.
6. What might you suggest to Mark to try to decrease stress among the SCRs? Why do you think this would work?
7. Are there other problems at the Viking Hotel? Explain.

The Housekeeping Department

The executive housekeeper, **Troy Jackson,** felt that he became the executive housekeeper at the Viking Hotel by accident. He graduated from college ten years ago. As an undergraduate, he focused on law and medicine and after doing well on both admission exams, he chose to attend law school. During his second year of law school, he became disenchanted. While pursuing a summer internship as a legal assistant, he found out about a position as front desk management trainee at a 112-room property. He applied for the job and was excited to be selected. He enjoyed the excitement of the job so much that he quit law school.

After spending the summer months as a trainee, he was promoted to front desk manager. The first year, he worked exclusively from 2 P.M. to 11 P.M. During his shift, Troy took reservations; answered the phone; did room service and laundry (facilities were near the front desk), which included washing and folding towels; and dealt with maintenance problems, even plunging toilets in guest rooms, if necessary. After 11 P.M., the night auditor oversaw front desk duties, answered the phone, and laundered bed linen.

After one year, Troy was promoted to the day shift and worked from 6 A.M. to 2:30 P.M. During this time, he set up the limited breakfast buffet, answered the phone, and checked out guests. He also set up the schedule boards for housekeeping because there was no supervisor. Hotel management was having no success in finding a housekeeping supervisor, so Troy got his first experience at working with housekeeping.

After that, Troy became well versed in how *not* to run a hotel. Over the two-year period he was there, Troy experienced a revolving door of GMs. Finally, after the owners recognized that the system of sending young managers to run the hotel was not working, a task force was brought in to run the hotel in the interim while a more experienced manager was located. Troy became very frustrated, so when a former night auditor told him of the opening at the Viking Hotel, Troy was very interested. He had been front desk manager for two years and was looking for a change. Troy became the manager on duty for the front desk area during the evening shift at the Viking Hotel.

Six months later, Jason asked Troy if he was interested in the position of assistant housekeeping manager. Troy had never really thought about taking a back-of-the-house position, but agreed to accept the challenge. After a year and a half, the executive housekeeper resigned to move out of state, the newly hired executive housekeeper was fired after two weeks, and Troy was promoted to executive housekeeper.

Troy supervises thirty-eight associates in the housekeeping department, including an assistant director, an inspector, twenty-four associates who clean rooms, six who clean public and utility areas, and six who work in laundry. Two of the public-area attendants have been cleaning for five years, and the six laundry employees (all male) are very experienced, with one having been at the Viking Hotel for fourteen years. Of the associates, only four housekeepers speak any English; thirty-one speak only Spanish, and one speaks only Bosnian. Currently, there are five employees who have worked six years in housekeeping and cannot speak any English. One of Troy's assistants, **Angel Rivera,** is bilingual and is extremely helpful when it comes to communication within the department.

About eighteen months ago, there was a male room attendant, **George Hanson,** who did a better job cleaning rooms than any female attendant Troy has supervised. However, Troy noticed that it was very difficult for the women to accept George, and they often tattled on him when he was off for the day. They complained that rooms previously cleaned by George did not meet standards. Although Troy tried to help George understand that it probably was a cultural issue, George left. Since that time, Troy has hesitated to hire any male room attendants without being sure they understand the working environment.

Troy's next job would be to move to a golf resort or to go to a property within the management company but from a new chain. He would like to do a year in food and beverage as a restaurant manager or director of banquets. He would then feel ready to be an assistant GM with hopes of moving to a GM position.

Compensation

Laundry employees are paid per hour and room attendants are compensated per room, after they complete the thirty to sixty days of probation. Before this rate structure was introduced, room attendants were paid per hour and chose to work in pairs. However, once they understood the current pay structure, all attendants have chosen to work alone.

The room rate for attendants is based on the expectation that an attendant will clean sixteen rooms during an eight-hour day. Using $8 per hour as a basis and multiplying times eight hours per day determined the rate of pay per room. The $64 was divided by sixteen rooms, and resulted in pay of $4 per room. Most employees like this system because if they get their assigned rooms cleaned in less than eight hours, they can leave early and still receive $64 (assuming that they cleaned sixteen rooms). This structure often has reduced child-care costs and has negated any overtime. This compensation system is driven by a consistency in room inspection. Since the system was implemented, Troy has noticed that scores on room inspections have increased. The room inspector inspects two to three rooms cleaned by each attendant per day. A flowchart is used to ensure that all rooms are worked into the inspection schedule and that specific rooms are not inspected repeatedly.

Room attendants are called in to work based on seniority. Troy schedules the number of employees for the day based on the forecast of rooms to be cleaned and dividing by sixteen. If the number of rooms per attendant is 15.5 rooms, the senior attendants will get the extra room. One way Troy manages his staff is to leave vacant rooms to be cleaned the next day.

Senior employees are assigned to the lower floors as the hotel fills up from the lower level. Troy assigns each employee the same rooms each day because he believes that familiarity with the room, how the closet is organized, and so on increase efficiency. If there is a problem employee, Troy assigns him or her to be a floater.

At the Viking Hotel, "full-time" is considered thirty hours per week for benefits, including holiday pay, vacation pay, and insurance. Housekeepers get one week of vacation after one year, two weeks after two years, and one additional day per year after five years.

With the compensation system for room attendants it is possible for an attendant to fall out of full-time status if he or she is too efficient. When Troy gets a warning that an attendant might move to less than full-time, he tells the employee that he or she needs to put in longer days. He is well aware of the impact on productivity and recognizes that housekeepers have no choice but to slow down.

Troy tries to be fair to his employees. For example, on New Year's Day he pays his employees for sixteen rooms, but plans that they will clean only ten. If a room is trashed, he pays the attendant for two rooms. He feels that his employees are quick to pick up on fairness, so he expects to meet them halfway. When new employees are trained, they work with a variety of housekeepers over the course of a week. As an incentive, the housekeeper who is training is paid for twenty-two rooms and the trainee is paid hourly.

Two years ago an incentive program was established. Incentives are awarded based on the average inspection score of rooms over one month. Associates receive gift certificates to use at the gift store, for a free lunch and/or dinner, or for a reduced room rate, and reward bucks to use at hotel rallies. The rallies were developed to bring employees together for a meal and provide them an opportunity to spend their reward bucks. The rallies are held over the lunch hour, when a meal is served. Although it seemed that this award system would be favorable to employees, some employees were upset because the employees who got to the rally first had a better choice of prizes, and competition among employees occurred. To alleviate this problem, employees were given lottery tickets that controlled who could purchase prizes first. It was decided to serve the meal first so that if employees were detained they were not penalized. Employees responded that they felt this format gave them a fair chance at the prizes. Employees do not need to spend their bucks and can keep them until a future rally if they choose. Accumulating bucks allows them to buy more expensive prizes. Troy believes that this system has produced the intended effect: to increase productivity.

Lost and Found

One major recurring issue related to housekeeping is dealing with the lost and found because it is the housekeeper's word against the guest's word. The state hotel law says that when a guest leaves, if the item is not locked up, the hotel is not responsible for lost items. It has helped that the hotel has electronic locks so there is a record of all who have entered the room since the guest checked out. It is not unusual for Troy to spend three hours each Monday dealing with lost-and-found items from the weekend. The hotel policy is that the lost-and-found items are kept for ninety days, and if they are not claimed, items go to the finder. When new housekeepers are trained, it is imperative that they know about the theft issue. Usually telling them that the hotel works with the local police is enough of a deterrent. There seems to be a positive impact in telling new employees that they will be questioned by the local police if there is any concern about theft, because the employees don't want to be involved in that questioning.

In four years, Troy can only remember two instances when the housekeeper took something home. One was a food basket the employee thought the guest didn't want, and the other was a pair of earrings that walked, but the employee admitted the theft and brought them back. Troy recalls one instance when he was on the phone with a former guest for fifteen minutes being told that his employees were thieves. When Troy checked back with the guest after investigating the issue, the guest said she had found the item and gave no further explanation or apology. When items are mailed to the guest, they are sent C.O.D. unless it is the fault of the hotel employees.

Troy estimates that the hotel loses $2000/month in linen. The hotel uses walnut hangers that cost $1/hanger and lose many usually during the weekend or during state tournaments when many guests are students. When car groups stay at the hotel, there will be an increase in towels stolen as they are great for shining car rims.

Guest Evaluations

The hotel management randomly sends sixty questionnaires per month to guests for evaluation of service and cleanliness. Although financially the Viking Hotel is ranked with properties in the whole company (including all operations), for cleanliness and service it is ranked only against similar properties. Since Troy became the executive housekeeper, the Viking Hotel has ranked in the top 25 percent for service and cleanliness.

Safety of Employees and Guests

Safety of everyone in the hotel is of prime importance and is stressed during training in the housekeeping department. Videos are used for training new employees as well as for retraining current ones on safety issues. All employees must view a safety tape during training. Videotape topics include what to do during a tornado or fire and how to handle bloody sheets or a hypodermic needle. Safekeeping of the master key, especially as it relates to security, is another topic that is a repeat for employees. Many employees want to be helpful to guests and want to open doors for them, and need help in understanding the dangers of doing so.

Troy believes that housekeeping employees can ensure guest security by checking rooms to verify that guests are not ill or in need of medical attention. When Troy receives a daily report from the front desk indicating stayovers, change in stay, and those who have left, he walks all unused rooms daily to ensure that they are vacant and ready for the next guest. In order to honor the Do Not Disturb signs, Troy waits until after noon to check those rooms to be sure guests are okay.

Communication with Other Departments

Troy's daily activities include communicating with all departments. He finds staff meetings to be a good way to increase communication among departments. When there is going to be a large banquet, it is important that he receive the forecast for linen needs. Several times he has been called at home because communication broke down when issues were not addressed at the weekly staff meeting. The restaurants' needs are more predictable than banquets because they need linens at specific times with little variance. Communication with the engineering department mostly relates to cleaning rags. Rooms sales employees, especially Kathy, sometimes don't communicate or think ahead when they have made promises to clients. For example, they have told the client that their group can check out at 2:00 P.M. rather than 12 noon, but failed to let Troy know. Or they have promised to have thirty rooms ready by 10 A.M. and never bothered to tell him.

Troy also has had problems with accurate communication from the front desk. In addition to guest safety, Troy checks rooms to verify what the housekeepers put on their room record. Sometimes the problems lie with the front desk associates who promise later checkout but don't communicate it to housekeeping.

Problem Employee—Sandy Paulson

Sandy Paulson, the assistant director of housekeeping, began her career at the Viking Hotel as a room attendant; she worked her way to public areas, inspector, and finally assistant director. Troy senses that she is a very nervous person. He blames part of her nervousness on her unwillingness to speak to her Spanish and Bosnian employees. This lack of communication affects her ability to ensure that housekeeping tasks are done correctly.

Troy wishes she would see the need to learn Spanish, as it would enhance her leadership skills. She doesn't spend much time communicating with the employees, because she is unable. Observations of Sandy show that when she does talk with them, she talks faster and louder as if that will help employees understand her. This frustrates Troy because he feels that working with employees is all about communication.

Sandy's leadership style is very authoritarian and she seldom smiles. Her philosophy can be summed up as, "I am the manager, you are the employees." On the other hand, Troy believes that he is a problem solver who treats employees as he would want to be treated. He doesn't see himself as the "boss" type, and makes it a point to be friendly to the employees. It is not unusual to hear him asking an employee about a sick child.

Troy has sensed that when employees have a problem or concern on his day off, they wait until the next day to talk with him rather than Sandy. As he was reviewing the schedules of management, he realized that he had been scheduling either himself or Angel to work with Sandy so she is never left alone. Now he wonders what impact that has had on her wanting or seeing the need to learn Spanish.

Troy would like to improve the Spanish/English problem, but when positions in housekeeping open, there are a hundred Spanish-speaking and three English-speaking applicants. One tool Troy uses to enhance his Spanish communication is a Web site where one can type in English and get a free translation to Spanish.

In the past, employees were given a half hour per week of paid time to work on their English skills. Flash cards with pictures and basic words were developed for their use, but employee interest was lacking. Troy has overseen the development of maintenance request forms that use pictures and include both Spanish and English words.

To encourage non-English-speaking employees to learn the language further, Troy worked with their schedules to ensure that they had free time to attend ESL (English as a second language) classes at the high school. Room attendants are aware that if they increase their English-speaking skills, they can move into the public areas and then to inspector, where they don't have to clean and can receive increases in pay. He is waiting for this idea to work. The employees have transportation problems, so many of them can't get to the high school.

A bigger problem that Spanish-speaking housekeeping employees face is that everything from human resources is written in English and must be translated: important announcements such as when the next rally will be held, when employees need to park in the back parking lot for one day, or what to do if they want to switch dental providers. This means that when Troy gets the employees together to give them a motivational push for the day, answer questions they may have, hand out room assignments and keys, and discuss any major changes (such as placing new TV programming guides in rooms), he must be sure that these announcements are given in Spanish. Troy is thankful for Angel, who is bilingual and can communicate extremely well with the room attendants. There is no value in hanging announcements by the time clock.

Troy is frustrated that upper management recognizes that non-English-speaking employees are hired, yet does not work on ways to enhance communication. It is evident to Troy that department heads who don't work with non-English-speaking employees don't understand the problem. Troy knows that without his ability to speak some Spanish, there would be a lot more running to rooms where employees have questions because he would need to do show and tell to get his point across.

Discussion Questions

1. The first hotel where Troy worked was always filling the GM position with young managers. Was that a good idea? Explain. What problems, risks, and/or opportunities does this provide?
2. Do you think there is value in employee rallies even when business has dropped off? Why or why not? What might be another form of employee appreciation the hotel management could use? Why do you think it would work?

3. Can managers develop "crutches" for employees? Identify some within this case and explain the impact. How would you deal with them? Why?

4. Does communication within the housekeeping department and between housekeeping and other departments need to improve? Explain your response.

5. How would you implement a communication program among departments? Why do you think this would work?

6. Do you agree with the way Troy manages his room attendants? Why or why not?

7. Should employees be disciplined for taking items from a guest room that do not belong to them? Justify your answer.

8. What are your feelings about how the hotel management handles the lost-and-found issues? Support your answer.

The Gabon Inn

The Gabon Inn is a small hotel and convention center situated one mile north of Mineral City. The inn has rooms and food service, consisting of a lounge, a cafeteria, and extensive banquet facilities. The inn has four small meeting rooms that can accommodate up to thirty-five people and a ballroom that accommodates 100.

Recently, **George Kumdo,** general manager (GM), has been experiencing problems with his management employees in both the rooms and food and beverage divisions. He is not sure what needs to be done, and for now has decided to let the managers work it out among themselves. He will get involved when asked, but believes in his managers and their abilities to handle the problems. One thing he is considering strongly is changing the organization chart for the rooms division (see the Gabon Inn organization chart). When George became GM three years ago, the current form was in place and things seemed to have worked fairly well, so he has left it alone. But, times have changed, and so might the organization chart.

The Food and Beverage Division

Kevin Jamison has been the food and beverage director at the Gabon Inn for four years. During his previous eight years at the Gabon Inn, he was assistant banquet manager and then banquet manager. He expects his managers to be available for their guests and provide the guests with high-quality food and service.

Bob Brown, the head chef for the past two years, has been going through a very trying divorce. His personal life has affected his ability to perform to his fullest, causing a chain reaction throughout the kitchen. Performance has dwindled greatly the last two months. Guests have complained about cold, bland food, resulting in higher food costs due to product waste from not following recipes and not paying attention to food quality.

**The Gabon Inn
Organization Chart**

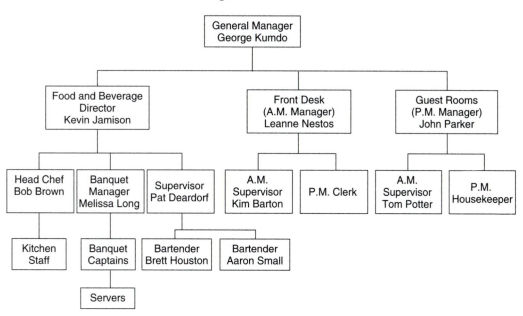

Melissa Long, banquet manager, scheduled herself to be the manager on duty to oversee a second annual holiday dinner and dance. She has been banquet manager for eighteen months, so she is aware of Kevin's expectations. Melissa scheduled her two best banquet captains to help provide quality service at this party.

On the afternoon of the party, Bob was not in good spirits, which was affecting the whole kitchen staff. Because the kitchen was in such chaos, a triple dose of bourbon was added to the dessert that was to be served. Two different cooks added the extra liquor at separate times.

An open bar with mixed drinks and beer was scheduled to begin at 6 P.M. with dinner to be served at 8 P.M. The dance was scheduled from 10 P.M. to 1 A.M. with champagne to be served at midnight. Melissa was somewhat nervous about the event because she had heard how this group's holiday party got out of hand last year. She was confident that with her background knowledge of the crowd, she could handle the evening.

At 6 P.M. the partygoers started to arrive. All was going well, and everyone seemed to be having a great time. After thirty minutes, Melissa checked with her bartenders, **Brett Houston** and **Aaron Small.** They reported that some guests were drinking quite a bit, but everything seemed under control. Melissa decided to take a break before dinner was served.

At 7:30 P.M., Melissa returned and found that a few of the partygoers had consumed too much liquor. The noise level was getting very high. Melissa questioned Brett and Aaron on why they had let things get out of hand. They both had plenty of excuses as to why they did not cut off the guests who had obviously had too much to drink. The guests were having a good time, and most of them were staying at the hotel. They thought that because the guests did not have to drive, it was okay to let them have more liquor. Plus, the more the guests drank, the greater the tips. They also told Melissa that their supervisor, **Pat Deardorf,** had told them to make sure the party guests were taken care of, and everyone had a good time. (Later Melissa found out that Pat had told the bartenders that this could become a big account, so it was okay to ignore some of the policies and procedures usually followed with other guests.) They assumed that this meant ignoring the crude behavior of some guests.

Melissa suggested that dinner be served immediately so that guests might settle down. As the banquet servers began bringing the meal, most guests took their seats. Several guests began harassing the servers. They were loudly demanding that their food be brought right away and more drinks be served to them.

When the meal was underway, several guests started playing pranks on the servers. They asked servers to bring condiments and additional silver, only to hide them and ask again. Some male guests began calling the servers derogatory names and making advances to female servers. When the dessert came, there was a pause in the action.

Melissa checked on Brett and Aaron and asked them to close the function at 1 A.M. Although they were hesitant, Melissa explained what needed to be done and where the keys were located, so they could lock up as needed. She then went to the front desk and told **Kim Barton,** the supervisor who was working, that she was leaving the hotel to attend another party. She told Kim that the banquet captains would take care of the dining room and the bartenders would take care of the bar area.

The next day, Kevin learned that the party got out of hand about 11:30 P.M. and the police were called to break up the party. Three guests were arrested. Kevin learned of Melissa's delegation to the captain and bartenders and decided that he had better have a discussion with her as soon as possible. When he went to look for her, she was nowhere to be found. He was sure she was scheduled to work.

Discussion Questions

1. Is there a communication problem within the food and beverage division? Give examples to support your response. How could the situation be improved? Why do you think your ideas would work?
2. What should the banquet captains have done to control the harassment from the guests? Why?
3. Disregarding Kevin's expectations of Melissa's presence during the party, how did her absence affect the outcome of the party? Support your answer.

4. Identify problems that are occurring in the kitchen. How would you work through them with your staff?
5. What does Kevin need to discuss with Melissa? Why would these issues be important? What action should be taken? Why?

The Rooms Division

Occupancy for the rooms division runs highest when Delta University is in session and falls to its lowest during school breaks and summers. Last year, the Gabon Inn had an average annual occupancy rate of 54 percent for rooms with an average room rate of $85.

The rooms division management team includes **Leanne Nestos,** A.M. manager; **John Parker,** P.M. manager; and **Kim Barton** and **Tom Potter,** two A.M. supervisors. There are no P.M. supervisors. However, if there is a need for a supervisor in the evening, John calls either Kim or Tom, whoever is on twenty-four-hour call.

Leanne and John are responsible for overseeing the rooms division. Kim is responsible for the front desk, and Tom is responsible for the rooms, laundry, and general housekeeping areas. Kim is especially pleased that employees in the rooms division get along reasonably well. She does not like confrontation, and does everything she can to keep guests and employees with whom she works happy.

Leanne graduated from college with a bachelor's degree in recreation management and attended graduate school for two years in family and children's services. For another year, she took additional business and management courses at Delta University. While attending school, Leanne worked twenty hours per week in the university residence department, where she supervised ten part-time employees, mainly college students. For eight weeks each summer during college, she was a program director at a camp for 200 teenagers, where she supervised fifty workers, including foodservice employees.

During her last year of school and for two and a half years after graduation, Leanne was employed full-time as a front desk clerk at a local motel. Although her primary responsibilities were registering guests and keeping all financial books up to date, she also did some housekeeping and laundry.

She quit the Delta Hotel when she began working at the Gabon Inn as a night clerk. Nine months later, she was promoted to assistant manager of the front desk and hotel. Her responsibilities were supervising the housekeeping staff, making schedules, and assisting George, the GM. Four years later, the assistant manager position at the front desk was eliminated, and Leanne was promoted to front desk manager. She has held that job for the past eighteen months. During her last performance evaluation, she received an excellent overall rating with high ratings in communication, leadership, and planning.

Leanne practices a participatory leadership style. She encourages her staff to participate in decision making, so she can receive ideas and opinions from employees who are involved in and/or affected by decisions. She also feels that, as manager, she should be flexible and open-minded to new ideas or suggestions from employees.

Leanne believes that organizational skills are very important because they are used when setting priorities, which helps employees know what is most important and what needs to be done first. She thinks that being well organized helps decrease stress because employees don't need to rush to get everything done at the same time, even doing what is unimportant. For example, every morning Leanne writes down her priorities: which tasks *have* to be done and which *should* be done. She then completes tasks according to this priority ranking.

Leanne has been spending some time thinking about Kim's upcoming performance evaluation. Because Leanne is the A.M. manager, Tom thinks she should do the evaluation. She is wondering how to help Kim see the impact of some of her behaviors. Although the performance evaluation is scheduled in three weeks, Leanne has to decide what actions she should take. Was Kim qualified for the job? Has training been adequate? Why does she do some things that put the hotel into such dilemmas? Why doesn't she see the importance of following policies and procedures? She recognizes that Kim is a hard worker, but wonders if some of her work could be eliminated if she improved her organizational skills and set priorities.

Kim attended college for two years but she didn't get a degree. Prior to becoming the front desk clerk at the Gabon Inn, she worked at a flower shop for two years and was a supervisor of a hospital gift shop for almost three years.

When Kim became the front desk clerk, she was trained in that position and received a copy of policies and procedures. **Sue Baldwin,** the previous manager, and Leanne, the assistant manager, did her training. About eighteen months later, she was promoted to supervisor.

The job description for the supervisor position lists the following duties:

- Ensure that the main desk policies and procedures are followed correctly, which includes updating the main desk manual, proper key control, lost and found, cash security, information center, and sundry candy sales
- Assist the front desk manager with hiring, training, supervising, and evaluating full- and part-time staff
- Evaluate problems, examine alternatives, and make recommendations to the front desk manager for efficient operations of the main desk
- Assist the front desk manager in maintaining effective budget controls and proper inventory levels
- Establish a sense of cooperation and harmony to hotel guests using services of the main desk and staff
- Assure control and responsibility for the operation of the main desk in the absence of the front desk manager

Most of the time, Kim does a good job. Although she knows the importance of the hotel policies and procedures and uses them to assist Leanne in training new staff, she sometimes doesn't follow them for registering guests and taking reservations. This results in lots of mistakes in her area.

Leanne recalls problems Kim had one night about three weeks ago. On the night of the holiday party, some guests who were staying at the hotel left the dance shortly before 1 A.M. and were quite loud around the pool area. Kim was concerned because she knew there were guests in the hotel who were not part of the function and were trying to get a restful night's sleep. When the noise got louder, some guests called the front desk to complain. Kim tried to talk to the group that was partying, but most of them had consumed too much alcohol to care. Kim didn't want to call the police because they had left the premises just forty-five minutes earlier. She didn't want to bother Leanne or Tom at home because she felt it was her responsibility to take charge.

As the party continued, calls to the front desk increased. Kim decided that she would not answer the phone, hoping the guests would think she was away from the desk. She also hoped that none of them would come down to the front desk to complain in person.

The next day, Kim comped the rooms of guests who complained when they checked out of the hotel. Most complainers were those who had rooms close to the pool area. She didn't leave a note for Leanne. Kim was scheduled to be off for two days following the party, and Leanne had three days off when Kim returned. Actually, when she finally saw Leanne, the incident had slipped her mind, and she never reported it. Kim was glad that no one had gotten hurt that night.

However, Leanne heard about the incident from Tom. She decided to confront Kim during the performance evaluation. In the meantime, there were notes to check and visits with Kim's co-workers to make in preparation for the evaluation.

As Leanne checked through her notes, she recalled the March 7 mixup. Kim had taken a call asking that a block of rooms be held for alumni association members to use the first Friday in June. However, because Kim didn't follow the proper reservation procedures, the rooms were not held and the alumni association representatives felt cheated.

Four months ago, several visiting scholars who had reserved rooms two weeks in advance had to wait in the lobby because Kim did not follow the hotel's procedures. She forgot to write the necessary information in the book that is used by the housekeeping department. Therefore, some of the reserved rooms were not cleaned at the time of check-in.

Another concern brought to Leanne by front desk employees is Kim's reaction when they suggest new ideas to her. They complained that she never considers them, often appears jealous of the clerks, and disregards their ideas totally. Leanne has noticed that Kim lacks organizational skills and at times tries to do so many things at once that many mistakes occur. While Kim spends valuable time correcting these mistakes, Leanne has to do part of Kim's job to get the situation under control.

Leanne is sure that Kim could avoid such mistakes if she would follow hotel policies and procedures and set priorities every day. Therefore, Leanne shared suggestions that had worked well for her with Kim. What a pleasant surprise when Kim started using her manager's suggestions! But after a week or so, Kim was back to her old routines and habits.

Leanne recalls Kim's strengths that were discussed during Kim's previous performance evaluation. Kim does a nice job accommodating guests' requests. For example, if a guest comes to the front desk and asks for a fruit tray to be delivered to the room, she won't tell the guest to call the room service number. Instead, she will call room service and ask them to deliver the fruit tray to the guest's room. When guests complain about something, Kim apologizes and tries to settle the problem for them. If the problem is not resolvable, she explains why it isn't, and usually guests are satisfied.

Kim's friendliness to guests results in many of them expressing appreciation to the manager. Kim explains everything to the guests. While they register, she talks with them about their trip to Mineral City and what events are occurring in the area during their stay. There have been times when guests have called the manager and said, "I just checked in with one of your staff at the front desk. Her name is Kim, and she really did a nice job."

Leanne knows that Kim works very hard so that she can get the maximum work done in any given day. Even though she spends some of her time correcting her own mistakes, she still gets a lot done. Leanne has thought about discussing Kim's evaluation and some of her weaknesses with George, but knows that he relies on her to take care of the problems within the rooms division. She decides she should handle it on her own. Tom doesn't seem to have much interest.

Discussion Questions

1. If you were Leanne, how would you prepare for Kim's performance evaluation? Why did you select this approach? Should Tom be required to participate in Kim's evaluation? Why or why not?

2. If you were Leanne, how would you help Kim (a) recognize her problems, (b) realize improvements that need to be made, and (c) take ownership of making changes? Why do you think this assistance will help?

3. What alternative courses of action are available? If you were Leanne, would you give Kim any alternatives? Why or why not?

4. Describe your reaction to the fact that there was no discussion between Leanne and Kim about comping rooms for hotel guests the night of the party. What should have happened? Why?

5. As a manager, how would you handle the situation with the potential guests who felt cheated because one of your employees did not follow the hotel's policies and procedures? How will this create a positive resolution?

6. From the job description, do you think there are too many duties and responsibilities for Kim? Why or why not?
7. What do you think of George's management style? Would you use it? Why or why not?
8. If top management believes in a participatory management style, should they require that middle- and lower-level managers use this style? Why or why not? If so, how can they ensure that all levels of management are using the same style?
9. Should George change the organization chart for the rooms division? Why or why not?

The Harrington Hotel

The Harrington Hotel of Moorestown is owned and operated by the Dalton Company. Although this company has numerous hotel properties, it mostly deals in construction and rental of business properties in huge malls. The hotel division of the Dalton Company has franchise agreements with various brand-name corporations.

The Harrington Hotel is situated in the rolling hills of a small city, about two miles from the downtown area. Within a ten-mile radius are the university campus and San Luis Creek Park. About 14,000 students are enrolled in the university. Occasionally the university hosts conferences and invites popular personalities, most of whom stay at the Harrington. Other guests include guest speakers who are invited from outside Moorestown to deliver a speech or attend a meeting.

San Luis Creek Park is within five miles of the downtown area and is basically known for its fishing facilities. It has a large playground that interests children. Most visitors to Moorestown are from nearby areas and normally go home before dark.

Tom Gilbert, the district manager for hotels, lives in Moorestown. He is a community leader who knows what he wants and will do what it takes to have top-notch hotels. Sometimes he steps on the toes of general managers (GMs) who are not doing as well as he expects. One GM who did a good job keeping his hotel up to par was **Rob Hunter.** Rob always was willing to give experienced advice to his exceptional staff and tried to protect them from Tom and his overbearing ideas.

Background

The hotel consists of seventy-five single rooms, fifty double rooms, twenty twin rooms, fifteen king rooms, and eight suites, all with color TV, radio, telephones, Internet capabilities, and video links. Each room has provisions for brewing tea and coffee. Some single rooms have minibars provided, and some double rooms are handicap accessible. All guests receive a free national morning newspaper.

Guests can choose from an à la carte menu from the San Luis Restaurant, which can accommodate ninety-five guests. It is open from 6:30 A.M. to 10 P.M. The menu offered in the San Luis Restaurant is fairly extensive and reasonably priced. The restaurant is known for fine dining, good food, and pleasant service. It offers a variety of entrées to suit the taste of its guests. To accompany the fine meals, a wide selection of cocktails, wines, and non-alcoholic beverages are offered. The San Luis Lounge, with a capacity of sixty guests, is situated next to the restaurant and can be used for seating during breakfast and lunch, if needed. The hotel also has a large ballroom for functions such as weddings, anniversary parties, meetings, and banquets. It can seat 450 people at a time in a classroom-style seating, but also can be divided into three conference rooms for smaller groups.

Staffing and Organization Structure

As can be expected with many medium-size hotel operations that are not unionized, the employees have no formal training within the catering industry. Most Harrington Hotel employees are housewives and high school students. No employee has a college degree except the GM, who has a B.S. degree in hotel management and an MBA (see the Harrington Hotel organization chart). The other managers have been promoted to management positions because of their experience, competence, and familiarity with the existing system.

Employees take a lively interest in the operation and work efficiently as a team. Suggestions for improvements generally are encouraged from employees. Because the pay and working conditions seem fair, the employee turnover rate is

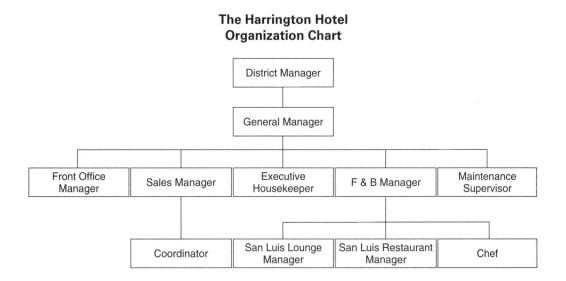

**The Harrington Hotel
Organization Chart**

much lower than those of other similar properties in the area. Almost all management-level personnel, excluding the GM, have been working in the same property for the past eight years. The sales manager joined the team just four years ago.

About three years ago, the hotel management ran into some problems dealing with minorities. They had several accusations of employing little or no Hispanic or African American employees. Although no charges were filed, shortly thereafter a Hispanic woman took the position of manager of the San Luis Restaurant. Rob was excited to have **Rosalita (Rosie) Guatemala** on board. Rosie had worked as a manager of a family restaurant. She did not have a college degree but planned to go back to college in the near future. Although the atmosphere in the San Luis Restaurant was initially tense, employees seemed to adapt to Rosie and worked well under her.

Accommodations

Most business from room sales is generated during weekdays by transit travelers. Room rates charged on the weekend are slightly lower than those of area competitors, so guests consider the rooms a good value for the money. Special packages are offered during the slack season. For example, free accommodations are given to the bride and groom before or after a wedding reception and to the couple of honor for an anniversary party, and special rates are given to those guests attending sports events at the university.

The Harrington Hotel has an excellent reputation due to its customer-focused management staff. Comment cards often express the guests' appreciation.

Change at the Top

Rob Hunter had been the GM at the property for five years. He believes that productivity increases with the development of employees. Thus, his attitude toward employees made him popular. He showed his appreciation to employees in many ways. For example, on a special occasion, such as the twenty-fifth wedding anniversary of an employee, he organized an informal party and invited every employee to attend.

However, Rob has just been promoted and transferred to the Westgate Hotel, a Dalton property 150 miles away. This larger property has 350 rooms and is located in the heart of the city. Rob was excited to receive the promotion and looked forward to meeting the new challenges that lie ahead of him.

The corporate human resources department manager of the Dalton Company, which is located in Jonesville, was in the process of selecting a new GM for the property at Moorestown. Just before the department got final signatures on hiring **Kevin Millstad** as the new GM, they received a resignation letter from Rob, who wished to leave the company completely. A multinational company that owns only luxury hotels situated mostly in metropolitan cities had recruited him.

Kevin became the new GM for the Harrington Hotel. Kevin was previously an assistant GM in a medium-size lodging property twenty miles away. He has an associate's degree in hotel management and had previously applied for the GM position of the Westgate Hotel. Because of his lack of experience and qualifications and his less positive attitude toward employees, he was not considered for the job at the Westgate.

A week after joining the Harrington property, Kevin found out that Rob was leaving the Westgate property. He still has aspirations of being its GM some day. He knew he needed to demonstrate his management abilities at the Harrington Hotel if he wanted to move to the Westgate. He began by calling all managers to a meeting. He emphasized that certain existing procedures were to be changed immediately.

Kevin had a feeling that the hotel was overstaffed and employees had too much time on their hands and too much freedom to make decisions. Kevin insisted that each department head cut operating costs by 5 to 10 percent. When challenged by department heads, he stated that he believed that the quality of products and services should not decrease.

Department heads heard Kevin's message and decided that one way to reduce costs was to cut labor. Most department heads began to incorporate a lean schedule in which fewer employees, as a unit, were expected to accomplish the same amount of work.

The Conflict

Six months after Kevin was hired, Tom, the district manager, was reading the hotel's annual report and noticed that the average occupancy rate had dropped from 65 percent to almost 48 percent. Food and beverage sales had also dropped by a considerable percentage. The Harrington Hotel, which had a reputation for the lowest employee turnover rate, now had one of the ten highest turnover rates in the company.

Kevin also had some problems working with Rosie. He didn't realize that six months earlier, Rosie had received several complaints regarding the quality of service. She dismissed the complaints as unreasonable and failed to take action. When she noticed that two of her employees were in a heated discussion, she grabbed one of them by the arm and said, "Shut up or I will have you both fired."

Unfortunately, under Rosie's control the restaurant was not meeting expectations of the hotel or its guests. Food costs were up 43 percent and guest complaints were beginning to come in regularly. As a result of Rosie's actions, Kevin is considering establishing new job responsibilities for her as assistant manager. He thinks it would be best if she had no specific control over any department or anyone reporting to her. Her job would consist of checking on customer needs and comment cards. She also would deal with night security and guest complaints.

Although Kevin is not excited about promoting her, he thinks Tom would support it. Kevin is afraid of the consequences he might face if he fired her. The other department heads are not happy about the decision because they have been at the Harrington longer than Rosie has. They believe it is a case of the inept being rewarded. Tom is concerned about the increased tension that might occur with the change.

Discussion Questions

1. If you were Dalton's human resources manager, what action would you take once Rob told you he was quitting the Dalton Company? Justify your response.
2. What are external, internal, and personal factors related to employee turnover? Is turnover ever desirable? Explain.
3. According to your judgment, what could have happened to cause a decrease in productivity? Why do you believe these are the reasons?
4. If you were Tom, discuss how you would work with Kevin to increase productivity and guest satisfaction. Justify your suggestions.
5. How would you have handled Rosie's situation? Why?
6. What criteria would you use to make the decision of promoting Rosie to assistant manager? Justify your response.
7. Discuss the disadvantages of employing individuals who are not qualified to do job tasks expected of them.
8. How would you work with other department heads as they respond to this "so-called" promotion? Justify your plan.
9. What action, as vice president of human resources, would you use to recruit the GM for the Westgate Hotel? Why would this action be important?

The Lakeside Inn

The Lakeside Inn is a full-service business hotel located on the southern end of a large college town (see the Lakeside Inn organization chart). This 200-room hotel was erected in 1979 and has recently received a prestigious award for being one of the best properties of its kind in the world. Lakeside Inn is a member of a large hotel chain that owns and manages more than 1,200 properties.

The Lakeside Inn provides a variety of services and amenities to its customers, including a heated indoor swimming pool, a game room for children, a television room just beyond the front desk, bell service, and a piano bar to entertain the lounge patrons. The large university just to the north of the hotel patronizes the Lakeside Inn almost exclusively for its off-campus meetings and overnight business stays.

During the last six years, the Lakeside Inn has expanded its front-of-the-house facilities and number of rooms to accommodate the high volume of guests. A luxurious lobby, a bar and grill, and twenty new rooms have been added to the hotel.

The food and beverage and conference services departments at the Lakeside Inn offer guests a wide variety of services, including two restaurants, catering, business dining, room service, and a lounge. The food and beverage director is responsible for all front- and back-of-the-house food and beverage operations.

Autumn Leaves is a full-service fine dining restaurant featuring midwestern cuisine. Autumn Leaves has complete breakfast, lunch, and dinner menus as well as breakfast and lunch buffets to serve the hotel guests and the college town residents. The Lobby Bar and Grille is across the lobby from the front desk and serves as a lounge area for guests. It provides a soothing atmosphere in which to relax and enjoy a cocktail or sample some appetizers. The conference services department has a well-equipped kitchen and skilled wait staff to accommodate guests, who may use any one of four conference rooms or one of the three ballrooms (which can be quickly changed into one large ballroom) for business or social events.

**The Lakeside Inn
Organization Chart**

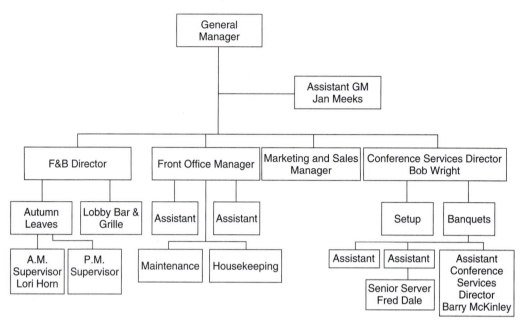

Fred Dale

Lori Horn, the morning supervisor, hired **Fred Dale** to fill the position of A.M. busser at Autumn Leaves three years ago (see Fred's résumé). Fred considered this a good place to gain food and beverage experiences to complement his hotel and restaurant coursework at the university.

Fred's shift lasts from 6:00 A.M. to 1:30 P.M. and is the busiest shift at Autumn Leaves. Business travelers arrive early in the morning to get a quick bite to eat before starting their day. After the breakfast portion of the day is finished, the restaurant is prepared for the lunch rush. From 10:30 A.M. to 12:45 P.M. the dining room is filled with hotel guests from the businesses that surround the area.

After five months, Fred was promoted to dining room waiter. Fred began to seek ways to become more involved with the restaurant and offer ideas to help with service. He noticed that during breakfast the servers were constantly rushing about trying to keep coffee cups filled and retrieve orders from the kitchen in a timely fashion. During his first shift meeting as a waiter, Fred suggested that the restaurant invest in some small insulated coffee carafes to aid the wait staff. These carafes would be filled with coffee and placed on patrons' tables, freeing the servers to deliver their orders and to perhaps handle a higher volume of guests. This would increase wait staff efficiency and speed the morning turnover of customers. Lori declined to take advantage of the idea. She said that a speedy staff could overcome the problem just as easily as purchasing new equipment.

Résumé

Fred Dale

Education	State University
	Bachelor of Science in Hotel and Restaurant Management, Expected May 2006
	Financed 100% of education through full-time employment, loans, and scholarships
Relevant Courses	• Quantity Food Production
	• Purchasing and Procurement
	• Hotel and Motel Law
	• Personnel Management
	• Hotel and Restaurant Accounting
	• Business Communications
	• Principles of Accounting
	• Labor Economics
	• Front Desk Management
Career-Related Experience	Lakeside Inn
	• Senior Server
	Department of University Residence
	• Food service worker (two years)
	• Served and performed variety of kitchen duties
	• Supervised and served dinner exchanges
	Unicorn Seed
	• Corn detasseler
Activities	University Scholarship Project
	Career Day—Student ambassador (two years)
	Residence hall house committee vice president

Three weeks later, the service staff was assembled in the employee dining area and was instructed to use the new carafes to aid in breakfast service. After the breakfast shift had ended, Fred was about to approach Lori to ask her why she had suddenly changed her mind. Just as he was about to get her attention, **Jan Meeks,** the assistant general manager (GM), praised Lori for her idea to use the carafes to aid in customer service. Fred turned away and decided not to discuss the carafes with Lori. Fred was upset that Lori had taken credit for his idea. From October to late December, Fred met opposition from Lori on most of his ideas. If any were implemented, Lori would take the credit.

Fred felt that Lori didn't want to give him credit for his suggestions because he was black. At one time, Fred was told that a group of senior wait staff personnel had taken his girlfriend out for a drink at another bar and attempted to persuade her to break up with Fred because he was black. Fred didn't let this get in the way of his good attitude and his desire to make quality suggestions at the Lakeside Inn.

The following January brought hopes of a new year and the new Lobby Bar and Grille. Seeing this as a chance to offer ideas in a new area of the hotel, Fred asked to have his time split between the restaurant and the Lobby Bar and Grille. The request was granted. After two months, Fred was offered a chance to work with the hotel's front office. One employee was on maternity leave, and all but one of her five-hour shifts had been taken. Fred agreed to fill the shift. He was now working in three different capacities at the Lakeside Inn and was gaining plenty of practice, knowledge, and experience.

Bob Wright

In April, **Mitchell Rhone** transferred from the position of conference services director to front office director. **Bob Wright** was hired to fill the vacated conference services director position. Bob had seven years of experience in the food and beverage field. He had been GM of a popular family restaurant in across town for the past four years. Bob Wright, like Fred, was also a minority.

Fred saw an opportunity to learn more about hotel and restaurant management and met with Bob to seek a full-time position with the conference services department. Bob talked with Fred's other supervisors to get an idea of Fred as an employee. After a few favorable comments, three days later Bob agreed to take Fred aboard as a server in the banquet department of conference services.

After six months, Fred became very useful to the department. He was well respected by his peers, and the two assistant managers relied on him to answer his co-workers' questions about the job. Many wait staff personnel directed their questions toward Fred before asking for help from the assistant managers.

During a slow period, the assistant conference services manager, **Mary Thompkins,** transferred to the front office. She said the work hours were more in line with what she needed to give her family more attention. Fred saw this as a chance to move up, and asked Bob Wright to consider him for the position of assistant conference services manager (see the position description). Bob stated that the department would conduct a formal applicant search and that they would not implement the search until late April because the slow period for the hotel lasted from late December to early May.

Bob confided in Fred that he felt Fred would need a little seasoning before he would be given an opportunity to advance. Because Fred was always eager to learn something new, he and Bob met to establish a set of tasks for Fred to complete before May. On January 12, Fred was given the status of senior server (a new position created especially for Fred; see the position description) and put in charge

---

Position Descriptions

Conference Services Assistant Director

An entry–level management position within the organizational structure. Directly monitored by the conference services director. Receives instructions and directives from the conference services director. Other duties include:

1. Supervise hourly staff
2. Schedule hourly staff
3. Train hourly staff
4. Conduct performance appraisals of hourly staff
5. Attend joint department meetings
6. Organize and supervise monthly department meetings
7. Supervise conference services functions
8. Evaluate and update training manuals and tools
9. Assist director and complete delegated tasks

Conference Services Senior Server

Liaison between the conference services assistant director and hourly service staff. Duties include:

1. Supervise conference room preparation
2. Secure all supplies needed for room preparation
3. Give actual guest counts to kitchen staff
4. Supervise service of guests
5. Monitor quality and food levels of buffet lines
6. Assist in training hourly staff
7. Complete delegated tasks
8. Attend monthly meetings

---

of training new servers and assisting managers with scheduling. In this capacity, Fred also acted as a liaison between the service staff and the assistant managers. Fred remained at the regular conference server wage.

After two weeks of training servers with an outdated manual, Fred revised the old manual and submitted it for approval. Fred also prepared a three-day orientation program to help new employees become familiar with the staff and other departments in the hotel. This was the first orientation manual ever created for the department, and the training manual and orientation program were approved very quickly for implementation.

During training, a server asked Fred how to earn a raise in pay. Fred wasn't sure, so he asked Bob, who said that there wasn't a written method of appraisal upon which to base a raise. Bob also said that most servers weren't around long enough because they were college students who left town during the summers. Fred began to work on an appraisal system that would reward those who stayed and met certain goals to earn a raise in pay. Fred left the raise amount to the decision of the managers and submitted the new system to them for approval. It was quickly approved with only a few modifications.

Barry McKinley

The time for the applicant search for the new conference service manager position was arriving, and with all of his accomplishments, Fred felt that he had a solid opportunity for advancement into the position. Around the middle of April (three years after Fred began at the Lakeside Inn), the conference services department held a meeting to introduce the new assistant conference service manager, **Barry McKinley,** to the department staff. Fred had not received the promotion.

Résumé	
Barry McKinley	
Education	University of Northern State Bachelor of Science in Personnel Management, May 2004
Relevant Courses	• Personnel Management • Business Communications • Labor Economics • Economics • Speech Communication
Career–Related Experience	Lakeside Inn: Server • Provided professional services to hotel guests • Utilized communication and organization skills 3M Intern • Applied human resources management skills in practical environment • Supervised office staff of 45 • Assisted in interviewing sessions
Activities	• Senior class vice president • Student advocate to dean of academics

Later, Fred scheduled an appointment with Bob to discuss the hiring of Barry. During their conversation, Bob stated that Barry had worked as a waiter for the restaurant for three summers while pursuing his human resources management degree at another institution (see Barry's résumé). During that time, he became friends with Jan Meeks, and she promised him a position with the hotel upon graduation. At the time of Barry's appointment, there were three other positions available: assistant front office manager, housekeeping manager, and assistant P.M. Autumn Leaves manager.

Fred's work performance began to decline. He became less involved with the department, and his working relationship with Barry was rocky at best. One month after Fred's appointment with Bob, Fred was evaluated for a raise. His raise was declined because it was cited that not only had his job performance decreased, but he also had an attitude problem and a lack of respect for his immediate supervisors. After three years of employment with the Lakeside Inn, this was the last straw for Fred. Fred seriously was tempted to give notice the next day.

Discussion Questions

1. What leadership style do you think Bob practiced, and how do you think this influenced the case? Explain.
2. What steps could Fred have taken to make this a better situation for himself? Why?
3. What qualifications do you think are needed to fill the assistant conference services manager's position? Justify your response.
4. Should Bob try to retain Fred? If so, what should he do? If not, why?
5. How could the Lakeside Inn improve its recruitment procedures? Why are they important? How would you implement the recruitment procedures?
6. Do you think Fred's minority status influenced management decisions? Explain.

The Bridgeport Inn

The Bridgeport Inn is a large five-star bed-and-breakfast inn located along the banks of the Fox River in a wealthy suburb of a metropolitan city. This luxurious forty-room European inn is large by bed-and-breakfast standards but very small on a hotel scale. The inn was renovated from its original structure of an 1800s creamery to its Eurocentric present-day structure. Considered a historical landmark, the Bridgeport Inn was rebuilt using the original limestone rock found at the local rock quarry.

The Bridgeport's highest ratings come from the interior decorating and overall ambience it portrays. Each room comes with a king-size canopy bed, a minibar, a two-person whirlpool bath, a fireplace, satellite television, a European marble bathroom (with bidet and shower phone), double vanity sinks, a European continental breakfast, and milk-and-cookie turndown service at night. No two rooms have the same antique furniture, and major differences are the size and location of the rooms. Along with its comfortable lodging facilities, the Bridgeport offers Atwater's, a fifty-person-capacity, four-star restaurant named after the original owner of the creamery, Henry Atwater.

From its opening, the Bridgeport has enjoyed a profit margin that is envied by many of its competitors. The location of the inn is a key factor in much of its business. It is an easy thirty-five-minute drive to the major downtown area, which eliminates most of the congested traffic. The suburb is known for its wealthy society that caters to the public by creating extravagant parks, bike paths, numerous rustic antique shops, upscale restaurants, and seasonal festivals that attract people from around the world. The suburb does not have any written laws that protect gay/lesbian employees.

Only five minutes away from the inn, a major consulting firm has employees, mostly corporate executives, flying in every day from all parts of the world, creating a need for a hospitality market. During a four-year period, the Bridgeport had an average of 87 to 90 percent room occupancy every year, much higher than major hotels near the airport. Reservations for the inn were usually booked four to five months in advance; thus, the inn is considered one of the busiest hotels in the area. Due to the small size of the dining room, revenue generated from food and beverage sales is minimal. The Bridgeport again counts on its sales department to book weddings and private parties for much of its food and beverage leverage on the general ledger. This makes the role of the sales department vital for booking special events throughout the calendar year.

Kent Laudson is the owner of the Bridgeport Inn. He started with his own land development and construction company. As his wealth increased, so did his company. He now owns much of the suburb and the surrounding areas. He has built many housing developments and shopping malls in the western suburbs of the city.

Ten years later, Kent decided to expand his company to foodservice and lodging, creating Laudson Hospitality. He now owns numerous restaurants and two hotels in the area, including the Bridgeport Inn. His greatest concerns are still toward his construction company. Because he has no experience in hospitality, he hired **Mario Vadi** to be his general manager (GM) and oversee all segments of Laudson Hospitality. Mario must send a daily flash report to Kent every morning to inform him about the progress of his properties.

Mario has been a manager of many fine dining restaurants in the area over the past ten years. He has a degree in business management from a local university. He has no previous experience in the hotel industry, but he is a quick study and a hard worker. These characteristics won the appreciation of Kent.

All assistant manager reports are faxed daily to Mario at the Laudson office building. He prefers to do the majority of his business work over the phone. He is excellent with numbers, but he sometimes gets too involved with one project. Once the Bridgeport was up and running, Mario focused all his attention on the Sweetwater Hotel, another property of Laudson Hospitality. He paid little attention to the other properties.

Danny McNider, the assistant manager at the Bridgeport Inn, is ambitious and a hard worker. Before the Bridgeport Inn he worked as a server in the finest restaurants in Chicago and was well versed in catering. He also has a degree in hotel and restaurant management. As an hourly employee, he was named the friendliest server in Chicago three years in a row. He also experienced some success in management by being named manager of the year by a nationwide travel club. Danny has been at the Bridgeport Inn since it opened and is greatly respected by many clients for his extra effort and professionalism. He oversees every aspect of the hotel; however, due to his background he concentrates greatly on the food and beverage department. Danny is openly homosexual and has no qualms about it. He often jokes with both female and male staff members about it, and sometimes makes the male employees a little uncomfortable. Yet once they get to know Danny, all worries are set aside and he is accepted.

Department Heads

Front Desk

Kelly Samson and **Susan Mitchell** are the front desk co-managers. They are in charge of all aspects of the front desk, including training front desk employees and handling reservations. If a special group of guests need a block of rooms, Kelly and Susan must clear that request. Kelly and Susan met in college and have been best friends ever since. They are very close and have a nasty habit of gossiping.

Housekeeping

Fran Moser is the director of housekeeping. She has had many years in the business and is very efficient at her job. Her personality is very dominating and she is loyal to very few people. The only people she really talks to are Kelly, Susan, and Juan. **Juan Kwok** is Fran's assistant and has worked with Fran for the last eight years. They are very close and can always be seen near each other. Juan is rather quiet but has a tendency to lose his temper quickly.

Because of the elegant and very delicate furniture at the Bridgeport Inn, housekeeping plays an important role. This makes the line of communication between front desk and housekeeping of vital importance; fortunately, the front desk gets along very well with housekeeping.

Sales

Maria Demarco is in charge of the Bridgeport's sales department and shares an office with Danny. She has an incredible work ethic and is very much in control of her situation. If anything were to throw her off, then her whole system would fall apart around her. She is very reserved about hurting anyone's feelings and sometimes tends to speak before thinking; therefore, she has found herself in trouble often.

The Problem

One July evening, Danny held a party for employees to show appreciation for all their hard work. Many employees brought dates to the party. A few people noticed that Juan had not brought a date. When an employee asked Maria why Juan hadn't brought a date, she said that Juan was gay and didn't want to feel uncomfortable. Maria said she had found this out through a male co-worker but would not say who it was. Fran was standing near Maria when she said this, and Fran overheard the entire conversation.

Later that week, Juan and Fran decided to confront Maria about what was said. They cornered Maria in one of the rooms and violently scolded her about making assumptions about someone's sexuality. At that point Juan admitted to being homosexual. Fran and Juan then continued to threaten Maria physically if she did not reveal who had told her of Juan's sexuality. Maria immediately left the room and decided it would be best to not mention the incident.

From that point on relationships at the inn were strained. Department heads took sides, and the stage was set for a classic decline in morale.

Due to the strong communication between front desk and housekeeping, Kelly, Susan, Fran, and Juan took sides against Maria. They made things harder for the sales department by sometimes not approving a room booking just so Maria might lose a client. A lot of messages that were left for Maria would somehow disappear. Often Maria would come to the front desk only to find the foursome in deep conversation about her. This made her feel very uncomfortable. Fran and Juan continued to badger Maria by walking past her in the halls and muttering obscenities.

The badgering continued for months. The foursome became so obsessed with badgering and hurting Maria that their jobs suffered because of it. They were so preoccupied with gossiping that much of their work was starting to slacken, and in turn, their subordinates started to slacken as well. Their employees were taking on the attitudes of their department heads, and those employees were gossiping about Maria even when they had no clue about the situation.

Service was at an all-time low in housekeeping, and customers started complaining about little things that weren't cleaned properly. It was obvious that Fran and Juan were not checking rooms. In addition, a lot of business was lost because Kelly and Susan did not approve rooms for occupancy if they were in any way connected to Maria, causing her to lose commission on her sales. The largest and most devastating loss was when they consistently rejected a group of consulting firm executives. The executives were so upset that they spread the word to the rest of the company about how the Bridgeport Inn was not accommodating its most valued customer.

There was little room for mistakes at the Bridgeport Inn because of its elegant and classic European style. No matter how small a complaint or mishap, the consequences would be very large. Finally, Maria could take it no more and decided to talk to Juan. She told him that Danny was the one who had told her that Juan was gay.

In retaliation, Juan went directly to Mario to explain what Danny had done. Mario then proceeded to call each employee into his office individually to ask him or her a series of questions about Danny. Mario was also tape-recording all of the employees' answers without their knowledge. This was all very discreetly done while Danny was on vacation.

Upon Danny's return from vacation, he was called into Mario's office. Without any warning Mario accused Danny of sexual harassment and proceeded to play back the employees' tapes. Each one had said that Danny was very open about his sexuality; some said they felt a little uncomfortable at first but never felt violated by Danny. The only one who felt sexually harassed by Danny was Juan. Mario asked Danny for his letter of resignation.

Discussion Questions

1. Do you think Maria handled the situation about Juan's sexuality properly? Why or why not?
2. Danny openly joked about his sexuality with everyone. Is this appropriate in the work environment, even though his employees didn't seem bothered by it? Defend your response.
3. How should Danny respond to the sexual allegations against him? Why?
4. If it was Danny that Juan was making sexual advances toward in the beginning, how would this affect Danny's case? Justify your response.
5. If you were Kent, what would you do when you were made aware of the situation? Why?
6. If you were Kent, how would you handle Mario? Evaluate the issue of tape-recording employees.
7. Explain the advantages and disadvantages of Mario's management style. What should be done? Why?

The Fairfax Hotel

The Fairfax Hotel, located on Interstate 25, is a major convention facility surrounded by two average south-central communities. The hotel has been open for nineteen years and is owned and operated by the Fielding Corporation. There are six large banquet rooms, a dining room, a coffee shop, and a lounge. The hotel has 201 rooms and is managed by **Malcolm (Mal) Spiller.** Business has continued to show a profit, and sales are increasing every year. Currently, the hotel is at 76 percent occupancy.

Moe's Place is a restaurant that is a separate business from the hotel. Moe's is managed by **Paul Liu,** who owns the restaurant along with three other people. The restaurant is operating at a 64.3 percent food gross profit and 81.5 percent liquor gross profit and runs a 28.9 percent labor cost. The restaurant area is leased from the hotel, but the general manager (GM) of the hotel has no authority over the restaurant.

During the last six months, problems have begun to arise. Employee turnover has increased, and morale is at its lowest since **John Cox** became employed at the hotel. John has been the night auditor for three years, and he worked at Moe's Place for three years prior to this position. John is working toward a degree in hotel and restaurant management and is very efficient on the computer. He wanted to learn auditing so he could become more familiar with the inner workings of the hotel business.

Mal has managed the Fairfax Hotel for eight years. **Melody Antonenko** is his administrative assistant. Mal began as a front desk clerk and has worked his way up the company ladder. Currently, he is in the process of getting a divorce and is dating someone who works for the corporation at a different location. This is one reason for the divorce.

The Front Desk

Presently, there is no front desk manager (FDM). **Loren Walsh** recently quit as FDM because his only son was killed in a car accident. After a period of time, Loren returned to work but the stress of the death and the job were too much for him. **Nancy Miller,** who is in charge of the front desk, was offered the job but she turned it down because she didn't want the long-term responsibilities. However, during this interim period, Mal has noticed that Nancy has the respect of the front desk employees.

There have been no performance evaluations in years, and raises are seldom and very small. This has angered many employees who have left to take positions at other area properties.

Mal will be gone for hours and not tell anyone how he can be contacted. When he arrives, he will not acknowledge employees or even say "Hi." The front desk staff feels as though he doesn't care. In effect, they have taken over the responsibility of managing the business. They handle guest complaints and problems as well as reservations and group bookings without supervision from management.

Nancy ensures that everything runs smoothly and that nothing goes wrong even through it isn't part of her job description. She feels very insecure and does not like the stress of her job. Fortunately, the front desk staff has few problems because they work as a team. Away from work, they often get together but try to not let the socialization interfere with their professionalism at work.

The relationship between the front desk and other departments is very poor. Front desk employees think that other department employees are their subordinates. This has caused much stress between the head housekeeper and the front desk staff.

Most guests are repeat convention bookings as well as regulars who are used to the old homestyle treatment they got from the "old staff." Out of the nine front desk employees, only three "old-timers" remain. Even though Mal has received many compliments about them, he doesn't openly recognize their hard work and dedication. Until Nancy found several complimentary letters and comments that were sent to Mal, front desk employees were not aware of them because he keeps them in a file and never posts them. However, he always posts the bad letters and then calls a meeting and chews out the staff. He has on numerous occasions "ripped" on employees for no reason. He waited six weeks before placing an ad to find a new FDM because he knew the job would get done. The three "old-timers," who have been there for three, eight, and ten years would see to that.

Finally after interviewing only two candidates, Mal decided to hire **Trent Lawson** to replace Loren. Trent had no front desk experience and was not familiar with the company's system. This decision was not received well by employees.

Nancy became aware of a problem with the audit. John suspected, along with the rest of the staff, that Mal was taking money from the company. One night while John was doing the audit, he discovered $500 missing from the guest advance payment fund. John found this odd because these funds had been rung out on the register as guest refunds. Normally, the most common reason for a guest refund is a reimbursement to someone for a bad night's stay.

John dug deeper and discovered that the money had come out of the advance payment fund. He now has evidence to discredit Mal, who has been mistreating him. Mal's security appears to be threatened by John. Mal is glad that John will be graduating and not returning to the Fairfax Hotel after next May. John has photocopied all papers to give to Nancy, who technically is in charge of the front desk.

Because profits have been declining over the last few months, the corporation owners are taking a greater interest in the business. The owners have allowed Mal freedom to do whatever he wants, whenever he wants to do it, and have given him full control because they felt the profit was excellent. Now rumors are filtering to the owners about all the problems.

John left to return to school. He realizes that in order to solve the problem, management needs to recognize what employees have to say and treat them as people with value.

Discussion Questions

1. What are the primary causes of the problems at the Fairfax? Justify your answer.
2. What should Nancy do about the possible theft occurring at the front desk? Why do you think your suggestions are viable?
3. As the new manager, how would you help solve the problems between departments? Support your responses.
4. What action would you take to reduce turnover? Why? How would you implement this action?
5. Do you think employee morale can be improved? Why or why not? If yes, what would you do? If no, what would you do?

Housekeeping

The housekeeping department is facing extreme staffing problems. Each week one or two of the eight full-time employees must work a seven-day stretch. To alleviate the problem, **Betty Stahlman** was hired.

Betty completed an application and interviewed on the same day. During this process, Betty never mentioned having any sort of mental or physical disabilities. During the interview, **Kendra Pepper,** the housekeeping manager, noticed that Betty was slow in her movements but seemed able to handle a housekeeping position. Kendra was happy to have one more "warm body" on board before she took her maternity leave.

Within a week after starting, Betty's progress was assessed as slow. She told Kendra she had epilepsy and was on medication for severe seizures. Her stories of illnesses and various causes of seizures change frequently. By the third week, Betty had begun skipping work because she was having seizures and her doctor had advised her to rest for a few days. She evaded regular duties and lied to her supervisors about completing them. Betty's rooms never passed inspection, and when she was told about the unsatisfactory rooms, she blamed her illnesses.

Because of the labor shortage, management did not feel that they could fire Betty. Other housekeepers, although frustrated with Betty, felt that even if she cleaned only three rooms a day, that would be three fewer rooms for them to clean. While Kendra was away on maternity leave, she came in only occasionally to check on things. **Nikki Burns,** the most senior housekeeping supervisor, was left to handle Betty.

Nikki has begun doing periodic checks each day on Betty. At first, this idea worked well; the room checks seemed to keep Betty motivated and moving. However, the checks became the cause of arguments between Nikki and Betty, who began to complain of getting "picked on."

The Fairfax Hotel supports a program that enables employees who are developmentally challenged to clean rooms at a set pay rate and not an hourly rate. Given Betty's behavior, Nikki believed that the program for the developmentally challenged might influence how Betty should be paid. Nikki started paying Betty according to the number of rooms she cleaned rather than by the hour.

Once she became aware of this change, Betty brought in her "coach" to help her. Up to this point, Betty had refused to admit that she had a coach. Despite the presence of the coach, Betty still did a poor job.

One day Betty said she was quitting. She told Nikki that she and Mal had agreed that in one week she would be done. Later that same day, Betty claimed that she could not finish her rooms and needed to go home so that she wouldn't have a seizure.

Frustrated with her behavior, Nikki told Betty that she must stay, and if she did leave she was not to return to work. Betty cleaned one more room and then took a break. When she returned from her break, she told Nikki she would not be quitting. Nikki, glad to be rid of her, told her that because she had given notice, she must quit. No papers were signed.

Betty took another break and went to the front desk to tell Nancy she was being fired. She told Nancy that today was her last day and she would not finish her last two rooms. Betty finished three months at the Fairfax.

After being fired, Betty went to Mal and caused a loud scene. She insisted on speaking to **Carol Simes,** the human resources manager. She told Carol that she was discriminated against, harassed by her supervisor, and fired. Betty claimed she had already talked with a lawyer and was going to collect unemployment benefits because she was fired. After talking to Mal and Carol, Betty went to the head office of the Fielding Corporation to tell her story.

Three weeks later, Betty returned to the Fairfax Hotel and asked for a personal apology from Nikki. During her visit, she told Nikki she could not let the situation rest. She said her lawyer was working on the case. Lawsuits would be filed against the Fielding Corporation, the Fairfax Hotel, Mal, Kendra, and Nikki. She said the legal action might even include Carol.

Discussion Questions

1. Identify the root problems in housekeeping. Support your response.
2. If you were Kendra, what action would you take to resolve the problems? Explain.
3. What should be done to prevent the Fairfax Hotel from future lawsuits? Explain.
4. Does Betty have a case against the Fielding Corporation? The Fairfax Hotel? Mal? Kendra? Nikki? Carol? Justify your answers.
5. What are the pros and cons of hiring Betty? Defend your answers.

The Riverfront Inn and Convention Center

The Riverfront Inn and Convention Center, a large full-service hotel adjoining a casino in Charles City, is located within an eighty-five-acre complex of shops, restaurants, and theaters. Across the street is a multi-unit office park. This four-star hotel hosts many big-name conventions throughout the year. The hotel is within short distances from the downtown shopping and sporting centers, and many famous people stay at the Riverfront Inn during their visits to Charles City. Guests are attracted to the hotel because of its location and the consistently high-quality guest services.

In addition to the usual amenities, the inn's 650 guest rooms have dual-line direct-dial telephones with data ports. In addition, there are forty-nine spacious suites. The award-winning, 2,600-square-foot presidential suite, with an elegant dining room, spacious living room, and fireplace, sells for $1,500 a night. Also unique to the hotel is its 254 guest office rooms, including 73 three-room suites that are designed especially with the corporate traveler in mind. These rooms include extra office supplies, a spacious work desk, and an in-room laser printer/fax/copier combination. The suites include a refrigerator with complimentary nonalcoholic beverages, a wet bar, two remote-control televisions, and a coffee maker with coffee. Three similar hotels with suite accommodations can be found within a six-mile radius of Riverfront Inn.

There are two dining facilities within the hotel limits and several within the casino complex. The most famous restaurant is the Manhattan Steak House, located on the rooftop twenty floors above the lobby. With its spectacular view of the city and its award-winning Sunday brunch, this restaurant is a favorite stop among repeat hotel guests. The Brasserie, another restaurant, is located on the main level and features all-day dining. With its continental specialties in an elegant bistro-style setting, this restaurant caters mostly to a large lunch crowd. The Brasserie's lounge features live piano music during evening hours and is designed so that guests can enjoy the a river view from all sides of the restaurant.

The spacious convention area makes the Riverfront Inn very popular. The thirty-three meeting rooms are of various sizes in order to host the large number of meetings that come through the inn each year. With its specialized convention staff and a high-tech, on-site business center, the hotel is able to pull off many large conventions in one week. Some examples of large conventions hosted within the past year were the national National Association of Science-based Educators (NASBE) convention (750 guests), a local national sport team's year-end banquet (525 guests), and a national distributors' group (835 guests). Evaluations of the convention coordinators are very positive.

The hotel's busy season runs from February through October. The front desk has been able to handle guest check-ins when the hotel is completely booked. Sometimes it is necessary to bring in more part-time help to assist in providing a smooth check-in process.

Department Structure

The front office staff includes one front office manager (**Rebeka Scales**), three assistant managers (**Jamie Berg, Frankee Lawler,** and **David Crawford**), two night auditors (**Jeannie Sawyer** and **Cathy Ching**), and twelve front desk employees. Each shift is eight hours, with the morning shift beginning at 7:00 A.M., the afternoon shift at 3:00 P.M., and the graveyard shift at 11:00 P.M. Employees usually show up, on their own time, fifteen minutes before their shift begins to get the bank ready and check voice mail for important messages. On busy days, an assistant manager quickly reviews changes or additions with each employee or, at least, informs them that they need to check their messages.

The housekeeping staff is a very diverse group of employees, with most of them speaking Spanish, Chinese, or Bosnian. The housekeeping department is made up of one housekeeping manager (**Jen Dirks**), three assistant managers (**Bryan Welson, Chau Chang,** and **Bona Chen**) and forty-two room attendants. There is one assistant manager scheduled for each shift, and the manager works from 7 A.M. to 5 P.M. most days. Jen is often on call when not at the hotel. Communication is a major requirement between the front desk and housekeeping staffs in order to make sure rooms are updated, clean, and available to be checked into when guests arrive.

Jerry Mullin

The Riverfront Inn offers a corporate rate to companies within the office park plaza, which seems to be competitive with other luxury hotels. There are times that company representatives have great demands on Riverfront employees. **Jerry Mullin,** a regional field recruiter for a large farm machinery company, is an example. He spends an average of four nights per week on the property and has been a long-term guest. His company provides the hotel with about thirty-five guests per night. Consequently, this is a good account for the property.

Jerry is a demanding guest, and on several occasions he has criticized the day-to-day services provided by the hotel employees. Each department has felt Jerry's presence; he has been verbally abusive to many employees, especially in housekeeping and the front desk. Being a VIP member, Jerry receives a fresh fruit basket upon arrival. In addition, he requests that a bottle of fresh lemon juice be placed in his room upon each visit. This request requires that a bellhop purchase the juice from a local grocery store. If the lemon juice is not in the room, Jerry yells at the front desk staff.

The front desk staff receives the brunt of Jerry's criticism, and generally **Angela Simon,** an intern, has to deal with him. Angela describes him as rude, belligerent, and demanding. Angela has noticed that he also picks on new trainees (interns and trainees are identified by their badges). On one occasion, Angela noticed that Jerry's reservation was not in the computer. Attempting to correct the problem before he arrived, she entered the reservation into the terminal and sent a bellhop to get a bottle of lemon juice. Satisfied with herself for heading off a confrontation with Jerry, Angela hand-wrote a registration card. When Jerry arrived, the handwritten card did not escape his notice and criticism. He berated her incompetence and demanded to see the front desk manager immediately. Jerry ranted and raved for what seemed like thirty minutes, finally bellowing, "I bet there is no lemon juice either."

Angela heard that Jerry also complained about valet service, housekeeping, and the newspaper deliveries. Angela silently hoped that there would be enough complaints that Jerry would be asked to stay elsewhere.

Although **Richard Camp,** the assistant general manager, expressed his concern about the hotel's well-being and employee morale, he was hesitant to talk to Jerry. After several weeks of dealing with Jerry's behavior, three full-time employees approached Richard and explained that they and several others would quit if something wasn't done about Jerry's abuse.

The following day, Richard brought Jerry into his office and explained that his abrasive behavior would no longer be tolerated. He explained how difficult it was to get any employee to serve him. Hearing this, Jerry became outraged. He stormed from the office bellowing. "If you no longer want my business, you have just lost my entire company's business. You will be sorry. I know lots of people. I can ruin this hotel!"

After much thought, Richard apologized to Jerry and allowed him to remain at the hotel. After all, he reasoned, the company's business is important because it's there during lean months. Richard than told the staff to do what was necessary to retain Jerry and his company's business. One employee who had complained to Richard quit, stating that it was a slap in the face to allow a guest to treat employees the way Jerry had done.

Communication between Departments

A year ago, with a full staff in the housekeeping and front office departments, management became lax in communicating with employees. Changes in the front office staff started to occur, with many new procedures implemented. Instead of holding a staff meeting to explain the changes and reasons for change, managers left messages at the front desk, in employee mailboxes, or on their voice mail. This lack of face-to-face communication upset several employees, and major problems started to occur. A few employees quit because the stress level became too high for them. Conflicts among employees occurred because each interpreted the messages in a different way.

The housekeeping staff also was going through many changes. Jen was hired when the former manager was fired for insubordination. She refused to implement some changes Richard was requiring. Bona and Chau did not speak English very well and were unable to communicate effectively with the front office staff. The assistant managers were not very friendly to front desk employees and often ignored requests made by the front desk employees. Front desk employees felt it was due to Bona and Chau's inability to understand the request, so rather than ask for clarification, they would ignore the request. Bona usually worked the night shift, when few requests were asked. Lack of communication was setting the stage for future problems. Jen seemed unaware of the situation.

An Unexpected Visit

March came and the hotel started to get extremely busy with conventions. Tuesday, the first day of a major four-day convention, was to be a big check-in day. With 550 reservations for check-in that day, the front office and housekeeping employees knew they had a busy day ahead of them. Unfortunately, that was the day that agents from U.S. Citizenship and Immigration Services (USCIS) made an unscheduled visit. The look on Richard's face showed that he had had no idea this was going to happen. By 10 A.M., employees from most departments, including food and beverage, housekeeping, laundry, maintenance, and the front desk, were dismissed. More than half of the housekeeping staff, Chau, and Cathy were told to leave, in addition to seven employees in the kitchen, because they had illegal alien status. This presented a very stressful situation within the three departments. Cathy had worked as a night auditor for the last year. She had graduated from a local college and obtained an optional practical training status for one year. At the end of the year, Richard had been unable to obtain H1 status for her. Richard appreciated Cathy's loyalty to the company and strong work ethic, so he kept her on as a night auditor. He had hoped that the next attempt at getting the H1 status for her would be more successful. Then he would work to get her a green card.

Because housekeeping was hit quite hard by USCIS auditors, Jen, Bryan, and Bona were forced to clean rooms. About half of the laundry staff was reassigned to housekeeping with very limited training. By check-in time, half of the rooms were not ready for guests. Rooms were assigned on a first-come, first-served basis. One convention speaker was very frustrated when his room was not ready. He was scheduled to give a presentation within an hour and a half of his arrival and wanted a room to refresh himself and complete final preparations of his speech. He was less than happy, and Frankee and Rebeka were involved in trying to find him a room. Several convention attendees were expressing their displeasure, and employees were instructed to not tell guests about the USCIS visit. The convention was scheduled to begin at 5:30 P.M. with cocktails, and the dinner and program was to follow at 6:30. Many guests wanted to change clothes and freshen up before the evening events began. It was close to 9 P.M. before all guest rooms were ready. The stress of the day caused Angela, the intern, to walk out on her shift. She thought about the grief she had experienced with Jerry and the lack of help she received from management. This, coupled with the current happenings, influenced her decision to leave. She decided the internship didn't mean that much to her. Another newer employee also quit at the end of his shift.

The week's activities decreased employee morale at the front desk and in housekeeping. Communication between housekeeping and the front desk deteriorated even further. Employees in each department took their frustrations out on employees in the other department. Housekeeping now had to hire half its staff and an assistant manager, while the front desk had to find a new night auditor. Managers in both departments had to find ways to reunite employees.

Discussion Questions

1. Identify some opportunities when hiring employees without legal documentation. Whom does this benefit? For how long?
2. Describe some risks of hiring employees without legal documentation. Why do you consider these risks? What problems may result? Explain.
3. Although the hotel was experiencing labor shortages, ethically should the company have hired illegal employees in the first place? Why or why not?
4. Whose fault is it if USCIS finds out about illegal employees at a property? Explain.

5. Is it appropriate to shift people from different departments to pick up the slack, such as moving laundry employees to housekeeping? Support your answer. What are the disadvantages of moving employees?

6. As a manager, when and what is too much to demand of your employees? Is it fair to ask them to pick up shifts until more front office staff is hired? Is it fair to ask the front desk employees to deal with Jerry? Why or why not?

7. Could anything have been done to improve Angela's internship? Why or why not? What should be expected of a company that has an internship program? Justify your answer.

8. Evaluate Richard's behavior concerning Jerry's demands.

9. As the management team, how you would you go about reuniting employees within your department? Between the two departments?

10. What are some ways that communication could be improved between housekeeping and front office departments? What problems can result as a lack of communication? Explain.

11. Describe how you would improve communication.

The Suite Hotel

The Suite Hotel is located in Marshallville, a medium-size southeastern city of 275,000. Marshallville is fueled by a booming high-technology industry. Many of the high-tech companies that are headquartered in Marshallville have contracts with the military. The city has two small colleges and one private religious college. There is a small local airport from which all major carriers fly. There is one nationally known museum that caters to groups of schoolchildren as well as a new convention center that is building its customer base for year-round conventions and cultural and social events.

The hotel has 100 two-room suites, forty-five one-room suites, and two honeymoon suites along with very limited meeting space. The two-room suites have a separate bedroom with two double beds or a king-size bed and a living area with a kitchenette. The kitchenette has a microwave, refrigerator, sink, coffee maker, dishwasher, and eating area for four. The living areas have a sleeper sofa, a recliner, and a twenty-five-inch television.

The one-room suites feature kitchenettes but do not have a separate living area. Instead they have a recliner and a small table for one. The honeymoon suites, similar to the other two-room suites with a king-size bed, have a two-person whirlpool tub in the bathroom. The hotel also has a sauna room; an exercise room equipped with treadmills, stepping machines, free weights, an indoor hot tub, and a NordicTrack machine; and a large swimming pool with inside and outside swimming areas.

The Suite Hotel has three meeting areas. Two areas are located on the second floor and can accommodate thirty-five people each. The ground floor meeting room can accommodate 115 people in a theater-style seating arrangement.

The hotel has a casual restaurant with breakfast, lunch, and dinner menus. The restaurant seats fifty people. Though the restaurant is not very profitable, it does not lose money. The restaurant does not have a manager, so the head cook, **Hattie Washington,** purchases the restaurant's food. Hattie purchases her food directly from the local warehouse in Marshallville. In addition to Hattie, there are three cooks, five servers, a dishwasher, and one cashier.

Julie Barry

Julie Barry was hired as general manager (GM) by the Suite Hotel owners seven years ago when the property opened. She was working as a sales manager at a larger property. Though she did not have any direct GM experience, she often substituted for the GM at her previous hotel when he was away on business or vacation. The owners of the Suite Hotel were former hotel company executives attempting to go into business for themselves. Julie assured them that she was committed to doing a great job for the upstart company. There are two properties in the state: one in Marshallville, where Julie works, and the other in the neighboring city of College Park. Other properties are located in Tennessee, Arizona, Virginia, and Ohio.

Julie is the mother of two teenagers and recently remarried. As GM she is committed to the Suite Hotel and a more stable professional life. She also enjoys spending more time with her family,

Though Julie's property was doing well, the other properties were not. The franchise had been experiencing financial trouble from its inception and had struggled to make a profit. Recently, the company became financially unstable and had to liquidate its assets. Many hotel employees became nervous about the stability of their jobs and began to look elsewhere for work. Julie decided that she would not abandon the hotel. She feels comfortable with the hotel's status because the owners keep her abreast of the developments. Many major chains immediately offered to purchase the Marshallville property, but the owners felt the bids were far below fair market value. The owners are desperately attempting to hold out for a better offer for the property that was making money.

The New Owner

Three weeks after the owners informed the employees of the need to sell the Suite Hotel, Julie received a call from the owners informing her that they had found a buyer. **Rad Rashad,** a retired economics professor from a local college, had invested his money well over the years and was looking for a business opportunity. Though he had no experience in the hospitality industry, he decided that buying the hotel was a sound financial investment. Rad is married and has two sons, both recent college graduates.

Within the week, Julie met with Rad, introduced him to the remaining staff, and told him about her job as well as the duties and responsibilities of the other management employees and back office staff. The back office staff includes an accountant, a sales manager, a reservationist, and a secretary. The hotel also has housekeeping, maintenance, and front desk managers. Rad didn't ask many questions of Julie but seemed friendly. Julie and the other staff noticed that he was very observant of their activities, but never commented on anything unless asked.

Rad informed Julie that he would be moving into the empty office next to hers and would begin handling some of her workload, especially the financial portion. Julie was excited to have Rad handling the financial aspect of the hotel because then she could concentrate on filling management positions. She hired **Shelly Hsu** as the front desk manager.

Shelly was a logical choice because she already knew the computer reservation system, was assertive, and had previous management experience. Julie informed her that the front office staff needed to be retrained so they would be very knowledgeable about the computer system, hotel, and city. Julie wanted the front desk to be a strong capable team. The front desk team consisted of Jay, Leslie, and Katrina.

Jay Lewis was a former army policeman who was in the National Guard. He worked primarily second and third shifts. Jay was somewhat abrasive toward other front desk employees and did not possess the patience to help train new employees. He was very friendly with guests and often personally took care of their requests. He also was able to make good decisions and maintain order during high-stress moments at the front desk.

Leslie Dinh, the primary night auditor, had been at the Suite Hotel for two years. Though she had been at the hotel for a long period of time, she was not very knowledgeable about amenities offered. She often was late for her shift.

Katrina Belgilee, a college student, usually worked first and second shifts. She was probably the best all-around front office employee. Katrina was polite to guests but did not possess the strong selling skills that Julie would have liked. Because she was an accounting major, she was very good with numbers, was rarely short, and made very few mistakes. She often found the mistakes of other desk employees and helped them correct their errors.

More Changes

Six months after taking ownership of the Suite Hotel, Rad brought his youngest son, **Sammy Rashad,** into the hotel staff. Sammy was 23 years old and had recently graduated from college with a degree in biology. He wanted to be a doctor, but his father had persuaded him to try out the hotel business. Sammy was tentative about assuming responsibility because he was not very assertive, but he was friendly. Soon after, Rad informed Julie that Sammy would assume the GM position and she would become sales director for the hotel. Fuming about the new decision, Julie's first reaction was to quit. But she decided to stay, convincing herself that the change in responsibility would give her more time at home.

With Julie as the director of hotel sales, the hotel now had two sales managers. Julie joined **Wendy Lyler,** a recently hired sales manager who was looking for a career change. Wendy had been an elementary school teacher who saw the advertisement in the local newspaper. Julie felt Wendy had some creative ideas and was excited to have her on staff.

Three weeks later, Sammy informed Julie that he would be making the managerial hiring selections. **Marcy Awa,** the accounting manager, decided that there were too many unknowns with the new owner, so she informed Sammy that she would be leaving in two weeks. Knowing this, Sammy placed an ad for an accountant in the daily paper. After interviewing a few applicants, Sammy hired **Jenny Barr,** a recent college graduate with a degree in business administration and a limited work history. When Sammy told Julie he was excited to have found Jenny, Julie asked him why he had chosen her over the other candidates. He responded that Jenny seemed nice, and he was confident that she could learn the hotel accounting responsibilities quickly.

Soon after, **Joyce Hwan,** the housekeeping manager, also quit; she could not tolerate the changes being made at the hotel. Though Sammy was the GM, Rad patrolled the hotel daily, watching and observing employees and often telling Sammy what should be done. Joyce frequently had noticed Rad peeping in on her while she completed paperwork in her office. This made her extremely uncomfortable.

Sammy came to Julie and asked her what he should do until a new manager could be hired. When she replied that he needed to get one of the managers to assist the housekeepers until a new housekeeping manager was found, Sammy asked her to find a temporary replacement. Julie was dismayed as to why Sammy could not ask another manager to assume the role of housekeeping manager temporarily. When he asked Shelly to split her time between the front desk and housekeeping departments for a short time, Shelly agreed.

Julie noticed more and more that Sammy was coming to her with questions. Attempting not to show her disappointment for having been replaced by an inexperienced manager as well as her disgust for the way things were being handled at the hotel, she assisted Sammy as much as possible.

One day Julie got a call from an electric company employee asking why the hotel's bill hadn't been paid for several months. Julie informed the caller that she was no longer the GM, but would check into the matter. Julie approached Sammy about the bill. His immediate response was, "I guess we need to get that paid. Do you know where the checkbook is?" Julie then asked why Jenny wasn't handling the payment of bills. Sammy responded that Jenny was busy with more important things. Julie went to Jenny and asked her to print a check so Julie could drop it off at the electric company on her lunch break.

Still fuming from the previous day's events, Julie noticed a new front desk employee. In questioning him, Julie learned that he was the father of Sammy's best friend. **Jack Dempsey,** a retired Air Force officer, had recently moved back to Marshallville. He had no previous hotel experience. In addition, he had chronic back pain and could not stand on his feet for long hours. Because Shelly was splitting her time between the two departments, Katrina was training him.

Four months later, Sammy decided to begin the first of many remodeling projects. He told Julie that within three months a bar would be open in the space occupied by the restaurant because it wasn't profitable. During morning hours, the former dining area would be used as an eating area for guests with a complimentary continental breakfast of muffins, danishes, cold cereal, hot beverages, and doughnuts. Weeks passed since the restaurant closed, and Hattie was still purchasing food for the breakfast and alcohol for the bar.

Rad noticed that some employees were helping themselves to the breakfast, so he sent out a memo stating that no employee was to eat the hotel's breakfast, including leftovers. Employees often saw him come in early on weekends to make sure employees were not eating any food.

Julie was not able to find a qualified person to manage the housekeeping department. Sammy asked Julie about the difficulty of finding a housekeeping manager, and she explained that the pay is the big issue in securing someone. Sammy suggested that Shelly stay in housekeeping, and he would make Jack the front desk manager. Julie reminded Sammy that Jack had been on the job only for a short while and had not yet mastered the system. Sammy assured her that Jack would do just fine.

A party was held the following afternoon to announce Jack as the new front office manager. Jack took his new position and the power that accompanied it to heart. Soon he recommended eliminating the position responsible for taking reservations to save money. Sammy liked Jack's thinking. They knew they couldn't ask **Andrea Banning** to leave, so they offered her a front desk position with a decrease in pay. Andrea quit immediately.

Rad, on one of his daily visits to the hotel, notified the sales managers that he was going to franchise the property. To comply with the new hotel chain standards, there would need to be a massive renovation. Rad hired a general contractor, **Morris Dee,** to do the job. Morris moved into two of the hotel guest rooms with his wife, young son, and large dog. Although the hotel does not allow pets, Rad didn't think that the dog would be an issue. The day after the Dees moved in, guests started calling the front desk to complain that there was a dog tied to the fence by the pool and they didn't like the barking. The guests also complained when Morris left the dog outside in the evening while he and his family went out to dinner or a movie.

Satcha Rashad, Rad's other son, oversaw the renovation. Satcha graduated from one of the local colleges with a degree in physics. He and Jenny began working together to assess the hotel's financial status. In reviewing payroll, Jenny noticed that Sammy was not listed. Jenny asked Sammy about the discrepancy, and he told her that his father pays him directly each month. Jenny decided that she did not want to know any more regarding how Rad compensated his sons. She didn't ask any more questions and continued to gather financial data for Rad.

Despite the problems, the Suite Hotel was doing quite well under Julie's efforts to keep the occupancy rates high. Since becoming director of hotel sales, she had managed to secure many new room contracts with the military, airline manufacturers, and a chemical company. When Rad decided that Satcha would become the GM of another hotel he had recently purchased, Jack began to supervise the hotel renovation.

Although Jack was salaried, he clocked in when he arrived in the late evening to check on the renovation crew. He made verbal notes in his handheld tape recorder as he toured the hotel, and left his notes for Sammy to review the next morning. During the day, Jack rarely left his office to help at the front desk. He was unable to answer most questions because he lacked experience.

Weekly mandatory meetings were held for front desk employees. Jack instructed employees on how to do their jobs better. He presented them with scenarios and instructed them how to handle them. During this time, back office managers staffed the front desk. Often Sammy volunteered, but because he did not know the computer system well, the guests were not served in a timely manner. There always was a line waiting for front desk employees when the meeting was over.

With renovations coming to an end, Sammy announced that he was going to become the GM at a third property his father had recently purchased. Jack would be the new GM at the Suite Hotel.

Discussion Questions

1. If you were Julie, what would be your next move? Why?
2. What problems exist in the hotel? Justify your responses. What potential problems could occur in the future? Why do you think these might occur?
3. As a consultant for an organizational development firm hired by Rad, what suggestions would you have for him? Support your answer. Describe how you would help him implement the changes.
4. Has Rad done anything illegal? Support your answer.
5. Evaluate Rad's decisions. Identify those you would support. Why would you support them? Identify those you would not support. Explain your response.
6. Do you think hourly employees are aware of problems within this hotel? Why or why not?
7. Think of yourself as a hospitality management student who has worked as a front desk employee at the Suite Hotel for one year. Sammy asks you if you would like to work full-time for his father. Would you accept his offer? Why or why not?

The Bern Hotel

The Bern Hotel is a four-star Swiss hotel located in the heart of Bern, the capital of Switzerland and a German-speaking area. The hotel has 150 rooms and seventy employees. Most guests are either business travelers or tourists. The hotel's location and efficient services make it famous for its food and beverage (F&B) outlets.

The hotel has four F&B outlets: a fine dining restaurant, La Monte; a quick-service restaurant, Berian; a piano bar, Lusian; and the banquet department. In the past, these F&B outlets had accounted for 60 percent of the total annual revenue, with 55 percent of the net being profit. The hotel's revenue had been growing by more than 20 percent per year, and shareholders and hotel owners were satisfied with the financial reports. However, over the last two years, revenue has declined due to a 30 percent increase in operating costs of banquets and a decrease in regular customers.

Bay Schenter is the general manager (GM) and an owner along with **Emily Schenter,** his wife (see the Bern Hotel organization chart). She is the housekeeping manager. She manages with an authoritarian style. Emily is fifteen years older than Bay.

Emily is overseeing the preparation of this month's management report to the other owners and is eager to locate the problems within the banquet department. She has given **John Bauquis,** executive manager, the responsibility for investigating, reporting, and finding problems and solutions for the Schenters.

John Bauquis

John graduated from a Swiss hotel management school and has seven years of experience in the industry with four years as executive manager at the Bern Hotel. He is responsible for hiring, firing, recruiting, and training all employees and managers. He is known by employees and managers for his ability to control quality

The Bern Hotel Organization Chart

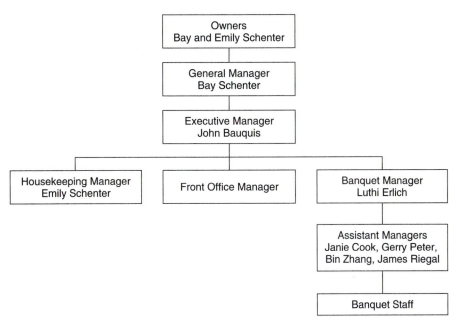

and costs, and is well known for his technical ability, high productivity, and tough management. John has an abrasive personality toward the staff, but is good at guest relations.

John works more than eighty hours a week, helping with service during busy hours to cut labor costs. Bay has given John full authority for supervision and management of all employees, even those supervised by Luthi in the banquet department. With all this authority, John set a policy that requires employees to work in other areas of the hotel when help is needed. For example, during lunch service for 1,000 guests for a recent conference, he required front office clerks to help with service for one hour in order to save overtime pay. The banquet staff is asked to work in laundry for four hours or in another F&B outlet when they have little work to do. This change saves money on overtime and keeps employees busy during slow times.

This policy has had a negative impact on employees. John's relationship with employees has been strained because he asks them to do tasks beyond what is expected in their job descriptions. However, profits have been good, and the operation has run smoothly to the satisfaction of owners and shareholders.

Food and Beverage Department

Luthi Erlich, the banquet manager, has been the F&B manager for the past two years. He started as a server five years ago and was promoted through the ranks. He reports to John, who evaluates Luthi more on his work in the banquet department than in all F&B outlets. Luthi is 27 years old and works hard while continuing his studies at a hospitality school. He is well liked by employees.

There are four assistant managers: **Janie Cook, Gerry Peter, Bin Zhang,** and **James Riegal.** Each takes a turn supervising the outlets on a two-week basis as determined by Luthi. When Luthi is on vacation, John arranges their work schedules. They are in charge of hourly employee work schedules.

Banquet Department

Organization

Luthi has four full-time employees, two interns from the hospitality school, one part-time employee, and two dishwashers reporting to him. The entire staff, except for Lucy, are foreigners who have a yearlong contract that includes a monthly payment, annual leave, lodging, three meals per day, and a minimum of fifty hours per week. Most foreign employees are from poor countries and come to make money. A yearlong work contract causes high turnover and frequent loss of good employees. For example, **Marie Diaz,** a former full-time foreign contract employee, had an outstanding performance evaluation but couldn't continue the contract because the hotel policy does not extend the contract with foreign employees.

Staff

Lucy Chalet: Six years as full-time staff; Swiss; in charge of breakfast; likes to take all gossip to management

Joe Arnez: Four months as full-time staff; Spanish; very cooperative with management; works hard, hoping to continue his work contract next year

Paul Digenaro: Six months as full-time staff; Italian; speaks German fluently, so he works more in "à la carte"

Helm Diaz: Ten months as full-time staff; Spanish; very experienced in beverage service, so he works more during cocktail parties

Ruth Kwon: Three-month intern; Japanese; mostly works with Lucy; complains that Lucy always stays inside the back office and works only when managers are present

Angel Juan: Three-month intern; Chinese; mostly works night shift and replaces Ruth when she is not scheduled; does not get along with Lucy

Mark Casteau: Seven months as part-time staff; French; has no responsibility with checks and no share of tips

Pan Sharma: Eight months as a full-time dishwasher; Indian; likes to drink leftover wine and takes leftover food home

Dinno Vahagan: Four months as a full-time dishwasher; Hungarian; speaks little German and has difficulty with communication

Operations

Personnel in the banquet department need the event orders from the sales department one week in advance. Receiving event orders weekly mandates that the banquet staff work schedules are arranged on a weekly basis. Therefore, banquet employees have no fixed work schedules or scheduled time off from work. Sometimes they finish working at 2:00 A.M. and begin working a breakfast event at 7:00 A.M. the next day. Little or no overtime pay will be given. In most cases, the only compensation given employees is shortening their working hours. This allows employees to finish work two hours earlier on a day when business is slow. Employees are not satisfied with the situation and are exhausted with their heavy workloads. Afraid of losing their jobs, they hesitate to complain.

After a new employee has worked one week in the banquet department, he or she is given $150 in pocket money and a key for the cash register. The employee must return the $150 cash and the key on the last contracted workday.

Each day the banquet staff needs to check the schedule to see what events they work or the events in which they may be in charge. Responsibilities include setting up and clearing the event rooms, taking orders, providing services, preparing guest checks using the cash register key, and receiving customer payments. The banquet managers are in charge of catering events only when the service is for more than 100 guests or the event is very important. The staff are allowed to keep their own tips.

At the end of the workday, banquet employees are required to hand in a cash bag that consists of total guest checks and cash received. A daily accounting report also must be given to the banquet management or an assigned manager before leaving the workplace. If the banquet manager is not free to receive this cash bag, employees either leave it in the manager's drawer or ask another colleague to deliver it later. If any shortage of the guest checks or cash is discovered, the employee who initially had the cash bag is responsible for the shortage. That amount will be deducted from the employee's monthly pay.

Problems

Sick Leave

Recently, several problems have developed in the banquet department. One of the problems involves the use of sick leave, and the other is about shortages in the beverage inventory.

Two months ago, Ruth was very ill and Angel had an operation during the same time. Ruth was given two weeks of paid sick leave, and Angel had one month. Their doctors approved both leaves. When John saw their sick leave forms, he was very angry. He sent them a letter stating the recently developed hotel policy. The letter stated that any employee who did not follow the policies would be fired. The two policies related to sick leave are as follows:

1. The sick employee has to stay in his or her room, and a housekeeper will check the employee's room on a random basis.
2. No sick leave will be granted beyond one month. After that, all employees must follow the work schedule.

Even though the labor union lawyer told Ruth and Angel that they could file a grievance because John was not following the Swiss Labor Regulations, they did not. They were afraid that John would get angry and fire them. If they were fired, they would not be able to continue their studies. Therefore, they didn't accept the labor union lawyer's recommendation to file a grievance against the Bern Hotel.

According to the regulations:

- Employers must follow doctor's instructions on the employee's sick leave approval indicating the days of sick leave needed and the doctor's recommendation for the level of physical work, such as light work or half-day, that an employee can do.
- All sick leaves must be paid fully by the employers.
- Employers have to give employees two weeks of paid annual leave for every five-month work period.
- Both employer and employee have to follow the work contract, which consists of the job description, payment, minimum work hours, work period, annual leave, work place, and work conditions.
- Hours worked over the minimum contract work hours are to be paid at the extra wage written on the contract.

After Ruth and Angel came back to work, John gave them a hard time. He specifically changed Ruth's work schedule so she worked from 6:30 A.M. to 9:00 A.M., 11:00 A.M. to 1:30 P.M., and 7:00 P.M. to 12:00 A.M. Angel's situation was worse than Ruth's; John changed her job description so she was not a banquet intern. He assigned tasks to Angel as he liked. He wanted to show the other employees what would happen as a result of being absent from work.

Ruth and Angel have been working under great stress. John's behavior has had a negative influence on other employees because almost all of them are foreign employees, and they realize that one day they may face the same situation. After observing John's behavior, no banquet employee called in sick or asked to be excused. However, productivity was lower than before, more guests complained about service, and the morale obviously decreased. Now the banquet employees only want to make money and finish the work contract.

Alcoholic Beverage Inventory

The other problem in the banquet area is the daily inventory of alcoholic beverages. All beverages are set up in the back, and servers are allowed to take them out directly for service. No one in the banquet department is in charge of daily beverage inventory.

Bob Huss, a beverage controller, sets out the beverages every morning and gives the monthly beverage inventory report to Luthi. Although Luthi has asked every staff member to take beverage orders carefully and check the actual bottle consumption, the beverage shortages and costs were still increasing. He asked the four assistant managers to supervise this problem and find out who was stealing the beverages and/or writing inaccurate checks.

The beverage situation continued to get worse. In order to make up differences, Luthi gradually began putting the shortages on separate guest checks. Sometimes several cash bags were stolen or the money inside the cash bag was short. In some instances, employees have reported that their personal wallets have been stolen.

During the time Luthi has been banquet manager, he has worked hard to correct several major problems that had existed in the food and beverage division when he assumed his duties. But this beverage shortage problem was getting to be too much. Unaccountable losses and shrinkages of wine and liquors were plaguing the hotel.

After an investigation, Luthi discovered that, due to poor planning, the hotel's dining room and bar area had inadequate wine and liquor storage space to carry them through a busy weekend. It was standard practice for the employees to pick up the keys for the main liquor storage area from the front desk when the restaurant or bar needed additional supplies. The employee would either get the items or give the keys to someone else to fetch the wares. While there were forms to record such emergency supplying, the wares missing from the storeroom never matched the completed forms left behind. Through a series of tests, Luthi determined that this was where the majority of shrinkage was occurring.

The food and beverage budget would not allow staffing of the liquor storage area on weekends. So Luthi worked with John, who wished to centralize all key storage, to devise a new system. Keys to all areas of the hotel were placed in individual lockable drawers in the office area behind the front desk. Front desk personnel were supplied with a log book and a list of people who were authorized to access keys. For example, if an employee needed to get supplies from the liquor storage area, he or she would go to the front desk and ask for key seven (the key to the drawer containing liquor storage area keys). If the employee's name was on the authorized list, the front desk person would note the time the key was taken, have the employee initial the log book, and give the employee the key to drawer number seven. The employee would open the drawer, take the keys to the liquor storage area, get the needed wares, and note the removal of wares on the appropriate storage room form. The employee would then return the keys to the drawer, lock the drawer, and return the drawer key to the front desk. The front desk employee would note the time at which the key had been returned in the log book and initial the entry. If the person requesting a key was not authorized to have that key, the front desk would note the request in the log book, but under no circumstance issue the key.

Luthi and John went through the system with their employees, stressing the importance of following *all* guidelines and steps in the procedure. They discussed disciplinary actions that could result from not following procedures. One action could be immediate termination. All employees were required to sign a statement following the information session indicating their understanding of the policies.

After the new procedure had been followed for two months, both John and Luthi were pleased with the results. Spot checks showed that employees were adhering to the policies, and liquor shrinkage had dropped considerably. The hotel director, who had been supportive of the idea, congratulated the two on their efforts.

Luthi also was pleased that a personnel matter he was dealing with seemed to be coming along nicely. Several months earlier, Luthi noticed that one of the hotel's longtime servers, Lucy, was frequently absent from work. The waiters' union had an agreement with the hotel that the union employees would cover any absences from their own ranks if the hotel did not hire extra "on-call" servers. Because servers worked on a percentage of sales, this arrangement was beneficial to both groups. Yet Luthi was concerned. Lucy was experienced and competent and an asset to the restaurant. It was unlike her to be absent so often.

Luthi contacted the representative of the waiters' union and shared his concerns. The representative told Luthi that Lucy was having major problems with alcohol and often could not work as a result of consuming too much alcohol. Together, the two men developed a plan to help Lucy. If the union representative could persuade Lucy to seek treatment, hotel management would pay for her stay and treatment at a well-known substance abuse center. Lucy would be given sick leave for the time she was undergoing treatment, the union employees would cover her position, and Lucy's job would be waiting when she returned. Luthi would take care of the necessary forms to ensure that Lucy's absence appeared to be some ailment requiring a lengthy absence from work, and no one would know the actual reason. Luthi shared his plans with the hotel owners, who gave him their total support. The union representative contacted Lucy's brother. The two men approached Lucy and, fortunately, she agreed to the plan.

Now it seemed that the hotel was reaping the benefits of helping one of its employees. Lucy had been back on the job for some time. She seemed happier, more energetic, and very positive, and she never missed work. The hotel director congratulated Luthi and the union representative on their roles in Lucy's rehabilitation.

Luthi had taken the weekend off and was out of his office on Monday. Tuesday evening found him trying to catch up on paperwork when the union representative came in and closed the door.

"It's about Lucy," he said.

The representative went on to explain that Lucy's brother had committed suicide on Saturday. Lucy, distraught at the news, had come to the hotel at 2:00 A.M. on Sunday, explained what had happened to the front desk employee on duty, and asked for the keys to the liquor storage. Lucy was given the keys. She "borrowed" two bottles of Scotch whiskey, returned the keys, and left the hotel. Lucy had not reported to work on Sunday or Monday, and was not here today. The union was, as usual, covering Lucy's station.

Luthi thanked the union representative and immediately began an investigation of what had happened. The log book at the front desk showed nothing. According to what was recorded, no one had requested the key to drawer seven, no one had received the key, and no one had been denied the key. The forms in the liquor storage area showed that no one had removed anything from the area since early Friday evening. And yet Luthi had just been told that it had happened.

Checking the employee schedule, Luthi found out who was on duty at the front desk when Lucy had been given the keys. Unfortunately, John, had already left for the day, so Luthi could not confront him with the information immediately. Finding nothing more he could accomplish, Luthi went home.

Sitting down to his desk on Wednesday, Luthi noticed that his left leg bumped something. Checking further, he found a brown paper bag containing two bottles of Scotch whiskey. Attached to the bottles was a note that read: "Thanks so much for the loan. Lucy." Luthi left the bottles under his desk and confronted John about the employee on duty when the bottles were removed. Expecting support, Luthi was surprised when John said, "Well, what do you expect me to do? After all, it was *your* employee who had the problem. And, anyway, you got the bottles back. What do you want? Blood?" He continued by saying, "Do you know how hard it is to get good night managers at the front desk? I can't afford to lose Lucy. She's doing a great job. Since no one was hurt, why can't we 'stretch' the rules a bit in this case?"

Returning to his office stunned, Luthi kicked the bottles as he sat down. He realized that their absence would show up in the monthly inventory tomorrow.

Discussion Questions

1. Is John an effective manager? Justify your response.
2. What do you think are the root problems in this case? Be specific and defend your answers with examples.
3. React to how cash bags were handled. Would you make any changes? Why or why not?
4. If you were Ruth or Angel, what would be your worst fear concerning this personnel situation? Why?
5. Do you think that accusing the hotel management of unfair treatment will improve the current situation? Why or why not?

6. Do you think the alcoholic beverage shortage is related to the sick leave incident? Why or why not?
7. If you were Luthi, what could you do to improve the beverage shortage? How would you implement your plans? Why do you think your plan would work?
8. Would you discuss the problems with John? Why or why not?
9. Most restaurants experience theft problems. If you were the manager, would you take action on the problems? Why or why not? What may be the hidden risks in the organization? Explain. Are there advantages to taking action? Explain.
10. If you were Luthi, would you:
    a. Confront Lucy?
    b. Go to the hotel director with your information?
    c. Return the bottles and do nothing about it?
    d. Confront the person who was on duty at the front desk the night the bottles were taken?
    e. Take some other action?
       Give specific reasons for your decision.
11. What ethical questions are addressed in this case?
12. What factors in this case make it difficult to decide on the "right" or "best" course of action in handling employees? In dealing with the alcoholic beverage shortage?

The Britton Hotel

The Britton Hotel, located in Trond, Norway (a city of 120,000), was built in 1896. The 150-room hotel was owned and operated privately by the Rudd family, who did little to improve and upgrade the hotel or to keep the hotel operations up to date. Ten years ago, Royal Hotels Inc., a new hotel corporation in the city, purchased the Britton Hotel in an effort to expand their services to guests. The purchase was big news for many older hotel guests but not well received by the Britton Hotel employees, many who had worked there for more than thirty years.

The Property

The hotel's flagship restaurant, The Palm Garden, was open for breakfast, lunch, and dinner seven days a week. The 175-seat restaurant was considered "the city's living room" by people in Trond and was known for its fine food and wine. Visitors enjoyed the daily piano music and the fine dance orchestras that played in the adjoining dance lounge, After Eight. The Palm Garden also had an adjacent oak-paneled reading lounge. The Palm Garden was the only part of the hotel showing a profit when the Rudd family sold the hotel. The Corner Restaurant, a popular lunch and supper restaurant, was currently losing money. An international piano bar featured a different pianist each month. The hotel also had a beauty salon.

Management

George Hoff was appointed director of the Britton Hotel. He was trained in Switzerland and came with extensive hotel and restaurant management experiences from an upscale hotel corporation in both Switzerland and Africa. Most recently he had worked as food and beverage director for the Royal Hotel during its building and opening phases. Although extremely competent in food and lodging, George came across as arrogant and unfeeling, a fact not lost on old-guard employees of the Britton Hotel.

When George took over operations of the Britton Hotel, **Kevin Thompson** had, for all practical purposes, been acting as director of the hotel, although his official title was food and beverage manager. While George did not care for Kevin or respect his abilities, he kept Kevin on as food and beverage manager. George then "headhunted" and subsequently hired **Fred Siefer** as executive chef and **Eve Berg** as hotel manager. When the hotel was sold, the personnel director, **Solman Rupel,** resigned and became the district director of the servers' union.

Remodeling

In May, the owners began an extensive remodeling and upgrading project of the Britton Hotel. A seventy-five-room addition was built on a former back parking lot. In addition to modern rooms, the addition included Club Britton, which was a floor with suites, a fireplace lounge, a sauna, and whirlpool facilities, and a small cluster of first-floor shops that were accessible from the hotel and street. All rooms and corridors in the original Britton building and the 1954 wing were refurbished or restored. Electrical service was updated, a sprinkler system added, the front desk area changed, the front entrance upgraded, and a computer system added. George, who acted as coordinator of the whole project, decided to keep most of the hotel open during all remodeling and building activities. However, The Palm Garden closed for two months for extensive remodeling.

There was other extensive remodeling of the hotel. The Corner Restaurant closed and the area became office space for hotel management. The former beauty salon and some storage space in the basement were remodeled to create a 120-seat informal dinner restaurant, Jonathan House. The reading lounge was converted into a quiet before-dinner lounge area called the Lobby Lounge. The international piano bar remained basically the same, as did the elegant private dining rooms in the old section of the hotel.

Employees

The strongest and most vocal group in the hotel, in fact the group that for all practical purposes dominated and directed all decisions made in the hotel, was the Palm Garden staff. The group of professional waiters and waitresses was strongly unionized. Many had been at the hotel for more than thirty years, with an average length of employment of twelve years. While Kevin was acting director, he had maintained peace with the group by trying to befriend them, frequently granting favors, overlooking discrepancies, and generally going along with their wishes. From his new position of authority, Solman closely monitored the changing events at the hotel. During the remodeling, the Palm Garden staff, as a group, opposed the changes made in the hotel. They disliked George as a director and had near-hatred for the executive chef, Fred. Kevin, secretly in front of the director and openly in front of the Palm Garden staff, agreed with them.

In July, against Kevin's wishes (Kevin wanted to promote from within), George hired **Craig Winter** as restaurant manager. Craig, who came with excellent references, had a four-year degree in hotel and restaurant management and extensive food and restaurant experience both in Norway and abroad. George had worked previously with Craig, knew his capabilities well, and looked forward to having him on the Britton team. Craig's main focus was to work directly with the Palm Garden staff on motivation, morale, service levels, and relations with other hotel employees. In addition, his duties would include the following:

- Daily operations of restaurant reservations (a new position filled by a rather difficult former maitre d' who had been with the Britton Hotel for twenty-eight years)
- Staffing and daily operations of the After Eight bar, the Palm Garden restaurant, the Lobby Lounge, Jonathan House, the private dining rooms, and room service
- Daily operations of the international piano bar
- Hiring and supervising of breakfast service personnel, coat check personnel, and doormen

Craig started by holding training sessions on service attitude for all restaurant staff. In spite of themselves, the Palm Garden staff found, over time, that they respected and even liked Craig. He was honest, straightforward, and fair, yet loyal to George and the hotel. Kevin often tried to circumvent Craig, going directly to employees with bits of information and gossip, and occasionally the employees bought into his tactics. But over time, they realized that their real supporter was Craig. Craig, realizing Kevin's tactics, confronted him on several occasions, but Kevin always denied any wrongdoing. Finally, Craig went to George with his concerns, but nothing seemed to change.

One of Craig's main concerns became obvious immediately: how to improve relations between Fred and his kitchen staff and the Palm Garden staff. Fred had been Craig's boss and had encouraged Craig to come to the Britton Hotel. Craig knew Fred as a no-nonsense, straightforward, and extremely talented chef who understood the need to make money as well as be creative. Though very different in their leadership styles, the two men got along well, and their styles seemed to complement each other. Both were highly motivated with strong work ethics. They not only respected each other, but also became good friends and often went out for long discussions about the hotel over a "cold one" after work.

In the short time he had been at the hotel, Fred's kitchen staff of thirty had completely changed twice, a fact that the Palm Garden staff was quick to share. The old faces familiar to the Palm Garden staff were gone, and it seemed that few people were willing to work under Fred's high standards and direct criticism. Yet over time George saw that Fred was developing a loyal group of hardworking individuals, and the standard and quality of food in the hotel had improved vastly. Unfortunately, it seemed that the new staff carried the same animosity toward the Palm Garden staff as Fred did. George also noted that Fred and Craig worked well as a team, and he encouraged their friendship.

The relationship between Kevin and Fred also needed attention. They did not get along. Kevin felt that he knew everything there was to know about food, while Fred had no respect for him and felt that he knew nothing. Fred never hesitated to tell Kevin exactly how he felt. The two rarely had a discussion that did not break into a full-blown temperamental argument. Kevin regularly made snide comments to the Palm Garden staff regarding Fred. George, on the other hand, supported and encouraged the changes Fred was making, and the two men respected each other.

When the Palm Garden restaurant reopened, Craig added three new maitre d's to the staff. First hired was **Helen Johnston,** a former flight attendant with a sunny personality, a mind and eye for service, and some management experience. She was willing to work only part-time. Next, Craig hired **Ruth Hansen,** an instructor in a hotel and restaurant management school who was on a one-year leave. The third maitre d' was **John Foster,** who had worked for fifteen years in the restaurant field, ten as a waiter and five as the manager of a small, upscale restaurant known for its quality food and service.

It became apparent immediately that John and the Palm Garden staff clicked, though Craig was concerned that John was "giving in" to them more than he was leading and directing them. Craig knew that John partied with the Palm Garden staff, suspected that he was having an affair with a waitress, and was concerned that John might be drinking too much. Though he was very good with the public, John did not like paper work, so either Helen or Ruth did most of the reports.

After Reopening

When the Palm Garden and After Eight reopened, they were full every day. The Lobby Lounge opened for business one month later, and the international piano bar was as popular as ever, although there seemed to be some employee problems that needed attention.

Jim Lunderson, a twenty-year part-time maitre d', assumed responsibilities for the two private dining rooms (which seated fifty and twenty-six, respectively) with a new, young staff of waitresses. The goal was to "freshen up" the previously stuffy service in those areas. It became clear quite rapidly that while Jim had been a maitre d' in the Palm Garden, he was actually afraid of the staff there. In addition, he rarely completed reports correctly, he often confused reservations, he did little training of new staff (there were a lot of guest complaints), and several employees suspected he was drinking too much. While Craig was aware of these concerns, he felt that he had little time to deal with them.

Kevin seemed unhappy with all of the food and beverage areas even though their profits were good. Although he offered no concrete suggestions for improvement, he repeatedly told Craig that "things *have* to improve." Craig met with Kevin on several occasions, explaining that he felt he had too many responsibilities to do a good job and asking for an additional restaurant manager. Kevin did not feel that it was necessary and suggested that if Craig hired more qualified people and organized himself better, things would function just fine. Kevin seemed to have other concerns. While Fred agreed with Craig that a second manager was needed, he was quick to criticize Craig for not "taking care of that Palm Garden gang."

Although Fred's and Craig's staffs, trained together by the two men, functioned smoothly, and the restaurants were more popular than ever, Craig was feeling lots of stress. Finally, one Monday night he collapsed. His physician sent Craig home to recuperate for one month. When he got home, he found flowers and champagne from the Palm Garden staff.

Craig contacted George with his plea for an additional restaurant manager and shared again his concerns about Kevin's ineffective management practices. George promised to take action immediately.

George began looking for another restaurant manager that same week. Craig contacted his old girlfriend and suggested that she apply. **Lilly Anterman** had a degree in restaurant management from a two-year college, had managed a small restaurant abroad for a number of years, and had been very successful as maitre d' of the prestigious international Hotel Alex for the past ten years. Lilly and Craig had worked together at Hotel Alex and were to be engaged when Craig ended the relationship. After a period of time, the two developed a friendship, though Craig was sure that Lilly still wished for more. Lilly interviewed and was hired as restaurant manager.

About six months later, it became clear that the rooms division of the Britton Hotel was not doing well. Numbers of guests did not make up for the additional rooms. Room percentages were startlingly low. While all food and beverage sectors were now showing a profit, overall sales were down.

Lilly was working out very well as restaurant manager. She was well liked and although she was not as assertive as George had hoped, she was an effective manager. Aware of Lilly and Craig's previous relationship, George was glad to see that they functioned well as a team. Unfortunately, there seemed to be some friction between Lilly and Fred. George also noted that the relationship between the Palm Garden staff and the kitchen staff had improved. He did not attribute the changes to Kevin. It was clear to George, however, that anywhere he could save money would benefit the hotel in the long run, and he began looking for ways to do so.

When Kevin resigned on March 1, George did not encourage him to stay on at the Britton Hotel. George felt that this was his chance to make some positive changes in the management team of the Britton Hotel. He needed to "right the ship," both financially and managerially. He saw several options open to him. Some of the options he considered were the following:

- Replace Kevin from outside the hotel (salary savings).
- Promote Craig to food and beverage manager (which he would accept) and fill his position with either John, Eve, Jim, or someone from outside the hotel (salary savings).
- Promote Lilly to food and beverage manager (although she really didn't want the position) and fill her position with either John, Eve, Jim, or someone from outside the hotel (salary savings).
- Divide the food and beverage position between Fred and Craig (which they would accept with reluctance), and then promote John, Eve, or Jim or hire a replacement from outside the hotel (salary savings).
- Divide the food and beverage position between Fred and Lilly (which both did not really want) and promote John, Eve, or Jim or hire someone from outside the hotel (salary savings).
- Divide the food and beverage position between Craig and Lilly (which both reluctantly agreed to) and eliminate the restaurant manager positions (larger salary savings).
- Divide the position between Craig, Lilly, and Fred (which Fred did not agree with) and eliminate the restaurant manager positions (larger salary savings).
- Eliminate the food and beverage position altogether, with George assuming the duties himself (largest salary savings).

Discussion Questions

1. If you were George, which of these solutions would you choose? Describe four reasons for your decision. Describe three negative repercussions of your decision.
2. List five reasons why you feel that George was justified in accepting Kevin's resignation without encouraging him to stay with the hotel. Why did you choose each?
3. Do you see any areas where George could have made or should have made better decisions as hotel director? Explain your answer. Be specific.
4. What are some reasons why George made decisions that later proved not to be very sound? Justify your response.
5. If you were George, would you change the organizational structure of the hotel? Justify your reasoning.

The Embassy Hotel

The Embassy Hotel, a property of Wayward International Hotels, Inc., is a luxury 520-room hotel located in the heart of a major North American city. Most guests are either tourists who are attracted by the city's cultural and historical landmarks or individuals attending conventions. The hotel is the choice of many meeting planners for annual conferences and meetings because of its accommodations.

The hotel has four food and beverage units: a well-renowned fine dining restaurant, open for lunch and dinner; a coffee shop serving breakfast, lunch, and dinner; room service; and a banquet-catering service. These units account for 35 percent of the hotel's annual revenue. The hotel formerly operated a bar on the top floor, allowing guests to socialize within the hotel and have a panoramic view of the city at the same time. However, over the last few years, business declined because guests preferred to attend nearby bars that appealed to a wide range of customers and offered a variety of music styles.

The hotel manager, in collaboration with Wayward International's corporate offices, decided to maximize revenue per square foot on the top floor by transforming the bar space into a meeting room, the Panorama. This room can be split into smaller rooms by using sliding dividers. Recently, a kitchenette was added so food could be assembled and dished close to the new meeting room to ensure efficient food service.

The hotel has a special agreement with the city for all the catering business at the city's convention center. This works out well because the hotel is located one floor above the convention center. When the hotel was built, the architects also planned a kitchen at this level so the hotel could cater to groups who booked the center. The banquet kitchen is equipped to serve up to 2,500 customers at one time and is run as an independent unit.

Food and Beverage Division

The Embassy Hotel's food and beverage division is headed by the food and beverage director, **Phil Peters,** who is responsible for all activities of the division: hiring and firing employees, training managers, controlling costs and quality, and making profits. He is also the liaison with other divisions in the hotel, such as rooms, sales, purchasing, accounting, and maintenance. He reports directly to the assistant hotel manager, **Helen Smith,** who reports to the hotel manager, **Ramona Knoll.**

Working under the food and beverage director is the executive chef, **Alex Roth.** He is associated more closely with the daily operations of the different parts of the division: main and banquet kitchens, pantry, butcher shop, bakery, and storeroom. Three sous-chefs—**Alan Jeon, Daniel Rogers,** and **Richard Lebeau**—who work closely with the hourly employees assist Alex. Richard is responsible for the banquet kitchen, while Alan and Daniel supervise the other parts of the division.

Food and Beverage Director

Phil Peters was hired two months ago to replace the retiring food and beverage director at the Embassy Hotel. He has a bachelor's degree in hospitality management, an associate's degree in food and nutrition, and seven years of experience in the hospitality industry. He started in the industry as assistant manager of a 120-seat family-style restaurant, the Family Haus, and worked his way up to general manager (GM) within three years. He gained great knowledge of cost control, as well as valuable experience in hiring and training employees through Family Haus's well-developed training program. His philosophy is to let each employee progress at his or her own pace, getting involved only when progress is too slow. Further, he encourages employee input on how to improve each position. He strongly believes that good performance comes with job satisfaction. Employees respect him, and his employers always have been satisfied with the financial results.

Phil held the position of GM of Family Haus for four years. He became weary of working seventy to eighty hours a week, having little or no leisure time, and missing out on time with his two young daughters. He also wanted to have more input into the company's policies, procedures, and rules, while staying close to the daily operations of the restaurant. Further, he knew that his next promotion would be to the restaurant chain's corporate offices in New York City, and he didn't want to move because he enjoyed living in his hometown. These factors caused him to seek another position.

Phil wanted to move to a formal dining restaurant because he believed it would allow more creativity in menu development. He could use his educational background to modify menus and recipes to be more nutritious, reflecting the recent health trends. He applied for the position of food and beverage director at the Embassy Hotel, which seemed to be the position for him. Two weeks later, he was offered the job. With little need to consider the decision to accept the job, he told Ramona he would join the Embassy team.

Executive Chef

Alex Roth has been with the Embassy Hotel for seventeen years. He started as a cook and worked his way up to sous-chef, then to executive chef. He has been executive chef for the past eight years and is very proud of his position. He was born in Europe and came to North America when he was 28 years old. His parents owned and operated a restaurant in the old world. Alex was, therefore, brought up in the restaurant business. In Europe, his father had been a chef, while his mother supervised front-of-the-house operations. Because of his father's example, Alex believed that only men could properly manage a kitchen. He learned all the basic culinary techniques and refined his skills by attending a well-respected culinary school for one year before coming to America.

Alex, like many old-world chefs, has an autocratic leadership style and does not believe in delegation. He insists on having total control over kitchen operations, even though he has three sous-chefs to assist him. He personally does all scheduling of workers—often too many or too few. The use of part-time employees is inconsistent. Some part-time employees work nearly thirty-five hours per week, while others work fewer than fifteen hours per week.

Alex's busy schedule does not allow for adequate training. Many new hourly employees learn their jobs by themselves or by asking others who themselves have not been adequately trained. This results in poor scheduling and new employees having to learn their job by themselves. Alex is also the type of person who believes that his way is best; he seldom accepts suggestions from co-workers and is resistant to changes.

Alex has been running the operations in this manner for a few years now because the former food and beverage director, **Paul Clem,** was just marking time, waiting for retirement. Paul was not supervising the division effectively. He also was very close to Alex and frequently left him in total control of the division. Over the years, Alex assumed most food and beverage director duties.

Upper management seemed to be unaware of the problems. Paul falsified reports presented to his superiors. Having faith in Paul's ability, the GM did not assume that there was a need to check reports. Paul had been with the hotel for several years and was well liked by Helen and Ramona. There was no indication that he could not be trusted. Therefore, the hotel appeared to be doing much better than what really was happening.

Decision Point at the Embassy

Upon assuming his duties as food and beverage director, Phil quickly realized that the division was not performing well. Food and labor costs in the main kitchen were too high compared to the standards set by Wayward International. Food quality was poor. Frequently customers complained about cold food, unattractive plate presentation, and starchy-tasting sauces. Often food was slow or late coming out of the kitchen.

The banquet kitchen also was in need of reorganization. The major problems with the kitchen operations were continuous overstaffing, resulting in high labor costs; misplaced catering orders; and food problems similar to those in the two restaurants. Phil realized that Richard was not doing his job adequately. Two weeks after becoming the food and beverage director, Phil caught Richard drinking on the job and immediately dismissed him.

After interviewing several good candidates to replace Richard, Phil hired **Julie Zinfandel,** a young graduate from a culinary school. Her previous work experiences showed that she was well organized and was very efficient in doing her work. Her latest position was as an assistant chef for a 156-room resort located in the mountains forty miles from the city. In addition to her impressive credentials, she stressed the importance of teamwork and indicated that without it, a kitchen could not be managed efficiently. She was exactly what Phil was looking for to improve banquet operations and assist Alex in organizing the opening of the Panorama kitchenette. He especially was excited about her teamwork attitude.

Within Julie's first month of employment at the Embassy Hotel as banquet sous-chef, she cut labor hours and improved food quality and service. She organized the paperwork to avoid misplaced catering orders and spent more time working with the cooks. The cooks of the banquet kitchen had been left on their own when Richard was their supervisor.

Julie also took the organization of the Panorama kitchenette in hand. Sensing that Alex would not approve her plan for reorganizing the kitchenette, she went directly to Phil to have her projects accepted. Phil was very impressed with her work and gave her his approval. He congratulated himself for hiring such an efficient sous-chef.

Phil's next task was to improve food cost and food quality in the division. He examined the work patterns of the executive chef and cooks and soon discovered that the company's procedures, policies, and rules were not being followed.

Alex was ordering wholesale cuts of meat and having the butcher shop cut them into specific items. Studies at Wayward International's offices showed that this increased labor costs and meat waste. Compliance with sanitation rules also was made more difficult. Further, standardized recipes were not followed and ingredients were not weighed. Alex believed that a chef's special touch to perfectly season a recipe could not be written down. Phil also noticed Alex's attitude toward his employees. The cooks and sous-chefs constantly were given orders with which they had to comply. Whenever employees brought in new ideas or suggested alternative methods, Alex would ignore their comments. He thought highly of himself and didn't want any competition from his employees. He also knew that he would need to recognize employees if their suggestions were used and improved on his abilities.

Phil met with Alex to talk over the food and personnel problems. He soon realized that Alex's cooperation would be hard to obtain. Alex got angry and clearly stated that his kitchen was run the way he had learned in Europe's best cooking school, and that the Embassy's fine dining restaurant was recognized as one of the city's best dining places. He said he saw no need to change the operations. Alex added that Julie was making too many decisions about the banquet operations without consulting him. He asked Phil to remind Julie that he was the one wearing the chef's hat and he should approve all decisions.

Phil told Alex that he was aware of Julie's projects, for he had personally approved them. Alex became upset and stated that he had not been consulted and did not appreciate being passed over. He left Phil's office furious. Alex decided to show Phil and Julie, the two newcomers, that he was the executive chef, and he should be the one running the kitchen.

Phil realized that his executive chef was very stubborn, and his new position as food and beverage director offered more challenges than he had foreseen. He decided to let Alex calm down a few days before trying again to talk with him about the situation. Meanwhile, he checked on Julie's work. Banquet operations were running smoothly with reduced personnel, the Panorama kitchenette was ready to start operating, and Julie had added new items, several of them healthy in nature, to the catering menu. He believed she was doing a good job and saw no need to talk to her about seeking Alex's approval for change.

A few days later, Phil again met with Alex. Phil began by discussing a topic other than the kitchen problems, in an attempt to calm Alex, who was ready to burst. He explained to Alex that the two restaurant menus needed improvements to respond to customers who requested a healthy gourmet cuisine. Phil's suggestions included replacing part of the salad dressing in creamy salads with low-fat yogurt, decreasing meat portion sizes while increasing the size of vegetable servings, using whole-wheat flour in more baked products, and offering a greater choice of healthy desserts. Alex immediately stood up, hit Phil's desk with his fist, and declared that the changes were "an insult to his ancestors' cuisine." He added that he would never approve of such changes in his kitchen. He also mentioned that before Phil was hired, he had run the division successfully and did not need the new director's help. Alex left banging Phil's office door.

Phil realized for the first time the difficulty he faced in stepping into Paul's shoes. He did not enjoy working with employees like Alex. In his many years in the food and beverage area, he had never encountered someone who did not want to make changes. He wondered if all chefs felt this way.

Ramona Knoll, the hotel manager, happened to walk by and witnessed the scenes. She asked Phil to follow her to her office. Ramona questioned Phil about the situation and to Phil's amazement, the hotel manager seemed to support Alex's point of view. Ramona gave Phil two weeks to solve the conflict with the executive chef, reminding him that Alex was a valuable, dedicated, long-term employee. If Phil could not solve the conflict, Ramona said she personally would take action to resolve the situation.

When Ramona left, Phil felt stunned. He knew that he had a good employee in Julie, and that Alex seemed to do a good job. Alex's high self-esteem seemed to play a large part in his work relationships.

Discussion Questions

1. What seems to be the cause of the many kitchen problems? Explain. Why are they occurring?
2. Do you think Phil was the right person to be hired for the food and beverage director position? Justify your answer.
3. Compare and contrast Alex's and Phil's backgrounds and styles of leadership.
4. What action would you take if someone with Alex's personal traits were your employee? Your co-worker? Your superior? If your responses differ, discuss why.
5. How could the conflict between Alex and Julie have been avoided?
6. Explain how a supervisor should handle a management employee who is waiting to retire and therefore is ineffective. How would you implement your suggestions?
7. Why do you think Ramona was on Alex's side?
8. Describe in detail one positive and one negative outcome that might result from the conflicts between:
   a. Phil and Alex.
   b. Julie and Alex.
9. If you were Phil, what would you do to handle Alex's attitude toward employees? How would you solve the conflict with the executive chef?

The Oak Tree Hotel

Kevin hung up the phone and sighed. It seemed that a food and beverage cashier mutiny was inevitable at the Oak Tree Hotel. Kevin wondered what he could do to minimize the tension. He decided to reflect on the events leading up to the current situation.

Background

The Oak Tree Hotel is a 400-room hotel located in suburban Tower City. The Oak Tree, one of ninety hotels in a nationwide chain headquartered in Tower City, is an upscale, full-service hotel that receives most of its income from the corporate meeting/convention market.

As with most hotels, the organization is divided into separate functional areas: rooms division, food and beverage (F&B), sales, catering, accounting, engineering, and personnel (see the Oak Tree Hotel organization chart). The F&B cashiers are employees of the accounting department. Kevin is their manager and reports to Jim, the controller. However, the cashiers work in the Coffee Shop, the Sycamore Room (restaurant), and room service. They also are responsible for any cash bars or cash coatroom functions booked by the catering department.

Although some line employee positions are union and others are nonunion, the F&B cashiers are represented by the Hotel Employees and Restaurant Employees Union (HEREU). HEREU also represents the servers and bussers who work in the Coffee Shop and the Sycamore Room.

**The Oak Tree Hotel
Organization Chart**

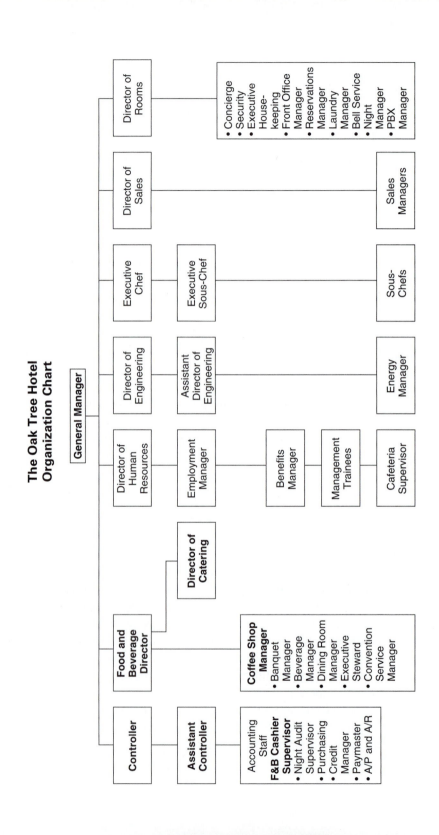

Cashier Duties and Responsibilities

As stated before, the cashiers are part of the accounting department. They may work in the Coffee Shop, the Sycamore Room, or room service, or they may be called upon to work a cash function for the catering department.

The Coffee Shop is the informal restaurant and is open from 6:30 A.M. to 10:30 P.M. When cashiers work in the Coffee Shop, they stand at the register (which also functions as the host station) at the front of the restaurant to process transactions. Guests may either pay the server, who brings the check to the register, or bring their checks to the register as they leave.

Room service is open from 6 A.M. to 12 A.M. (1 A.M. on weekends). The room service cashier in the morning is responsible for taking orders, ringing them up, and posting charges when checks come back. After the morning rush is over, the cashier works the lunch shift in the Sycamore Room. At night there is no room service cashier, so the Coffee Shop cashier handles all room service orders in addition to the Coffee Shop duties.

The Sycamore Room, the specialty restaurant, is open for lunch and dinner Monday through Friday and for dinner only on Saturday. The cashier station in the Sycamore Room is located in the servers' area, so the cashier is not visible to guests. The servers are responsible for bringing the checks to the cashier.

Because each outlet has good and bad points in terms of cashier duties, Kevin feels it is important to continue the practice of rotating cashiers among the outlets in order to keep morale high. Although cashiers with more seniority could take the easier shifts, they feel rotation is important because it adds variety to the job.

To staff the outlets completely, a total of three full-time day cashiers and three full-time night cashiers are needed. Permanent on-call cashiers (between three and five) are used to staff catering functions. (See the list of cashier duties.)

Cashier Duties

The major responsibilities of all cashiers are as follows:
1. Assign guest checks to servers, ensure that all unused checks are returned, and account for all used checks.
2. Settle charges to the correct accounts—cash, credit card, room charge, city ledger, staff, or promo. Room charges must be posted immediately to avoid having guests check out of the hotel without paying for the charge.
3. Write down charged gratuities for each server.
4. Handle all telephone calls—take reservations, room service orders, and special requests; answer questions; and give information.
5. Balance all work with the report generated by the cash register.
6. Count the drawer and drop the correct amount of money.

Current Employees

Kevin Sankar is the F&B cashier manager. He is the third manager since the department was given its own manager two years ago. Kevin knows the cashiers' job very thoroughly because he started as a cashier early last year. He was promoted that December after the previous manager, **Joanne Newell,** was fired. Kevin is 20 years old—a little younger than the cashiers he supervises. Although he is personable and well-liked by all, Kevin has not completed any formal hotel/restaurant education. He is a hard worker and really wants the department to succeed.

Jim Baummer is the controller and has been at the Oak Tree a little more than two years. Although Jim originally was controller at several other hotels in the chain, he worked in the corporate office for several years before coming back into the field. Jim is very knowledgeable about the function and theory of the accounting department, but the cashiers feel he doesn't really know what they are doing or supposed to be doing. Because the cashiers work in the restaurant and not in the office, they often feel that Jim isn't interested in them unless something goes wrong.

Craig Sipe is manager of the Coffee Shop and room service. He has been employed at the Oak Tree for several years, starting as a houseman in convention services and working his way up to department manager. Subsequently, he became an assistant manager in the stewarding department and later an assistant manager in the Coffee Shop. Craig has an associate's degree in hospitality management from the local community college. Although he is just 21, Craig seems to be going places with the company. He has a great network and knows the right strings to pull. Craig is popular with guests, but his employees feel he's a bit hypocritical. He tells them to be enthusiastic about the company, yet in the next breath he talks about getting a better job elsewhere.

Alex Milke is the F&B director. He has been at the Oak Tree for almost three years. He came from another property in the chain. Employees describe him as "the ghost" because he is seen only occasionally around the F&B outlets. He is not very outgoing, and many employees have never had a conversation with him. The corporate office recently placed Alex on probation because of subpar performance.

Peg Hays has been the director of catering for more than four years. She transferred from her position as director of catering at the airport property. Although Peg is successful with her clients, she is not popular with employees. Her abrasive manner and penchant for berating employees in front of guests make her a manager to avoid, if at all possible.

Darren Sawyer is the general manager. He has been at the Oak Tree for almost two years. Although Darren lives at the hotel, employees do not see him too often. His calm, mild, and reserved demeanor is unnerving to many employees, who are used to working with more outgoing managers. Darren seems to be more of a "numbers person" than a "people person."

Joyce Dimitrova, the assistant controller, has been at the Oak Tree for three years. She originally came from a chain hotel in Texas. After graduating from an HRIM program four years ago, she completed the chain's intense management training program. Joyce is very good in her position and is well respected by the hotel employees. Because she takes care of many day-to-day details in accounting, Kevin finds it easier to deal with her than with Jim.

The Current Situation

The cashiers are concerned with several recurring problems related to their jobs. There are two major issues: (1) policies and procedures currently are not standard and seem to be set on a daily basis, and (2) the Coffee Shop managers are expecting cashiers to do more and more work for them, even though the cashiers have more than enough to do in their own jobs.

Although the cashiers have a manager, Craig and Alex are setting procedures related to the cashier position. For the most part, these procedures are never discussed with Kevin or Jim before being issued to the cashiers. Because neither Craig nor Alex is very familiar with the cashier position, procedures that are set are often unrealistic given the job constraints. Policies also are subject to change without notice, and new procedures often are in direct conflict with procedures set previously.

As an example, Craig posted a memo to the cashiers stating that they are never to leave their position at the register at the front of the restaurant. This was acceptable to the daytime cashiers. However, at night, because there is no cashier in room service, the Coffee Shop cashier must take orders and walk them out to the room service waiters. When the cashiers brought this to Craig's attention, he assured them that the room service waiters would come and pick up the orders. In practice, the waiters are not doing this in a timely manner, and orders are often late. Then guests call the cashiers and complain. Room service waiters also are not bringing checks back to the cashier, and several checks have been lost.

Policies and procedures for running cash bars and cash coatrooms also are being changed constantly. Peg, the catering director, does not see the value of having standard procedures, but neither does she see the value of communicating changes from the established standard. She has a habit of promising special services to clients that are never communicated to Kevin or written on the contracts. When these details are not taken care of, Peg belittles Kevin and the cashiers, frequently in front of the customers.

The cashier's job is often frustrating because the Coffee Shop is very busy. It is not uncommon to serve between 275 and 350 customers for breakfast on weekends. Room service also is busy all mornings and most evenings, and room service employees handle many small meetings held in guest floor suites. Many Saturdays, the phone continually rings with reservations for the Sycamore Room and personal calls for employees. Cashiers often complain that the restaurant managers don't take enough responsibility for what happens in the restaurant. They like to walk around the hotel and let employees handle everything.

Another source of irritation for the cashiers is that a host is not scheduled for all shifts. A full-time host works five days a week from opening until after lunch, but there is no host to cover her two days off or to work at night. The restaurant managers are not consistent about watching the door when there is no host, so often the cashier has to seat all guests. When the restaurant is busy, tempers flare over this issue. Because the cashiers are responsible for taking cash and closing guest checks, they feel that these duties take precedence over seating guests. The cashiers are not, as a rule, inflexible or uncooperative, yet they feel the managers should recognize that cashiers are cashiers and not hosts. The cashiers are willing to help the manager or the host when they are not busy, but they think it was ridiculous to expect cashiers to seat 250 guests, take all guests' checks, answer the phone, take carryout orders, take room service calls, and balance their work on the nose—all for $1.00 over minimum wage! Besides, Craig has told them they are not allowed to leave the stand.

The labor market is tight in both Tower City and the suburbs, and there often are times when the Coffee Shop is short on bussers. When the Coffee Shop is busy and tables are dirty, Craig expects cashiers to help bus tables. This irritates the cashiers as much as the host situation does. The consensus among cashiers is that they already have too much work to do and that the restaurant managers are just using them to make their own lives easier.

Unfortunately, these problems have been going on for several years without a continued successful resolution. Turnover of new cashiers is very high, and it takes several new hires to find one who will stay and work under these conditions. However, some cashiers have worked at the Oak Tree while they are attending college, but they don't have any intention of staying with the company after graduation.

In the Past

The troubles with the cashier position started five years ago, when the Oak Tree completed an expansion that added 100 guest rooms and increased conference and meeting space in the hotel. However, these new problems were never addressed, because cashiers did not have their own manager. The general cashier in charge of the hotel bank and the daily audit of cash drops also was in charge of scheduling the cashiers. The cashiers, for the most part, managed themselves.

Two years later, the general cashier decided to quit, and the decision was made to split the position of general cashier into two—general cashier and F&B

cashier manager. **Bonnie Van Gerpen,** who had been an assistant manager in the Coffee Shop, became the first F&B cashier manager. The paymaster assumed the position of general cashier.

The morale among cashiers increased dramatically when Bonnie became department head. Because Bonnie had always helped the cashiers when she worked in the Coffee Shop, the cashiers knew she would be both fair and knowledgeable. With a full-time manager, the cashiers suddenly were getting new supplies and equipment they had needed for several months. When two cashiers left the Oak Tree to return to school, the cashiers all pulled together and worked extra shifts because they saw Bonnie working shifts daily in order to cover all outlets and banquet functions. Teamwork and camaraderie were evident and the department was given much praise for its new coordination.

However, discontent concerning the host position and the extra work being demanded by current Coffee Shop managers was becoming a major issue. Although there had never been a host in the Coffee Shop, there had never been cause for concern. Teamwork among cashiers and employees of the Coffee Shop was strong enough to ensure successful coverage of the host position. However, all three of the current managers in the Coffee Shop were new to that department, and two of them had come from another hotel chain. Craig was the only one from inside the organization. Collectively, the managers were not concerned with watching the door; thus, it was up to the cashiers to seat all guests. In time, the need for a host became a major issue; after meeting with the managers and getting no cooperation from them, Bonnie brought it to the attention of the controller, **Phil Ferreira.** Phil did nothing about the problem, so Bonnie brought the problem to the attention of the F&B director, **Ron Peyton.** Still nothing happened. In the meantime, Phil resigned and Jim took over. Bonnie brought the issue to Jim and ultimately, a hostess was hired.

At first, the cashiers thought all their problems were solved. However, they were really just beginning. A new debate raged over whose responsibility it was to seat guests on the host's days off. Because there had never been a host, it was unclear who should cover his or her days off. Of course, the cashiers felt it should be the restaurant manager's duty, and the managers thought it should be the cashier's duty. The debate wore on and on. Bonnie again raised the issue with the restaurant managers, and they agreed they would try to "watch the door" more carefully. Bonnie explained to them that the cashiers were not trying to get out of helping, but her employees' job responsibilities did not include covering the host position. If the managers did not want to schedule a host, they should make sure they covered the position.

This verbal commitment lasted about a week. The managers began slacking off again, and the cashiers became substitute hosts. To make matters worse, the host resigned and the cashiers were left to cover all host duties. Frustrated, Bonnie went to Jim and told him that her employees were fed up with what was happening. They were not hosts nor were they hired to be hosts. Nowhere in their job description did it say cashiers were responsible for seating guests. She told him her employees were ready to call the union to seek advice on filing a grievance. Bonnie told Jim that, although she was not a union employee, she supported her employees completely. For months they had tried to work through the proper channels, yet no concrete action other than hiring the first host had been taken.

During the next week, Alex (the new F&B director), Jim, Darren, and the human resources director assessed the situation in the Coffee Shop. The Coffee Shop managers were informed that they had to take more initiative in running their restaurant. They were to be on the floor at all times, unless they had a very good reason. The servers were to "seat the door" if they were not busy and customers were waiting. Whether there was a host or not, cashiers were not to seat guests unless absolutely necessary.

Finally, the cashiers felt certain of a victory! The managers of the Coffee Shop had no choice now except to follow the orders of the executive committee. It became comical to see them race for the door from the far side of the restaurant if guests were approaching. However, the success was short-lived. In March, Bonnie turned in her resignation, effective May 31, because she was expecting a baby in late August. This alone caused morale to drop considerably among the cashiers. Bonnie had been their first manager and had done a tremendous job of building and strengthening the department. She was fair and treated the cashiers with respect.

Before Bonnie left the company, she helped Jim and Joyce hire a new F&B cashier manager. First, they considered two in-house cashiers. One cashier was full-time during the day. He was only 19 and was not mature enough to handle the responsibilities. The other employee was an on-call cashier who worked full-time at a bank. In the end, it was decided to hire someone from outside the industry who had considerable experience managing cashiers at a grocery store. **Joanne Newell** readily accepted the position of F&B cashier manager. Although she was to start in the middle of May and have two weeks of training, a series of car accidents kept Joanne from starting until three days before Bonnie's last day.

From the beginning, Joanne didn't seem to take to her new job, although she attended both new employee orientation and an orientation with Bonnie and Jim. During the three days she spent with Bonnie, Joanne was not inquisitive or eager to take over the reins as manager. Bonnie expressed her doubts to Jim, and he had a pep talk with Joanne. Jim and Bonnie felt that Joanne was probably overwhelmed with the position but would adjust after she became familiar with the workings of the hotel.

After Bonnie left, she kept in touch with Kevin, whom she had hired and trained. From Kevin's reports, the situation was deteriorating rapidly, and the department was losing much of its hard-won credibility. Joanne was unorganized and frequently did not come in at her scheduled time. She missed meetings and was unaware of many details cashiers needed to know concerning incoming groups. Although the cashiers had all promised Bonnie and Jim they would continue to work hard for Joanne, they were becoming unhappy with her nonchalant attitude. Kevin tried to give Joanne the benefit of the doubt, but he was becoming increasingly concerned about the department's welfare. His conversations with Bonnie frequently focused on the current problems, and he often asked her for advice.

More and more it appeared that Kevin was the one calling the shots in the department, although he tried to coach Joanne on how to deal with different people in the hotel and different situations. Many managers started going to Kevin instead of Joanne, because they knew he would make sure things happened. Joanne became increasingly careless, and many functions were left unscheduled and uncovered. Other times, Joanne scheduled all on-call cashiers for a particular weekend evening, forgetting to cancel them when functions failed to materialize.

Understandably, the cashiers were becoming more upset with the situation. Joanne told Kevin that she had asked Jim and Joyce to make Kevin her assistant because she was so bogged down with work.

In November, Jim met with Joanne and told her that her performance was not up to the hotel's expectations. Joanne said she felt she had not been trained adequately and blamed her poor performance on Bonnie. Jim said that, whatever the case, Joanne had thirty days to improve her performance. Unfortunately, no final action, such as termination, was specified. Later that day, Joanne told Kevin she thought she would probably be transferred to a different department, which would be great because she hated cashiering. Kevin went in to talk with Joyce about his own promotion. Joyce said she hadn't heard anything about it, but that she would get right on it. Several days later, Kevin was promoted to cashier supervisor under Joanne.

Although Joanne had been placed on notice, her performance did not improve. In fact, it seemed as if she was determined to get transferred to another department. Kevin did not think they actually would fire her, if they did at all, until after New Year's because of the huge amount of business booked at the hotel. However, the weekend before Christmas, Joanne called in sick and when she returned to work, she was terminated.

Kevin was promoted to department head. The cashiers were excited that Kevin was chosen to replace Joanne, despite the fact he was not the most senior cashier in the department. They respected Kevin as a hard worker and knew he had been well trained by Bonnie.

Even with departmental support, Kevin is finding that the job is not easy. In fact, he is spending a considerable amount of time trying to restore relations with other departments that were damaged badly by Joanne. The host issue is still on the front burner, and now Craig seems to feel that *he* should be setting cashier policy unilaterally. Although he is really excited about being department manager, Kevin knows he needs help from a lot of people to bring it to its past level of success and move it further. His first thought is to call Bonnie.

Discussion Questions

1. Why do you think problems in the cashier department started after the expansion? How effective was Bonnie as a manager? Explain.
2. Describe what you think caused Joanne's poor performance. What could have been done differently to increase Joanne's chances for success? Why do you think your suggestions would work?
3. Discuss the concept of letting managers make their own decisions.
4. Cashiers often complain that the restaurant managers don't take enough responsibility for what happens in the restaurant. What is your reaction to this statement? Defend your answer.
5. What should Kevin do first? Why?
6. What are the main issues he needs to address? Why are these important issues? Describe how Kevin should go about addressing these issues.
7. Should the F&B cashiers be placed in a different division than accounting? Why or why not?
8. What should be done about the hosting and bussing issue? Explain why your actions would work.
9. Who (departments and/or specific individuals) should be involved in making decisions affecting the cashiers? Why?
10. As Kevin, how would you encourage more cooperation between the cashier department and other departments, specifically the Coffee Shop and catering? Explain.
11. Because the threat of calling the union produced results last time, would you advise Kevin to encourage this tactic again? Why or why not?
12. Evaluate Bonnie's involvement with employees going to the union. Do you think she should have the involvement that she does? Why or why not?
13. As Kevin, if you decided to use this tactic, would you call the union representative or would you have one of your employees make the call? Why?
14. Evaluate the structure of the Oak Tree Hotels' organization chart. Does it have possibilities? Why or why not?

The Palm View Hotel

It was Monday morning at the Palm View Hotel when Andrew went for his daily meeting with Henry, the general manager (GM), to discuss Ntinos, a cook, and the kitchen situation as a whole. After thirty minutes, the GM came out of his office shaking his head saying: "I can't believe that all this was happening in the kitchen, and the chef didn't tell me anything before now."

Background

The Palm View Hotel is a three-star unit of the Paradise Tour Corporation. Paradise owns cruise ships, tour buses, travel agencies, and about 8,000 guest rooms in hotels all over the island of Cyprus. Business is extremely good between March and October, when about 1.3 million tourists visit Cyprus. The Palm View Hotel was built in 1977 and is just five miles from Larnaca City. The Palm View is a tourist attraction because it is fifty feet from the beach. It has 111 guest rooms that can accommodate up to 230 guests at a time.

The Starvoso complex was constructed next to the Palm View in 1986. The Palm View and Starvoso complexes share the same manager. The complex consists of thirty-one apartments, a souvenir shop, a swimming pool, and two tennis courts. It accommodates up to 110 people. The occupancy rate during the summer is 80 to 90 percent, and the average length of stay is ten days. Because there is no foodservice at the Starvoso complex, all customers eat at the Palm View Hotel. Therefore, the foodservice at Palm View normally serves from 200 to 290 people at each of its three meals. The largest number of meals is produced for the evening meal.

The Palm View has an upscale dining room that features a wide menu variety at reasonable prices. It is known for its high-quality food, and local people often come to the Palm View for a nice, relaxing evening with dinner in the dining room.

However, nearly 75 percent of its guests are those who stay at the hotel or complex next door. There are times when the waiting list for dinner, and sometimes lunch, gets quite long. However, guests seem to wait patiently or make a reservation if they have a tight schedule. Many guests can be found lingering near the pool area.

Employee Shortage

The population of Cyprus is 600,000 people. Excluding the elderly and children, the Cyprus workforce becomes very small. In addition, the government cannot allow enough foreigners into Cyprus to meet its workforce needs because the union caps the number of foreigners who can get into the country.

The employee shortage at the Palm View is obvious in the foodservice department and at the front desk. The seriousness of employee shortage is illustrated by a recent incident. **Andy Haan,** a front desk employee, got married on a Sunday in July, and she could not take vacation time because of the employee shortage at the Palm View Hotel.

There is no attempt by management to assess other ways to deal with the employee shortage. They do not review procedures to see what changes could be made to increase efficiency with the shortage of employees. For example, purchasing a larger steam jacket kettle would increase the efficiency of the foodservice department, but management will not do so. Consequently, the foodservice employees work harder to produce the same amount of food.

New Management

Three months ago, the Paradise Corporation opened a four-star hotel, the Princess Hotel. The GM, the assistant manager, the chef, and the most experienced cooks at the Palm View were transferred to the Princess Hotel. These individuals were replaced in different ways.

Henry Akis was promoted from another two-star hotel to be the new GM of the Palm View Hotel. **Kit Spyros** was promoted from a smaller hotel (175 guest rooms) to be the assistant manager, and **Andrew Paul,** who was the assistant chef of the Palm View, was promoted to chef (see the Palm View Hotel organization chart) without further training. In other words, the management team was new to its duties.

Henry has a bachelor's degree in hotel and restaurant management from a Bulgarian college. After he graduated, he had two years of training at a Bulgarian four-star hotel. Later, he joined the Paradise Corporation and worked three years as an assistant manager of a three-star hotel. From there he was promoted to GM of a two-star hotel (213 guest rooms). After working for five years in that hotel, he was promoted to his current position at the Palm View Hotel.

Kit graduated five years ago with a bachelor's degree in hotel and restaurant management in Bulgaria. After graduating, she had two years of training in a Bul-

Organization Chart for Palm View Hotel

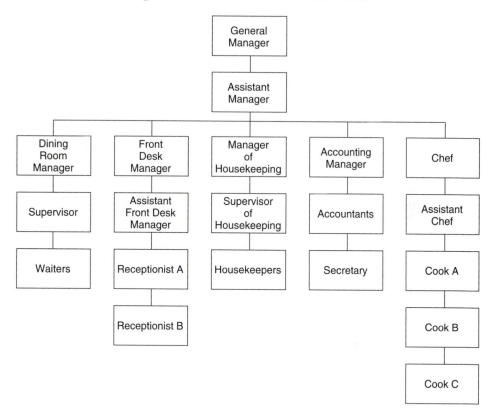

garian hotel. She then joined the Paradise Corporation as an assistant manager for a two-star hotel (175 guest rooms) for three years before being transferred three months ago to assistant manager of the Palm View Hotel.

Andrew has been working in the hospitality industry exclusively for Paradise Corporation for thirteen years. His education included a two-year degree from a Cypriot college and twelve months of training in Holland. Andrew worked at the Palm View for three years as an A-ranked cook and five years as an assistant chef. Prior to the Palm View, he worked as a B-ranked cook in a four-star hotel owned by Paradise Corporation.

The Cooks' Rankings

In Cyprus, there is a ranking system for cooks (A, B, C) with A as the highest-ranked cook and C the lowest (see the organization chart). The assistant chef is one level above the A-ranked cook. The chef often oversees the foodservice department employees.

A cooks are responsible for preparing the entrées of the day with the aid of B cooks. They also are responsible for the foodservice department when the chef and the assistant chef are absent. The B cooks are responsible for the à la carte preparation and appetizers, and they supervise the C cooks while preparing breakfast. C cooks are responsible for the pantry area and prepare a variety of salads and fruits. The dessert area is assigned to an A cook with the aid of a C cook. During serving time, all cooks participate in serving guests, with the most experienced cooks doing the most critical tasks.

In Cyprus it is much more difficult for hospitality operations to hire an A-ranked cook than to hire a B or C cook. Employees generally don't leave an operation after they are hired because it is difficult for them to get hired by another company. Due to the Cypriot culture, employees don't easily change organizations. Therefore, A-ranked cooks are not available for hire. The Palm View Hotel has thirteen B cooks, nine C cooks, and no A cooks.

The Assistant Manager's Responsibilities

Kit was above all food/beverage and lodging departments. However, it seems she was most involved with the front desk activities and the accounting department. She got involved with the foodservice department only when the GM was not on duty. Kit had daily meetings with the chef. However, the chef's indifference towards the foodservice department broke down the communication channel between the foodservice department and Kit.

The Cooks-Management Gap

The cooks at the Palm View Hotel were complaining about the cook shortage. The cooks were very concerned about the weekends, because on Saturdays there were about 150 additional visitors in the dining room, and every Sunday there was a party or wedding reception for 500 to 800 people. Consequently, over the weekend, the cooks worked around the clock (the overtime pay is one and one-half times the regular pay). Because of the workforce shortage, management was unable to accommodate employees' requests for time away from work. At the same time, management continued to look aggressively for more large parties to increase sales and ultimately profit. In addition, the four most experienced B cooks were demanding promotions because their duties were equivalent to that of A cooks. The manager appeared rather reluctant to promote anyone because he believed that those cooks were not ready for promotion based on their skills. If these

B cooks were promoted to A cooks, they would receive more pay, therefore decreasing profits.

The Current Situation

On August 10, Henry informed Andrew of a plan to serve lunch by the swimming pool, where currently only à la carte items were served. The plan originated because the atmosphere by the outside pool near the trees was much better than in the hotel dining room. In order to implement the new plan to serve guests in the dining room and at poolside, the cooks prepared the food in the kitchen and transported it to the very small poolside kitchen. Besides the à la carte, this kitchen also was scheduled to serve two entrée items for lunch.

The poolside kitchen has a small bain marie, two ovens, one broiler, and one fryer. The space available for cooks is so limited that it is very difficult to move fast during busy times. The cooks did not like the idea. They knew it would cause extra stress for them. Because they would not have enough equipment and space, they knew that food quality would decline and service would be slower. However, nobody asked the cooks for their opinions. Andrew, in spite of knowing the cooks concerns, supported Henry's idea.

One Saturday lunch, three weeks after the poolside service began, an order came from Henry for a steak with French fries. That day 270 customers from the hotel and about 130 people from outside the hotel were served. **Ntinos Kumo,** the most experienced B cook, took care of Henry's order. Two hours later, when all the customers had gone, Andrew asked who cooked the French fries for the manager. Ntinos responded, and Andrew asked, "What kind of French fries did you serve him? They were terrible. It appears you cooked them a couple of times." Andrew also told Ntinos that Henry was very upset and wanted to see the cook who prepared his food.

Ntinos answered, "I followed the proper procedure while preparing the fries. Tell Henry to come down to the kitchen and fry his own fries and see the conditions under which we work. We can't continue working in this little kitchen with a shortage of cooks and extensive overtime. If we have to show him that we mean business, Mike [another B cook] and I will quit."

Andrew told him to calm down. He said he would talk to Henry about the situation.

Discussion Questions

1. As the manager, what might you have done to prevent this tension between the manager and employees before and after the Ntinos incident? Defend your actions.

2. Evaluate all options the manager has concerning the employee shortage and serving food by the pool. Which would you choose? Why?
3. Describe the problems you see in the communication channel between the foodservice employees and management. Why are these problems?
4. Is the manager an effective employee? Why? Describe his style.
5. Analyze the transition of the old management of the Palm View Hotel to the new one. Identify any problems.
6. What problems occur when there are no A-ranked cooks? How would you solve this problem? Why would your solution work?

PART 3
Country Clubs

Cedar River Golf and Country Club
Jakarta Country Club
Prairie Creek Country Club
West Oaks Golf and Country Club

Cedar River Golf
and Country Club

Cedar River Golf and Country Club is a private organization with an eighteen-hole golf course, swimming and tennis facilities, workout rooms, a pro shop, and several food and beverage outlets. Cedar River is a very exclusive club, with net worth requirements for prospective members. The club is forty-five years old with many longstanding family memberships. Once younger family members have experienced the club facilities, they tend to maintain membership as they become adults. Recently the country club was host to a national, professional golf tournament. This tournament exposure has brought renewed interest in membership applications.

The members who are at least 18 years old elect a board of directors. The board oversees the operation of Cedar River. The board consists of influential individuals who are interested in maintaining a high-class operation. The twelve-member board is made up of nine men and three women. Officers of the board of directors are elected among its board members, and currently all positions are held by men. The general manager reports to the board during each scheduled board meeting. There are times when special board meetings are called and the general manager may be asked to provide an update or report at that meeting.

The club boasts a membership of more than 1,800. The club offers its members a variety of social activities in addition to fine food served in its two dining rooms. There also is a lounge area where members can order off a minimal menu as they enjoy a cold beverage. Members are required to spend a predetermined amount for food each month. If they do not spend the money, they forfeit it to the club because it cannot be carried over from one month to another. Consequently, members often bring guests to dine at the club.

Cedar River is open year-round, with the busiest periods for dining during summer and the Christmas holiday season, which lasts from Thanksgiving through mid-January. The club's primary source of income, besides initiation fees and monthly dues, is from catered events held at the club. During the busy months there are as many as five or six major events per week, including golf tournaments, wedding receptions, and business banquets. Most banquets are held in the ballroom, where more than 600 guests can be seated.

The Dining Rooms

The Cardinal Room sports an informal atmosphere and is popular with members who have children and those who use the club's recreational facilities. This room seats 250 and has a menu of basic grill items, sandwiches, soups, and salads. Members often eat in the Cardinal Room after playing a round of golf because it has an informal atmosphere. It is not unusual for family members to have dinner with a parent who has just finished playing golf. Members also frequent the Cardinal Room after swimming or playing tennis.

The Atrium Room seats 100 and is the club's formal dining area. Reservations for the Atrium are required because it is so popular. The menu is varied including a number of gourmet dishes that befit the elegant atmosphere. Business people often take their clients to dinner in the Atrium Room. During much of the year, the Atrium Room is very busy and members call early to ensure reservations.

The Management

The general manager (GM) of Cedar River is **Don Reynolds.** Don has managed the club for almost seven years and has worked in the country club segment for twenty-three years. He has earned the members' respect for keeping the club in a strong financial position by controlling costs and fully utilizing the club's spacious banquet facilities. There are very few weeks when the banquet facilities are not used to some extent.

Don's experience in food production is highly respected by his peers, club members, and the board of directors. However, his reputation for producing high-quality food is offset by his personality. Although most employees would agree that the food served at Cedar River is excellent, they would admit that Don's status with employees is not so good.

Don has been characterized as having an abrasive personality and a bad temper. It is not uncommon to see him walk into the kitchen and start screaming at a food production worker for doing something incorrectly. Usually he reacts before consulting with the executive chef, **Sean Lewis,** to determine why the employee is working in such a manner. He doesn't consider the circumstances that might affect production. Often times his screaming results in female employees shedding some tears and male employees making faces when his back is turned.

Don also has been guilty of criticizing Sean in front of his subordinates. In most cases, Sean had things under control and easily could have explained the situation, if Don had given him a chance. Many employees become rattled at the mere presence of Don, for fear of being reprimanded. He is famous for changing procedures for no apparent reason. It appears that doing so gives him the feeling of being more in control of employees. Even though employees are aware that Don's actions reflect his need for power, his behaviors still have a negative impact on employees and production slips somewhat.

The management team, in addition to Don, includes **Tara Nixon,** the clubhouse manager, who reports directly to Don. Tara oversees the work of four additional management team members who report directly to her. She acts as liaison between Don and the other managers.

Tara is responsible for hiring, firing, and scheduling hourly employees who work in the clubhouse, including employees who work in the Cardinal Room, the Atrium Room, and banquets. Reporting to Tara are the catering manager, **Sandy Porter;** the banquet manager, **Brian Bushnell;** the Cardinal Room manager, **Jerry Carlson;** and the Atrium Room manager, **Pat Shaw** (see the Cedar River organization chart). While Tara works closely with each manager, it is Don who makes most major decisions.

Each member of the management team has worked at the club for a minimum of two years. Tara began working at the club as a waitress and received some management experience while in college. She has been promoted through the ranks to her current position as clubhouse manager, which she has held for almost three years.

After graduating from college, Tara taught business courses at a local high school for two years. During the summer months she worked at Cedar River. After

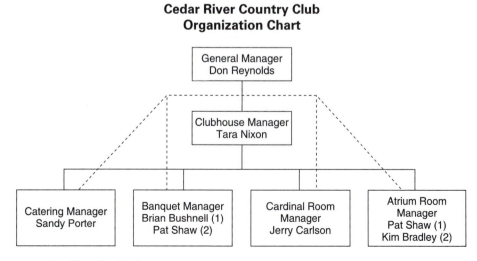

**Cedar River Country Club
Organization Chart**

—— Indirect line of authority

two years of teaching, she realized that her first love was working at a country club, so she resigned her teaching position and returned to the club as catering manager. After learning the ropes in all food and beverage outlets, Tara was promoted to clubhouse manager. She enjoys her job and believes she has a great team with whom she works.

Tara is excited about the coming months. She feels that the club has sufficient employees, and this holiday season should be less stressful than previous ones.

The Problem

Just as Tara was feeling good about the situation, Brian gave notice that he had accepted a new position at a club in northern California. He informed Don that he will be leaving in three weeks (at the end of October). Brian is well liked by his staff and certainly will be missed. He is very knowledgeable about the club's operations, having worked there for over six years. He started as a busser in the Cardinal Room, later worked as a waiter in the Atrium Room, and then spent some time as a helper in the kitchen. He was thrilled to be promoted to banquet manager almost three years ago.

Tara left her office in a daze and as she walked toward the banquet room, she heard some part-time employees discussing how much they enjoyed working for Brian. She did not look forward to telling them of his resignation. She knew they would find out about Brian's decision in the next few days, so she decided to meet with many of the more tenured and full-time employees.

Don wasted little time in taking action to fill Brian's vacancy. He informed Pat, manager of the Atrium Room, that Pat would be taking Brian's job. The move is considered a promotion because the banquet job involves working with other management team members when coordinating banquets. Currently, Pat spends very little time working with the other managers. He works with the public only in a pinch. That is one reason he enjoys this position. He is not comfortable working with the public and has voiced his displeasure to many employees.

The current, harmonious conditions in the Atrium Room are a far cry from the chaotic conditions that existed prior to Pat's promotion as manager. Pat has worked very hard to earn the respect of his staff and feels that his team works very well together. Pat can be counted on to help employees when they are short of staff or when the activity becomes stressful and hectic. Pat's subordinates truly appreciate his interest in them. Even though he is more reserved, they know that he speaks well on their behalf.

Officially, Don has not announced his choice to replace Pat in the Atrium Room. However, strong rumors have surfaced that Don has decided to rehire **Kim Bradley,** the former Atrium Room manager. Kim worked at the club three years ago before leaving to become the club manager at Lakeshore Country Club.

During his previous stint at the club, Kim was not well liked by his employees because they felt he could not be pleased. He was always quick to criticize his staff in front of club members in the dining room. Seldom, if ever, did he take the side of his staff in their dealings with members. He had, however, become one of Don's favorite employees.

Additional rumors indicate that Kim left Lakeshore after being ousted by the board of directors. He currently is unemployed and would be happy to return to Cedar River. The likelihood that Kim will be rehired has created quite a stir among staff, especially employees in the Atrium Room. They are apprehensive, and many of them say they would rather quit than work for Kim again. The employees see Kim's personality as an extension of Don's personality.

Based on their hunch that Kim will be returning, key Atrium Room staff asked to have a meeting with Tara to discuss their feelings. Tara agreed to meet with them within the next few days when her schedule becomes less hectic.

Tara does not look forward to meeting with her employees. She knows that they will ask her to try to influence Don, but Tara feels as though her hands are tied. On one hand, she faces the possibility that many hourly employees may quit. Many of these employees have worked at the club for several years and will be difficult to replace. The timing is especially bad because the Christmas season is rapidly approaching, and Tara is counting on her experienced employees to take on more responsibilities this year.

Last year, Tara worked 90 to 100 hours per week during the holidays, splitting her time between the dining rooms and the catering business. This year, Tara felt that Pat really had the Atrium Room under control, which would make it possible for her to focus her attention on the banquet business. Tara also is concerned about Pat's attitude toward the change. She's afraid he might leave to work in another club. She knows that with his skills, he is very marketable. What will she do if she is short of staff? She cannot even think of what that would mean to her life and the amount of time she would have to be at the club. She has worked hard to get the management team working well, and employees were responding nicely to her managers. Is it possible that all this work was for naught? Will Kim really be rehired?

Tara remembers the days when Kim was there. She gladly took his resignation when he decided to leave. He had an air of power about him that employees did not appreciate. Pat had been a refreshing force for the employees in the Atrium Room.

On the other hand, Tara is hesitant to confront Don about the potentially explosive situation, for fear she might be viewed as a complainer. Tara has gotten where she is in the club partly because she doesn't question Don's actions. In fact, some employees feel that she has started to adopt his leadership style. Employees would define her personality as more abrasive each year, and they have noticed that her temper flares more often.

Tara doesn't enjoy this reputation, but she doesn't want to look for another job either. Tara is well aware that anything she says about Kim is not likely to be given much credibility by Don.

Discussion Questions

1. What options does Tara have? What are the pros and cons of these options? If you were Tara, what would you do? Why?
2. Is there any truth to the theory that managers tend to hire employees like themselves? Explain.
3. What are the pros and cons of bringing Kim back?
4. Is it good for a general manager, such as Don, to wield so much power in a country club? Why or why not?
5. What role should the board of directors have when it comes to the day-to-day operation of the club? Justify your answer.
6. Is Don an effective manager? Justify your answer.
7. Is the fact that the board of directors and other club members think Don is doing a great job justification for his rather harsh managerial style? Why or why not? Do the ends justify the means? Explain your responses.

Jakarta Country Club

Mary Lee recently graduated from a hospitality management program at Central State University. Because of her excellent academic performance and previous work experiences, she was accepted for a position as food and beverage manager in Jakarta Country Club, a privately owned golf and country club in Indonesia. She heard about the job opening from an Indonesian host family with whom she stayed for ten months during a student exchange experience five years ago.

Having been born and raised in a midsize town in the midwestern United States, Mary was eager to get more international experiences. She believed that Indonesia was the best place for her to relocate. She realized it was a big decision, but she felt quite confident because she already knew several Indonesians and spoke the Indonesian language to some extent. Based on her ten-month student exchange experiences, Mary also loved Jakarta, the largest city in Indonesia with a population of more than nine million people. She was excited to think of Jakarta as her new hometown. To her, the city offered excitement and many opportunities. The salary and fringe benefit package offered by the Jakarta Country Club was very attractive relative to other job offers she received. In addition, Mary felt that her previous working experiences as a food service production worker and a food and beverage supervisor in a small midwestern country club had helped prepare her for the job. She believes that her participative management style, which she practiced at her previous supervisory job, also will help her do well in the new position.

Indonesian Culture

Indonesia, like most other Asian countries, has a very different culture from that of Western countries. Besides cultural and traditional differences, Indonesia also has relatively more complicated and implicit guidelines that regulate proper

249

interaction between individuals. The unavailability of written rules contributes to the complication, especially for nonnatives. In addition, most Indonesians are less outspoken compared to people from Western countries. In Indonesia, it is considered impolite to criticize others openly. Most people hold their opinions to themselves unless asked to voice them. The young also know that respect for the elderly is demanded. Younger people are expected to treat the elderly as more knowledgeable than themselves. Women also tend to be less outspoken than men in Indonesia, even though this is less prevalent now. Indonesians handle conflicts very privately. To confront others, including co-workers and subordinates, private conversation is a must. Instead of direct confrontation, most Indonesians prefer to point out the problem with carefully chosen words to lessen the chance of hurting the other person's feelings.

The Club

Jakarta Country Club is a privately owned club. Roughly one-third of its 2,500 members have shares in the club. All members pay initiation fees and semiannual dues. The club's facilities include a golf course, two Olympic-size pools, fifteen tennis courts, five squash courts, four badminton courts, a gym, and a jogging track. In addition, the club has a formal dining room called the Hourglass, a family-style restaurant with an adjacent poolside grill called the Atrium, and a ballroom named the Grand Ballroom.

The board of directors has elected MBC Inc. to provide management services for the club (see the Jakarta Country Club organization chart). MBC is a U.S.-based hospitality management company. The agreement between Jakarta and MBC allows MBC to select the club management team. The management team includes a general manager, a food and beverage manager, a sports facility manager, a marketing manager, and an account manager. In addition, the food and beverage manager supervises a banquet manager and two managers for each of the club's dining facilities.

Native Indonesians who speak fluent English hold all positions but sports facility manager. They all hold at least B.S. degrees from U.S.-accredited hospitality management programs. The current sports facility manager is an American named **John James** who has been living in Indonesia for eight years and speaks fluent Indonesian.

The club has a good reputation partly because it is known to hire knowledgeable Western-educated foreign managers such as John and Mary. These individuals have skills that are rather rare among the native Indonesians. For example, few native Indonesians have experienced formal education in human resources management, including the proper practices of hiring, firing, and disciplinary action. Even fewer native Indonesians have the proper culinary education. Among those who have received such education are those who study overseas, mostly in Switzerland

**Jakarta Country Club
Organization Chart**

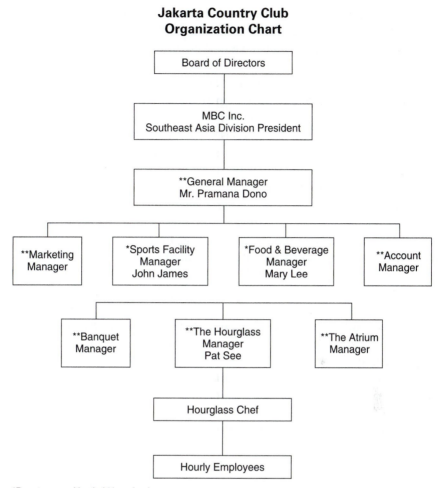

*Denotes a position held by a foreign manager
**Denotes a position held by a native Indonesian

and the United States. In addition, club members are upper-class Indonesians. Most members are well educated and speak English without much difficulty. The members often look at the foreign managers in their club as conversation partners who give them the opportunity to practice and use their English.

Mary Lee's Responsibilities

As a food and beverage manager in the club, Mary is responsible for supervising the banquet and restaurant managers. Her primary duty is to ensure the smoothness of operations in the club's dining facilities. Twice annually, she has to prepare a report to **Pramana Dono,** the GM, about major activities in the club's dining facilities and its financial condition.

During the first three months on the job as food and beverage manager, Mary found one major weakness in her department. She observed that **Pat See,** the Hourglass manager, does not have knowledge of proper sanitation methods. Mary noticed that Pat never wears a hair restraint in the kitchen and often tastes food with used flatware. Pat often interrupts the chefs' and hourly employees' workflow by helping in the production area even though she's not needed. Pat adds ingredients to recipes according to her personal preference, ignoring standardized recipes. As a result, Mary has observed that product inconsistency often occurs, even though she is not aware of any customer complaints.

In the kitchen, Mary sensed that the hourly employees did not like Pat's unnecessary help and improper practices. Mary also realized that most Indonesians prefer to keep quiet when seeing someone doing something wrong. It is almost considered taboo to confront a person openly about his or her mistakes, especially if the person is a superior. Nevertheless, the atmosphere in the kitchen often turns tense as many hourly employees try hard to ignore Pat's habits. On some occasions when Mary is in the kitchen, the hourly employees give her indirect clues about Pat's inappropriate habits. They tell Mary they appreciate the fact that Mary, unlike some other managers, wears a hair restraint and trusts their ability to work independently in production areas. Yet, with her limited Indonesian language skills, Mary does not feel confident in having further conversations with hourly employees.

However, on the other hand, Mary also has observed Pat's strengths. Because of her outgoing personality, Pat has a good relationship with club members. Several members have commented to Mary about Pat's friendliness. They told Mary that Pat is considered a friend because of her seven years of excellent service.

Mary knows that Pat has the potential to be a good manager. She delegates properly and never acts rudely toward the hourly employees. The problem is that sometimes she interferes with the job that she has delegated to someone else. For example, she delegated the job of creating standardized recipes for the Hourglass to the chef, yet she often gets into the production area and changes the recipes as she pleases. However, Pat does not seem to irritate others intentionally with her undesirable habits. Mary believes that Pat just simply does not realize that her habits are less than acceptable.

Mary talked to John about the problem with Pat. Mary thought that John, who obviously is more accustomed to Indonesians and their culture, could give her valuable input on how to solve the problem. John did not take her problem seriously. He simply said that Mary is too Westernized and that she needs to adjust better to the Indonesian culture of never openly confronting a problem. John suggested that Mary ignore the problem because, after all, members perceive Pat positively. In addition, John also explained that most Indonesians are used to quietly accepting inferior-quality service and products, so Mary does not need to worry about product inconsistency and such. The chef and hourly workers, who are all

Indonesians, were able to work with Pat for seven years before Mary arrived. John advised Mary to dismiss her concern about the hourly employees as well.

After talking to John, Mary felt discouraged about confronting Pat. She honestly believes that Pat's habits are improper, unacceptable, and disturbing to the hourly employees. Mary also wants to improve the quality of service and products for Hourglass customers. She feels responsible for carrying out MBC's mission and reputation of providing excellent management services to its customers. However, she also is afraid that John is right. She starts to think that maybe she just needs to adjust better to the Indonesian culture. She even thinks maybe it is easier for her to be accepted by the club management team if she ignores the problem with Pat.

Mary feels like a failure. She thought that having lived in Indonesia for ten months, she was prepared adequately for the Indonesian culture. She wonders what she should do.

Discussion Questions

1. What would you do if you were Mary Lee? Would you look for more information about Indonesian culture, especially the norms that Indonesians follow in interacting with each other? Why or why not? Where do you think such information can be obtained?

2. Do you think Mary has a sufficient background to work in a foreign country with a totally different culture? Why or why not? Should MBC be responsible for helping Mary understand Indonesian culture and prepare her before she actually goes to Indonesia? Defend your answer.

3. If you were Mary, would you follow John's advice? Justify your response.

4. Even though Pat's unsanitary habits have not caused any customer complaints, what are potential risks associated with the behavior? Are these serious enough for Mary to be concerned? Why or why not?

5. Hospitality has become an increasing global industry. If you are hired by an international company and later find that you are to be relocated to a foreign country, would you be willing to do so? Why or why not? Describe how you would prepare for this position.

6. How can a manager who is about to hold a position in a foreign country better adjust to the cultural differences? Why do you think these suggestions would be helpful?

7. Should a manager working in a foreign country adjust to the culture of the country? Why? Can such a manager follow his or her own culture, beliefs, and management styles? Why or why not? Justify your responses.

Prairie Creek Country Club

Carol is thinking about the conversation she had at lunch with **Jane Cleary** and **Angie Lehman,** two servers at the Prairie Creek Country Club. She remembers when she began working there several years ago. She spent lots of time with staff on a day-to-day basis. Recently she noticed that there were ups and downs, but she hadn't really been in tune with how other employees have been treated. Carol has become more involved with her family and looks forward to the time she can spend with them. She doesn't think about work after hours, and her interaction with other employees has been limited, quite different from when she began at Prairie Creek. She had not been prepared for the earful that she received.

Prairie Creek Country Club is a private club with approximately 1,500 members. It consists of two eighteen-hole golf courses, a banquet hall, a casual dining room, a formal dining room, a main kitchen, and a separate kitchen for the casual dining room. The management staff consists of the general manager, **Carol Watne;** the clubhouse manager, **Laura Wangberg;** the banquet manager, **Brandi Takke;** the formal dining manager, **Peter Polaski;** and three casual dining managers. There are various captains for different areas. Prairie Creek is well known for its high-quality food and services.

Two issues are causing some frustration at Prairie Creek; one of them is related specifically to Angie, and the other affects all employees, but especially Jane. Angie was there to support Jane and provide some information regarding performance appraisals. They both maintain that the performance evaluation for hourly employees was not appropriate and have asked assistant managers to bring it to the attention of the general manager. They know that this never happened, and the last evaluation of Jane's performance has angered her. Angie agrees and supports Jane.

Angie also wants to discuss another problem. The friction between her and Peter in the formal dining room is escalating, and Angie wonders if Peter is getting back at her for being vocal concerning his treatment of her and **Scott Wong,** another server, that she thinks is unfair.

Employee Evaluations

Previously, all employees were to be evaluated during a two-week period each April. Appropriate raises were given to employees who received a positive evaluation. The problem noted by Angie and Jane was that all employees are hired at a base wage that is paid during training. When the training period of approximately two weeks was over, a fifty-cent raise was given. Employees who finished their training in April or after would get only one raise of fifty cents in that year, and they had to wait another year to get the next pay increase. An employee who completed training before the end of March could very well have two raises during the first month or so on the job. Angie has been very dissatisfied with this approach and has explained her concern to Carol on more than one occasion.

Finally, the labor market dictated that something needed to be done to attract better employees while reducing turnover. An all-employee meeting was conducted to explain the new procedures:

Immediate supervisor conducts evaluations on a quarterly basis.

Club manager reviews evaluations to ensure that any unnecessary prejudices were countered.

The base rate is increased by fifty cents after training

Additional pay increases are based on the evaluation score:

79 and below:	No raise
80 through 89:	Average increase
90 and above:	Maximum increase

Not meeting standards on a subsequent evaluation can result in losing the previous raise. For the initial implementation, there would be a cap at $3 above starting wage for all food servers, bartenders, and captains. Before this system, each group of employees was under a different pay scale.

Initial problems were as follows:

1. The fine dining staff have a much more complex job than the banquet staff, who would now receive the same pay rate.
2. The bartenders started at a higher level than the servers. Plus, the captains were a notch above the bartender level. Previously, they were paid for the knowledge and responsibility required for that job.

Jane was one of the more senior servers. Three months after the new pay schedule was implemented, Jane had her first evaluation. During the evaluation she lost points for cosmetic reasons. The following were pointed out to her:

1. Jane wore her hair up every day as the rules stated, but with the layers she had some "wispies" at the end of the night. Other female servers who disregarded the rule completely told Jane it wasn't even mentioned in their review.
2. Jane was told that she was too pale and didn't wear enough makeup.
3. Jane was told that management didn't like her glasses and that she should wear contacts. She was told it was especially bad when her eyes got red. Jane's eyes get red due to allergies; she had been told by her optometrist never to wear contacts.
4. Jane is shy around the club members. She doesn't think it is right to interrupt a guest's meal with unnecessary chatter. However, she believes she is not rude or unpleasant.
5. Jane was criticized for her lack of wine knowledge. She accepts that there is a lot to know, but she was upset that she got the same score as a server who couldn't pronounce the names of the most common wines.
6. Jane used the wrong color side towels several times. On numerous occasions, Jane had seen others making the same mistake. To her knowledge, she had committed this mistake three or four times in the last six months. Several servers told her that they were not docked for this mistake.

Jane was disturbed with her evaluation and talked with Angie. Although Jane felt that she does not pat herself on the back, Angie agrees that Jane is one of the hardest and most dedicated workers at the club. After the evaluations, she saw herself surpassed by others who did the minimum required for their job, barely getting by with their quality of work.

Out of 100 points, Jane was docked 11, giving her an 89. She received an average increase. She told Angie that her disappointment wasn't with the small raise but with the principle of it as well as the criticisms. It really blew her self-esteem, which was not too high in the first place. Jane remembered when she was selected as employee of the month. As the general manager was giving her the award, Jane felt like the manager's tone of voice sounded like she was giving out a death sentence. This incident has affected her opinion of the manager who she once thought was so great.

Jane discussed how she graciously accepts criticism—when there is a basis for it—but was not willing to accept criticism for these issues, especially when others were not evaluated in the same manner. She recognizes that one must live and learn, and she will deal with her evaluation scores.

Angie shared with Jane how some other employees got the same shaft. Two servers who had worked at Prairie Creek for more than ten years would occasionally help bartend for special parties if extra help was needed. Or they would help at a small party by serving as both the bartender and server to save the cost of additional help. This was not a trained position, just an acquired job. They were docked for not being quick and efficient enough, plus they didn't always set the bar up in the right manner. It appeared that helping out resulted in punishment. This task was definitely not in their job descriptions.

At this point, Angie and Jane discussed some of the happenings in the formal dining room. Jane was well aware of the situation that was affecting Angie. Jane got along with the dining room managers, so she didn't have any issue with their treatment of her. They decided they should talk to Carol about the evaluation process, and Jane agreed that Angie also should talk with Carol about her situation with Peter.

Discussion Questions

1. Evaluate the performance appraisal process. Is it fair? Why or why not?
2. What suggestions do you have for making changes? How would you implement these changes?
3. If you were Carol, what you would do? Defend your actions. Should Carol override the decision about Jane's evaluation? Why or why not?
4. Do you think Jane was evaluated fairly? Support your answer.
5. Should Angie be allowed to be part of the discussion or should Carol ask her to leave? Explain.

The Angie–Peter Conflict

Angie has worked at the club for several years, the last two as a server in the formal dining room. She explained that two weeks ago when Carol was gone for two days, Peter took charge of an evening banquet party. She felt that she generally got along with Peter, so was surprised by what transpired.

Angie and Scott were scheduled to set up for the party. They finished setting up and looked for Peter, who was nowhere to be found. He had gone over the party briefly with both of them and they hadn't seen him after that. Meanwhile, the guests were showing up, and Angie and Scott had been serving cocktails. As the time for serving dinner approached, Angie and Scott reported to the kitchen to begin serving. A few minutes lapsed. Then out of nowhere, Peter appeared and began to yell at them. He said the setup was incomplete. When they questioned Peter, he said the napkins were missing, and this was an important party. Angie explained to Carol that she then suggested that they take napkins out and place them on the guests' laps. Peter had agreed, and Scott and Angie both thought it worked well and actually appeared to be planned as an extra touch to the service. Some guests even made positive comments.

The dinner party continued without any more problems. When Angie and Scott were taking a break later in the employee lounge, Peter came by and was verbally very abusive to Scott. He accused Scott for the mistake with the napkins and yelled at him in front of several employees. Then he looked at Angie and said, "You are not any better, it's your fault too."

The next day Angie talked with Scott, and he said he was thinking of quitting. When she suggested they visit with Carol, Scott didn't want to carry it that far; he would just quit. He also commented that he wasn't that pleased with how his performance evaluation had been conducted either. He further stated that it was probably time to begin looking for another job.

Angie approached Peter and explained that he was going to lose a good employee. Peter didn't seem to care and said he didn't think he needed to apologize to employees when he got upset because they messed up. Angie told Carol that she thought she and Scott worked well together, and didn't want to see him leave. She assured Carol that she was not happy with the treatment she had received either.

Discussion Questions

1. If you were Carol, what would you do? Why?
2. Is Angie right in going to Carol? Why or why not? Should Carol listen to what Angie has to say? Defend your response.
3. Should Peter have disciplined Angie and Scott? Why or why not?
4. If Peter decides to discipline Angie and Scott, describe how he should go about administering the discipline?

West Oaks Golf
and Country Club

As **Harold Sykes,** the director of marketing of West Oaks Golf and Country Club, drove home that quiet Saturday night, he thought about the events that had gone on that evening. Harold hoped that nobody found out about the evening at West Oaks. He questioned what would happen if others found out about the evening. Would he lose his job? Would the staff lose respect for him? What would happen if members became aware of what occurred?

Harold knew that there had been other human resources problems at West Oaks. Just recently, **Chris Bowman,** the head chef, had had a problem with **Beth Linder,** a server, who eventually was terminated. He is worried that what had happened under his direction could be reason for immediate termination.

Background

West Oaks is a beautiful, secluded country club on the outskirts of a small town of 15,000. The club offers many benefits to its 1,050 members. There are two gorgeous eighteen-hole golf courses, a twenty-five-meter swimming pool, two formal dining rooms, and the more casual Golfcourse Café. Because the town is so small, members have very close relations with one another. An extremely strong board of directors that consists of five members runs West Oaks: president, vice president, secretary, treasurer, and event coordinator. The board basically has total say in club activities. Also, they keep close tabs on improvements that need to be made. After all, it is the members' club. All in all, the board and management work very closely with one another to make West Oaks the best club possible.

Through hard work of the board and management, West Oaks offers its members many activities at the club. Every Tuesday night, there is a couples' golf tournament. After the couples play eighteen holes, the club hosts a theme buffet. Also, Wednesday through Saturday formal dinners are served in the club's dining room. In addition, there are the annual pool and Christmas parties and the huge Fourth of July celebration. Attendance at the club's activities is high. Because of this, the addition of more activities is always an option at West Oaks.

Management at West Oaks consists of four job titles: general manager (GM), two assistant mangers (one of whom is the head chef), a dining room manager, and director of marketing. In addition to the management team, there are thirty-two clubhouse service personnel, a maintenance crew, and a pool staff.

Jackie Fraser, the GM, oversees all club operations and is well liked by all of the employees. However, she is a very autocratic leader who wants things done her way. The service personnel understand her expectations and rarely fail to meet them. Jackie always explains her high expectations. She feels that employees work harder when they understand the reason for her expectations. When Jackie is not able to be at the club, Chris, the assistant manager and head chef, or **Simon Douglas,** the assistant clubhouse manager, is left in charge.

Simon is an assistant manager who oversees the front of the house and often works in the casual café. He usually works the dinner shifts Tuesday through Friday. He has been at the club for three years. Simon is well liked by the employees, but he is known for being hard to please and very particular. He is a very high-strung and stressed person who tends to blow up at his employees when certain situations arise.

Chris is one of the top chefs in the state and has been at West Oaks for ten years. The membership at West Oaks has increased significantly since he came to the club. Chris ran his own gourmet restaurant for six years before it burned to the ground. Instead of rebuilding, he looked for a chef's position elsewhere. Because Chris is at the club from open until close nearly every evening, he has been made assistant manager. Chris was very happy about being offered the position. Chris does the work of the assistant manager but is much different from Jackie. To put it nicely, it's best when he and Jackie are not at the club at the same time. Often when Chris is left in charge, mass confusion arises.

Chris is in charge of six cooks, writes all weekly specials and does the kitchen scheduling. He is a hard worker who tends to be a little high-strung. He tends to work twice as fast as the other cooks. He is very critical of other people, especially the front-of-the-house employees. He is known to criticize certain servers more frequently, and one of those servers is Beth.

Chris is a more lenient manager with his cooks than Jackie is. Jackie trains the club staff, and therefore they work under her guidance. When the staff is working under Chris, he tries to change their work ethic. For example, servers are only allowed to serve one table at a time. This is written in their employee handbook and stressed by Jackie. When Chris is in charge, he pressures the servers to handle as many tables at a time as they can. This creates a great deal of confusion for servers; especially when Jackie comes in the next day and demands service of one table at a time. Because of this, the servers change their habits, depending on who is in charge that day, Chris or Jackie.

Next in line, behind Simon, is **Robin Johnson,** who oversees operations of both formal dining rooms. Robin is a hotel and restaurant management (HRM) graduate. She did her internship at West Oaks while attending college. Once she graduated, Jackie offered her the position of dining room manager. Robin is a very quiet and reserved manager. She basically allows employees to walk all over her. Needless to say, employees love her. Lately, Robin has been absent from work a great deal. One day it will be car problems, and the next her dog is sick. Jackie has become very suspicious of Robin's absences.

Jackie has never confronted Robin about her frequent absences. Currently, however, Robin is on maternity leave, and Jackie is very considerate of this matter. When Robin is not in, Harold takes over as dining room manager.

Harold is a recent college graduate with a B.S. degree in marketing. He has worked at West Oaks for two years. His job responsibilities include the club's newsletter, public relations, and some general office work as delegated by Jackie. Harold works very closely with the board. They feel that Harold does a wonderful job of promoting the club's activities to members. The entire West Oaks staff likes Harold.

The majority of clubhouse staff consists of college students working as intern students or earning a little extra money while in college. Harold often finds it difficult to delegate responsibilities to employees who are not only his age, but often are his friends.

The Problem with Beth

Harold recalled what he knew about Beth's termination. In his mind, he wasn't sure that she wasn't set up for failure and should not have been terminated. He had his own feelings about Chris and Simon. He didn't quite understand all the "politics" in this situation, so couldn't sense what might happen.

Chris and Simon have very similar personalities and work together through the week. They have formed the same vision of how the café should be run. They both are very strict and professional at work, but they believe that all servers must act as Chris and Simon perceive the servers' roles. One server they did not work well with is Beth.

Beth worked as a server in the café. She had worked at West Oaks for a little over two years and was a full-time server. Beth was a great asset to the club because she was cross-trained in many areas and knew the members very well. It was not uncommon for members to request her as their server because they liked her friendly personality. Generally, Beth was the closing server.

Chris and Simon believed that all Beth did was cause problems and act immature. Beth usually was the first one to get yelled at when things went wrong. Although Beth tended to be very hyper and did deserve to be reprimanded most times, Chris usually took it too far. At times they would gang up on her and yell at her in front of other employees and sometimes members.

One Thursday night, Beth, Chris, and Simon were all working at the restaurant. It was 8 P.M. and the restaurant was getting ready to close. Just as the last table left and everyone was about to leave, three parties arrived. Following club policy, all parties were welcomed and seated. Because Beth was the only closing server, she was given three tables. The members in these parties were all very demanding and required a lot of attention. Beth ran the food out to all her tables and didn't get a chance to check on her six-top after she delivered their food. At West Oaks, it is the servers' responsibility to check on their table after delivering the food to ensure that everything is to the members' satisfaction.

Beth did not do this until about ten minutes after her table had received their food. All of their food was prepared wrong and was not to their liking. The members became very irate at Beth and began screaming at her, stating that along with the bad food, the service was ridiculous. By this time Simon had heard the upset table, so he apologized for Beth and comped their meals. After that, Simon and Chris began yelling at Beth for not checking on her table. This occurred in the kitchen, which is visible from the dining room. The fight among the three employees escalated to screaming and cursing. When the members heard the commotion, they walked out of the café. Simon was so upset at Beth that he sent her home.

The next day, Chris wrote a letter to the club president and the GM explaining the incident and also explaining why he felt Beth should be fired. He listed all the things Beth had done wrong in the past and stated that he felt she caused too many problems at the club. The club president, **Thomas Speas,** called an emergency meeting with Jackie, Chris, and Simon to discuss what should be done. The decision was made to terminate Beth because no one, other than Chris and Simon, had been present at the time of the incident, so the group took the word of the assistant managers.

Discussion Questions

1. Evaluate Chris and Simon's treatment of Beth before the incident.
2. Should Beth have been the only server left to close? Why or why not? What, if anything, should be done about scheduling servers? Support your response.
3. Describe how you would have handled the situation in the kitchen if you were Simon or Chris. Support your plans.
4. Should Beth have been sent home? Why or why not?
5. If you were Chris, would you have written a letter to the club president? Defend your answer.
6. Do you think Beth should have been terminated? Explain why or why not.

That Saturday Night

It was a Saturday night, and the club was hosting a wedding party for 250 guests. That night, the management staff was all in attendance, including the entire clubhouse staff. Everyone was very busy serving dinner, drinks, and cake. About 11:00, the wedding began to slow down as guests started to leave. Jackie and Chris decided to delegate management responsibilities to Harold so they could leave early. Harold agreed to his responsibilities of supervising cleanup.

Tammy Chen, a clubhouse server, asked Harold if she and a few of the employees could finish off the champagne and keg of beer left from the wedding. All of the alcohol was paid for; however, it was club policy that employees could not drink while at the club. Harold firmly stood his ground, saying "No," until a couple of staff members said, "Come on, we can't let good alcohol go to waste!" Harold gave in and replied, "After we finish cleaning up, we can party, but don't let the word out!" The employees cleaned up the dining room faster than ever.

At 2:30 in the morning, all of the alcohol was gone. Needless to say, the staff, including Harold, had consumed a great deal of alcohol. Their partying did not end here. Harold and the staff decided to go for a swim in the club's swimming pool, which was against club policy. The pool was only supposed to be used by members. It had been locked since 7:00 that evening. The staff and Harold swam in the pool for a bit. Finally, after the fun was over, Harold and the staff drove their separate ways.

Discussion Questions

1. What is the problem Jackie faces? How should the problem be dealt with? Support your answer. Whose responsibility is it to correct the problem? Defend your response.
2. Should Harold have been delegated the responsibility of dining room manager? Explain.
3. If you were Harold and friends with the staff, how would you have handled the situation? Explain.
4. How should Jackie reprimand Harold's behavior? Through the board of directors? Should the staff also be reprimanded? Explain.
5. Do you believe that the club could be held liable for the actions of Harold and staff? Why or why not?
6. Have you ever worked where the supervisor had problems managing staff members who were the same age or were his or her friends? Describe the situation.

PART 4
Business and Industry

Ambassador Manufacturing In-Plant Cafeteria

The Ambassador Manufacturing Company is located in a midwestern city of 250,000. It is one of several companies that employ a substantial number of employees. The Ambassador has enjoyed a reputation for being a good place to work, so there always have been sufficient applicants on the waiting list for employment.

About fifteen years ago, the management of Ambassador offered its employees another benefit when it converted some of its space to a cafeteria. At that time, the decision was to hire an outside company to operate the foodservice. Although the foodservice department had different employment guidelines, its reputation of being a good employer seems to be inherited from the overall company's reputation. The foodservice and plant managers have had a good working relationship. Six months ago, **C. T. Smith** became the new foodservice manager of the cafeteria, which caters to 1,200 employees.

C. T. is frustrated as the result of a major conflict among the A.M. and P.M. production supervisors. It appears that **Kim Stone,** A.M. supervisor, is requesting every Saturday off in honor of the Sabbath. Kim is one of the more senior supervisors on the staff, having transferred from another company facility. After hearing about Kim's request, two less senior supervisors, **Leslie Crane** and **Jerry Jones,** are requesting every Sunday off in honor of *their* Sabbath. They insist that if Kim is given Saturdays off and they are not given equal consideration, they will contact the local Equal Employment Opportunity Commission (EEOC).

The cafeteria and plant are non-union, and C. T. wants to handle the situation equitably. Although supervisors are not allowed to cooperate with union organizations, a human resources manager has informed C. T. that reputable sources saw Leslie talking with union representatives. It appears that he has been involved actively, during his off hours, with a local union's attempt to contact plant employees concerning a potential union campaign to organize the entire plant.

The human resources manager has advised C. T. that Leslie should be elimi-nated from the staff. The manager is concerned that if the problem within the food-service department results in unionized activity, there may be some union activity in the plant. None of these union contact incidents concerning Leslie's activity have been documented, although the information was received from both identi-fied and unidentified callers on an in-plant employee hotline.

The plant has allowed cafeteria managers to establish and enforce their own departmental personnel policies and procedures, as is done with many contract companies. However, differences in policies have been discussed with representa-tives from the human resources department. Representatives of the foodservice company and Ambassador managers have agreed that the human resources depart-ment staff would provide assistance to all employees. Consequently, there has been a good working relationship between these two entities.

Kim's Sabbath request stated that **Kelly Schaaf,** the previous manager, had promised him every weekend off. Six months later, C. T. replaced Kelly. Kim had not received anything in writing to document this promise. However, a recent state law was passed stating that all nonessential personnel should be allowed to be off on their respective Sabbaths. Kim and Leslie are classified as essential employees by human resources. Jerry is classified as a nonessential employee. In fact, the human resources director has told C. T. he prefers that Leslie be off on weekends. He fears that Leslie will use this time for the purpose of campaigning and solicit-ing for the union with plant employees.

C. T. has overheard Leslie and Jerry making prejudicial remarks about Kim's religious and ethnic origins. Leslie and Jerry reported to C. T. that Kelly, the previous manager, had given preferential treatment to Kim. They stated: "Whenever Kim requested a special day off, it was granted." However, C. T. dis-covered that Kim's requests always had been made in writing. Copies of these re-quests were found in Kim's personnel file. No copies of Leslie's and Jerry's requests were in their respective files.

In six months, as manager of the cafeteria, C. T. has discovered many in-stances where there was no written documentation for promises that had been made to other employees in the department. Because the previous manager be-came known as one who did not document personnel activities well, many of the departmental employees began documenting most of the verbal agreements that were made with cafeteria supervisors. It appeared that employees who kept note-books and complained the loudest were able to achieve personal results during pe-riods of stress and crises.

According to others, it was determined that Kelly was a poor communicator. This was the main reason the parent foodservice company transferred Kelly to a smaller plant in another state. C. T. had never been told the reason why Kelly was transferred. He was excited about his new promotion and the opportunity to man-age a larger in-plant cafeteria, and he never thought to inquire.

C. T. recently has discovered that Leslie is contemplating accepting a position with another company offering a substantial increase in salary. Jerry has threatened to leave unless she is given the same consideration offered to Kim. Right now, C. T. would rather not deal with resignations and finding new employees who may need substantial training.

Discussion Questions

1. If you were C. T., how would you determine which, if any, supervisors should be allowed the Sabbath off according to their religious beliefs?
2. Should individual department managers be given the authority to determine the department's human resources policies and procedures? Explain.
3. Describe problems that can result when employees who work for a foodservice management company interact with the plant employees. Should anything be done about these problems? Why or why not?
4. If you were C. T., what action would you take regarding the prejudicial remarks made by Leslie and Jerry? Support your answer.
5. Why is documentation important to employees and the organization? How would you ensure that it was done?
6. Should anything be done about Leslie's apparent unionizing activities? Why or why not?

BiDesign Dining Services

BiDesign is a very expensive, upscale office and custom home furnishings company. Its corporate headquarters is located in a sprawling city in southern California. The company has manufacturing plants, distribution centers, and sales offices positioned in four key geographical areas of the country.

BiDesign is a well-established company enjoying a highly successful growth rate and possesses an intelligent plan for future development. Corporate officers are contemplating a strategically located overseas site as part of its future. BiDesign is facing a bright future as a specialty business serving an affluent clientele, largely unaffected by changes in the economy.

The corporate headquarters employs approximately 125 people including executives, designers, administrators, department heads, consultants, and its own marketing staff. Heads of these vital areas frequently are required to entertain current and potential clients. Additionally, corporate officers provide "special occasion" events at their homes for chief executive officers of companies from whom they buy products. The company operates its own kitchen and dining rooms to provide for these various high-quality luncheons, dinners, and catering requirements.

Staffing

The director of dining services, **Ann Dow,** has eleven years of experience in managing various types of foodservice operations. Her previous position at a national contract foodservice company where she was responsible for multiple sites impressed the BiDesign director of human resources, who hired her two years ago. Ann had considered herself fortunate when the position at BiDesign suddenly opened due to the unexpected retirement of the former director. Ann was excited to get a position that did not require the extensive traveling she was doing with her previous job.

Dining services operates three food outlets. Executive dining for breakfast and lunch each day is offered in the Linden Room, where senior corporate officers and their guests dine. Special dinners are scheduled approximately twice a month. Other corporate officers, administrators, designers, and staff are served breakfast, lunch, and light dinners in the Capitol Room. Business meals, entertainment luncheons, and dinners must be scheduled in advance and are catered in the Sutter Room.

As dining services director, Ann is responsible for the organization, supervision, and fiscal accountability of the entire dining services operation. Her business expertise is considered excellent. Her immediate supervisor, **Patricia Kerry,** is the human resources director.

The fact that both directors share similar interests and have similar personalities is an added benefit. They work closely on a daily basis in scheduling the many dining and catering requirements for the various company officers.

There are twenty employees in the dining services division (see the BiDesign Dining Services organization chart). Most employees have been with BiDesign for twelve or more years, enjoying excellent pay, benefits, and working conditions. Ann's dedicated employees enjoy their work and fulfill their responsibilities quite well.

Patricia has been with BiDesign for ten years and is known to be a very firm and direct supervisor. Patricia and Ann often have lunch together in the Capitol Room and appear to have a very close relationship. Employees and managers at

BiDesign Dining Services
Organization Chart

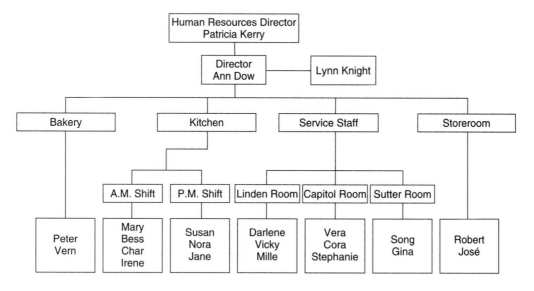

BiDesign have come to regard this pair as a mutual admiration society. Some employees and managers are concerned that this close relationship may give Ann a free hand in running the dining services division.

Dining services has never been asked to make a profit. In fact, the company subsidizes all meals and catered functions in order to keep meal costs low and employee morale high. Company guidelines related to food costs and charges have been given to Ann. The guidelines indicate the subsidy amount her operation can expect. Ann has interpreted the guidelines to mean "break even" and has slowly raised prices on selected items to meet her personal goal to show a profit. She hopes her friend (and supervisor) will be pleased with her initiative.

There are established firm guidelines on hiring at BiDesign in order to maintain a good mix of expertise, experience, and personalities. However, over lunch six months ago, Ann received special permission from Patricia to hire a secretary. She claimed that dining services requirements have increased beyond her ability to manage them effectively without additional administrative assistance. Ann alleged that due to her new financial control systems, the office work was more complex. No request for additional food preparation or service staff was brought forward by Ann.

Ann ultimately selected **Lynn Knight,** a single parent, as the new secretary. Lynn has been a homemaker and volunteer for many years. She recently reentered the workforce after completing an office skills class at a community college. She is an eager, highly motivated employee who quickly developed a strong allegiance to Ann. Lynn has been impressed with Ann's business expertise, leadership abilities, and gentle patience in helping her achieve a high degree of efficiency. Ann has become fond of Lynn as well. Three weeks ago, Ann recommended Lynn for a merit pay increase based on her dedication to work assignments.

Changes in Assignments

Initially, Lynn was well liked by employees. She performed her administrative tasks quickly and accurately and always had a kind word for everyone. The period of adjustment, while learning her new position and getting to know fellow employees, was very short-lived.

Recently Lynn has been given increased responsibilities with respect to supervising kitchen and dining room staff assignments. Lynn often delivers special work instructions from Ann, even when Ann is absent. The kitchen staff, in particular, have noticed that Ann seems to know virtually everything that goes on in the kitchen even in her absence. Lynn has slowly, almost imperceptibly evolved into a working–assistant manager position (without an official title or formal announcement).

Even more disturbing to the other dining services employees is that Lynn now receives extra hours at catering assignments held at corporate executives' homes. In addition to overtime pay, tips received at these catering functions are typically very generous.

Complaints

The kitchen and dining room staffs, predominantly female, have become agitated. A formal written complaint about unfair treatment as a result of Lynn's addition to the staff has been given to Ann. Employees allege that Lynn is now "adjusting" the work schedule so that she receives the best catering assignments. They also allege that Lynn has become a spy for Ann whenever Ann is not in the kitchen. Employees complain that they now must receive "permission" from Lynn to see Ann, as Lynn controls Ann's appointment calendar.

Ann defends Lynn's position and dismisses the complaints as trivial, unfounded bickering. Ann claims that BiDesign is a growing company, and employees must recognize that as businesses mature and expand, each section of the operation must adjust with the times, including dining services. Ann further recommends that if employees want to improve their opportunities for advancement, they should return to college for additional training. Ann cited Lynn's college experience as an example.

More Complaints

The dining services employees were not satisfied with Ann's response. The senior employees were especially upset, as they never experienced anything like this in the past. **Mary Rosario,** a fourteen-year kitchen employee, is the most senior kitchen staff member. She is respected and well thought of by all her co-workers. Mary was asked by her colleagues to take their concerns to Patricia with the hope that some resolution could be obtained at a higher level. Mary made an appointment with Patricia to discuss employee concerns about poor management practices and unfair treatment they were experiencing.

Two days before the appointment, Mary received a memo from Patricia requesting that Mary bring any two dining services staff members with her to the meeting. Further, Patricia asked Mary and her colleagues to provide any documentation that might support their allegations. Lastly, Patricia changed the time of the meeting from 2:30 P.M. to 5:00 P.M., stating that her calendar has become unexpectedly busy. She apologized for any inconvenience this change may have caused.

Mary became upset because she and the two employees who were to accompany her to the meeting all work the early shift. This change in schedule means that they either need to hang around after work or come back later. Mary and her co-workers wonder what this inconvenience and change in meeting time means.

Discussion Questions

1. What are the root problems at BiDesign? Be specific in their identification. Defend your selections with examples.
2. What action(s) can the dining services staff initiate to obtain a resolution in this matter? What are the risks, if any, involved with the action(s) you recommend?
3. Was Patricia's response to Mary's appointment agenda proper? Why or why not?
4. If you were Ann, what would be your worst fear concerning this personnel situation? Why?
5. If you were Patricia, what would be your worst fear concerning this personnel situation? Why?
6. What organizational changes can be made to prevent a similar situation from developing elsewhere in this company? Justify your response. How would you implement these changes?
7. If the CEO hired you as a human resources specialist, what suggestions would you offer to alleviate the tension being experienced? Explain. Is it possible to achieve a harmonious operation again? Explain.
8. What human resources issues need to be considered in overseas expansion? Why?

Food Service Management Corporation

Food Service Management (FSM) Corporation is a contract company that oversees food and beverage services for various healthcare facilities; schools, colleges, and universities; and business and industry companies. FSM has numerous contracts throughout the United States, including Global Tech Inc., which has its home office in the southeastern United States. There are two types of management structures within the clients' settings. In some contracts, there are two managers, and in others a manager, unit clerk, and chef constitute the management team; the latter manager structure exists at Global Tech.

Global Tech employs 1,200 people who work Monday through Friday at its high-technology corporate office. As a benefit to employees, Global Tech has contracted with FSM to provide an on-premise foodservice for breakfast and lunch. The operation is open for breakfast from 6:30 A.M. to 8 A.M. Lunch runs from 11:00 A.M. to 1:30 P.M., and the cafeteria is open until 2:30 P.M. for employees who want to purchase a beverage or snack. In addition, special events occur on a daily basis, sometimes taking place on weekends. FSM also supplies the vending machines located throughout the premise.

Approximately 30 percent of employees eat breakfast, which includes a continental breakfast; choices of pastry, bagels, yogurt, or fresh-cut fruit; and hot entrées of eggs, pancakes, or waffles. About 40 percent of employees eat lunch, which includes a deli bar, a grill line, and a salad bar. Gross income from food sales during the day approximates $2,500 in cash and $1,200 in vending in addition to credit card purchases. An employee who assumes the role of vending attendant collects all monies from the vending machines. The employee removes all bills and currency in excess of a base amount.

All Global Tech employees are issued a key card with an identification number as part of the security program. The key card is necessary to enter the building and food production areas, use the elevators, or enter any conference room or office. The security system monitors the use of key cards so that on any given day, each employee's activities throughout the building are logged on its system. If employees flash a badge to enter a room to which they don't have access, the system records that action.

As part of FSM's security system, a password control log for access to the safe is maintained and kept in the safe. A six-digit number is needed for access. There is no set schedule as to when the password must be changed. The only requirement for changing a password is to know the current one to gain access to the safe. The password security system allows one to reuse a password after a six-month period.

Generally, the unit clerk is the only other person who needs to have the safe password so that after the clerk has balanced the day's receipts, it can be placed in the safe. However, it is the manager who changes the password code as desired or as the need arises. Further, when the chef is in charge of a catering event, the chef is given the password to the safe. At the end of the function, the chef places the money in the safe.

Karl Pitzur is the food and beverage manager at Global Tech. Karl graduated from a four-year hospitality program. After several years with other contract foodservice companies, Karl became the manager at Global Tech five years ago. Karl is a team player who is well liked by the two other management team members and ten other foodservice employees. He is respected by corporate managers because he turns a profit for FSM.

Karl serves as the primary representative of FSM to the Global Tech account. Karl is responsible for coordinating and directing all foodservice employees' activities within the account. He works with **Megan Villar,** the district manager, on an as-needed basis to ensure a solid and mutually beneficial business relationship with Global Tech. Important components of Karl's job include client and customer satisfaction and a positive work environment that retains employees to achieve the financial goals of FSM and Global Tech. Karl is responsible for ensuring that quality standards are met and that all employees comply with government regulations and corporate policies and procedures.

Karl oversees a management team of **Marcia Seaburg,** the unit clerk, and **George Nguyen,** the chef. They have worked together for one and a half years and have a great deal of mutual trust.

Marcia is responsible for accounting procedures and financial reports, scheduling appointments, and operating the computer. Marcia operates a cash register, counts the cash from register and vending sales, and provides Karl with a daily cash flow report for verification. She prepares daily deposits for pickup by armored car service. Marcia administers employee benefits and processes payroll and time cards.

When Karl is off premise, Marcia is expected to make decisions and handle all situations. She ultimately is responsible for all funds when Karl is away. Marcia generally works from 6:30 A.M. to 3:00 P.M.; however, her time can vary depending upon Global Tech's needs.

Each day Marcia is responsible for balancing the safe to $4,800, which includes money left in the cashier drawers for the next day. After ensuring that each drawer contains $330, Marcia returns them to the safe. Because the armored car service for Global Tech comes at 1:30 P.M. (before the cafeteria is closed), Karl decided that the current day's deposit should be left in the safe and picked up the next day.

George is expected to provide the highest-quality food and service to customers. He develops menus, oversees preparation and service of a wide range of food products, and leads a preservice meeting before lunch begins. George is responsible for keeping all food production records and following HACCP rules and food safety requirements. Because George is in charge of the client's catering needs, he has a key card that gives him access to production and the production office areas twenty-four hours a day. His normal day begins at 6:00 A.M. and ends at 2:30 P.M. When a catering event occurs after hours or on weekends, George is given access to the safe.

A Cash Shortage

One Friday morning before a holiday weekend, Karl received word that **Rick Pierson,** his nephew, had passed away shortly after midnight. Although the death was not unexpected, it was very hard on Karl as he had a fairly close relationship with Rick, even though Rick lived 500 miles away. Upon hearing the news, Karl made plans to leave town immediately to be with his only sister's family and attend the funeral the following Monday morning. Before leaving, Karl took time to review his expectations of Marcia while he was gone. He also changed the password to the safe and gave the six-digit number to Marcia.

The following Monday morning, Marcia arrived at work by 6:00 A.M. to pull the drawers for the cashiers during breakfast service. The deposit from Friday's sales was in the safe, ready for pickup by the armored car service.

The day's activities were fairly normal, and most things went off without a hitch. After the cafeteria closed at 2:30 P.M., Marcia took the cash register drawers to the office to balance out the day and prepare the deposit for the next day's pickup by the security service. At this time she noticed a shortage of $400. She recounted each drawer to ensure that she had not left too much money in either of them, and she recounted the money in the deposit bag. Everything checked out.

Marcia knew that she was the only one with the combination, so she immediately called Karl on his cell phone to report the discrepancy. Karl instructed Marcia to recount the amount of money she had in each drawer for the next day and the amount of money that she had in the deposit bag. Marcia told Karl that she had checked each of these at least three times. Karl told Marcia to call Megan, as he would not be returning for another two days.

Megan notified FSM's corporate office, who said they would send out **Sharon Tiller,** one of their security investigators. Megan also notified Global Tech management of the reported missing money. When Karl returned, he reported the theft to the local police. All other transactions were held internally.

During the investigation, Megan and Sharon talked with Karl, Marcia, and George. Karl and Marcia continued to work during the investigation, but George was given time off with pay. Marcia relayed her story to Megan and Sharon. She later told Karl that she was becoming very resentful of George. She suspected he was guilty and couldn't understand why he would do such a thing to her. He knew that she was the only one with the combination, and the guilty finger would point to her.

The keycard access report showed that George had been in the production/office area during the holiday weekend. He defended his action by stating that he had some work to do. Any paperwork that George needed to do could be done from his desk located within the production area. Although he had used his card to enter the food production area, there was no record of him entering the office, which was readily accessible because it was within the production area and left unlocked.

When questioned, Karl explained how he had changed the combination before going out of town. The six-digit combination was his birth date, a combination that he had used earlier when George had access to the safe. During the time George had access to the safe, three different combinations had been used. Karl suggested that George might have tried the three combinations and one of them worked. It was difficult to ascertain fingerprints because Marcia had opened the safe the morning on the day the money was found missing.

In the end, FSM's corporate management staff used money from a general fund to replace the $400. George was told that it would be best if he parted company with FSM. George hung on for a while, but he no longer had a key card to enter the production area. Within a couple of weeks, George quietly resigned and was offered vacation pay as well as one month's salary in severance pay. Any work reference given for George would follow corporate's policy to provide only factual information of employment dates, position, and pay rate. If asked about rehiring George, the response was to be "no comment." George since has found a position as a chef in a healthcare facility.

Discussion Questions

1. Who is responsible for the theft of $400? Support your answer. Why do you think only $400 was taken?

2. Do you think the amount of trust among the management team members affected the situation in the case? Why or why not?

3. As a corporate manager, what would you have done in this case as you interacted with Karl? Marcia? George? Explain your action in each situation.

4. Can Marcia be ruled out as a suspect? Why or why not? Does a guilty person make calls to his or her manager and district manager? Support your answer.

5. Does Karl share any responsibility or liability in the theft? Why or why not? Do you think he would be treated differently under other circumstances? Why or why not?

6. Why do you think George was asked to resign? Explain your response.

7. George didn't resign immediately. Do you think he became tired of being accused and took severance pay? Justify your response. Was he guilty of theft? Why or why not? Why wasn't he arrested for theft?

8. Do employees take advantage of situations such as the one Karl was facing? Explain your answer.

9. Evaluate the procedure used for not picking up the day's deposit until the following day. Should changes be made? Why or why not? If changes were to be made, how should they be implemented?

10. What message do you think FSM sent to other employees? Justify your response.

11. As a corporate security investigator, what changes would you suggest? Explain.

Kirkwood Foods

Jay Barker, district manager of Kirkwood Foods, Inc., is reviewing the notes from a recent meeting with fifteen Kirkwood employees who work in the SCG Company foodservice department. Unfortunately, the focus of the meeting centered on the lack of interpersonal skills of the foodservice director, **Sandy Carter.** Jay wondered what went wrong as he recalled how Sandy became the manager of SCG.

Background

Sandy had outstanding academic credentials from a highly respected hospitality management program at a local university. She demonstrated a lot of the enthusiasm, drive, and self-confidence necessary to be successful in industry. She seemed to be the ideal trainee for Kirkwood's intense six-month training program. This training program provided opportunities for the trainee to experience all areas of contract foodservice, including planning, purchasing, production, service, and human resources management.

Kirkwood had been working on obtaining the foodservice contract with SCG Company for the last five years. Five years ago, Kirkwood lost the bid for the contract to TNX, Inc. However, this August, TNX decided it was having too many difficulties with its employees. Additionally, the number of SCG employees using the cafeteria had decreased below precontract level. Therefore, TNX decided not to rebid for the contract. Kirkwood had to act quickly—a second chance like this didn't come along every day. Only two months remained before the new contract period would begin. After modifying its former proposal, Kirkwood rebid and was selected to provide foodservice for SCG beginning October 1.

SCG is a manufacturing plant operating three shifts per day, six days per week. If necessary, the plant operates one shift on Sundays. There are approximately 1,400 employees, including administrative personnel. Roughly two-thirds of the employees are women, and men fill most management positions. SCG has been located in Rock Lake for forty-seven years and has a solid reputation for treating employees fairly. Employee benefits are great, and most employees are happy working at SCG. One benefit is the in-plant cafeteria, which until recently, had offered quick service and good food.

Kirkwood was excited about this new contract. However, they did not have a manager available who wanted to transfer to this smaller operation. After some management discussion, it was decided to offer this managerial position to Sandy. However, this would mean ending her training program three months early. On the other hand, Kirkwood would now have a woman in a management position.

Sandy was pleased about the offer. This was the opportunity for which she had been waiting *and* it was happening three months earlier than she had expected. Sandy immediately went to SCG to begin planning the production and service areas. Because Kirkwood was changing the cafeteria structure, equipment had to be ordered. Some employees had to be hired.

Jay knew he would have to devote extra time at SCG helping Sandy get started. During this intense interaction with Sandy, he realized that she had excellent technical skills and fairly good conceptual skills, considering her lack of experience and shortened training program.

Jay was a firm believer in participative management and, whenever possible, allowed his managers to make decisions on their own. He often provided suggestions for consideration and, in some instances, hoped the suggestions would be accepted completely. However, he began to notice that some of the suggestions he made to Sandy about the new foodservice operation were not well accepted. The manner in which Sandy presented her plans to Jay indicated that she did not expect to be questioned and desired to do the job on her own.

Jay worked with Sandy to develop her conceptual skills more thoroughly. He felt it was important for Sandy to see the consequences of different alternatives in serving meals during the first shift as compared to the second and third shifts. He also helped her to see the impact that self-service areas would have on production, service, and profit. However, Sandy also had many ideas for new menu items and planned to make use of a quantity food production recipe file, available through Kirkwood, anticipating that the new recipes would increase employees' patronage.

The Current Situation

Jay returned to the present. He continued to review his notes from the meeting. Comments from employees indicated that Sandy had a tough personality and was overbearing and demanding. Employees, many of whom had worked for TNX, felt that Sandy had an authoritarian leadership style and, at times, appeared to abuse the power inherent in the position. Their comments compared Sandy to their previous manager while working for TNX. They indicated that they now realized how good the TNX manager was, and some even commented that they wished he were back as their manager.

Jay decided to call Sandy in for a meeting. During this meeting, he asked her how the food service operation was going at SCG. Sandy replied that things would be much better if the employees were halfway competent. She stated that if employees spent half as much time learning the operation as they did telling her how to manage the foodservice, everyone would be better off. Jay then told Sandy that some employees had come to him with several concerns. He informed her that employees were not happy with her management style and felt she was a dictator. He also told her she was not measuring up, in the employees' eyes, to their previous TNX manager. Jay asked Sandy to try to relate better with the employees. She agreed to be more understanding and patient.

Unfortunately, things at SCG did not improve. Three weeks later, Jay stared at a stack of termination and resignation slips. More than half of the SCG employees had either quit or been fired.

Jay was livid. He immediately called Sandy in for another meeting. When questioned about this mass exodus of employees, Sandy replied that she had been trying to be nicer to the employees, but when she did, they began breaking rules and slacking in their productivity. Therefore, she had been forced to take disciplinary action.

Jay sighed. Fortunately, a trainee from another district was ready to be placed and had agreed to relocate to Rock Lake. Jay told Sandy that, based on her performance, he felt he could not justify keeping her in her current position. He informed her that he had recommended that she be transferred to a larger site as an assistant manager at the same salary.

Sandy was furious! First, the company had pulled her from the training program to take this position and now, because *employees* were not performing well, *she* was being demoted.

"No way," she said. "I quit!"

Discussion Questions

1. Should Jay have pulled Sandy from the training program before the scheduled completion date? Describe the benefits and risks in doing so.
2. After the employee meeting, Jay called Sandy in for the first time. Do you agree with the way Jay handled the meeting? Explain your decision. Describe what he could or should have done differently. Defend your suggestions.
3. At the second meeting with Sandy, Jay recommended that she take a demotion. Do you agree with this action? Why or why not? What other alternatives might there have been to remedy the situation? Support your suggestions.

4. Now that Sandy has quit, Jay is faced with an operation that has no manager and is short-staffed by 50 percent. What are some options? What should Jay do? Discuss why this is the best action.

5. Another new manager is coming to take over operations. What advice would you give him or her? What things could or should the new manager do differently at SCG? What should Jay do differently this time? Defend your suggestions.

6. Many Kirkwood employees at SCG had worked previously for TNX. Do you feel that they should have been retained by SCG? Why or why not? Explain how this could affect the situations presented in this case.

Optimum Catering Company

Richard Dodge founded the Optimum Catering Company fifteen years ago. His parents owned a little diner, and he turned the place into a catering company. Now, fifteen years later, it is the third most popular catering company in the metro Atlanta area. Richard is very proud of his business. Optimum is busy year-round, usually catering at least three events during the week and two events on weekends. The business has forty-three full-time and ten part-time employees. Because catering events often require different service styles, about fifty banquet servers are on call. Although his business is successful, Richard doesn't have many managerial skills or any formal human resources training, so he relies on **Mark Taber** his general manager (see the Optimum organization chart).

Mark has a four-year degree in HRIM and has worked for Richard for nearly six years. Prior to Optimum, he worked as a production manager at a local high school foodservice for two years following graduation. He was promoted from catering manager at Optimum to GM four years ago. His responsibilities include monitoring and coordinating all events among departments, hiring and firing employees, and maintaining good customer relationships. After he was promoted, **Lisa O'Holleran,** the chef, was promoted to catering manager.

Lisa has formal training from a chef's school and worked in an upscale restaurant in France for one year. During her five years at Optimum, she has generated great ideas for each event. She pays a great deal of attention to each event to ensure that customers are satisfied with Optimum's services. Her work has not only improved Optimum's reputation but has also increased repeat business.

Lisa is considered a great chef but an average manager. She does not have training in human resources, which appears to be a severe hindrance to her management style. For example, two of her kitchen staff consistently are late for work, and Lisa covers their jobs for them or finds someone else to do their work. When

**Optimum Catering Company
Organization Chart**

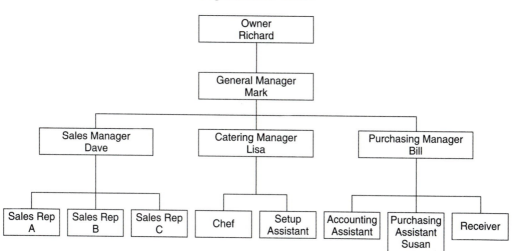

Mark noticed Lisa delivering prime rib to the walk-in cooler last Thursday, he questioned her about why she was doing that job. Lisa replied that she didn't mind helping the kitchen employees; in fact it kept her in tune with them.

At the following weekly meeting, Mark asked Lisa about the problem of her two employees being late. Lisa stated that occasionally they are just ten to fifteen minutes late. She went on to say that they are really experienced employees who are familiar with their jobs, so they still get everything done on time even if they are late. Mark wondered about other employee reactions to this situation and if there were complaints. Lisa replied that she didn't feel that there were any problems, and everyone seems fine with the situation.

Dave Bilyeau, the sales manager, has worked for Optimum since it opened. He has a degree in business and is responsible for all sales contacts and contracts, developing new markets, promoting repeat business, and filing complete customer records. Mark is very pleased with the job Dave does in promoting the business. He has been engaged to Lisa for a year. Mark doesn't think this relationship is causing any concern among employees. Lisa and Dave work quite a bit together and sometimes are found chatting about personal things rather than work-related topics.

The Real Problem

One month ago, Richard introduced his nephew, **Bill Dodge** as the new purchasing manager. Richard is very proud of Bill and gave the employees a short summary of Bill's career since receiving an accounting degree from a local business college. He began his career as an accounting clerk with a national retail chain.

After two years, he didn't feel challenged with that job, so he became an accounting assistant for a regional chain restaurant and was promoted to accounting manager within eight months. For two and a half years, Bill learned about foodservice purchasing, so Richard feels confident that Bill can do the purchasing at the Optimum. Not wanting Bill to change his mind, Richard hired Bill at once and wanted him to begin within the week.

Bill heard about the job from his uncle when the previous purchasing manager was fired for poor inventory control at a catered family picnic. The Sunday before Bill began work, Richard called Mark to inform him of his decision.

Bill was good at purchasing control and accounting. After he took over, inventory was handled properly. His goal was to find the cheapest suppliers for the variety of food items and also to monitor food issues closely. There was soon an obvious cost saving, and Richard was happy with Bill's performance.

Bill talked a lot about his relationship with Richard on the job, such as how close they were and how much Richard liked him. It seemed that he liked to put his nose into everyone's business to prove his superiority. During Mark's meetings with other supervisors, he found that Bill had already had several arguments with Dave about some decisions in the sales department. For example, Bill thought Dave should not take small banquet contracts, even though those contracts came from repeat customers. He pointed out that no matter how small the events, the labor cost for a minimum number of employees who were needed to carry through on the event could not be eliminated. Bill stressed that those contracts were not cost-effective.

Lisa also reported that Bill often asked her to compromise and order lower-quality food items. Lisa told Mark that she had explained to Bill that quality is the company's first concern, but Bill just joked, "That is what qualified cooks are for." Moreover, she said that Bill had more than once blamed her late employees for not adhering to walk-in cooler security. Lisa and the entire kitchen staff heard him yell at them, "If there are any expensive items missing from the cooler, would you take responsibility or will 'nice Lisa' cover for you guys one more time?"

Mark also noticed that the purchasing assistant, **Susan Zhan,** who works directly under Bill, was acting quite differently lately. She seems to have been influenced by Bill and has started to give her opinions to others regarding their order requests. For example, when the setup assistant orders carnations, Susan replaces them with roses, which she prefers. Mark knows that employees are upset with Bill's superior attitude, and he plans to talk to Bill about his attitude soon.

Three days later, Lisa and Dave came to Mark's office and Lisa firmly stated, "I can't work with Bill anymore. If you don't do something, I will quit my job." She also explained to Mark that she had gone into Bill's office and noticed a chef's knife sticking into a bulletin board. When she questioned Bill about it, he told her he was just releasing some built-up tension. Lisa said she completed the conversation very quickly and left the office. She was so shocked, she didn't think anyone would believe her, so she kept quiet. As she relayed the story she was obviously upset.

Mark calmed her down and once again promised to talk to Bill. Dave was quite angry and said to Mark, "The person who should leave the company is Bill, not Lisa. If you let Lisa quit, I will go with her!"

Mark finally called Bill into his office. Mark asked him if there was anything wrong between him and Lisa. "What did she tell you?" Bill asked. Bill was not in a good mood. Mark asked again, "What is really happening?"

Bill replied, "This morning, Uncle Richard called Lisa in and told her she shouldn't let her staff get out of control." In Mark's memory, Richard had seldom made direct comments about a supervisor. He usually talked to Mark first and let him handle problems his way. Mark was confused and asked, "Does Richard know something about Lisa?" Bill replied frivolously, "I told Uncle Richard that Lisa was doing the work for her two late employees at a family party last Sunday. That's all. When I check the inventory, I often see Lisa doing someone else's job."

Mark asked, "Is anyone complaining about Lisa to you?" Bill was becoming furious and asked Mark, "Are you blaming me for telling the truth to my uncle?"

Discussion Questions

1. If you were Mark, how would you gather facts?
2. What should Mark do when he finds out what is happening? Be specific.
3. If you were Mark, how would you handle the knife situation? Be specific.
4. What do you think about close relationships among employees? What are advantages? Disadvantages?
5. How should Lisa deal with the two staff members who are consistently late for work?
6. What are Mark's options? Which option should he select? Why?
7. According to Optimum's organization chart, would you make any suggestions? Why or why not? If so, describe how you would implement these changes.

PART 5
Healthcare

Apple Valley Retirement Community
Broadview Medical Center
City Medical Center Food Service
Culver Community Medical Center
Forest Lake Hospital Foodservice Department
Lake Regional Hospital
Memorial Medical Center Foodservice Department
Walnut Hill Retirement Community

Apple Valley Retirement Community

Apple Valley Retirement Community (AVRC) consists of the board of directors of the university retirement corporation, the Apple Valley Resident Association, and the Health Care Services (HCS) management company. It is also made up of a team of employees who render a variety of services to the residents of the community (see the Apple Valley organization chart).

The AVRC concept was developed to provide elderly people with a viable retirement alternative. This alternative is a special combination of housing, support services, and health care. The support services provide assistance in day-to-day living, including transportation; on-site facilities for dining, exercise, and crafts; exterior and minor interior maintenance; biweekly housekeeping; and emergency medical services. The purpose of these services is to make life for the retirees very attractive by providing them freedom, dignity, independence, and security.

Management of Apple Valley, including the day-to-day maintenance, is the responsibility of HCS. HCS is headquartered about thirty miles away and has been serving retirement communities like Apple Valley for the past thirty-five years. It is not only a local provider of these services, but is actually a well-known leader in the development and management of retirement communities. HCS is responsible for planning, developing, and managing more than eighty retirement communities throughout the United States that are similar to Apple Valley.

Foodservice Department

The foodservice department's main responsibility is to provide meal service for independent residents (those living in townhouses and condominiums) and to residents of the on-site care facility. Currently, three meals per day are provided to

291

Apple Valley Retirement Community
Organization Chart

Apple Valley Retirement Community Organization Chart

- AVRC Board of Directors
  - HCS Administrator Carol Burns
    - Medical Director
    - AVRC Advisory Council
    - HCS Operations
      - Director of Plant Operations
        - Maintenance/Grounds Staff
      - Accountant
      - Director of Housekeeping
        - Housekeeping/Laundry Staff
      - Activities Director
        - Activities Assistant/Laundry
      - Sales/Marketing
      - Assistance-in-Living
        - Assistance-in-Living Staff
    - Consulting Dietitian
    - Administrative Assistant
    - Receptionists Bus Drivers
    - Director of Food Service Joan Dixon
      - Cooks Dietary Aides Wait Staff
    - Director of Nursing
      - Nursing Staff

about forty people in the health care center, plus those experiencing temporary difficulties providing their own meals. Meals for independent residents are provided two nights during the week as well as Sunday noon. The foodservice department also is responsible for any on-site catering for individuals or large groups.

Foodservice Director and Managerial Duties

The foodservice director for the past three years has been **Joan Dixon,** who has fifteen years of experience running various types of operations. Most of her experience has been in healthcare foodservice operations. Before she was hired, the responsibility of providing foodservice was contracted with an off-site provider. When Joan was hired, she was required to develop the on-site foodservice department, including equipment and layout of the kitchen, development of job descriptions and specifications, hiring and training of personnel, and developing menus. She is under the supervision of **Carol Burns,** the administrator of HCS operations at Apple Valley.

Joan also is responsible for providing safe and healthy meal service to residents. She is responsible for maintaining the overall quality of service required by HCS, the residents' association, and the board of directors. Other supervisory functions expected of her include scheduling and supervising employees, managing special diets in cooperation with the dietitian and head nurse, and keeping employees up to date on company policies and changing job duties.

Foodservice Staff

The foodservice department consists of an assistant supervisor, a cook, a dietary aide, and wait staff. Men and women of various ages and abilities fill both full-time and part-time positions. Every employee, including department directors, has been given a handbook regarding all employment policies. The handbook contains policies for rule violations and a termination procedure to be followed in every department.

Dale Roberts is the assistant supervisor and full-time cook during the day shift. He is 25 years old and has worked in foodservice operations for the past five years. Dale is an extremely organized individual with a good command of food preparation techniques. He is well liked and respected by other employees in the department and is often the first person to whom employees take their problems.

Jane Brown, 30 years old, works full-time and is the main cook on the evening shift. Prior to her employment at Apple Valley, she worked for three years as a baker and cook. Jane's primary attribute is her attention to detail, as reflected in the appearance of her menu items and their attractive presentation on the plates. Jane has epilepsy as a result of a head injury and has had several small seizures, lasting one to two minutes, while on the job. These seizures are characterized by a period of unresponsiveness and memory loss. This memory loss occurs at other times as well, so she compensates for it by keeping notes on everything she does at work. For example, she keeps detailed records of recipe adjustments, serving diagrams, and the organization of menu item production.

Jill Stevens and **Chris James** hold the full-time dietary aide positions. Jill, 28 years old, has a two-year associate degree in foodservice from a local community college. Her work experiences have mostly been in quick-service restaurants and in retail. Jill is very efficient at performing her job duties. She has a firm grasp of tasks she performs, but she has a tendency to be inflexible and overreacts to major and minor changes in routine. She is a very timid individual and has trouble expressing her thoughts to others. Her self-image seems poor, as demonstrated by the fact that she often feels that her job is threatened by mistakes she makes.

Chris works directly alongside Jill. He has had various experiences in foodservice, most recently in a college dormitory kitchen as a cook. He is 45 years old and has a master's degree in elementary education and was employed as an elementary school teacher for several years. Chris is an extremely fastidious person who is always cleaning, often with disregard for his other job duties. The manner in which he communicates with others is often brusque and sarcastic, and he is often construed as being combative.

Marge Baxter

Marge Baxter is 37 years old and is employed in the foodservice department as a cook and dietary aide. She has worked at Apple Valley for a little over a year. Several years before, she was involved in an accident that left her vocal cords paralyzed. Through therapy and treatment, she is now able to talk somewhat, but she is difficult to understand unless one listens very carefully. Even though her ability to communicate orally, including answering the phone, has been affected, she has no physical disabilities that limit the performance of her job duties.

The only previous work experiences listed on her application form were baker and cook at a local restaurant. When she was hired, she desperately needed the job and seemed willing and able to do what was required. She started on a part-time basis but due to employee turnover, she moved quickly to full-time status. After four and a half months, she requested and was granted part-time status. She claimed that she was not happy working full-time and had other personal reasons as well. It seemed that she had just received a disability allowance from the government that required her to work only part-time.

The quality of Marge's work and her ability to perform her job duties shows some definite problems. These problems have occurred with regularity, which suggests a pattern of conduct rather than a string of chance incidents (see the observation sheet). Most problems, if not all, have occurred when she was scheduled as a cook rather than a dietary aide. These incidents, especially the tardiness and calling in sick, started to occur after she returned to part-time status.

OBSERVATION SHEET

Observations and Incidents of Marge's Behavior

Basic Skills

Organization and Time Management

Marge has trouble preparing menu items so they are finished and ready to serve at the appropriate time. If she is having trouble, she rarely asks for help and proceeds to try and finish the work herself, which often results in poor-quality products (appearance is unattractive, and food temperatures are not what they are supposed to be).

Attention to Detail

The visual appearance of Marge's menu items needs improvement. Her overall plate presentation is sloppy, and often she will use the wrong dinnerware for the menu item. She also has to work on the appearance of her side dishes, salads, and desserts. These tend to be portioned incorrectly and in a haphazard manner.

Food Preparation

Although Marge started with limited knowledge of basic food preparation, she still has trouble preparing certain menu items that she has prepared frequently. The department operates on a four-week menu cycle. All meals (breakfast, lunch, and dinner in a group) are served for four weeks and then repeated. The four-week cycle changes with the season of year.

Following Recipes

Marge is able to follow recipes given her. However, she often overcooks or undercooks foods when a recipe calls for a judgment for doneness to be made.

Portioning Food and Following Special Diets

Marge's portioning of menu items is inconsistent with what is recommended. She will usually give all residents the same size portion rather than the size required on their diet cards. Marge also has trouble providing special foods required for residents who have special diet requirements. These requirements are written down both on the diet card and on the cooks' production sheets (a list of foods to be prepared for the meal).

Safety

Marge does not appear to be flagrantly violating safety rules. She seems to have more accidents (mostly minor) than anyone else in the department. She filed a total of ten accident reports for the year she has been employed (no other foodservice employee has filed a report). One severe incident was when she almost cut the tip of a finger off while using her hand rather than the hand guard to hold a roast she was slicing.

Rule Infractions

Tardiness

Marge is tardy by five to ten minutes almost every time she works. The time she was an hour late she failed to call until fifteen minutes into her shift. However, she always shows up for her shifts.

Calling In Sick

When Marge calls in sick, she gives short notices (thirty minutes).

Following Directions of the Supervisor

Most times Marge follows the directions given her. One time when she became ill at work before the supervisor arrived, she left a note on Joan's desk rather than calling her or having someone else call Joan. When Joan arrived and asked her if she was still ill, Marge said she was. Joan called a replacement. When the replacement arrived, Marge said she was fine and refused to leave even after Joan told her to leave. Joan took her into the office and talked with her and she eventually left.

Misuse of Equipment

Marge often ignores the maintenance and cleaning of equipment she uses. For example, she does not fill the steam table with enough water to complete meal service. On one occasion, the steam table boiled dry.

Reactions to Marge's performance have come not only from Joan but from other employees in the department, nursing staff, and residents. The other foodservice employees feel sorry for her and her personal situation, but they have lost sympathy for her mistakes on the job. They don't think Marge is putting forth the quality of work expected and is not being disciplined. Consequently, Marge's lack of quality performance is making the department look bad. Some employees have expressed their concerns to Joan directly with little or no apparent effect.

Dale also has received comments concerning her performance. He has taken them to Joan, and he sees little impact from those discussions. Each time Marge commits a rule infraction or makes a mistake on the job, Joan reprimands her. This occurs as soon as possible or in a conference at a later time. In addition, Joan places a written report of each incident in Marge's personnel file. Even though Joan is reprimanding Marge, other employees feel that Marge is allowed to continue her behavior.

Some residents have been given the wrong foods in the wrong amounts because Marge ignored their diet cards. Because the nursing staff is responsible for the health and well-being of residents, the head nurse has reported these incidents to Joan when they occur.

Finally, residents also have complained to Joan about food quality when Marge cooks. These complaints center on the way the food is prepared. Residents have told Joan that the food is cold, overly soggy, or too dry, and is often just plain inedible.

Joan's Expectations and Philosophy

When Joan hired Marge, she expected her to be able to perform according to the job description, just as anyone else in these positions would be required to do. Though the incidents in her file suggest that she does not have a good understanding as to what these expectations are, Joan insists that Marge is still expected to perform them.

Even though Marge listed only one previous job on her application form, Joan hired her for several reasons. The main reason is due to Joan's philosophy, developed over the years through her work as a healthcare foodservice supervisor. Joan believes that due to the low-paying, routine, repetitive, noncareer-oriented nature of the jobs, it is difficult to find individuals to perform them. Often this means hiring less skilled and disabled workers rather than those with more education and skills. This tends to reduce the rate of turnover and conflict with job expectations.

Joan also hired Marge because of her availability. She was having difficulties filling vacancies on her staff, which surprised her due to the reputation of Apple Valley and the fact that it is located in a college town. When Marge approached Joan for a job, Joan had been looking to fill the position for three weeks, and Marge was the only one who had applied. After interviewing her, Joan felt that she seemed to have enough basic skills that she could be trained to perform the tasks required for the position.

To maintain the quality of service required by Apple Valley, especially HCS, Joan's supervisory role is very important. She is aware of the employee handbook that states all policies. However, Joan is under the impression that the policy regarding rule violations and termination is meant as more of a guideline because it is rarely used, if at all, by other department supervisors. Joan also feels that there are so few incidents that would require its use, it seems unnecessary to enforce it. Instead she has decided to follow a plan of her own that involves maintaining a file on each employee within her department. The information in these files is used during employee evaluations. However, Joan has no formalized plan as to what she should do when an employee, such as Marge, accumulates a large number of these incidents at work.

Joan believes that Marge's situation is a particularly perplexing one, even though to others it might not appear this way. On the one hand, she feels that she must remove Marge from her job to maintain the required level of quality and desired performance. Yet she also feels that due to Marge's personal situation she should continue to work at retaining her.

Discussion Questions

1. What are some common management pitfalls into which Joan may have fallen? Describe them in relation to this case.
2. Evaluate Joan's employment philosophy. Is it appropriate? Why or why not?
3. Consider the employee handbook's rule violation and termination policy. Should Joan use this policy? Why or why not? (Take into consideration the risks and opportunities involved.)
4. If you were an employee in the foodservice department, would you consider expressing your concerns about Marge to Carol? Why or why not?
   If you were Carol and an employee came to you with his or her concerns, explain what you would do.
5. There are definite problems that can occur when hiring unqualified people. What are these problems? Relate these problems to this case. What examples are given in this case to show they have occurred?
6. How important is it for Joan to know about Marge's previous work experience? Explain.
7. If you were Joan, what kinds of questions would you ask Marge in order to obtain information about her previous work experience? (Consider the fact that this information is not complete on Marge's application form.)

Broadview Medical Center

Broadview Medical Center is a 180-bed hospital that provides medical and surgical services within a large metropolitan area. Occupancy has averaged between 130 and 140 in-house patients for the last six months. The foodservice budget is slightly less than 1 million dollars. In addition to patient meals, the foodservice department prepares food Monday through Friday for 200 Meals on Wheels recipients and five to six staff caterings. Approximately 350 meals are served to employees and visitors in the cafeteria. The drop-in employee meals during the weekend are compensated for with more visitor meals.

For the last three years, a college student who is majoring in dietetics or foodservice management has been employed on a part-time basis. Depending on the student, he or she may be given supervisory responsibilities.

The Staff

Julia Strasburg has been employed as the foodservice director in a 100-bed hospital for the past nine years (see the Cloudy Cafeteria organization chart). She has a master's degree in human nutrition. The cafeteria and kitchen are managed and run by a small staff of employees ranging from the foodservice director to a handful of mentally challenged hourly employees.

Julia has two daughters; the younger one has a physical disability as a result of a car accident. Because Julia understands the challenges her daughter faces every day, she strives to provide employment for individuals with disabilities.

Julia uses a participatory management style with her staff, which consists of two full-time and two part-time dietitians, ten full-time and fifteen part-time cafeteria/kitchen workers, and two full-time and four part-time diet clerks. Julia

Cloudy Cafeteria Organization Chart

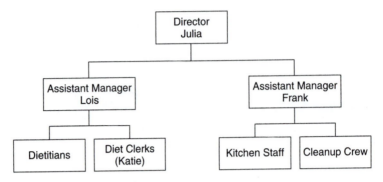

usually works the 8:00 A.M. to 5:00 P.M. shift and rarely stays late. She also avoids working on weekends. When she is absent, managerial duties are carried out by Frank.

Frank Romero, the assistant manager, is an autocratic leader who has been employed by the hospital for ten years. Because Frank shows favoritism and tends to micromanage employees in his charge, he is not very well accepted. Frank is perceived as being insecure and has a tendency to criticize anyone whom he considers a threat to his job. This criticism contributes extensively to the high turnover rate among the kitchen staff.

Long-term employees typically are those with only basic mental capabilities, resulting in a high percentage (40 percent) of employees who are mentally challenged. Frank detests dealing with these employees and manages to disappear soon after Julia leaves the office. When Frank is not available, he assigns the managerial duties to either a diet clerk or the evening shift cook, whomever he considers the most qualified person on duty. He knows that Julia will always back him if there is a conflict between an employee and himself.

Frank's management consists of some strict rules and procedures for maintaining order and a high level of productivity in the kitchen operation. Due to this high productivity, Frank is viewed by Julia as her right-hand man. Because operating costs are kept low, Julia receives a bonus every year. She relies on the bonus for her family's vacation each year.

Lois Nyland is the assistant manager in the dietitian's office. Her duties include management of the dietitians and diet clerks. She also procures all food items and kitchen supplies within the foodservice department. She uses a passive management style and is rarely seen enforcing rules. Lois has developed this style of management because most of her employees are self-motivated and rarely need her guidance. As a result, she hardly ever converses with them. Lois and Julia do not get along, and even though their offices are next to each other, they never communicate. Their communication is done via written messages to each other.

Katie Gould is a full-time college student majoring in foodservice management at the local university. She has worked in the foodservice department for the past three years. She is a part-time diet clerk who is fourth in line behind Julia, Frank, and Lois. Katie is well accepted among the kitchen staff and works well with the dietitians. She works the evening shift and rarely sees her supervisor, Lois, who works the early morning shift. This arrangement makes it hard for Katie to get feedback from Lois, and creates tension when Katie receives conflicting instructions from Frank.

Frank often tells Katie what to do and how to do it, which differs from the training Lois provided when Katie began her job. When this happens, Katie leaves notes for Lois but never receives any responses. Twice when Katie e-mailed Lois that she never received a response to her latest message asking for input to a recent request by Frank, Lois responded that she never received the message. Only Katie, Frank, and Julia have a key to Lois's office.

Other times, Frank asks Katie to perform certain duties that are not in her job description. Although Katie is agreeable to doing the task, she points out the discrepancy between his request and the job description. Frank goes into his office, changes the computer-generated job description, and brings it to Katie with the task listed.

Lois is responsible for Katie's performance appraisal. However, Lois has never met with Katie to discuss her performance. Usually, the appraisals are very positive, but Katie continues to be surprised when Lois leaves the completed form for Katie with a note asking her to review the evaluation. If Katie agrees with the evaluation, she is asked to sign the form and leave it on Lois's desk.

Katie also has personal experience dealing with people with special needs because her best friend recently suffered severe brain damage as a result of a skiing accident. Katie takes great pride in helping employees who are challenged and demonstrates inexhaustible patience with them.

Katie always feels a little uneasy working around Frank, whose behavior borders on sexual harassment. Frank has made comments about how well her body fills out the scrubs she often wears. However, it is hard to find a job that fits so well with her college schedule and pays her a sufficient wage, so she chooses to ignore Frank. Katie often thinks that Frank feels threatened by her intelligence, and she becomes exasperated when Frank treats her unfairly. Fortunately, Katie rarely has to deal with him because Frank normally vanishes shortly after Julia leaves.

Bob Fitzpatrick works the afternoon or evening shift in the dish and supply rooms. He has been employed by the hospital for five years. Bob is a friendly, simple man with limited cognitive abilities. He is a hard worker and makes few mistakes in his job. Bob is able to function at his job with a little prompting from his co-workers. Even though Bob has limited abilities, he has never been diagnosed with a mental disability. However, in the past few months he is having an increasingly harder time remembering how to do his job. Frank has stated openly that he does not care to work with Bob.

Hourly Employees

Even though employees who are mentally challenged require special training or extra supervision, Julia has spent a lot of time working with these employees, helping them fit into the workforce and perform at an acceptable level. Hiring individuals with disabilities helps maintain good public relations with the community. However, simple problems such as not being able to find the cart they used to haul supplies can prevent them from accomplishing the task of restocking supplies.

Frank is frustrated by this behavior and does not enjoy working with employees who have mental challenges. He feels that they ask too many questions, and he doubts their abilities to perform their job responsibilities. Most of these employees hide from Frank because he is so disrespectful of them. Katie, in particular, finds this mistreatment very offensive, which has resulted in disputes with Frank. In the past two years, six employees with disabilities have quit working in the foodservice department because of Frank's treatment.

Julia is concerned about the high turnover, but she has never confronted Frank about it. Employees have started to question Julia's integrity because she is so oblivious to what is happening in the department. Julia always has supported Frank when employees have complained about him. As a result, employee morale and productivity have started to decline.

The Incident

Katie was walking from the parking lot toward the front doors of the hospital ready to begin another evening shift. As she approached the entrance, she saw Bob running out the door in the direction of his truck. She thought to herself, "I wonder what he is doing? Should he be leaving this early? I hope there isn't an emergency."

As the power doors slid opened, she could see a dense white fog spreading across the lobby. Katie cautiously entered the lobby. Her eyes instantly started watering and burning from the intense fog. She could feel her face turn red, and she began to sweat. Her skin burned, and the acid odor took her breath away. People were running past Katie toward the sliding doors she had just entered.

Out of the fog, Katie saw a figure approaching her, and she heard a voice call out, "Katie, I'm glad you are here. Come with me."

Jan Tusmo, a dietitian, seized Katie's hand and started pulling her toward the stairway to the basement, where the kitchen was located. Katie wasn't sure who was guiding her through the dense fog. The fog in the stairway was much worse than the lobby. It became thicker the farther they went down the stairs. When they reached the side entrance to the kitchen, the door to the dish room was wide open, and no one was in sight.

Katie surveyed the room and saw some empty bottles lying on the floor. One was a bottle of CLR (calcium and lime remover), and the other bottle was industrial-strength chlorine, which the hospital used as the sanitizer in the dish machine.

A maintenance employee approached Katie and asked who was in charge. In her mind, Katie started down the chain of command. She realized that with Julia, Frank, and Lois gone, she was the one in charge.

Katie was surveying the situation when it hit her. It was a chlorine gas cloud! She remembered a warning from her chemistry instructor that excessive exposure to chlorine gas fumes could be fatal. All the kitchen staff were currently in the emergency room after becoming sick from the fumes. To make matters worse, the dish room was only fifteen feet from the six elevator shafts and two stairways connecting the basement to the rest of the hospital. Both elevators and stairways had negative air pressure, which meant the fog was transferring through the shafts to the patient floors. The phone was ringing off the hook—patients were getting sick from the fumes, and no one was sure what should be done.

Katie's first responsibility was to call Frank, who did not appear to be on the premises. After repeated attempts to contact him, Katie gave up and tried to contact Julia. The phone rang and rang at Julia's home but Katie couldn't reach her either. This meant only one thing: Katie had no other option but to take charge.

Katie called security and instructed them to open all doors to the outside. While she was trying to contact other managers, a maintenance employee with a gas mask entered the dish room to find the source of the chlorine gas cloud. He discovered that the sink was full of chemicals and the drain was plugged. He began frantically trying to free the drain so he could dilute the chemicals with water. It took almost forty-five minutes before the maintenance employee could free the drain and dilute the chemicals to safe levels.

With all the commotion in the kitchen, Katie didn't realize how much time had elapsed. She realized she had only thirty minutes to prepare dinner for 100 patients and 150 staff members because most kitchen staff and servers were sick in the emergency room. Katie, Jan, and one server were the only employees left to tackle this challenging situation. Fortunately, a cook had covered the entrées and placed them in the airtight steam ovens to prevent them from becoming contaminated. The three employees hurried to prepare side dishes to complement the dinner selection.

Eventually Katie learned that Bob had mixed the chemicals that created the gas cloud. Apparently he had been making a sanitizing solution, and when he discovered that he had put too much bleach in the sink, he drained the bleach to refill it to the proper level. When he realized the sink was clogged, he poured CLR into the sink to unstop it. Instead of using a small amount, however, he used a gallon of CLR, which created the chlorine gas cloud.

As Katie reviewed the events of the day, she realized her degree of exhaustion. She had successfully determined the cause of the gas cloud, kept patient exposure to a minimum, handled the service of food, accounted for sick and missing employees, and dealt with complaints from the first four floors of the hospital.

Discussion Questions

1. Identify the problems in this case. Justify your response.
2. Who is responsible for the high employee turnover? Support your answer.
3. How should Katie have handled the sexual harassment? Why?
4. Who should have been notified about the sexual harassment incident in the beginning? Why?
5. What should she do about the notes that she leaves Lois and Lois says she never gets? Why?
6. What is the first thing Katie should have done when she saw people running from the building and discovered the intense fog? Explain.
7. Should Katie have been the one to take charge? Why or why not?
8. Were the emergency procedures adequate? Why or why not? What would you consider to be the most appropriate procedures to follow? Justify.
9. How could this incident have been prevented? Support your response. What measures can be taken to prevent a recurrence? Explain why your alternatives would be the best.
10. Should Julia have been more instrumental in the prevention of this incident? How?
11. Should disciplinary action be taken with Bob for his actions in the dish room? If so, explain your answer. If not, why?
12. Should employees with limited cognitive abilities be given responsibilities that involve harmful chemicals? Why or why not?

Epilogue

Later that evening, after the gas cloud had dissipated, Bob returned to work. He claimed to have gone on break, and when he returned the gas was so overwhelming that he began to feel sick. He thought it best to go home for a while and come back after meal service to clean the dishes. Katie thought Bob's behavior was very strange when he returned to work.

A few months later, Bob was diagnosed with type 2 diabetes. After he received education on how to manage his diabetes with diet and exercise, Bob's quality of work improved greatly.

A few months after that, Katie graduated from college and quit her job. When she turned in her resignation to Lois, she included copies of all the job descriptions that she had been given by Frank. She also asked for a one-on-one exit interview with Lois, but she was told there was no time. She received a ten-page exit interview form to be completed and returned to Julia within two weeks of leaving the job. Katie looked at it, thought a moment, and threw it away.

In the four months that followed, the next three people hired to replace Katie left because they could not get along with Frank. Julia has not made any changes in the management style used in the cafeteria. Frank has not changed his style of management either. He continues to be hard on the people with whom he does not wish to work, and he refuses to change. The employee morale has dwindled to just an occasional smile from time to time. Most employees don't care about their jobs, and the food quality reflects their lack of motivation.

Discussion Questions

1. Should Julia make any changes in the management system used in the cafeteria? If so, explain what changes should be made. How should she implement these changes? If not, explain your reasoning.

2. What should hospital management do to help people who must deal with medical problems (such as diabetes) while working in the facility? Justify your response. What strategies should they use? Why?

3. Why do you think Katie was not given a one-on-one exit interview? Why do you think she did not complete the exit interview form? If you were Katie, would you have completed the form? Why or why not?

4. If you were Julia, would you be concerned when Katie did not return the exit interview form? Why or why not? Why do you think Julia never contacted Katie about the form? Should there be a record of resignations and receiving the exit forms? Why or why not?

City Medical Center Food Service

Liz smiled as she read the hospital newsletter about City Medical Center (CMC) being named employer of the year by the county chapter of Arc (Association of Retarded Citizens). A year ago when Alice, a high school student with mental disabilities, had interviewed for a volunteer position, Liz never imagined that this would be the result.

Background

CMC is a 200-bed, city-owned medical center. **Liz Trueblood** has been a manager in the foodservice (FS) department for more than thirteen years. The FS department employs more than seventy people, with sixteen full-timers and the rest part-time employees. The part-time staff includes working moms, college and high school students, people with mental disabilities, and semi-retired persons. Some employees are from foreign countries. In the past, high school students with mental disabilities interviewed and volunteered in FS to get experience. They wiped tables and assisted the salad prep person.

Alice Wyant was a 21-year-old high school student when her teacher brought her to interview. Liz's first impression of Alice was, "She's a young Missy!" **Missy Kongland** was a 49-year-old woman with a mental disability who had worked at CMC for twenty years.

Alice was physically strong and appeared very capable of pushing the heavy carts to and from floors, a job that could use Alice. She seemed good-natured but quiet during the interview, and her teacher helped her answer questions. She was difficult to understand. She was neatly dressed and well groomed.

During the interview, Liz decided to show Alice and her teacher the basics of the cart job. "We may as well train her on something truly useful rather than have her wipe tables," Liz thought to herself. Fortunately, Alice could identify numbers, even though she could not read. After showing them basic job tasks, Liz offered Alice the opportunity to learn the job as part of her schooling. Alice shook her head yes with her teacher's approval.

Alice on the Job

Liz introduced Alice to the unit secretaries in each patient unit on her first day. Liz explained that Alice, a volunteer from high school, would be helping **Jane De-Witt,** one of the cart people. Alice smiled and said "Hi." Liz told the secretaries to call if they had any concerns or problems and asked them to keep an eye on Alice. Liz introduced Alice to the FS workers, including two employees with mental disabilities. Several employees in the department had children or siblings with mental disabilities.

For each meal, eleven patient carts are delivered to the floors. The cart person delivers a cart to each unit, and nurses deliver the tray to the patient and remove it when the patient has finished the meal. On some floors, nurses place the tray in a pass-through compartment, cubicles, by each patient's room. The cart person pushes the cart through the hall, picking up the trays from each cubicle. On other floors the nurses return the tray to the cart.

Alice volunteered two hours a day with the assistance of her teacher, **Mrs. Barton,** who was committed to helping Alice become independent. Mrs. Barton had the expertise and tools for training people with mental disabilities. She noted that FS employees were very friendly and accepting of Alice. Liz appreciated the conversations she had with Mrs. Barton as they discussed Alice's progress and how they would work together to improve her performance. At first, Alice followed Jane, and then Alice pushed the carts and Jane followed. When Mrs. Barton thought Alice was ready, they did certain units by themselves. Mrs. Barton made flashcards to help Alice find the units. She also insisted that Alice push, rather than pull, the carts to avoid injury.

Jane liked having Alice because it was less work for her; pushing the carts was physically fatiguing. Alice's cheerfulness and good nature also made her popular with the employees in FS. Two unit secretaries, **Peggy Shekhar** and **Pam Lindeen,** became Alice's friends and she looked forward to seeing them.

During the semester, Alice continued to improve and worked with the other cart people as well. These four workers would go with Alice when Mrs. Barton was absent. Sometimes these employees would "help" Alice by picking up a cart for her or going with her to the cubicles. This change in procedure confused Alice. Also, they would not correct Alice when she pulled rather than pushed the carts. Liz made a sign explaining these concerns. Liz also explained the sign to each cart person and answered their questions. However, Liz would still discover the employees "helping" Alice.

Mrs. Barton and Alice's parents noted Alice's positive experience. They hoped that Alice could continue to work there. Liz thought it might happen if Alice continued to improve and there was money for her pay. They agreed to have Alice continue to volunteer because the job provided a stable routine for her. Her parents assured Liz that if Alice needed a job coach they would obtain one.

Liz was glad that things seemed to be working out and she sent a memo to the FS director, **Mike Weinstein** (see memo #1). Mike responded that as long as FS was not adding hours, Alice could continue. When Liz checked with **Karen Ritter,** the other daytime manager, Karen replied, "As long as it doesn't take any of my time."

After arrangements were made to have Alice continue volunteering, Liz took a vacation. When she returned, she realized there were some problems developing with "the Alice project." Because Alice was no longer in school, her aide was no longer available. She noticed that the regular cart people were not able to prompt and direct Alice effectively. Liz contacted Alice's parents in June asking for a job coach to be assigned to Alice, but said it was not urgent.

Memo #1

May 10

Alice is graduating at the end of May. I propose the following plan in order to help her obtain future employment at CMC.

Alice would come in at 7:30 a.m. M–F and volunteer on carts. She would be learning how to deliver the carts and the rest of the morning cart job. She would then eat lunch and leave at 11:30 a.m. to attend her afternoon program. Mrs. Barton (the teacher's aide) said that realistically three and half hours a day is all Alice could do right now. After Alice has learned the complete morning cart job, we could put her on payroll and see how we could fit her into the schedule, including weekends and evenings. The complication here is that once Alice is on payroll in FS, she can no longer volunteer in FS (hospital policy prohibits this). I have contacted Beth in linen services about having Alice volunteer in laundry when Alice is not scheduled in FS. Beth said that would work out for them. This way we can provide Alice with some paid hours and a routine, and help ensure that she will be available to CMC.

I need to let Alice's parents know ASAP.

Thanks,
Liz

The Problems

Things seemed to be going along well until July 19. Liz received a copy of a memo sent to Mike from **Miriam O'Dell,** the director of a unit detailing several concerns about Alice (see memo #2). Later that same day, Mike forwarded another memo. This one was from the supervisor of housekeeping, who said that he had received numerous calls from patient floors about spills by the cubicles that needed to be cleaned. The supervisor asked FS to work with this person to reduce the number of spills. Mike included a note with this memo stating, "I assume this is about Alice. Can you please talk to her?"

Liz wondered if the nurses were uncomfortable with having Alice on the floor without Mrs. Barton. She also wondered if Alice was a convenient scapegoat for the spills.

Liz decided to address the spill issue first. She talked to the housekeeping supervisor and asked to be kept posted on spills. She then worked at getting a job coach, which was now very urgent. A job coach was promised by July 24. Liz e-mailed Mike to let him know what she had done about the spill issue and personally delivered the memo in person on July 21 to each unit supervisor (see memo #3).

Memo #2

July 19

Mike,

Something occurred to me today. You know that young lady who picks up and delivers trays to our unit who has the cognitive limitations and appears to be a volunteer. I don't mean to discriminate but a number of red flags occurred to me today. In the past we have had a number of patients elope (escape) from the unit when nonstaff held the door for them. Does this young lady have the cognitive ability to direct them to the nurse's station? What if she was assaulted up here; would she have the ability to protect herself or initiate a response? Has she been informed of the safety risks of coming to and from this particular unit, and if so, does she have the cognitive ability to weigh her options related to this experience? Now, Lord forbid that anything would happen, but there might be some serious liability questions if she were injured up here and she was not informed of the risks and/or capable of making a conscious decision not to put herself in that risk. She has done a great job. The only problem we have had is trying to teach her that she does not need to ring the bell multiple times to have us release the door lock mechanism to allow her to exit. Appreciate your thoughts on this.

Miriam

Memo #3

July 21

Unit Supervisors:

Alice is a volunteer who has been doing the cart job M–F mornings. We hope that Alice's performance will improve to the point that CMC can hire her to do this job part-time. A job coach from an agency outside CMC will be coming beginning the week of July 24 to assist in working toward the goal of getting Alice's work performance to the desired level. I would really appreciate any observations you have concerning Alice's performance. Would you please call me at Ext. 1234 and report if she is spilling trays, going into patient rooms, running into the wall, or interfering with patient care in any way? I hope this will not be too taxing for you. Let me know if you are unable to do this, and I will try to obtain this information another way. Alice has done a good job but needs to improve, and with your assistance and that of the job coach I hope CMC will gain a valuable employee.

Thank you very much for your cooperation,
Liz

Liz gave a copy of the memo to Peggy and Pam and asked them how they thought Alice was doing. Both agreed that Alice needed some help, but they had not seen her spilling trays. Liz was thankful that Peggy and Pam liked and helped Alice.

Liz then spoke with **Carla Ropenski,** the employee who checked trays and loaded them into carts. She thought Alice was doing fine but thought that getting a job coach was a good idea. Carla had been terrific about prompting Alice, and Carla saw Alice's potential. Liz knew that Alice really liked Carla.

Next, Liz called **Dee Foley,** the secretary to the vice president of nursing, who was a frequent customer of FS's catering. Liz explained that Alice would soon have a job coach. Liz asked Dee to inform the VP before he heard second-hand. Dee thought that employing Alice was a pretty cool idea, and she promised to pass the information on to the VP. Liz hoped she had reassured everyone she needed to about Alice.

Next, Liz called Miriam and arranged a meeting with her because Liz thought she had valid concerns. Liz was concerned that there might be an unconscious bias against a person with a mental disability. Her simple solution was to have the staff do some of Alice's work.

Liz knew the staff would not be enthused about the idea. In the meeting, Liz listened to Miriam and reminded her that CMC was committed to making reasonable changes to accommodate Alice's disability. Also, Liz pointed out that FS routinely employed high school students to do the cart job on evenings and weekends, and they might not display good judgment either. Liz then suggested her solution, which Miriam liked but which she had some concerns about. The meeting ended without a decision being made. Everyone would meet the next week and try to figure out what to do. When Liz called about the concerns, she found there weren't any.

A New Job Coach

Liz was glad to see **Gloria Molnar,** the job coach, on July 24 because she was pretty stressed out about "the Alice project." Liz introduced Gloria to Alice, and Gloria immediately followed Alice. Later, Liz provided Gloria a copy of the work schedule and discussed what she had done about the previous week's problems. Liz felt better and hopeful just talking to Gloria.

Gloria and Alice hit it off immediately. Every morning Alice asked, "Is my boss coming today?" Gloria observed other issues, such as Alice interrupting doctors working in front of the cubicle. Gloria came up with a cart person checklist to address these issues. Gloria or the regular cart person would record Alice's performance on the chart. The checklist made it easier for the regulars to remind Alice about behaviors she needed to display. The problem of spills never recurred, and Liz never received any calls expressing concerns about Alice's performance.

Alice continued to improve. In September, Gloria and Liz developed a plan to help Alice be on the payroll by December 1 (see memo #4). Alice was meeting the goals, and Liz kept the regular cart people informed of changes. Liz posted Alice's plan for the regulars to read.

A couple of the regular cart people told Liz they were worried that Alice might take some of their hours. Although Liz was not sure how it would all work, she reassured them that would not happen per CMC's policies. This satisfied most employees; however, those with attendance problems continued to express concern. Overall, it seemed that most FS employees enjoyed Alice and were proud of her accomplishments.

As December approached, Alice was meeting the performance standards, so Liz told Alice she would be paid to do her job. Alice was not very impressed until Liz told her she would get a name badge similar to those of her co-workers. That was very important to Alice, and she asked Liz every day about getting her name badge.

When Alice went on payroll, Liz arranged a celebration. She invited the vice president to whom Mike reported, and he shook Alice's hand and welcomed her. Alice acted shy but perked up when Liz gave her a name badge. Liz thanked all the employees and told them they should feel a sense of accomplishment because without all their efforts, Alice never would have grown to this point. Her employee friends responded positively when Alice showed her new badge.

Memo #4

Alice's Plan
September 27

Long-Term View: Alice will work at CMC in a paid position by December 1.

Objective 1: Alice will independently deliver and pick up food carts by December 1.

Date	Steps
10/13	Delivers carts independently to all floors using color-coded cards provided by job coach.
10/27	Picks up carts, independently, on floors 1–3 and returns them to the kitchen.
11/7	Picks up trays independently from cubicles on floor 4, puts them in carts, and returns them to the kitchen.
11/14	Picks up trays independently from cubicles on floor 5, puts them in carts, and returns them to the kitchen.
11/28	Picks up trays independently from cubicles on floor 6, puts them in carts, and returns them to the kitchen.
12/1	Completes all tasks independently.

Five months later, things were going well. Gloria has reduced her visits to once every week or two. Through attrition, Alice is scheduled Monday through Friday on carts without affecting anyone's hours. Alice did not miss a single day of work during the harsh winter.

Liz knew that some employees thought Alice was her favorite. Liz would think, "Yes, and you too could be a favorite if you showed up for work every day."

Discussion Questions

1. Workers in FS expressed concerns about the changes Liz made to help Alice. Were their concerns valid? Explain. How should Liz have handled those concerns? Explain.
2. What would you need to do if you were considering hiring a person with a mental disability? What resources would you want available? Why?
3. What expectations does a manager have for staff to help co-workers who are different from them? How can you help employees work with people who are different from them? Describe.

4. What was happening at CMC that helped Alice become successful? How crucial were these actions in Alice's becoming successful? Explain.

5. Politics can be defined as the complex relations between people in a society. Do politics play a role in the work environment? Explain. Give examples on how Liz worked the politics of CMC. How could she have improved her interaction with others? Explain.

Culver Community Medical Center

Kelly is wondering whether she made a mistake in accepting the dietary services director position at Culver Community Medical Center (CCMC). After three weeks on the job, there seemed to be many more problems than were revealed during the interviews. Kelly wonders whether the large increase in pay caused a halo effect in her decision to take the job. Was Kelly going to be able to meet the many department challenges? How is Kelly going to handle Carol O'Shea's requests?

Background

Kelly Wickson has a degree in HRIM and had been the foodservice director at a 150-bed hospital for the past three years. When she was offered the position as dietary services director of CCMC, a 500-bed American Hospital Association–accredited medical center, it seemed like a nice stepping stone. The department is divided into three major areas—cafeteria services, patient nutritional services, and catering services—providing Kelly with great experiences in supervising a more extensive operation.

CCMC is one of three privately owned medical centers. Each of the facilities contains an average of 500 acute hospital beds. The three medical centers were founded during the early 1950s by a physician who now serves as CEO (chief executive officer) of the corporation. His management style has been that of a benevolent autocrat, with very little delegation of authority. Although the CEO employed a hospital administrator for each medical center, he continued to bypass each administrator, interacting directly with many department heads.

After two interviews with the hospital administrator and the human resources director, Kelly had a tour of the department. The starting salary, negotiated at $60,000 per year with the option for a review upon completion of the first ninety days of employment, was more than a 50 percent increase in pay. Further, Kelly was to be paid an additional $40 per hour plus expenses for any consultation services requested by the corporate offices.

Carol O'Shea, the director of social services of the CCMC, is the founding physician's sister. She initially was given the title of foodservice supervisor for two years prior to offering Kelly the director's position. During her time as food-service supervisor, she actually left the day-to-day operation of the department to one of the head cooks and a clinical dietitian. She had very little influence within the department except for the responsibility of selecting the food and supply vendors. She set up most of these vendors as sole-source accounts.

Two months before Kelly's first interview, the founder of the three medical centers died in his office at work. At the same time, the CCMC's administrator received a written warning from the county health department. County officials stated that if a qualified dietary services director was not employed full-time, the hospital would be placed on probation. Additionally, an inspection agency of the American Hospital Association would be notified of the deficiency.

After long deliberation, Kelly decided to accept the position and began work. However, Kelly was concerned that the hospital administrator and director of human resources had not identified any major problem areas, nor had they specified any long-range goals for the department. When they discovered that Kelly had been in the military for five years before attending college, they appeared more interested in sharing old military experiences than in discussing departmental goals.

On the Job

During Kelly's first week on the job, she needed to have a letter of correspondence typed to send to administration. Kelly discovered that no secretarial support had been provided to the dietary services department. Historically, the secretarial pool in medical records had provided any typing. In addition, during the initial department tour, Kelly had thought the two clinical diet offices were administrative offices. In reality, Carol had functioned from a large desk and file cabinet located in the main kitchen's production area.

The medical complex contains two major production and assembly areas for patient and cafeteria foodservices. One area supports 150 patients in one building, while another area located in a high-rise structure supports 350 patients. The areas are half a block from each other on opposite sides of the street. The 150-bed production area recently had been cleaned, repaired, and repainted following a food-borne illness outbreak. Although eighty elderly patients were affected, fortunately no one's life had been threatened. However, the reputation of the dietary services department had been damaged severely.

Each building contains a cafeteria. The larger, more modern 300-seat cafeteria in the high-rise has never been able to reach a breakeven point since it was opened three years ago due to a reputation for poor-quality food and very slow service. In contrast, the seventy-five-seat cafeteria in the 150-patient building has a longstanding reputation for its individualized service and high quality standards. The smaller cafeteria always has a long line of waiting customers during the hours of service, while there is rarely a line at the larger cafeteria. In fact, it is used at less than 50 percent capacity. With the exception of the salad and dessert bar, neither cafeteria offers any self-service stations. All foods and beverages are dispensed by cafeteria employees. A recent time-and-motion report stated that the cafeterias were 35 percent over standard staffing levels.

After two weeks as director, Kelly was informed that the inspection agency had scheduled an inspection of the hospital within three months. While checking the department policy and procedure manual, Kelly found only five pages of non-specific information that had been written in order for the department to pass a sanitation inspection by the county health department, and no departmental job descriptions. Information used by the human resources department included rather vague job specifications with no salary ranges listed for any position.

Kelly discovered that many production workers were extremely unhappy in their positions because they had not received a merit pay increase within the last three years. Upon investigating, Kelly also discovered that many supervisors had not received an evaluation during the same three-year period. Only those employees who complained to the human resources director (about 40 percent) had received any evaluations or merit increases within the last five years. All employees had been given the annual standard cost-of-living allowances (COLA).

The professional staff of CCMC is extremely active with their daily luncheon meetings catered by the dietary services department. Many of these luncheons are ordered and arranged for in telephone conversations from medical staffs' secretaries. There have been many complaints concerning late and missing catering deliveries. Improperly received foods and incorrectly set meeting rooms are frequent problems. The costs for all of these catered functions are being absorbed by the dietary services department's budget.

During an inspection of storage facilities, Kelly discovered that almost all foods are purchased from only one source. As a result, many close relationships have developed between vendors and some members of hospital management. Many Christmas gifts offered by the vendors have been accepted by their respective friends working within the hospital's management staff. For example, the department's source for fresh poultry products has been a longtime friend of Carol's. In fact, they eat lunch together every day. Carol always has been able to influence other department head purchasing decisions due to her relationship to CCMC's founder. Kelly estimated that the current food and supply costs are double the current wholesale rates. During the third week of work, Carol asked Kelly to have lunch in the cafeteria with her.

Discussion Questions

1. In your opinion, what are the five most important problems facing CCMC? How would you approach these problems? Why would you select these approaches?
2. If you were Kelly, what might you have done during the interviewing process to reduce the number of unforeseen problems? Why?
3. How might you increase the proper utilization of the larger, more modern cafeteria? Why do you think these suggestions would work?
4. Is there danger in sole-source purchasing agreements? Explain.
5. What policy might you have for accepting gifts and other perks from vendors? Why would this be important?
6. If you were Kelly and were aware of the problems at CCMC, would you have accepted the job? Explain.
7. If you were Kelly, what discussion would you have with Carol during your lunch meeting? Why?

Forest Lake Hospital Foodservice Department

Cathy Henn is the manager of the foodservice department at Forest Lake Hospital. She was appointed to her position six months ago. The hospital provides medical, surgical, and intensive-care services to 500,000 people from both rural and urban areas. The foodservice department produces about 1,400 meals per day, which includes feeding 220 patients, 400 Meals on Wheels recipients, staff, and visitors who frequent the hospital cafeteria. Department employees also produce special catering. The department operates a central tray service, and the cafeteria is completely self-service. The annual department budget is $1.9 million with expected $250,000 revenue from the cafeteria and special catering.

There are two managers, including Cathy; two foodservice supervisors; and thirty cooks and kitchen assistants who are responsible for seven-day-a-week meal production and service. The stability of the staff is an important feature as there is a shortage of experienced workers and supervisors in the local labor market.

Because of financial pressures, Cathy has been charged with increasing the catering service to bring in more dollars. She has advertised the foodservice department's services to various organizations, hoping to increase the number of customers for whom the department could cater. She has distributed information to all departments telling them about what foodservice offers and about the cafeteria's monthly theme day.

When a request for special catering is received, Cathy and the customer decide what food will be served. A worksheet is developed, and these instructions are given to the foodservice supervisors to be initiated. The increased workload resulting from the marketing effort is to be managed with existing staffing levels. Cathy hopes to make the department more efficient by maintaining present staffing costs and increasing the number of meals produced.

The increased workload will produce additional demands on the staff in two ways. First, they will have more work to do than they have had in the past; therefore, they must work more efficiently. Second, they are entering the commercial and competitive market, so it is extremely important that all food leaving the department consistently be of high standards and meet the customer's requirements.

The Problems

In the first three months of advertising the foodservice and its special catering services, the output in the department increased. However, when Cathy examined her fourth and fifth month meal figures, she noticed that the department output was starting to decrease. When Cathy investigated further to see what was causing the decrease in customers, she discovered many complaints about late arrival and inconsistent standards of the food that left the department for special catering functions. Cathy talked with her foodservice supervisors who were in charge of the daily meal production to determine why these problems were occurring.

Theresa McNally is one of two foodservice supervisors employed in the foodservice department. She has been with the department thirty-two years and has worked her way up from kitchen assistant to cook to foodservice supervisor. She has been a supervisor for ten years and has reached a ceiling in her career with the hospital. She has no motivation to participate in further training or to apply for any positions outside the hospital. Cathy is the sixth department manager with whom Theresa has had to work. All department managers have been younger than Theresa, did not have the experience in the department she has, and usually arrived to their new positions with a lot of new ideas. Cathy is no exception.

Theresa is a large and aggressive woman with an authoritarian management style. She can be insubordinate and manipulative, and often doesn't follow procedures. Because she could be difficult to handle, former managers often bypassed Theresa when issuing instructions or looking for information. Cathy did not. However, Theresa has an enormous base of knowledge about the department and always knows exactly what the staff is doing. When she is doing her job properly, she is an excellent foodservice supervisor.

Richard Burras, the other supervisor, has been employed in the department for five years. Previously, he operated his own contract foodservice business, but due to health problems he sold it and accepted the position at Forest Lake Hospital. Richard is an agreeable person who is very approachable and willing to do what is asked of him. He seems to have difficulty keeping track of everything that is happening in the kitchen, and at times he forgets important instructions. His problems are the result of poor time management. He can spend too long solving one problem that is done very well, but this leaves him no time for the rest of the work.

Neither Richard nor Theresa felt that the problems in the kitchen were their fault. Their arguments were that the cooks and kitchen assistants knew what standards were expected of them during production and service, and as supervisors they couldn't be everywhere at once keeping an eye on things. Another argument was that the delivery of the special catering is the responsibility of another department, and therefore beyond their control.

The Till

With the increased workload generated by advertising the cafeteria service, it has become necessary to extend the hours the cafeteria is open. The part-time cashier in the cafeteria needs to be relieved for her thirty-minute lunch break because she is working longer hours. Cathy decided that this could be a part of the foodservice supervisor's duties, and at the regular monthly meeting with the foodservice supervisors, she told them about the proposed change. Richard was quite happy to work at the till and felt it easily could be fitted into his duties, as it is at a time of the day when the kitchen is quieter. Theresa, however, refused to do the job. When pushed, she said she would leave if she had to work on the till. When Cathy asked her why she didn't want to do the job, she said it was for cultural reasons. Theresa is part of a religious group that is very shy and doesn't want to be in the limelight.

Cathy is beginning to wonder if the increased efficiency of the department due to the additional workload is worth the problems it is generating. However, she knows that for the department to survive the increasing financial restraints, it must become more efficient. Cathy knows she has to take responsibility to solve these problems.

Discussion Questions

1. Who is responsible for the problems with the special catering? Why? Should Richard and Theresa be concerned about the delivery of catering? Why or why not?
2. How would you improve Richard's performance? Theresa's performance? Why do you think these ideas will work?
3. Do you think regular performance appraisals of the supervisors would improve the situation for Cathy? Justify your response. What characteristics would identify an effective performance appraisal?
4. Describe how you would solve the problems with the special catering. Justify your response.
5. Would you insist that Theresa spend time on the till? Justify your answer. Do you consider cultural sensitivity to be a good excuse? Why or why not? Would it be fair to Richard to not require Theresa to work on the till? Explain.
6. Would empowering employees help in this case? Why or why not? If it would, how would you go about empowering them?
7. What standards should be in place to ensure that the customers' needs are met? How would you ensure that these standards are met?

Lake Regional Hospital

Betty has just received the vending revenue figures from July. Revenue has increased $3,000 from June, a 50 percent increase. She's wondering why this has happened and reflects about possible reasons for this increase. In reviewing costs, she notes that $420 of the increased revenue is from soft drink sales, probably due to hot weather. A 10 percent price increase in candy bars occurred in mid-July, accounting for $400 in increased revenue. What is causing the other $2180 increase? Everything else is stable.

Betty asks herself what other changes have been made that might affect the vending area. She reflects that even though she has been the foodservice director since April, several changes have been made. Then she remembers Ron, whom she fired on July 3. One of his duties as store person was collecting money from the vending machines.

Background

Lake Regional Hospital (LRH) is a 200-bed secondary-care hospital. It serves a population base of 100,000 people and is located in the Mideast. There are sixty physicians on staff. The church-affiliated hospital is classified as nonprofit. It offers a wide variety of services such as dialysis, skilled care, psychiatric treatment, a chemical dependency unit, and the usual services associated with an acute care hospital.

The foodservice department has fifty-nine employees (42 full-time equivalents, or FTEs). **Anne Moschins,** the previous director, was in that position for ten years. Although Anne had an authoritarian management style, the supervisors were very lax and did not follow through when given direction. Consequently, the department deteriorated and Anne was asked to leave.

Betty Smith, a registered dietitian, was hired recently. She has a background in foodservice management, consulting, and inspecting health care facilities. She has worked in government and the private sector. Betty has found that private, nonprofit facilities generally have less bureaucracy, are more responsive to patients and staff, and have a very supportive administration. She likes the idea of that work environment.

Betty has a participatory management style. However, she finds it difficult to delegate because many supervisors are nonfunctional and ineffective. Consequently, she is deluged with endless questions and complaints from the staff. One of her goals is to develop effective supervisors. Another goal is to improve purchasing and storage procedures.

The Situation

Betty has just learned that **Rita Bass,** the production supervisor and a twenty-year employee, was promoted to supervisor when the dermatitis on her hands would no longer allow her to be a cook. Previously, a dietitian had held the supervisor position. Betty has learned through the grapevine that many problems have been left untouched. The department's history for not being clean has gotten worse under Rita's supervision. There have never been standardized recipes. Policies and procedures are written but not followed.

One of Rita's responsibilities is to do the purchasing. She buys from all sales representatives because she doesn't want to hurt anyone's feelings. She says that she takes inventory; however, with the unorganized storage areas, it is evident that she likely orders without taking inventory. The result is shortages of some items and an oversupply of others.

A related problem to the storeroom's lack of organization is that it is very dirty. **Ron Ferreira,** the only male in the department, is responsible for cleaning the storeroom. Word is that the previous director hired him more than two years ago because she felt sorry for him. He had been fired from a fast-food chain. Further, current employees have indicated that he is a "ladies' man" and sees many part-time workers socially. Frequently, Ron is paged through the hospital-wide paging system because he does not answer his beeper. Many of the numbers given for him to return a call are not related to his work. Betty has received reports that Ron spends a lot of time sitting in the laundry area or in the ambulance garage. This has been difficult to document because Ron works independently, and his duties take him throughout the building.

Betty's secretary receives daily complaints because the vending machines are empty. Filling the machines is one of Ron's duties (see the job description, job specifications, and work schedule). The secretary also reports that Ron does not follow correct procedures when checking in food and supplies. He often signs for an order without checking for accuracy. Betty has documented that the storeroom is not locked, stock is not rotated, and the storeroom is dirty.

Job Description—Storeroom Person

Job Title: <u>Storeroom Person</u>   Dept <u>Services</u>   Job No. <u>　　　</u>

Promotion Information: To this job <u>　　　None　　　　　</u>

From this job <u>　　None　　　　　　　　　　　　　</u>

Job Description Information:

Responsibilities
Coordinates own work with those of production, patient tray line, cafeteria and vending areas. Maintains proper inventory of all stores through rotation of stock and notification of supervisory personnel of outages and overstocks. Under the direction of foodservice director, accepts or rejects shipments on the basis of specifications. Denies access to storeroom to all unauthorized personnel.

Supervision Received
Limited. Foodservice director/food production supervisor.

Guidance and/or Supervision Exercised
May guide trainees in learning process. No supervisory responsibilities.

Special Qualifications
Must have valid driver's license. Ability to communicate well with fellow workers, supervisors, and the public. Must demonstrate responsibility in handling large sums of money and supplies. Able to organize work without supervision. Able to read and write clearly and legibly.

Material and Equipment Used
Unpacking and shelving equipment. Occasionally required to pick up and deliver supplies in hospital vehicle.

Work Performed
Checks in all supplies. Unboxes and shelves all supplies in their respective storerooms. Cleans the departmental storerooms on a weekly basis or as needed. Rotates all inventory on a first-in, first-out basis. Fills requisition sheets, delivers the needed items, and stores them in the correct areas as directed. Maintains stock in the beverage machines. Maintains change in bill changers. Prepares cash deposits for vending machine revenue.

Rita, as Ron's supervisor, is responsible for completing his performance appraisals. Evaluations show that she usually gives everyone very good ratings. However, she has recorded Ron's performance problems on the appraisals and has started the disciplinary process with him.

Betty has given specific assignments to Rita concerning Ron. Rita is to collect vending money with Ron three days a week, but Rita does not do this. Rita is

Job Specifications—Storeroom Person

Job Title: Storeroom Person   Dept Services   Job No._____

Standard	Specification	Notes
Education	High school or equivalent.	
Ingenuity and Initiative	Requires considerable amount of initiative and ingenuity to isolate problems and solve them or refer to appropriate personnel.	
Physical Effort	Walking, bending, lifting, shelving shipments on a daily basis. Must be able to lift 100-pound sacks on occasion.	
Training and Experience	Former stockroom experience helpful.	
Working Conditions	Works in isolated environment, closed rooms, some poor ventilation.	
Job Hazards	Lifting heavy cases of food.	
Cooperation and Contact	Demonstrates ability to communicate accurately and pleasantly with fellow workers, supervisors and visitors.	
Access to Confidential Information	None	
Tools and Equipment	Shelving and stockroom equipment.	
Supplies and Valuables	Access to departmental supplies. Should deny access to unauthorized persons.	
Mental and Visual Demands	Able to keep legible records and fill requisition orders.	
Accuracy	Must keep accurate inventories.	
Responsibilities	Coordinates own work with those of production, patient tray line, cafeteria, and vending areas. Maintains proper inventory of all stores through rotation of stock and notification of supervisory personnel of outages and overstocks. Under the direction of foodservice director, accepts or rejects shipments on the basis of specs. Denies access to unauthorized personnel.	

Work Schedule—Storeroom Person

Monday
8:00 A.M.–9:00 A.M.: Pick up money from all vending machines.
Between 9:00 A.M.–12:00 P.M.: Truck A comes in.
Fill requisitions while waiting for Truck A.
After Truck A comes in, take all frozen vegetables, produce, and frozen bakery goods to kitchen and put away.
Unload boxes in storeroom. Make sure to rotate stock.
Mark the date on all meat and all boxes that aren't opened. Mark at the end of the box facing out.
Mark sugar, flour, noodles, cereal and canned goods opened.
Fill pop machines.

Tuesday
8:00 A.M.: Fill all pop machines. Don't fill the lobby machine until 4:00 P.M.
Fill requisitions.
By 10:00 A.M.: Do special items inventory and give to secretary.
Clean storerooms.

Wednesday
8:00 A.M.–9:00 A.M.: Pick up money from all vending machines.
9:00 A.M.: Fill pop machines.
Fill requisitions.
Clean storeroom.
11:00 A.M.: Receive coffee delivery.

Thursday
8:00 A.M.: Fill pop machines.
Fill requisitions.
Truck A comes in usually by 11:00 A.M.; repeat Monday procedures.
Fill requisitions.
Make out Truck B order and bring it to foodservice director's office. Lay it on the secretary's desk.
Fill lobby pop machine.

Friday
8:00 A.M.: Pick up money from all vending machines.
Fill requisitions.
Check Truck C in, put food away, and rotate stock.
Check Truck D in, put food away, mark dates on boxes, and rotate stock.
Check Truck E in, put food away, mark dates on boxes, and rotate stock.
Check Truck B in, put food away, and rotate stock.
Fill requisitions.
Fill pop machines.
Routinely check vending/change machines to see that they are properly functioning.
Clean storeroom shelves and dust cans.
Once a month, clean freezer in basement, wipe off shelves, scrub floor.
Vending machines: Change prices in machine as needed.
Check in other suppliers that don't come in weekly.

to work with Ron so he will clean the storeroom. When Betty inquires why the storeroom is still not clean, Rita responds with her usual, "I told him, but he doesn't listen."

Employees have told Betty that Rita is ineffective. However, when checking Rita's files, Betty has been unable to find any evidence of her poor performance as cook. The employees don't understand how Rita got promoted to supervisor, let alone is allowed to keep her job. Yet, the employees go to break with her and are generally nice to her face.

Betty recognized that Rita gets along well with others but is not assertive enough to be a supervisor. She offered Rita a position in the special functions area where Rita could use her interpersonal skills but would not be in a supervisory role. Rita agreed to the change even though it meant a decrease in pay of about $2,000 per year. Betty agreed that Rita's present salary would be frozen until the new rate reaches her present level. She is doing very well in her new position but needs assistance with organizational skills.

Until the production supervisor position is filled, Ron will report directly to Betty. In reviewing Ron's file, Betty found performance appraisals from the last eighteen months. Problems identified were as follows:

1. Is checking in items without the purchase order.
2. Frozen meat sits at room temperature too long.
3. Stock is not rotated.
4. Has unauthorized people in work area.
5. Is careless and leaves loose dollar bills in the soft drink machines.
6. Does not clean storeroom.
7. Leaves storeroom unlocked.

Ron's written response was, "I thought the conference went well, and I will try to improve my bad qualities."

In the file were the following written warnings:

8/21: Does not keep storeroom clean. Ron's response: "I will keep it clean."

11/7: Ron failed to put meat away when it came in. It sat out for three hours. Ron's response: I will not forget to put it away again."

5/19: Storeroom floor and cans were not clean. Jell-O was spilled and had not been cleaned up. Empty candy wrappers were on the shelves. Ron's response: "A cleaning schedule might help." Noted on the form was: "The next step is suspension."

Betty decided to hold a counseling session with Ron to review his job description with him. She specifically addressed cleaning, use of proper check-in procedures, and rotating stock. Betty knew that this could be a potentially volatile situation and asked another management employee to attend the conference.

The Final Incident

Six weeks later, the director, the secretary, and two dietitians took the year-end inventory. The following problems were found in the storeroom:

1. Stock was not rotated.
2. The floor in the freezer was filthy. Items were freezer burned.
3. The storeroom was very dirty—shelves, floors, and cans.
4. Like items were not stored together.

The next day Betty met with the human resources director about the seriousness of the violations. They discussed what problems there could be if Ron was terminated instead of suspended. Ron would probably file for unemployment compensation. However, there was support for termination. It was decided to terminate Ron because of misconduct.

During the termination meeting Ron's only response was, "I thought I'd get suspended, not fired."

Follow-Up

A few days later, Betty was notified that Ron had filed for unemployment. She learned that many unemployment cases are decided on how much money is in the hospital's state fund, not on the actual facts of a particular case. Unemployment was awarded to Ron. The human resources director made it clear to Betty that hearing officers generally rule for the former workers.

Betty decided to appeal the decision. There was nothing to lose at this point, and perhaps the monetary award would be reduced. In preparing for the hearing Betty found that she needed to prove misconduct. Poor work performance means that the worker did not have the ability to perform the job. Misconduct means that the worker had the ability but chose not to do the job. Unemployment compensation is awarded for poor work performance.

During the appeal hearing the judge asked Betty to describe what happened. She responded with the problems documented in the performance appraisals and written warnings. She also reviewed the problems found when inventory was taken. The judge also asked why this problem was allowed to go on for so long. Betty responded that she started in April and couldn't address what had happened prior to that time. The appeal was won, and Ron was directed to pay back the unemployment compensation that he had received.

Discussion Questions

1. Describe how you would conduct the conference when demoting Rita from being a supervisor to a special-function worker. Why would you use these

tactics? As manager, how would you work with her to accept the change? Explain. What would you do on an ongoing basis? Why do you think your ideas would work?

2. If you were Betty, how would you deal with what had gone on before your arrival as foodservice director? What problems do you think Betty should have discovered during the interview for the director's position? Justify your responses. Explain other ways she could have discovered major problems that existed before she decided to accept the position.

3. How would you investigate the source of the $2180 increase in revenue from June to July? Defend your plan.

4. Evaluate the job description. What changes would you make? Why? Evaluate the job specification. Would you make any changes? Why? Would you make any changes to the work schedule? Why or why not?

5. If you were Betty, what characteristics would you look for in the new foodservice production supervisor? Why are these important? What characteristics would you want in the new storeroom person? Why have you selected these?

6. The starting wage for the storeroom person is minimum. How do you find a competent person who will accept this wage? Defend your response.

Memorial Medical Center Foodservice Department

Recently **Rachel Hopkins** has been wondering more and more whether she should have taken the job as the foodservice department's human resources (HR) manager in a large university teaching/research hospital. Rachel was surprised when her director, **Jackie Lapar,** encouraged her to look at the opportunities the job provided. Jackie told Rachel she liked the way she worked with employees. After Jackie told Rachel she had faith in her ability to solve problems, Rachel decided she was up to the new challenge. Rachel had a couple of HR classes in college; other than that, she has had no formal HR training.

As director, Jackie had been handling all the HR issues. One thing she recognized was that when dealing with the variety of issues, there is no time for trial and error. She believed that Rachel was the person for the job. Rachel is very patient, a required attribute. Although there are times when Rachel finds it is very difficult to work with employees, she reminds herself to be nice and try to find options that work for both the department and employee.

Now Rachel is having second thoughts. She is glad that the incident with Clinton has been solved. Some days are just too long! She wonders what action Brenda will take after learning that she did not get the job for which she recently applied. **Brenda Garcia** is a full-time employee who is not doing the work described in her current job description. Further, she is a Filipina who believes that whenever she does not get what she wants, she has been discriminated against.

Rachel has been surprised at how many grievances have been filed on the basis of discrimination related to ethnicity, race, national origin, and age. Ever since she began working in the department, the importance of working effectively with a diverse work population has been stressed. Jackie has insisted that the management team understand the backgrounds from which the employees come. And Rachel's feeling is that Jackie believes they do a good job working with a diverse population.

Brenda's Complaint

Rachel wasn't kept in suspense about Brenda very long, as Jackie just informed her of a letter she received from the affirmative action (AA) compliance officer. It stated that Brenda had named the foodservice department as a respondent to a formal complaint alleging a violation of the human rights policy. She alleged that she was not hired for a recent position (a promotion), and that she was discriminated against in the hiring decision because of her race and national origin. She also stated that she was the victim of discrimination because of retaliation for her prior complaint to the state civil rights commission and the Equal Employment Opportunity Commission (EEOC). (See the formal complaint procedure.)

Brenda stated that the last time the job was vacant, she applied for the job and was not hired. She maintained that she was told to reapply for the job because she was qualified. Brenda had filed a previous discrimination complaint against the department, and she believes that has had a negative impact on her unsuccessful try at being hired for the position. Previously, she had filed an internal informal complaint with the AA office as well as complaints with the EEOC and the state civil rights commission. She says she has heard from another employee that she will never be promoted within the department because of her previous complaint.

The next day, when **Anne Potter,** the compliance officer, began her investigation, she found that Brenda was interviewed for a position for which she was not qualified. **Janice Roberts,** a Caucasian female who is a new employee to the operation, was hired. The department director, an associate director, and the HR director deny that the hiring decision was based on discriminatory or retaliatory reasons. Brenda was the only person within the department asking for a promotion. All other candidates were original-entry applicants. Only two applicants (Brenda and Janice) were interviewed, and the decision to hire was based primarily on the candidate's communication skills as demonstrated during the interview. There was also concern about Brenda's inability to document her education.

In talking separately with the interview committee members, Anne found that they were consistent in stating that both candidates met the minimum educational requirements for the position. They said Brenda's application indicated that she had earned a B.S. degree from a college in the Philippines. When additional information was requested, Brenda did not provide any documentation and was not able to explain the subject matter or nature of her education. She was told it was necessary to verify her education for the job she was seeking. Janice currently is enrolled in distance-education courses in pursuit of a second degree. Her B.S. degree is in a related field.

Anne found that the interviewing committee members asked both candidates the same set of questions during their interviews. (Rachel gave Anne a copy of the questions.) The committee members agreed that Janice interviewed extremely well and elaborated on her answers with pertinent information about herself and her prior work experience that addressed the questions posed. In contrast, they said Brenda gave general answers without much detail. Her answers were not concise and were hard to follow. Sometimes she did not answer the question that was asked. In Rachel's opinion, Janice displayed much better communication skills than Brenda. The committee concurred. Thus, the decision was made to hire Janice, who the committee members believed was the better candidate for the job.

Rachel told Anne that at times during the interview, Brenda's credibility was on the line. On her application she stated that she had experience using the current software program. Rachel was surprised to see that, because Brenda did not use it in her job. When questioned, Brenda was unable to explain how or when she had used the program.

The department committee members stood by the decision to hire Janice. They told Anne that Janice's communication skills and prior work experience provided qualifications to perform the job. It was noted that Brenda discussed having

---

Formal Complaint Procedure

An individual may obtain information about the complaint procedure or discuss an incident without filing a complaint.

If a formal complaint is filed, an impartial investigation of the complainant's allegations is conducted by the affirmative action (AA) office to determine whether reasonable basis exists to believe that the human rights policy has been violated as alleged. During the investigation, the AA office does the following:

- Notifies the accused party of the complaint, identifies the complainant, and provides general allegations of the complaint.
- Interviews the accused party about specifics.
- Gives the accused an opportunity to respond fully to the accusations.
- Interviews others, if necessary.

At the conclusion of the investigation, the AA office will determine whether a violation of the human rights policy has occurred. If so, a written outline of the basis for the finding is provided.

- Copies of findings are given to the complainant and the respondent.
- The AA office will attempt to resolve the complaint within forty-five days.

If discrimination has occurred, the department chair will determine appropriate sanctions, if any, to be administered within the established procedures.

If the complainant is not satisfied, the decision may be appealed.

Confidentiality is essential. Failure on the part of the respondent to keep information confidential can be regarded as retaliation.

The AA office will obtain written consent from the formal complaint to obtain information with appropriate individuals.

to argue with other professionals (at a higher level) in order to get the job done. The committee members were concerned that Brenda had taken such an adversarial stance for the situation she described. There were other examples of her ineffective interpersonal interactions.

Anne questioned Jackie about the statement Brenda had made that she would never get the job. Jackie clearly indicated she that she had not decided or given direction that Brenda will never be promoted because of her prior complaint. She is not sure where Brenda heard that information. Later, Anne checked with Brenda about the complaint that she would never be hired for the position. Brenda admitted not knowing the source of the statement.

During the investigation process, it was never brought out that Brenda had been in a physical fight with a fellow Filipina, **Alicia Eduardo,** in the main kitchen. Brenda filed a lawsuit against Alicia stating that she started the fight because she was jealous of Brenda and her possibility for getting promoted.

Jackie and Rachel have learned that Brenda also has filed a personal lawsuit. They were aware that Brenda had substantial financial means, so they were not surprised to learn of the lawsuit, which, unlike most other employees, she can afford. Brenda's personal lawyer has been showing up unannounced and talking with her in the hallway. Although no attention has been given to these visits, Janice has become aware of his visits and has told Rachel she was feeling lots of pressure when Brenda and her lawyer stared at her as she walked by them while they were visiting. It seemed that there was tension among other employees too.

The Decision to Hire Rachel

Jackie recognizes that it is for reasons like Brenda's complaint that she designated Rachel to be the department HR person. There are always issues in the foodservice department, and Rachel keeps busy working on them. Before Rachel, Jackie did all the work with the union representatives and found that it was too time-consuming. In addition, she was unable to keep abreast of all the contracts, and this knowledge supported her decision to hire Rachel. Rachel had been Jackie's assistant in dining services. When Jackie was promoted to assistant director, Rachel moved to the manager position vacated by Jackie. Jackie is sure that she made the right move in making Rachel the HR person.

Rachel tries to keep her cool when she hears members of the management team talking about firing an employee who has caused them problems. Their eagerness to fire the employee could get the department in deep trouble with the union. They forget that just because supervisors see an employee take a candy bar without paying, they can't accuse the employee. She reminds them that it is their word against the employee's word, which is really worth nothing. They forget how important it is to treat people fairly and to have concrete evidence to support the accusation.

Rachel shares with them the story of the broken window of a door in the production area. A supervisor approached her with evidence that **Matt Steuk** was the one who broke the window when he was angry about something that **Jake Place** had said to him. Rachel got a list of witnesses and talked with most of them. Every witness said he or she saw something different, and Rachel's hands were tied.

Rachel helps supervisors slow down in the discipline process and gets them involved in the investigation rather than allowing them to just wait to "catch and fire" an employee. She explains to others that it is important to be fair and objective, and often uses open-ended questions when interviewing employees about their complaints or grievances. She builds on their responses. She also has learned that it is important to have another person present when confronting an employee.

Rachel is the liaison between the department and the central HR office. Until two years ago, whenever she had a problem that she didn't know how to handle, she would call the central office and whichever HR employee was available would work with her. For the last two years, **Joe Burras** has been assigned to work with her. It is his responsibility to conceptualize HR problems from a larger perspective. All materials and grievances are reviewed by the central HR staff to ensure that they are in line with the collective bargaining contract. Rachel perceives Joe's assignment to the foodservice department as a positive move because she now knows where to turn when the need arises, and she feels more comfortable with Joe. Although Rachel needs to be very familiar with the union contract and know what needs to be done and how to do it, Joe is there to provide assistance.

When a problem arises, Rachel first seeks out the needed information from management staff. She keeps her eyes wide open and looks at the big picture, a task for which Joe has provided assistance. She believes that the mission of the union is to "trip" the organization and win the grievance. It is through experience that Rachel has become savvier in working with the union.

At first, when the union told her that they needed an immediate answer, Rachel would be intimidated and thought she needed to give it. She now believes that they were taking advantage of her in this new role. She also has found that the steward, who is elected by the employees, doesn't just deal with his responsibilities as a steward, but tends to get into problems with the employees' personal lives that are then brought into the workplace.

Employees seem to relate lots of problems to their jobs. For example, an employee, **Carol Hromatica,** reported being sexually harassed because **Kent Hart** followed her to the car and then called her at home. Although these activities happened off the property, they were not left at the door when the employees came to work. So Rachel had to tell Carol to stay away from Kent while at work.

Rachel and the rest of the management staff have experienced violence in the workplace, and they have heightened their awareness of its growing possibility. They all felt their hands were tied because they were told they needed to find just cause to release Clinton, an employee covered by the union.

The Problem with Clinton

Clinton Fletcher had been a cook in the department for fifteen years before serving in the Persian Gulf. When he returned, other employees recognized that he was more aggressive and did not respond to small requests by his superiors, such as, "Take the lasagna out of the oven." Most of his behavior bordered on insubordination, but his comments were made when no manager was present. Some employees felt that they were in danger. But they did not want to "rat" on him for fear he might find out who the "ratters" were and retaliate. They were afraid of what Clinton might do.

When management was finally able to document his behavior, Clinton was suspended for one day. He returned to work, but after two weeks he was suspended again for three days. He worked fairly well for about six weeks, but then became insubordinate and was suspended for three more days. Each suspension was without pay, and each time he received a letter indicating the department's expectations of him when he returned.

Clinton grieved the third suspension, and the process automatically went to step 3, where the grievance went to the central HR director. A meeting was held with the director of staff relations to decide whether the contract had been violated. Rachel and a union representative also attended the meeting.

Rachel knew that at this stage no new information could be brought to the attention of others. She also knew that if it was determined that Clinton should not have been suspended, he would be paid for the suspension. If the director ruled against Clinton, he then would be told that he could ask for the grievance to go to arbitration. If this occurred, the department and the union would share the bill, each paying 50 percent. Rachel was relieved when the director ruled against Clinton all the way, and he received no pay while he was suspended.

Soon after returning to work after his third suspension, Clinton got on the intercom and threatened to bring a gun to work and blow everybody apart. Even though there is a policy of zero tolerance for guns in the workplace, the department managers had to investigate the reason for his threat. Rachel and **Phil Kepley,** associate director of production, investigated the situation, with Joe's assistance, to determine what type of behavior was occurring.

They determined that Clinton was on medication because of flare-ups as a result of being in the Persian Gulf. He wasn't conscientious about taking the medication, and the days he forgot his medication, his anger would get the best of him. Clinton was suspended for one day, and he filed another grievance.

During the grievance process, it was stated that Clinton was sick and needed to see a doctor about taking medication, although his doctor practiced at a veterans' hospital 120 miles away. It was agreed that Clinton needed to have the doctor document his adherence to his medication. However, Rachel is quite familiar with that process. It has been shown that doctors sometimes fall short on keeping track of these patients and simply sign off on the report forms when requested. **Jim Henrichs,** a steward, was with Clinton when he went through the grievance process. It was interesting to note that even though there are two stewards in the foodservice department, Clinton chose a steward from another department. Rachel and Phil assumed it was because Jim had been in the war and Clinton felt an association with him. Clinton lost the grievance and eventually was fired.

Language Problems

Rachel and Joe have been working with the union on another issue. They don't seem to be getting any where with helping the foodservice employees learn to speak English. All the hourly foodservice employees are covered by the union. Because many of them don't speak English, Jackie has attempted to get them into English as a second language (ESL) classes. However, the union dictates the hours the employees can work, and there has been a conflict between working hours and the classes. Although unable to understand the thinking on the part of the union, Rachel and Joe lowered the priority of the problem to deal with Brenda and Clinton.

The Importance of Documentation

Jackie is wondering what she can do to get good documentation from her management staff. Just maybe that would reduce the number of complaints filed, or at least stop them at the first level of the process. She wonders if better documentation would have prevented the lawsuit that Brenda filed. It is taking so much of her staff's time. Would life be better without the union? In fact, with the job classification of employees under her, Jackie works with two collective bargaining contracts. Further, what is not covered in a contract falls into the university policies and procedures. The collective bargaining contract covers hiring, compensation, and jobs performed. A great majority of the grievances come from the hourly employees and don't seem to go beyond the department. When she and Rachel have reviewed records, it seems there are more grievances in the foodservice department than in most other departments in the organization.

Jackie knows that the staff does an excellent job communicating with employees orally, but they forget that talking to them is not the same as written documentation placed in the employee file. When asked about showing the documentation, her managers will say, "I talked with her, and told her she needed to improve on her attendance," or "I talked to him about the way the food is brought to the serving line."

Jackie's Background

Jackie first stint with the foodservice department was when she was recruited for the production and purchasing manager, a position she held for five years before resigning to become a consultant to foodservice operations. Four years later, she was recruited once again and became the manager of dining services for four years. She then was promoted to assistant director, a position she held for ten years under **Rosemary Halder** who had been the director for thirty-five years. **Michelle Gilloon,** the next director, served only two years before being told her services were no longer needed.

Jackie was appointed interim director for one and a half years. Two years ago she was named the director of the unionized department. Her staff of six associate directors report to her (see the foodservice department organization chart) and are responsible for 250 full-time equivalents (FTEs), or 330 employees, including part-time. Thirteen FTEs are management and thus nonunion employees. All hourly employees are covered by the union because the hospital is located in a right-to-work state.

Foodservice Department Organization Chart

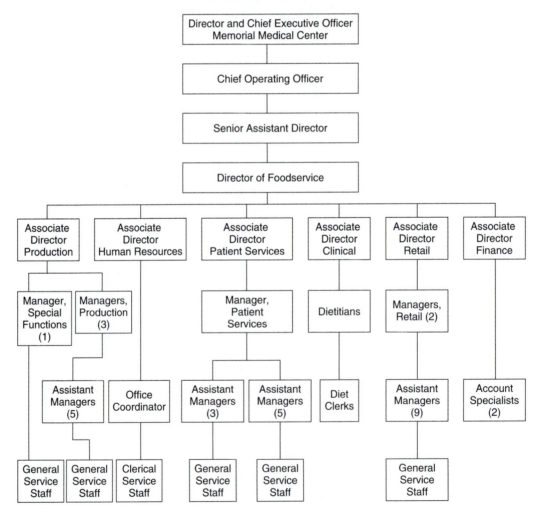

The department is committed to providing quality service to all customers in a caring and professional manner. Their focus extends to the community through efforts to support community needs that can be addressed by the department.

The foodservice department serves 2.5 million individuals a year, approximately 7,000 meals per day. It does about 800 catering events per month, all within the hospital setting. Sixty vending machines are located throughout the hospital, and revenue generated from them amounts to about $750,000 per year. Jackie calculated that about 60 percent of her revenue is from nonpatient meals.

When Jackie became director, she gradually changed the organization chart from one assistant director to five associate directors. She also changed the title of the associate director for dining services to associate director of retail. Eventually she added a sixth associate director position to oversee HR activities, working with the union and employee complaints and/or grievances.

On average, her thirteen management team members are fairly young, but Jackie has a lot of confidence in them. She likes that they don't play the "blame game," but rather are supportive of each other with open communication. When a grievance is filed or they recognize that one might be filed, several team members discuss it from all angles, hoping to forestall any mistakes on the part of the manager who is involved with the grievance. Jackie stresses the importance of being able to listen and focus on the issue rather than on themselves or the director.

Tenure for the associate directors ranges from two to twenty years, with three associates having less than six years and three associates having more than fifteen. The associate directors are equally divided in regard to gender. They get along very well and assist each other when possible and necessary. Although they don't all agree on every aspect, when a decision is made they accept it and move ahead.

Jackie believes that her success in having a team atmosphere comes from the interviewing process. She works hard at recruiting individuals who will complement the current team and add value to it. As a result, her team members share the same values and tend to think and respond similarly. When Jackie reviews her team members, she recognizes that they may work well together because she knew each one before hiring them. **Beth Warner** worked under Rachel as an assistant, and **Doug Turpen, Gretchen Quinnell,** and **Phil Kepley** all did their internships at the hospital and were recruited when positions opened. She was happy to get **Steve Letsky,** the director of patient services, because she believes he is a shining star.

Discussion Questions

1. How would you judge the quality of the management team? What factors did you consider in making your judgment? Why would these be important? Do you agree with the organization of the department? Why or why not?
2. Is it good that Jackie knew her management team before hiring them? Why or why not?

3. Do you agree with Jackie's decision to hire a human resources director within the foodservice department? Support your response.

4. Was Rachel the right choice? Why or why not?

5. Does documentation affect grievances? In what ways? Explain.

6. What guidelines would you provide to managers who have a grievance filed against them? Justify your response.

7. If you were Joe, are there suggestions you would provide Rachel to help her with the HR problems she has and is facing? Why would these be important to her?

Walnut Hill Retirement Community

Jack was coming to the end of his first year at Walnut Hill Retirement Community (WHRC). Managing the dining services department had gone well until just recently. He knew that Sue was not happy with the results of today's meeting. He was surprised to learn that Julie had scheduled a meeting with him to discuss the difference in hourly wage between her and Brett. He needed to do some information gathering before tomorrow afternoon when Julie reports to work.

Background

WHRC is located in Lakewood City, population 250,000. The property is owned and managed by Atlas Corporation, a national for-profit organization. Atlas is a recognized leader in retirement communities and has more communities than any other company. WHRC facilities include a continuum of care, with independent-living and assisted-living apartments as well as an on-site healthcare center. The independent-living apartments include a full kitchen in which residents can prepare their meals. The assisted-living apartments are furnished with a 1-cubic-foot microwave and either a full-size or room-size refrigerator. The healthcare center is professionally staffed for those residents who live in either an independent-living or assisted-living apartment. It is not open to the general public. However, in some facilities, when the census has been low, outsiders have been admitted to the healthcare center.

WHRC's concept started as independent living, and assisted living was added as the current residents had need. Later, as more and more residents needed extensive healthcare, the on-site center was added. WHRC is designed for residents who are physically capable of independent living and financially able to afford the rates. A nonrefundable fee charged to residents guarantees them living arrangements as needed. At least one spouse must be 60 years old or older and financially able to afford residency.

Amenities include a dining room for assisted-living residents to have their meals, a private dining room for residents to have meals with family members, a library, a beauty salon and barbershop, a chapel, garden areas, recreation/activity rooms, several unit kitchens, and regularly scheduled transportation to theaters and shopping centers. Most independent-living residents have access to their own transportation, and garages are available for another fee. Ample parking is available for other residents and the guests.

Independent-living residents (108 units) pay a monthly fee to live in an apartment. They can contract for one to three meals per day and eat at their own tables in the Garden dining room with the assisted-living residents. They have use of all amenities. Generally, older adults move into the independent units to ensure a spot when assisted living is needed. These units are very comfortable and may be as large as 1,700 square feet. Housekeeping services can be purchased.

Assisted-living apartments are the next level of care. They are smaller, often one-bedroom apartments. All residents contract with two meals per day and more than half have a three-meal-per-day contract. Residents eat their meals in the Garden dining room and have assigned tables. Assisted-living contracts include weekly housekeeping services and laundry. Snacks are available throughout the day. Limited nursing services can be provided for a fee. If residents want to have an outside individual spend time with them or take them to outside events, the theater, or other activities, the activity director provides the resident with a list of people with short biographies who have applied to be companions. The activity director arranges for that person to interview with the resident to determine acceptability. The resident pays an hourly fee for the service, and the facility pays the person.

The healthcare center (forty-five beds) has a 24-hour, round-the-clock nursing staff that assists residents with eating, bathing, medications, and other basic daily needs. The healthcare center residents eat in a separate dining room.

The management structure consists of an administrator and directors of dining services, nursing, marketing, activities, engineering, utilities, and human resources. **Jeff Kramer** has been the administrator at WHRC for four years (see the Walnut Hill organization chart). He was the director of dining room services for two years before he was promoted to administrator. Jeff is a creative, caring person who interacts well with the residents. He empowers his team members, the directors, to make departmental decisions, and he has a team meeting each month. He frequently visits different departments of the facility unannounced to perform random quality checks. The directors consider Jeff fair in his evaluations.

Dining Services

Jack Walden is the director of dining services. He has an associate's degree in hospitality management and is working toward a bachelor's degree at a nearby university. Jack has been at WHRC for a little less than a year. He worked in

Walnut Hill Retirement Community Organization Chart

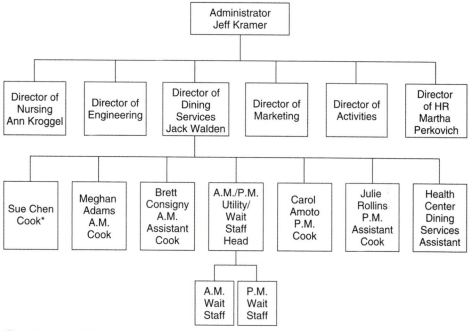

*Floats between A.M./P.M. shift

school foodservice for about ten years before he was accepted at WHRC. He also had three years of restaurant experience. Jack is perceived as strict, fair, and open-minded. Jeff and Jack work well together because Jeff allows Jack to run his own department. Jeff evaluates Jack's work highly because he has controlled food costs and developed more exciting menus.

Jack's biggest problem currently is dealing with Meghan and Sue. He was aware of the conflict but felt comfortable that it was more latent rather than out in the public. It had not reached the explosive stage. After discussion with Jeff, he decided that as long as productivity had not been affected, he would leave it alone.

The Staff

Dining service personnel are responsible for the production of three meals per day every day of the year. The utility workers provide the service and are not under the direction of the dining services director. **Meghan Adams** is the head A.M. cook and **Brett Consigny** is her assistant. **Carol Amoto** oversees the P.M. production as head cook and is assisted by **Julie Rollins. Sue Chen** floats as an additional cook between A.M. and P.M. depending on the complication of the menu and the prep that needs to be done for the next meal. There are six part-time dishwashers who work split shifts. High school students often do P.M. dishwashing tasks. The twenty utility workers cover service of all meals. The number at any one meal varies with the number of residents who are eating. There is no consistent pattern to how the utility workers are assigned.

Meghan has been working in dining services for about eight months. She has only a high school diploma but received good training as head cook in a local restaurant for a couple of years. Although she enjoyed the restaurant job, she applied at WHRC because they provide a better salary and benefits. She is a single parent of two children. She knows that she is limited by her high school education. Jack has found her to be an excellent employee, just as her references indicated. She is friendly and willing to help others. She enjoys visiting with residents when they come for snacks, and sometimes the visiting interferes with her work.

Carol has been the P.M. cook for three years. She is well-liked by her employees. They find her to be an excellent trainer and very patient. She has a two-year degree from a local community college. Carol has a very supportive family and often stays at work later and lets the other employees leave if cleanup seems to be completed. She is an effective worker, and Jack is happy that she is the one in charge when he leaves for the day.

Both assistant cooks are excellent workers and have been at WHRC for a little over two years. In fact, Brett has been employed by WHRC for one month more than Julie. They seem to get along with their co-workers. Julie has a certificate from a three-month cook's school she attended a few years ago. She also is certified in food safety. Brett has two years more work experience than Julie.

Sue floats between morning and night shifts. She moved to the United States from China about eight years ago. She has been working in dining services about five years. She did not complete high school, so she is happy to have the job that she has. Sue began as a utility worker before moving to the cook position a year ago. She is well-liked by the people who work with her because she works hard and will help them if needed. Although Sue is very quiet, Jack has perceived that she has a negative attitude toward her work. She does not like constructive criticism and is defensive.

The Problem

Sue feels that Meghan dislikes her because she is Asian. They argue most of the time when they work together. Meghan feels that Sue tries to ignore her when Meghan is talking to her. Sometimes Sue gets so irritated that she talks back to Meghan. Most arguments are petty, such as when Sue did not like the way Meghan talked to her or when Meghan did not like Sue's presentation of a dish to residents.

Sue gets along well with Carol. Lately, Carol has been concerned that the conflict is getting out of hand. Sue shares her problems with Carol and Julie when she works the P.M. shift. Carol is surprised that Jack has not become involved.

April 7

Sue was assigned to work on the morning shift with Meghan. When Meghan arrived at 5:45 A.M., she found that Sue, who was supposed to have done some prep for breakfast during the P.M. shift, had not done anything. Meghan was upset. When Sue arrived at 6:00 A.M., Meghan yelled at her for not getting the prep done. Meghan told Sue that she had to do the prep and was running behind. In fact, she called Jack and requested a change in the menu because there was not time to do all the preparation that was required.

Because Sue had not received any notes about her prep duties, Sue became very defensive. Sue accused Meghan of not yelling at Brett when he showed up late for work. Sue told Meghan, in a very loud voice, that she thought Meghan was discriminating against her. Meghan accused Sue of purposely not doing the prep because she wanted Meghan to look bad.

When Brett arrived at 6:40 A.M. (ten minutes late), he found two very angry employees yelling at each other. Brett tried to calm them. Brett realized that other employees were observing the argument, and several residents who came early for breakfast were appearing distressed about the situation.

By the time Jack arrived, all he saw was chaos in the kitchen. Jack directed all the employees to return to work. He instructed Sue and Meghan to go to his office. Brett was left in charge of the kitchen for a few minutes.

Jack told Sue and Meghan that it was inappropriate to argue about who made what mistakes when the dining room was to open in less than thirty minutes. Because they needed to finish breakfast preparation, he had no option but to send them back to work, but after the rush hour, he wanted them to return to his office to set up a meeting for the next day (April 8).

In the meantime, Jack went to talk to other employees about the incident, and he documented the information he collected. Jack talked to Brett to get his side of the story. He also called Carol at home to discuss Sue's behavior during the previous P.M. shift. Carol had not noticed anything out of the ordinary, and really hadn't been made aware that there was no prep for Sue to do. It had been a busy night. Jack was perplexed that Sue could get along with Carol but not Meghan. He invited **Martha Perkovich,** the human resources director, to observe the meeting and take any appropriate notes.

When Meghan and Sue returned to his office, Jack told them he was disappointed that they chose to handle their problem in such a manner. He noted the poor example they showed for other employees as well as the impact their behavior made on the residents.

April 8

Jack scheduled a short meeting with each employee before he brought them together. He started each meeting by telling the employee how valuable she was as a team member and the role she had in WHRC's success. He asked both of them to tell him what happened.

Sue explained that she had worked the night shift on April 6. She said that she did not receive any prep instructions, as she had expected, of work that needed to be done for the morning of April 7. She assumed that Meghan might have done the prep by herself. She indicated that she had not talked to Carol about the lack of directions because it had been such a busy night. She was not aware that Carol and Meghan talked outside of work.

Meghan told Jack, in her individual meeting, that she forgot to leave a list, but Sue should have checked the refrigerator or called her at home to make sure that everything was done. She admitted that Carol did not know about the preps and that there had been one or two times that no preps needed to be done.

After finishing his meeting with Meghan, he asked Sue to join them. As the conversation continued, more problems surfaced. Sue felt that Meghan did things on purpose because she did not like Sue. She told Meghan that she does things to make her look bad, such as not giving clear instructions about what needs to be done.

Meghan responded that she never said that she did not like Sue. She pointed out that when she tried to talk to Sue it appeared that Sue was ignoring her: "When I suggest how the plate presentation might be more aesthetically pleasing, you think that I am criticizing you. I don't think you show me the respect that I deserve."

Sue said she had been told that Meghan told other employees that she did not think Sue should be in the kitchen because she was slow and did not communicate well with others. Meghan denied saying those things, but stated that she might have mentioned that sometimes she had difficulty talking to and understanding Sue.

Sue complained that sometimes when she was busy doing something, Meghan took over and took the credit. Meghan responded that she did not do it on purpose, but when it needed to be done quickly, she didn't have time to wait for Sue to do it at her pace. Sue admitted that she did not feel comfortable asking for help. She further stated that asking for help would demonstrate her incompetence. Sue felt that Meghan acted as if she were superior and treated her with less respect than she should be treated.

Jack didn't think the conversation was going anywhere. He had another meeting to go to, so he told Sue and Meghan to evaluate where they might have some misunderstandings. There was no choice other than having them work together. He indicated that if they wanted to continue to working at WHRC, they needed to work well together.

Jack did not blame either employee. Sue expected him to discipline Meghan because she had failed to leave the necessary instructions for the prep and then started yelling at her the next morning. He told Sue that the next time she worked the night shift, she should make sure she did the prep for the next morning.

At the end of the meeting, Meghan promised Jack that she would try her best to get along with Sue. However, Sue did not promise anything. She told Jack, in front of Martha, that she felt that she had been discriminated against because she was Asian and Meghan was Caucasian. In her mind, there was no other reason why Jack did not take the problem seriously and discipline Meghan. A friend told her to consider taking legal action because Jack shouldn't discriminate based on nationality and lack of education.

April 9

It appeared that the Meghan-Sue conflict was the beginning for other problems to be aired. When Julie heard about what had happened to Sue, she decided it was time to bring her frustrations to management. Julie had just recently learned that Brett was receiving $1.50 per hour more than she was. He had been at WHRC for one month longer than she had.

Julie considers herself an excellent worker, and she has received many compliments from Carol about her performance. She knows that Brett is dating **Ann Kroggel,** the director of nursing, and wonders if that might have an impact on his recent raise. Julie also has been told that Brett comes to work late at least once a week. Although employees like Brett and he gets along well with Meghan and Sue, Julie also was told by a friend who is a utility worker that Brett spends lots of time talking with Ann. Because Julie does not work the same shift as Brett, she can't verify the rumors. She wants to know why Brett got a larger raise than she did as a result of their recent performance evaluations. She thinks they should be getting fairly similar wages. She intended to discuss the issue with Jack in the morning.

Discussion Questions

1. When the conflict occurred on April 7, do you feel the Jack handled the situation appropriately? Explain.
2. Should Jeff get involved in the Meghan-Sue confict? Why or why not?
3. Should Jack have let Meghan and Sue air all their problems at the meeting, or should he have focused on the prep problem? Why or why not?
4. What basic steps should Jack take when dealing with the conflict? Justify your actions.
5. Should Martha, director of human resources, get involved? Why or why not? If yes, to what extent should she be involved?
6. How can management prevent discrimination in a working environment? What is the best solution to this problem? Support your answer.
7. Should WHRC management take Sue's threat of discrimination based on nationality and education seriously? Why or why not?
8. Discuss how managers can prevent conflicts due to culture and education background differences. Why should managers be concerned about these types of conflicts?
9. What should Jack do to get ready for Julie's meeting? Support your answer. What reasons might be given for Brett's pay differential?

PART 6
University/College/
Public Schools

Brookes University Residence Dining Services
Greenhill Student Center
Kalamazoo University
North Central State University Campus Dining Services
Rocky Mountain University
Twin City Schools Food Service
University Memorial Center
Wellman State University

Brookes University Residence Dining Services

Brookes University is located in the Southwest with enrollment around 20,000 students. This university has five dining facilities on campus that are operated and managed by the residence department. The director of dining services, **Dean Bennett,** is in charge of these operations and has held his position for fifteen years.

Dean is well respected by his staff. There are times when he makes decisions that his staff does not agree with, but they also realize that his decision is in the best interest of the department. Dean does not typically intervene when there are disputes among his managers. His hands-off approach can be beneficial in that the parties involved must come to an agreement on their own, but sometimes managers feel that he should intervene and he does not.

Each dining facility on campus has a manager and two assistant managers. One assistant covers the A.M. shift, which starts at 5 A.M., and the other assistant manager oversees the P.M. shift, which ends at 8 P.M. The manager's hours range between 8 A.M. and 6 P.M. The ages of the assistant managers range from twenty-five to thirty-five. All the managers on staff have been members of the management team in this department for more than ten years. The ratio of women to men in any given dining unit is 3:1.

The main responsibilities of the managers are scheduling full-time employees, coordinating catering, and planning for the next semester. The managers' focus seems to be more on the "big picture," and assistant managers tend to focus on the day-to-day operations of the unit. The management team supervises between eight and fifteen full-time employees and an average of 100 student employees who are involved in the preparation and service of more than 2,000 meals each day.

The assistant managers' duties include scheduling and training student employees; forecasting and ordering food and supplies; supervising meal production and service; overseeing catering activities; overseeing sanitation; ensuring facility maintenance and safety; and maintaining positive relations and communication with student residents. Dean expects assistant managers to be competent, have past work experience, have enough confidence to make decisions based on what they think is best, and have a commitment to customer service.

The residence dining services department also employs graduate students of the university hospitality management department in dining units as graduate assistants. These students work an average of twenty hours a week. These individuals cover the full-time assistant managers' days off and are expected to fulfill the same responsibilities.

Staffing Changes

Last November, two assistant manager positions became vacant, effective immediately. Evan was a graduate assistant currently on staff in the residence department and was interested in full-time employment with the university. Two other staff members, Susan and Angie, were classified as "extra hourly" assistant managers and were interested in the vacant positions as well. The "extra hourly" classification is given to individuals who receive hourly wages but do not receive benefits. This assistant manager is hired to fill vacancies that occur in mid semester or to cover for another assistant manager who is on maternity leave, for example. These three current staff members applied for the two positions and a nationwide search was conducted as well.

A search committee was formed of two managers and two assistant managers. The committee evaluated all résumés received and held interviews with the top four candidates. The committee held a one-hour interview, and then Dean interviewed each candidate. After interviews, the committee decided on the best two candidates and this recommendation was given to Dean, who would make the final decision.

The top four candidates were as follows:

Evan Higgins has been on staff as a graduate assistant in the residence department for two years and works in the busiest dining unit on campus. In another year he will receive a master's degree in HRIM from Midstate University, and he hopes to continue employment in a university setting. He also has experience in a fast-food restaurant chain. Evan is a dependable employee with an above-average attendance record and knows how to get work done to meet deadlines. However, sometimes he is not as thorough as he should be in doing his work, which leads to problems that could have been avoided with a little extra time and thought. Evan has a good relationship with his staff and has their general respect even though he has been known to be short-tempered.

Susan Graber has worked for dining services for seven years. She was a student employee for two years, a student supervisor for two years, and an "extra hourly" assistant manager for three years. She currently works in one of the smaller dining units on campus and supervises the evening meal Monday through Friday. She also works one weekend a month in another unit as the "manager on duty."

Susan has little involvement in the ordering of food and supplies for her unit, but is responsible for hiring and scheduling student employees. Susan is well respected by her student and full-time staff. She is a hard worker and has the ability to think ahead and anticipate situations. These characteristics contribute to the efficient operation of the dining facility. Perhaps her greatest weakness is the discipline of employees. It is difficult for her to confront students so that she is taken seriously.

Angie Tabke graduated with a dietetics major from an accredited university and has been an "extra hourly" assistant manager for about a year. She works in the largest dining center on campus and essentially "answers" to the A.M. and P.M. assistant managers (because of the size of this dining unit, it has three assistant managers on staff). During her undergraduate work, Angie was employed for three years by a local hospital. She worked in the cafeteria as a cook, server, and night shift manager. One's initial impression of Angie would be that she is a timid, reserved individual; however, she is friendly and warm. She is willing to help out whenever needed and is very efficient in the performance of her duties. She has a personality that is compatible with just about everyone.

Jill Renze is an assistant dining services manager at a major university in a neighboring state. She has been at that university for six years and is looking for new challenges. Her previous work experience includes managing a family-owned restaurant for three years and coordinating banquets and special events for an entertainment management company. She has a bachelor's degree in business administration. Jill is a dedicated employee who at times takes that dedication too far by asking more of her employees than they can provide. She is very organized and has the ability to coordinate events. She is respected by her employees because she "knows her stuff" but she is not a very personable individual.

Discussion Questions

1. What qualities, in addition to those listed in the case, do you think the committee should be looking for? Why?
2. As a member of the interview committee, what questions would you ask the references of these four candidates? Why would these be important questions?
3. Because three of the four candidates are internal, is it still worthwhile to do reference checks? Why or why not?
4. If you were Dean, discuss the concerns you would have in offering a position to a candidate who is currently on staff.
5. As a member of the interview committee, what two candidates would you recommend for the two positions? Why? Explain why you did not choose the other two candidates.
6. Should Dean make his decision based on the committee's recommendation? Why or why not?

Greenhill Student Center

It is almost lunchtime. **Joe Smith,** operations manager of Greenhill Student Center (GSC), has no appetite and is still thinking about the problems his night/weekend (NW) managers reported during their weekly meeting an hour ago. One problem is absenteeism, which frustrates many on-campus managers who hire student employees. He also is reflecting on the earlier decision to establish the NW manager position and wondering whether it was a good idea. After the NW managers started working, some student employees quit while others seemed confused by the change. What went wrong?

Further, Barb, a current NW manager, certainly wasn't working out as well as he had hoped. And what about finding that fourth manager? Would that ever happen? Would one of the two applicants meet the specifications?

The Center

Joe thinks about his twenty-year career at GSC, located on the south end of a state university campus. GSC is a private, nonprofit property that provides meeting space, foodservice (including a food court), hotel rooms, and recreational facilities for students, faculty/staff, alumni, and guests. GSC's purpose is "devoted exclusively to the social, moral, religious, literary, scientific, and educational development and welfare of students, faculty, alumni, friends, and guests."

As the operations manager, Joe is responsible for the center's meeting and events business. He is in charge of general services (GS) employees, who set up meeting rooms; custodial employees; NW managers, who oversee the center's operations on evenings and weekends; and reservation office employees, who handle reservations of meeting rooms for all events held at the center.

Joe has no college degree; he started as a custodial supervisor and worked his way up to operations manager ten years ago. Although he lets his employees do what they think is right and does not take care of them, he is well respected by other center employees. Although he is even-tempered, he does not hesitate to discipline subordinates when he spots problems.

The GSC has fifty-five guest rooms on the top floors, with various-size meeting rooms on floors 1–3. The center's three major departments are lodging (rooms), general services (GS), and foodservice. The GS employees are responsible for setting up three large banquet halls that have a capacity for 400–800 guests, five medium-size halls for 150–300 guests, and fifteen small rooms for ten–fifty guests. Approximately 230 events take place each week during the fall and spring semesters. Nearly every Saturday night there is at least one large event, such as a wedding reception, dinner event, or student activity.

The three departments normally get along well with each other, but at times foodservice and GS employees have small conflicts over incorrect or late room setups or catering equipment and leftover food left in the meeting rooms. These problems frequently delay each other's work. Before the NW manager positions were established, the conflicts usually were more serious during the nighttime, because no one coordinated or supervised these two departments during that time period.

Joe takes full responsibility and credit for establishing the NW manager positions. Joe discussed his decision to hire four NW managers with **Carol Albright,** the center director. He justifies the decision because the center has had some serious problems in managing the operation during the night and weekend hours. All regular or full-time employees work from 9 A.M. to 5 P.M. with no one having final responsibility for the nighttime management. Guests staying in the center's rooms often had to wait until the next morning with problems or complaints, even if they were urgent. Meeting rooms often were not set up on time, and equipment such as a TV/VCR or a slide projector and screen was not provided promptly. Joe saw that the situation in the foodservice department was a little better because one of their assistant managers usually stayed until 8:30 or 9:00 P.M.

Carol agreed with Joe's plan and suggested that he consider graduate students for the positions. After he left her office, he agreed that would seem logical. He called the department chairs in hospitality and business to discuss the recruiting process. They both agreed to help him find three hospitality graduate students and one business student.

Prior to establishing the NW manager positions, Joe managed the GS department with one assistant manager, **Doug Peters,** who has a college degree in an unrelated major and was promoted from NW manager six years ago; one secretary; and two full-time clerks, who were in charge of reservations and scheduling. Doug supervised forty to fifty daytime building services employees (who worked fifteen to thirty hours per week) identified as the GS crew. They set up meeting rooms and halls according to daily worksheets prepared by Doug and the clerks. Sometimes the same room was set up three to five times a day. There were three student supervisors, and three more were about to be promoted to supervisory positions. Although the pay was minimum wage, the turnover rate was low and several employees worked in GS throughout their college years, with the more senior employees often promoted to supervisor.

Establishing NW Managers

Joe formally announced the hiring of the first two NW managers, **Steve Wentz** from hospitality and **Wendy Willson** from business, just before they started receiving training. He was certain that the addition of these managers would reduce conflicts between departments during nights and weekends. Joe, Doug, and the senior GS crew conducted the training. Steve and Wendy began working as soon as they had completed a twenty-hour training session over two weeks, which included the center's history, policies and procedures, building and departmental tours, electrical and alarm systems, and various room setups.

The NW managers have the responsibility and authority for making decisions that affect the total operation of the center. They plan, coordinate, and supervise the evening/weekend activities of the GS department. They are responsible for people, functions, services, and the entire building in the absence of full-time staff members. The NW manager supervises the GS employees directly and cooperates with the main desk, custodial, and catering employees.

They also are responsible, together with the manager, for hiring, training, supervising, and evaluating employees. Security of the building, cooperating with all center departments, and interpreting and implementing building policies and procedures are other responsibilities. Each manager covers one short shift on weeknights and one long shift on weekends. The shifts are flexible, depending on events being held at the center.

The NW manager nearly always will be backed in decisions made. Decisions are to be made in the best interest of clients and the center, with the NW manager meeting any reasonable customer request. Sometimes customers don't provide enough information to ensure that rooms are prepared ahead of time; however, this cannot be an excuse for not making requested changes. In addition, some policies are not understood by customers and not addressed by GS staff when they are broken. For example, some guests at wedding receptions or parties carry alcoholic drinks while walking in the hallway outside the banquet rooms, which is not allowed in the center. If the NW manager encounters dissatisfied or belligerent people, he or she can call campus safety officers for assistance.

Problems

Soon after Steve and Wendy started, five senior crew members notified Joe that they were going to quit in two weeks because the student supervisor positions were cancelled when he started the night manager system. The senior crew was very familiar with their jobs, and three of them were supposed to be promoted to student supervisor very soon. In fact, the senior crew was in charge of training new crew members even though they had not been formally trained. The morale among the GS crew dropped very quickly, and six of them decided to quit for one or more reasons. Two had personal reasons, one got a new part-time job offering higher wages, and the rest wanted more time to study.

The remaining crew often ignored the NW managers' orders, and acted as if the two managers did not exist. Even employees in other departments did not feel comfortable with the NW managers. They often stopped the conversation and went somewhere else if Wendy or Steve came near them. Most of them were not used to having a supervisor during the night hours and had problems interacting with the new managers. The crew believed that the NW managers' insufficient knowledge of their jobs and their lack of experience made the crew's jobs much harder. The managers often could not answer customer or employee questions.

Even though Wendy and Steve had some difficulties in carrying out their duties, department heads, including Joe, found improvement in the nighttime operations. The meeting rooms were set up correctly and on time and were cleaned properly before each event. Most of all, the number of complaints from customers had decreased noticeably.

Wendy and Steve really wanted to improve their relationship with the GS crew and other employees. Steve seemed to get along better with the crew than Wendy did. When the schedule was busy, Steve helped them set up rooms. He moved tables and chairs and sometimes did the laundry too. On the other hand, Wendy did not help because it was the crew's job, not hers.

One day Wendy found that two senior crew members, **Alex Bergar** and **David DeAngelis,** had cheated on their time cards. They had punched in three hours earlier than their actual working times. At first she thought she should tell Joe about their cheating. But later she decided not to tell Joe because she was worried that they would quit. Because many experienced crew members had already left, the department had difficulties training new crew members and working efficiently to complete a work schedule. This problem was more serious during the nighttime because most senior employees were working during the day.

Discussion Questions

1. Evaluate the training program for the night managers. What changes would you make? Why?
2. How much authority should be given to night managers? Support your answer.
3. What might be a viable process to improve nighttime management, other than hiring the NW managers? Explain.
4. How would you prevent senior employees from quitting their jobs? Justify your response.

5. Describe what you would do to improve the relationship between the GS crew and the NW managers.
6. If you were Wendy, what would you do about Alex and David? Support your actions.
7. Compare the relationship of Wendy and Steve with the GS crew. What are the strengths and weaknesses of each? Why do you consider them strengths and weaknesses?

Jason, Marilyn, and the Foodservice Department

Joe decided to make some staffing changes within GS. Doug is still the assistant manager. Technically, he is on the same management level as NW managers but has little interaction with them.

Only three of four NW manager positions have been filled. Two are in hospitality management and one is in business. The center offers jobs to them as graduate assistants so only graduate students are qualified for the job. Joe is still looking for the third graduate student in hospitality.

The big change was that Joe decided to reestablish the student supervisor position but with less responsibility and very little authority (see job description for GS supervisor). These supervisors would be upper-class undergraduate students who would work on different days, except when there are two of them working together on Monday and Friday nights. They would be promoted based on their continual good, hard work and leadership qualities within the department. They would report to the NW managers and would need at least one year of experience in the department. Student supervisors would be responsible for checking the GS employees' work.

There currently are thirty male GS employees, all students at the university. Because of the job demands, Joe has deemed it essential that the setup crew be all men. Major responsibilities include the setup of meeting rooms, placement of signs, inventory, or audiovisual equipment for meetings, and care and maintenance of equipment used in the department. For each shift, the work schedule has a combination of old and new employees. Pay starts at minimum wage and can be raised fifty cents per hour within one year and ninety cents per hour two years after employment, depending on performance. In addition, GS employees receive a 15 percent discount for one meal eaten during work at certain outlets in the center's food court.

The GS department uses a fixed work schedule. At the beginning of each semester, employees sign up for the time of day and days of the week when they would like to work. The operation manager then assigns them to different shifts: early morning (5 A.M. to 8 A.M.), morning (8 A.M. to 12 noon), afternoon (12 noon to 5 P.M.), and evening (5 P.M. to close). At least two employees are scheduled for each shift. The earliest meetings usually start at 7 A.M., and most evening meetings finish by 11 P.M.

Job Description—GS Supervisor

Work Title: GS Supervisor

Job Description:
Under general supervision of the GS director and/or NW manager, this position is responsible for the GS area.

Duties and Responsibilities:
- Perform all duties of GS.
- Assist in planning and performing setups.
- May lead or coordinate work assignments of other GS staff.
- Perform duties that are technical and complex, that is, that involve a high degree of responsibility and judgment.
- Take care of inventory (remove broken inventory from service and put repaired inventory back into service).
- Be able to lift a minimum of 75 pounds.
- Perform related tasks as assigned.

Knowledge and Experience:
Minimum of one year (two semesters) of GS. A significant amount of specialized training or experience required.

Responsibilities:
- Provide room sets for meeting, banquets, and other activities in the center.
- Responsible for neat and tidy presentation of meeting rooms.
- Must be able to set up and operate equipment such as public address system, movie projectors, tape recorders, audiovisuals, spotlights, and light boards.
- Attend meetings with GS director and NW manager to assist with planning activities when applicable.
- Assist with training GS employees.
- Assist with supervision and leadership of GS crew.
- Assess repairs that are needed with equipment or the physical part of the facility and use the work control program to get it repaired.
- Make a complete inspection of meeting rooms to check for accuracy of setups.
- Make decisions in the best interest of operations, events, and clients of the center.
- Use the guiding philosophy of the center to provide outstanding service and facilities to the university community. Whenever possible, accommodate any reasonable request. Often groups will have shown no forethought in planning an event or lack understanding of our policies. They must be accommodated and educated. Do so, whenever possible, in a positive manner.

Getting back to the problems at hand, Joe remembers that he also needs to deal with Jason and Marilyn. He also needs to talk with the foodservice department management team.

Jason Van Bergan has been working as a part-time student employee in the GS department for more than two years. He is the most senior and most ambitious of the student employees and takes pride in saying he knows everything about room setups. He tries to learn various tasks that the GS crew is asked to perform in order to foster dependence on him by the student employees and management. He has an outgoing personality and is good at leading student employees in setting up rooms for large events. He is charismatic and easily affects the output of other employees.

Taking advantage of his leadership ability, Jason urges other student employees to clock in early for him, sometimes up to several hours. He in turn clocks in early for students who do him this favor. The previous NW manager caught this unacceptable behavior, and Joe gave Jason an oral warning. Jason also will not set up rooms until the very last minute and tries to prolong the work in order to earn additional hours. He does not respond quickly to clients' requests for minor room setup changes. Most of the time he is late in reporting for work, and sometimes he does not even bother to come at all.

Because of GS employees' lack of interest in their jobs, they tend to generate the least work effort and seldom offer quality service to clients. A typical crew of two people on one shift must change a room from theater setup for 500 people into a reception setup using round tables for 300 people in less than one hour. This environment results in a very high employee turnover rate, and most student employees work in the GS department for less than one year.

Several times Jason has caused the GS crew to be late in the setup for important events because only one person was on the GS crew instead of the required two people per shift. Joe issued a written warning for Jason's absence and tardiness. However, Jason is aware that the management at the center is not eager to fire a well-experienced employee like him. The purely physical hard job at minimum wage is not appealing to many individuals. When the NW manager program started at the center, Jason had difficulty accepting supervision from outsiders with little or no prior knowledge about room setups.

The Foodservice Department

Luke Spencer is the director of foodservice. He is supported by three full-time foodservice managers: **Philip Duncan, John Gray,** and **Alan King.** The foodservice department satisfies its staffing requirements by hiring university students as hourly employees.

The youngest of the three managers, Philip, is a flexible and easygoing person. Being a part-time student himself, he treats student employees in his department, as well as the GS department, fairly.

John, on the other hand, is a very strict, autocratic manager and does everything according to set policy. He carries a small calculator and calculates the numbers of tables and chairs in each room. He will summon the GS crew just to shift a table or move a chair two feet away from the original place. He wants the GS crew to know that he is the boss.

Alan is an experienced foodservice manager, but he is notorious for his short temper. He has no patience for anyone and always shouts at his foodservice employees. He treats the GS crew in a heavy-handed manner and demands immediate compliance with his instructions. He typically comes to an event room fifteen to thirty minutes before the scheduled starting time and demands changes even though the rooms have been set up since the previous night.

Most events at the center request catering. Therefore, members of the two departments, foodservice and GS, must interact closely with each other to satisfy the client's requests.

Marilyn Campbell

Marilyn Campbell, a newly hired NW manager who replaced **Patricia Denton,** has supervisory experience in the hospitality industry as well as a business administration degree. On her first day, Joe introduced her to the directors of each department and showed her around the building. She received the NW manager manual to study at her own pace. She observed the room setup while working with student employees. Most of the time she learned by trial and error. For example, she was shown how to shut off and reset the emergency fire panel only after there was a false alarm.

After two weeks working with student employees, Marilyn learned about employee job dissatisfaction and the communication gap that existed between the foodservice employees and GS crew. She also discovered that most of the GS crew, especially Jason and the foodservice assistant managers, had disliked Patricia. Significant personal conflicts had existed while Patricia was working at the center. A potential reason for the dislike could be that Patricia was the only female manager at the center. A second reason was that she did not listen to employee reasons or communicate very well with employees. All staff and employees found it hard to accept the NW manager program. They did not know what the responsibilities of the NW managers were and how to handle the change in organizational structure.

One month after Marilyn began working at the center, the student supervisor position finally was re-established by Joe in concert with Carol. Two students with less seniority than Jason were given the positions. Jason was not promoted because of his poor work performance and uncooperative attitude toward clients' requests. As a result of not being selected, Jason became an extremely difficult employee and tried to sabotage the entire operation. He was very careful not to have open conflicts with anyone but avoided compliance with rules. In the meantime, Marilyn continued adjusting to the work environment, trying to cooperate with the staffs and employees of the GS and foodservice departments and satisfying clients' needs. Jason made Marilyn's work at the center as difficult as he could.

After six months, many student employees graduated from the university, including one student supervisor. Jason suddenly changed his work habits and began to report on time. He also recruited many of his close friends to join the GS crews. He tried to be on time for his shift. He went to Marilyn's or another NW manager's office to confirm the setups for last-minute changes. These changes in performance and attitude impressed them, and they reported this to Joe. As Jason was the most senior employee and had more followers than ever before, Joe decided to give the student supervisor position to Jason.

Discussion Questions

1. Is Joe's requirement that GS setup crews be all men discriminatory? Why or why not?
2. Is Joe's decision to promote Jason a wise one? Explain. Do you think Jason will continue to demonstrate improved performance? Why or why not?
3. Why do you think Marilyn informed Joe of Jason's improvements, given the fact that he had given her a hard time in the past?
4. Did John and Alan's management styles contribute to Jason's becoming a difficult employee? Explain. Give other contributing factors, if any.
5. Based on Jason's personal history of being a difficult employee, how would you help him improve his productivity? Why would your plan work?
6. If you were a newly appointed NW manager like Marilyn, how would you deal with John and Alan's management styles? Why?
7. Do you think that Marilyn's orientation and training were adequate in view of her responsibilities? If yes, why do you think so? If not, give suggestions on how to improve the training.

Absenteeism

Absenteeism is not something new for the GS department. After all, most employees are college students who always have numerous assignments, quizzes, papers, and exams that conflict with work. According to the center's policy, the employee is supposed to inform the operations manager before his or her expected absence and find another employee to substitute.

"Why was it not a problem before?" Joe asked himself. He remembers the GS staff as being close to one another. Whenever someone was absent, he or she always could find another employee to fill in. He really missed the "good old days" when GS staff would bring their friends for interviews, and he never had labor shortage problems. However, things have changed. Now it seems that nobody likes to help when other employees need to be absent. To fill this semester's work schedule, Joe has had to run an advertisement in the campus newspaper.

People just don't take this job as seriously as before, Joe mused. A senior GS employee who had worked for him for three years once made this comment. It seems to have some truth as he has found several chronic absentees. One of them is **Andy Bundgard,** who is scheduled to work on Tuesday night from 6 P.M. to close. He often is absent and never gets another employee to fill in for him. Andy always has some excuse and promises to come in on time the next Tuesday. After one or two weeks, he falls back to his "habit" again.

One NW manager suggested that Andy be terminated. However, there is no policy at the center to deal with student employee absences. Moreover, being already short of labor, Joe would rather call the absentees and give them a warning than take the time and effort to recruit and train new employees. So far, the absentees seem to take his warning seriously, at least for a short period of time.

However, the NW managers have reported complaints from some evening-shift employees who follow their schedules accordingly. They feel that it is unfair for them to take up extra work and stay longer at night while their co-workers can get by with being absent. As a rule, the evening-shift employees cannot leave unless all assigned rooms are set up. Joe worries that, if he continues to be lenient to the absentees, it could hurt the morale of good employees. What was more, absenteeism has had some impact on the NW managers' jobs too. Rather than spending more time overseeing operations of the center and dealing with customers' requests, they sometimes have to set up rooms.

There also seems to be some pattern in the absenteeism, thought Joe when he studied a copy of the GS work schedule. Employees on the early morning shift were more likely to be absent than those on any other shift. The early morning shift was a newly added shift this semester. Joe expected it to relieve some responsibilities of the evening-shift employees by setting up some meeting rooms in the morning. Usually the evening shift was the most demanding one because employees had to set up rooms for meetings held in the evening as well as those held the next day before 1 P.M.

At the beginning of the semester, employees showed up at 5 A.M. every morning. Gradually, some of them started to come later. Eventually, many of them ceased to come at all. Ironically, all early-morning-shift employees also work on other shifts and have no problem coming to work on time for those shifts. When Joe found that he could not count on the early morning shift, he had to fall back to the "safe" practice of having the evening shift set up all rooms for meetings scheduled before 1 P.M. the next day.

At first, the evening shift was happy with the addition of the early morning shift, because they felt they had been doing most of the work of the GS department even though the hourly wage was the same across shifts. However, when they discovered that they had to do the same amount of work after the addition of the new shift, dissent appeared. They complained a lot to the NW managers about the early morning shift having nothing to do. In the meantime, Joe started to hear complaints from the early morning shift about the haphazard work of the evening shift. It seemed that the early morning shift was now doing many minor adjustments to meeting rooms set up by the evening shift.

Probably it has something to do with our schedule, Joe thought as he took off his eyeglasses and put the work schedule aside. He wondered how other center departments made their work schedules. The catering department did not use a fixed schedule. They hired mostly students and determined the work schedule on a weekly basis. Because compensation included an hourly wage plus a portion of the gratuity collected from catered events, students were usually willing to come when they were called. Apparently, the GS department could not provide any extra money other than hourly wage due to the tight financial budget.

Joe looked out the window. It was a sunny April day and the spring semester would end in a couple of weeks. He wanted to plan for next semester's work schedule early. He wondered what he should do about the problems that probably would occur next semester.

Discussion Questions

1. What are some problems Joe is facing? Prioritize them.
2. How should Joe deal with absenteeism? Support your recommendations.
3. Should Joe keep the early morning shift? Why or why not?
4. What could Joe do to boost the morale of evening-shift employees? Explain.
5. Do part-time employees lack commitment? Why or why not? If yes, what would you do to increase commitment?

Barbara Wilson

Joe doesn't know what to do about **Barbara Wilson,** a new NW manager who replaced Wendy. Barbara is from hospitality rather than business, but Joe decided to hire her and continue looking for a manager from business. Barbara graduated from college two months ago and had no work experience. After two weeks of training in early August, she started work. Her fixed shifts were Monday and Saturday nights, and she has a rotating shift every fourth Wednesday.

On Monday night, there were two supervisors, **Tyler Versteeg** and **Bill Fletcher.** Tyler had worked for the center for more than three years, while Bill had been there for two years. They knew everything about the job and got along with each other. Whenever they differed on work matters, they discussed the problem rather than trying to force one's opinion on the other. Besides these supervisors, there was another employee working on Monday nights. He was quite new, but did not affect the efficiency of their teamwork because he was willing to accept instructions from others. Monday night always was easy, so Barb felt very comfortable.

On Saturday night, there were three employees plus Tyler, all with at least two years' experience. They worked very efficiently, making Barbara's job easier. Although there was more work on weekends than weeknights, Barbara was very satisfied with her staff.

Because Barbara was very new, she was not familiar with the system. At the beginning, she tried to learn everything. As time went by, everything ran smoothly because of her competent staff, so she stopped learning and relied a lot on her staff. Every time guests needed something, she called her staff on the radio and asked them to deal with it. At the end of the first semester, Barbara had not made any mistakes because of her staff. There were even times she did not check rooms set up by her staff because she was certain that they were done according to requirements.

Although Barbara was not as competent as her staff, she was well-liked by them. She treated them like friends. It was not unusual to see her sitting in the GS office chatting with them. Barbara never yelled at anybody, even when they made major mistakes. She did not keep a very close eye on what they were doing. She gave them lots of freedom, letting them do what they felt comfortable doing. Sometimes when they worked very late on Saturday night, Barbara bought food for them. She noticed several times that the GS crew took drinks from the kitchen, but she pretended not to see them because she did not want to make them angry with her and not work hard.

Most of the GS staff liked to work with Barbara because they could take breaks without asking her. As long as they got their work done, she didn't care what they did when it was not busy. They even asked Barbara to do some things for them. Barbara was never strict. Even when the GS staff violated policies, she just reminded them instead of blaming or reporting them. They did not feel any pressure working for her. Time went fast. Now Barbara realizes that she is in a very difficult situation.

The Problem

It is spring semester, and Tyler graduated in the fall. Barbara is scheduled to work Tuesday and Saturday nights. She has seldom worked with the three GS employees scheduled on Tuesday night. One of them has worked for half a year, and the other two started at the beginning of the semester. At first Barbara did not notice the difference between the experienced and inexperienced employees. After working on Tuesdays for two weeks, she found that she finished her work much later than on Monday night. She thought it was because that night was busier than usual. When the problem lasted for four weeks, she realized it was the employees' inefficiencies instead of the events.

What happened in the fifth week confirmed Barbara's guess. She started work at 4:30 P.M. and, as usual, she did not give the GS employees any instructions. She was used to letting them finish everything. After reviewing the schedule of events for that night, Barbara realized that it was a busy night, and she probably would not go home until midnight. She was not happy because she had an exam the next day. So most of the time she stayed in her office and studied for the exam. Only once did she go out to solve a guest's problem.

About 11:30 P.M., Barbara started to check the meeting rooms that she thought the GS staff should have finished. She was surprised to find that half the rooms were not set up at all, including one big room in which there would be a lecture for 500 the next morning. She called the GS department and found the employees chatting in the office. When she checked their schedule, she did not find any GS plan for that night. She was angry because it meant she had to stay at least one and a half hours later than she thought. Because she was always very kind to them, she just kept her anger inside and asked them to set up the rooms. This time she followed them and noticed that they were much slower than experienced employees not finishing until 2:00 A.M. As Barbara reflected on the employee schedules, she felt that they were not fair. There were two supervisors on Monday night but no one on Tuesday night, and Tuesday night was always busier than Monday night. However, she did not bring the issue to the staff meeting.

Another two weeks passed. Barbara attended the weekly meeting as usual. This time Joe mentioned the work on the previous Tuesday night. He said that there were quite a few mistakes in the setup of one big room. It was the first time he had pointed out the inadequate work. Barbara felt ashamed and decided to check the rooms carefully next time. But the same thing happened again the following week when Joe mentioned the setup mistakes. Barbara was embarrassed because she had not found the mistakes in the setup. Her confidence wavered more.

Again it was Tuesday night, and an important meeting was held in the biggest room. Barbara was walking around when she was informed that a guest wanted the microphone adjusted. Barbara asked a GS employee to do it. But after only a few minutes, she was called again for the same problem. She went to the room and saw all the GS staff there, but none of them knew how to adjust it. Barbara realized the seriousness of the situation, because she did not know either. Again Joe mentioned it in the staff meeting.

Compared with Tuesday night, Saturday night seemed much easier. Although Tyler was gone, the same employees who had worked with Barbara last semester were there. She had become closer to them because they always did a good job. She never expected anything to be wrong when they worked—until Joe talked with her personally instead in front of the other staff. He said that somebody had reported that she signed time cards for more hours than the Saturday night employees worked. All employees were paid by hours calculated from their time cards. Sometimes when they forgot to punch in, they asked the manager to sign the time card for them. Barbara always signed for them without checking for accuracy.

Barbara really was upset and worried about her job because it was her only source of income. The spring semester was ending, and eight experienced employees were ready to graduate. Among them, three worked with Barbara on Saturday night. After the summer semester, Joe will decide whether to continue employing Barbara.

Discussion Questions

1. What kind of a leader is Barbara? Justify your response. Are her leadership qualities related to her management ability? Why or why not?
2. Did Barbara have a good beginning? Explain. If not, describe what could have been done differently.
3. What problems troubled Barbara? Prioritize them in terms of importance. Describe how you would handle each.
4. Is Joe a good supervisor of Barbara? Justify.
5. If you were Barbara, describe what you would do to keep the job.
6. If you were Joe, would you decide to keep Barbara? Why or why not?

Night/Weekend Manager Shortage

As Joe recalls the responsibilities of the NW manager, he wonders if he will find a fourth manager. The three current NW managers—Steve, Barbara, and Marilyn—are from hospitality. After Wendy graduated, Joe has not been able to find someone from business because no one has applied. Because the managers are full-time students on assistantship, they can't work more than twenty hours per week. Therefore, Joe must do something to fill that fourth position.

In the meantime, Joe must decide how to staff his management positions. One solution for the fourth manager is to use one of the GS employees. **Ron Lee,** who has worked at the center for several years, could take part of the NW manager's responsibility on Saturday and Sunday mornings. Currently, Ron works these mornings as well as on weekdays. On weekends, he supervises other GS employees and on weekdays they are peer workers. Ron is a good worker but lacks leadership skills. He complains that the other GS workers won't obey him when he wants them to set up some rooms. Some GS workers become slack; they are absent from time to time without good excuses and often leave early. It is hard to find substitutes for GS employees.

The GS employees (including Ron) are not satisfied with the custodial staff. Usually at the end of a day, the custodial staff is responsible for cleaning the floors of rooms. But when rooms need to be turned over for the next events, the GS employees have to dust-mop the floor before they start the room setup. They frequently complain because they think it is custodial work. Although the operations manager and the NW manager on duty have told them several times that it is their responsibility, not the custodian's job, they are not happy. There are no written job descriptions for the GS employees. Sometimes the custodial staff asks GS employees to empty rooms so they can do floor work even though the work is not scheduled.

One night, the custodial supervisor asked the GS crew to empty a middle-size meeting room so that the custodians could scrub the floor, which was not scheduled. The GS employees were eager to go home. They finally left without clearing the room because the event in that room would not be over until 1:00 A.M. The custodial staff couldn't do the floor work that night. Joe wonders what Ron or a new manager would do in this instance.

Joe also thinks of Ron's effectiveness with other issues. The NW managers don't get along with the catering manager, **Pat Montabon,** and his assistant managers because they usually order GS employees to do work without informing the NW managers. It seems Pat and his assistants must be satisfied immediately no matter what the GS employees are doing at that time.

To keep costs low in the catering department, from time to time, Pat asks GS employees to work for him when they are having large wedding receptions, so the employees from the two departments have a chance to interact with each other. The GS employees are glad to help in the catering department because they can get free food. However, sometimes the catering staff doesn't clear the food left in meeting rooms until the next day and doesn't answer when paged to clear rooms. This upsets both the GS manager and crew because it delays the GS employees' work. When he was informed of this situation by the NW manager, Joe talked with Pat, but the rooms are still not being cleared.

Customers sometimes complained that the room setups were not correct, the tables were not clean, and some equipment was not working well. They also complained that the assigned room was not the one they requested. Sometimes the customers were not on the schedule, although they had called and reserved rooms.

All these problems bothered Joe. The managing director told him to improve customer satisfaction as soon as possible. He also has to solve the problems among different departments. He is hoping that one more NW manager will help change the situation. Is Ron the right person?

Just as Joe was preparing to offer Ron the NW manager position, he received a fax from the business college: the résumés of four candidates. However, before the interviews, two of the candidates informed Joe they had taken another job. Most students have financial aid at the business college and hold quarter-time assistantships, not half-time. The center has to select one from the remaining two candidates, **John Wang** and **Lucas Abraham** (see their résumés). When interviewing John and Lucas, Joe found that they didn't have any idea of their responsibilities as NW manager (see the job description). Apparently, the business college hadn't given them enough information about this job.

Résumé

John Wang
1245 Almond Street
College Town, MN
(234) 555-9000 *Jwang@compute.net*

Highlights of Qualifications

- Practical experience in designing export products.
- Effective management of technical team with high achievements.
- Excellent communication and presentation skills both in Chinese and English.
- Strong commitment to cooperative teamwork.
- Teaching experience in real world.
- Outstanding academic background and extreme activities on campus.
- Excellent adjusting and adapting abilities overseas.

Professional Experience

Independent Distributor, Market America (2001–2004)
- Initialized independent distributor network in Midwest to sell natural health products.

Volunteer Sales Associate, Worldly Good Art (2001–2004)
- Promoted sales of art goods from developing countries in order to help artists and keep the special arts alive in those countries.

Artist, Lansing, MI (2000–2001)
- Designed and made angels with clothing for Christmas season. Sold at an art store in Bloomington, MI.

Assistant Manager, Chief Designer and Designer, Shenyang Woolen Textile Company, China (1996–2000)
- Supervised 5 designers, assigned tasks, and evaluated their performance. Cooperated with marketing, sales, and production departments to determine the strategies, varieties, timing, and priorities of design and production of export products. Helped negotiate with foreign countries.
- Taught principles and application of color in textile for the designers and technicians in training programs company-wide. Created 2 textbooks and 16 training materials for workers and technicians on various topics.
- Designed patterns and processes for export fabrics. Coordinated the implementation of assembly lines in each workshop and supervised the product quality control.

Education

MBA Candidate, South West State University, 2003–present
Intensive English, South West State University, 2000–2001
ESL English, South West Adult Continuing Education Center, 2000–2001
ESL English, Indian Hill Community College, 1998–2000
B.S., Major: Textiles Engineering, TianJin Institute of Textiles Engineering, China, 1996

Activities

Member, Toastmasters International (1997–2000)
Student Leader, TianJin Institute of Textiles Engineering, China (1992–1996)
• President, Student Union
• Vice President, Textile Information Club

Honors

• Informational Friendship Fair (IFF) to give presentation about Chinese culture, 2000
• The Forest Series of Men Suite "Best Product" Prize winner in Liaoning Province, 1999
• Second Prize in the National Quality Evaluation Competition, 1997
• Honor Student and Best Student Leader

Résumé

Lucas Abraham
777 W. 9th Street
College Town, MN
(234) 555-1414

Work Experience:

Summer 1999   Tekfen Construction Company, Istanbul, Turkey
                       Office Assistant at Istanbul Subway Construction
                       Responsibilities and duties included:
                       • Supervise construction company workers (some-
                         times at the construction site)
                       • Help process project support requests
                       • Do typing and layout of weekly company newsletter
                       • Perform routine secretarial functions
                       • Produce graphics (about TQM models)
                       • Serve as Employee Activities Committee member

Summer 1998   Bayindir Construction Company, Istanbul, Turkey
                       Internship at Construction Site
                       Responsibilities and duties included:
                       • Supervise construction workers
                       • Type daily report to site engineer
                       • Serve on total quality achieving team to operate
                         7 management tools
                       • Perform all day-to-day engineering functions at
                         the construction site

Education:

1995 Uskudar Fen High School Graduate
2000 Bogazici University Civil Engineering Department Graduate (Rank: 3/77)
2000 State University, MBA

Office Skills: Windows 98, Office 97, Fortran 77, SAP 90

Activities:

• Member of Bogazici Univ. Ski Team (1995–2000)
• Member of Bogazici Univ. Soccer Team (1995–1999)
• Member of Bogazici Univ. Construction Club (1997–2000)
• Vice President of Bogazici Univ. Construction Club (1997–2000)
• Member of Project Team, Design and Construction of Underground
  Petroleum Tanks (Winner of Senior Projects) (1999–2000)
• Member of MBA Student Association, South West Univ. (2000–2003)

Job Description–Night/Weekend Manager

Work Title: Night/Weekend Manager (NW)

Job Description:

Under general supervision of the director of GS, this position is responsible for the operation of the center evenings and weekends after normal work hours. The NW manager has the responsibility and authority for making decisions that affect total overall operation of the center.

Duties and Responsibilities:

- Plan, coordinate, and supervise daily activities of GS department, including meeting room setups; placement of signage, inventory, and audiovisual equipment for meetings; and care and maintenance of equipment used in the department.
- Work with director of GS to hire, train, supervise, and evaluate part-time employees.
- Oversee evening and weekend operations.
- Ensure security of building, making decisions when assistance is needed.
- Handle money safely during off-hours.
- Work with departments in coordination of activities, functions, and schedules for efficient and effective running of center.
- Interpret and implement building policies and procedures.
- Maintain high level of building appearance.
- Check areas/departments, making sure all are locked and secure.
- Submit billing information to reservations office for billing purposes.
- Prepare required daily/nightly reports and other reports as needed.
- Attend weekly staff meetings.
- Perform other duties as assigned.

As NW manager for the center, you will be responsible for many people, functions, and services. In the absence of the full-time staff members, your decisions should be made in the best interests of the operations, events, and clients of the center. Even though supervisors of the various areas may be present in the building, the sole responsibility and authority for the operation of the building lies with the NW manager. You are granted the authority to make decisions and will be backed in those decisions.

The NW manager's role requires active monitoring and direction of operations. It is essential that you make a complete inspection of the building every hour, because you personally will be held responsible for building lockup at the end of each day. This is the only means by which the manager can observe and control the operation, particularly as the shifts have reduced supervisor and employee staffing. In addition, special or large events will require a great deal of your attention to ensure proper overall service to the center's clients.

The guiding philosophy of the center is providing outstanding service and facilities to the university community. Whenever possible, the manager should accommodate any reasonable request. Often groups will have shown no forethought in planning an event or lack understanding of our policies. They must be accommodated and educated. Do so, whenever possible, in a positive manner. Firmness is also required in enforcing policy, ensuring the orderly operation of the building, and providing for the security and safety of our facility users. In these cases, polite and informed enforcement is required.

Also, keep in mind that there will be situations in which you will need help in dealing with dissatisfied or belligerent people. Do not hesitate to call campus public safety officers.

Discussion Questions

1. Which candidate would you choose from the two students? Why? Would you consider Ron? Justify.
2. What are the other choices besides finding a fourth NW manager? Explain.
3. Is it the business college's responsibility to introduce the responsibilities of the job to student applicants? If so, what should the college do? If not, explain.
4. Describe what you would do to change the current situation of the catering and GS department. Why would this work?
5. What is your opinion of the GS crew's being asked to take on some custodial responsibilities? Justify.
6. Is there a problem with the GS crew working in catering? Why or why not?
7. As NW manager, describe what you could do to improve customer satisfaction.

Kalamazoo University

Kalamazoo University (KU) is located in a northwestern city with approximately 60,000 residents. KU has approximately 29,000 students, with on-campus housing available for about 15,000. The remainder of students live in off-campus housing, apartments, or other alternative housing arrangements.

The campus has its own foodservice operation, consisting of eight units. Each unit feeds about 3,200 students a day. (Meal plans are available to all students; however, they are not mandatory.) Students have a number of meal options available. They are allowed to eat at several venues throughout campus.

One goal of the foodservice department is for all units to operate in the same way, including use of standardized recipes and production forms and providing the same dining experience in each unit. The department also believes that quality of product and service is important. Therefore, the manager of each unit can authorize changes in products, policies, or procedures as needed to improve food quality and service.

Until recently, each unit was run by a manager with two assistant managers who help take care of day-to-day activities and duties. Each unit has an entrée, bakery, and salad department plus line service coordinators. For the most part, employees within each unit get along fairly well. One unit has a manager who has an abrasive personality, and often the human resources manager gets requests from student employees to be transferred out of her unit.

The foodservice department offers many work opportunities for students. It is no longer necessary to live on campus to be employed at the university foodservice. The foodservice managers work hard to give hospitality students a positive experience. Students often remain with the foodservice department upon graduation.

The Problems

Because of last year's budget cutbacks, two units, East Hall and West Hall, have been sharing one manager. **Jolene Hofmeyer,** the manager of these two halls, does her best to divide her time between the two places, but each unit has employees with different abilities, and Jolene is finding it harder to give each unit half of her time.

Although this is the second year of the shared arrangement, Jolene has noticed that as the school year has gotten into full swing, her absence is felt in both halls. Jolene's responsibilities include making final decisions on disciplinary matters, authorizing changes in recipes, and coordinating financial matters. She relies on her assistant managers to train all new employees, but it is her responsibility to evaluate them, so she feels that she must keep on top of the overall situation in both halls.

Because Jolene cannot be in both units at once, major decisions are delayed until she arrives at the hall. The delay in decision making is creating problems in the operation of the business and the attitudes of employees. Some employees are concerned that products that do not meet quality standards are being served to customers. For example, employees in the salad department of East Hall prepared a pasta salad according to the standardized recipe. The salad had a very bland taste and very little color. Jolene was not available to authorize changes to the product. Because the recipe was followed exactly, the salad was served as scheduled. Students took very little salad, and most of what was taken was not eaten. The remainder of the salad was discarded.

Disciplinary actions for some problem employees who are arriving late or not following instructions have been delayed. The problems are getting worse. For example, in West Hall, one student employee has been known to fix her own sack lunch. She fills her sack with more than the allotted amount of food. Such action could result in dismissal; however, nothing has been said to the employee because Jolene has not been available to witness the problem.

Because there may not be a manager in the hall when employees have a disagreement over policies or procedures, the issue doesn't get solved. Employees have been known to develop the issues to where there are sides between groups of employees. When Jolene hears of the conflict, it seems to be blown out of proportion, and she isn't sure of the facts. Jolene knows that there are dominating personalities who rub each other the wrong way. Power struggles can arise when these employees have differing opinions. A few times when Jolene has reported to a hall, the environment has been so tense one could cut it with a knife.

These situations are having a negative effect on the operation of the units. Employee morale is quickly decreasing, and the operation's efficiency is falling. Some long-term, full-time employees are considering taking the situation to the union. Full-time employees in all foodservice units at KU are members of the local union, so union involvement could affect all units. No one has shared the possibility of union involvement with Jolene. However, she probably is so busy that she hasn't even thought about it. How to keep the union out of management decisions has been discussed often at their meetings. They are fully aware that if the union gets involved in one unit, it will soon be in all units.

Sherry Isenhart, a key employee in West Hall, has shared the union possibilities with **Jane Slutzki,** another hall manager. She will not discuss who is planning to take the issue to the union, but has given some specific details about what employees have discussed. Jane is not sure whether she should bring this to the managers' meeting because she doesn't want to hurt Jolene's feelings. If this is just a rumor, it could do some damage to Jolene's self-esteem. On the other hand, Sherry's information has merit. It seems best to take care of the issues before the union gets involved.

Tom Besser, the director of foodservice, is sympathetic to Jolene's situation, but can do little for her. Because of lack of funding, an additional manager cannot be hired. Tom has, however, authorized Jolene to take whatever measures she feels she needs to make East Hall and West Hall operate as efficiently as possible. Whatever Jolene decides to do, she will have Tom's complete cooperation. Changes must be made soon, and whatever Jolene decides must have a positive and timely impact on the operation of the units.

Discussion Questions

1. Is Jolene being treated fairly? Why do you think Tom decided to share a manager between these two halls?
2. If you were Jolene, what would you consider viable solutions? Why? Which would you choose? Support your decision.
3. Should Jane share Sherry's information about employees going to the union with how things are being run in East and West Halls? Why or why not?
4. If you were Jane, what would you suggest to Sherry, if anything, when you are informed about the possibility of involving the union?
5. Should Jolene consider empowerment? Explain.
6. Will empowerment help the morale and efficiency in the foodservice units? Explain.
7. How can Jolene go about implementing empowerment? Why are these important steps?
8. What is the downside of employee conflict when it goes unsolved?
9. Do you agree that Tom's hands are tied? Support your answer.

North Central State University Campus Dining Services

PART I

It is late July and the director of campus dining services is getting nervous. **Steve Chupina** only has four weeks until school starts, and there is a lot of hiring to be done. He has been the director of six dining halls, each located within a dormitory on the North Central State University (NCSU) campus, for more than twenty years. Recently he was promoted to president of NCSU dining services and needs to make some changes in management personnel.

Steve chose **Carla Bahmen** to serve as interim director of NCSU dining services. Carla quickly accepted the position and was willing to begin as director whenever it seemed appropriate. Carla thought this opportunity to serve as interim director would give her the chance to decide whether she would apply for the permanent director position.

The catering department was becoming very profitable, and Steve created a position of catering manager. His second decision was to confirm who would be asked to fill this position. He had been planning to promote **Kari Lorimor** to catering manager for some time, and this seemed to be the right time to make the switch. Kari was excited about the opportunity. Both Carla and Kari have been dining hall managers for nearly fifteen years.

Three months ago, **Peg Kaur,** the Walker Hall dining manager for five years, told Steve that her husband had accepted a new job upstate, and her family would be moving in July. **Margaret Gurik,** the current dining manager at Dinan Hall, gave her one-month notice today; she is making a career change so she can spend more time with her family. She has been employed with NCSU dining services for about nineteen years.

NCSU Campus Dining Services
Organization Chart #1

President of NCSU Dining Services Steve

New Director Carla

Dinan Manager Opening
- P.M. Assistant Manager Rodney
- A.M. Assistant Manager Jim

Slater Manager Opening
- A.M. Assistant Manager Janet
- P.M. Assistant Manager Ross

Burgum Manager Sam
- Assistant Manager Diane

Locken Manager Marian
- Assistant Manager Chris

Walker Manager Opening
- Assistant Manager Morgan

Smith Manager Opening
- P.M. Assistant Manager Lynne
- A.M. Assistant Manager Elaine

New Catering Manager (Kari)

Thus, there are four manager positions to fill within four weeks (see the NCSU campus dining services organization chart #1). Applications have been collected from seven dining service assistant managers, and six applications have been received from outside applicants. Steve has elected a committee to do the interviewing and recommend who should be hired. The committee consists of Carla, Kari, Steve's administrative assistant, the on-campus grocery store manager, and the dining service's computer technician. Steve will review the committee's recommendations and ultimately make the final decision.

The Six Dining Halls

Walker Dining Hall

Walker Hall, the smallest of the six dining halls, serves 500 students per day. With Peg's move, there is no manager. It is well known that Walker is the easiest facility to operate. The meals are served buffet-style three times a day, Monday through Friday, requiring nine full-time staff. The manager must be capable of working in all areas so he or she can fill in if an employee is absent. Walker has one assistant manager, **Morgan Ervin,** who has also been there for the same five years as Peg has been but is not interested in becoming the manager. She is very happy in her current position, but is nervous about the new management.

Locken Dining Hall

Locken Hall is the second smallest operation, serving 800 students each day Monday through Friday. **Marian Kruzich,** the manager, is very happy with her job and how her hall operates. She is the person whom everyone calls when they have a question, and she always has an answer. Students serve themselves buffet-style, which requires a full-time staff of ten. In addition to serving a small number of dormitory students, Locken's specialty is serving pregame meals to all campus athletes and providing breakfast and lunch meals for the campus day-care center. Marian's only assistant manager, **Chris Salazar,** has not applied for any of the four manager openings.

Burgum Dining Hall

Burgum Hall, a medium-size facility, serves an average of 1,200 students each day. **Sam Van Osdel** is the current manager; he enjoys his position at Burgum and wants to stay. This hall is the only one where a vegetarian entrée is served each meal Monday through Saturday and Sunday brunch. All twelve full-time employees enjoy working at Burgum Hall because of its management staff, kitchen setup, and office space. The dining room is very open and bright, creating a pleasant atmosphere for employees and students. **Diane Underwood,** the only assistant manager at Burgum, has applied for a manager position.

Smith Dining Hall

Smith Hall has a medium-size production area and dining room with a very small dish room. About 1,500 students are served daily. Smith Hall also contains the centralized campus catering and bakery departments, the only departments open on weekends. Kari, who was recently promoted to catering manager, has two assistant managers, **Elaine Ritter** and **Lynne Mutungi,** who both have applied for a manager position. Smith Hall has a full-time staff of fifteen, plus thirty student employees. Because all meals for the catering department are prepared in Smith Hall, it is hard to project staffing needs due to unpredictable bakery and catering sales. The catering department has to prepare meals for a variety of customers, which tends to frustrate the kitchen staff.

Dinan Dining Hall

Dinan is the second-largest hall on campus and is open all year excluding holidays. Dinan runs three serving lines to serve 2,000 students daily, except Sundays when it is closed for the evening meal. There are two assistant managers, **Jim Luehrs** and **Rodney Jackson,** and a part-time student manager. It requires eighteen full-time employees and 125 student employees to operate effectively. This hall is known to be the "clean and organized" hall, a result of Margaret's management strategy. It also has a reputation for having many employee arguments and has the highest turnover rate of the six halls. During the summer, sporting camps, church groups, conventions, and annual business conferences are housed and served in this hall. When no groups are scheduled during the summer, the staff is kept busy cleaning for the next year because they have a twelve-month contract and must be provided work. Jim and Rodney have both applied for the manager positions.

Slater Dining Hall

Slater Hall is the largest and most popular dining facility on campus, yet has only two serving lines to serve 1,250 students per meal. Weekend counts vary due to students going home and participating in extracurricular activities off campus. Slater is open every day for every meal except Sunday evenings and holidays. There are thirty-five full-time staff and 175 student employees. Slater Hall is considered the hardest to manage because of its customer count, staff size, and facility size. It was decided that Carla will leave Slater when her replacement is named. The assistant managers, **Janet Kula** and **Ross Holbrook,** both have applied for manager positions. Students enrolled in summer school stay in Slater Hall and are fed in the dining room. The campus grocery store is attached to Slater Hall, making it easy to get menu items that are needed at the last minute. Other halls typically contact Slater Hall when they are in need of a food item on an emergency basis.

The Candidates

The search committee reviewed thirteen applications and chose to disregard the six outside applicants and interview the seven current assistant managers who applied. The candidates are applying for *any* manager position. The committee will decide which hall is the best fit for each candidate and make recommendations to Steve. Manager salary is directly related to the size of dining services. The committee is not charged with filling assistant manager positions; a second hiring will be done to fill these positions.

Diane has her B.S. degree in animal science from NCSU. She completed her coursework in a hospitality management graduate program and has been working on her research for the past two years. She was a student serving line coordinator at Dinan Hall throughout her undergraduate studies. After entering the graduate program, she was promoted to the assistant manager position at Burgum Dining Hall and has held that position for three years. The full-time employees at Burgum enjoy working with her because she is very personable and has no known enemies. In the summer months, Diane works in the Dinan Dining Hall office.

Elaine has a B.S. degree in nutrition and a master's degree in Hotel and Restaurant Management (HRM). She started working for dining services five years ago as a student manager at Dinan Hall. She has helped out with the busy summer months at Dinan for the past two years. She has been an assistant manager at Smith for three years. Her professional goal is to become a professor in HRM. Currently, she is on bed rest and expecting a baby in a few weeks. She is planning to take ten weeks of maternity leave. Dinan Hall employees hope Elaine doesn't become the Dinan Hall manager because they feel that she is bossy and tends to doubt full-time employees' judgment calls in the production area.

Lynne has been the assistant manager at Smith Hall for two years. She married Slater Hall's assistant manager, Ross, this past summer. She was encouraged to apply by her husband and her current manager, Kari. She enjoys her work and has done a decent job with paperwork responsibilities. She tends to be moody toward her employees and other managers in dining services. She had wait staff experience prior to obtaining her current assistant manager position. Lynne is a graduate of the dietetics program at NCSU and is a registered dietitian.

Jim has a B.S. degree in art and an M.S. degree in HRM. During his master's program, he was a student manager at Dinan Hall. He didn't finish his master's degree until he was offered his current A.M. assistant manager position. He signed the employment contract, with the agreement that he would finish his master's in less than one year. He uses his creative abilities in catering large functions. He has been the A.M. assistant manager at Dinan for the past seven years. He has worked under his manager, Margaret, longer than any other assistant manager. All others have quit. Jim oversees small catering events outside of Dinan Hall. He is known as a team player, and employees go to him before Margaret with any questions they may have. He has been working extra hard this summer training the new P.M. assistant manager, Rodney. Jim has been Steve's buddy for the past seven years.

Rodney has a B.S. degree in HRM. He has been the P.M. assistant manager at Dinan Hall since spring. He just told his manager, Margaret, that he has decided to get his master's degree in education at NCSU. His classes will be two nights a week for three hours each. His prior work experience includes assistant manager at a buffet-type steak house, manager at a quick-service restaurant, and assistant catering manager at a large hotel. His major responsibilities at Dinan are to control the meat and produce inventories. Recently, he has had to throw many items away due to his failure to forecast those items accurately. Dinan Hall employees appreciate his humor, but dislike his loud voice and his attitude that he can do no wrong. Just lately he has been confronted about his frequent personal phone calls while working. Rodney is the only African American applying for the position.

Janet has a B.S. degree in business and a MBA. As a student, she was a student supervisor at Locken Hall and a line coordinator at Dinan Hall. After graduating from college, she left dining services to become an assistant manager at a family restaurant for two and a half years. She then managed a busy cafeteria for the next nine years and eventually found herself back at dining services. She has been the assistant manager at Slater Hall for nine years. She remains active on the university's recipe development committee. Rumor has it that two full-time Dinan Hall employees will quit if she is assigned to Dinan as manager, because of past conflicts they had with her at Slater Hall. Slater Hall's employees respect her abilities, although she puts work second to her family.

Ross has a B.S. degree with majors in business and nutrition. Immediately after graduating five years ago, he was hired as an assistant manager at Slater Hall. His employees feel that he is very particular in the way things should be done, causing tension in the workplace. He also has a reputation for being "cocky." He is the head of special-event dinners held at all six halls, and he chairs the recipe development committee. His manager, Carla, thinks very highly of his organizational skills and ability to control food costs and employee turnover rates.

Discussion Questions

1. Predict who will be placed in each manager position at each hall.*
2. If you were Steve, would you use the same approach in filling four manager positions four weeks before school starts? If yes, why? If no, how would you have filled these positions?
3. Is the committee composition appropriate? If yes, justify your response. If no, whom would you add or drop? Why?
4. Do you agree that Steve should have the final say? Please explain.

*See the NCSU campus dining services organization chart #2 to find out what happened.

NCSU Campus Dining Services
Organization Chart #2

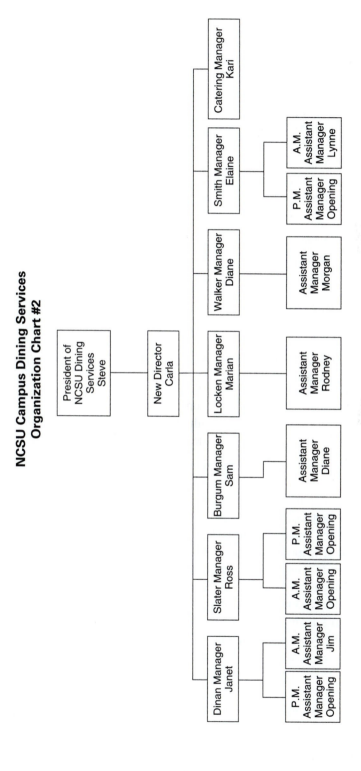

5. What other reasons, besides being happy, would you expect Marian and Sam (the only managers who are staying) might give you to justify why they want to stay in their current positions? After all, they would be getting a major salary increase if they went to a larger hall.

6. What manager qualities do you feel are needed in each of the following halls?
   a. Slater
   b. Dinan
   c. Smith
   d. Walker

7. Please list a weakness and a strength (if either applies) for each candidate, as you perceive them.

	Strength	**Weakness**
a. Diane		
b. Elaine		
c. Lynne		
d. Jim		
e. Rodney		
f. Janet		
g. Ross		

8. What do you think of the search committee's decision to disregard all outside candidates? Be specific.

PART II

The committee checked the seven candidates' references and discovered the following:

Diane's manager, Sam, highly recommended her for a position but felt she was stressed easily with work overload.

Elaine's manager, Kari, felt Elaine was a perfect fit for a manager's position. She had appropriate work experience and education.

Lynne's manager, Kari, told the committee that she felt Lynne was not mature enough for the position. She also expressed concerns about both Janet and Ross getting a manager position.

Jim's manager, Margaret, expressed her concerns that Jim was not a team player. She also stated that he was not involved enough with the dining services committees on campus. Margaret stated that he worked only his scheduled hours and never put in any overtime.

Rodney's manager, Margaret, told the committee that he was too new to be a manager. She said he had not excelled as expected. She reminded the committee that he was going to graduate school soon and might not dedicate himself to manager duties.

Janet's manager, Carla, thought Janet could handle people problems well and was very organized when it came to paperwork.

Ross's manager, Carla, thought Ross had proven that he could be a qualified manager.

During the interviewing process, each candidate was ranked by the committee and placed in a hall. The ranking was as follows:

1. Ross → Slater
2. Janet → Dinan
3. Elaine → Smith
4. Diane → Walker
5. Jim → no change
6. Lynne → morning assistant at Smith
7. Rodney → morning assistant at Locken

The committee shared their reasoning with Steve, and the time has come for him to make the final decision.

Discussion Question

1. If you were Steve, would you agree with the committee's recommendations? Why or why not? If not, what would your rankings be?

What Really Happened

Steve agreed with the committee's decision. Each candidate was brought into his office to receive the final decision. Jim, Rodney, and Lynne, reacted in the following manner.

Jim was shocked when he was told he did not receive a manager's position. He was told that Margaret had strongly discouraged promoting him. He felt he was dedicated to his career, Margaret, his employees, and his friend Steve. Now he will be responsible for training the new manager, Janet. He was very upset and has told the student manager at Dinan Hall that he is not sure if he will stay.

Rodney was told he was simply too new for a manager's position. Steve offered him the A.M. assistant manager position at Locken Hall, if he wanted to focus on his classes in the evenings. The A.M. position is considered more desirable to most assistant managers. Rodney accepted immediately. Steve thanked him for applying and encouraged him to apply for a manager's position in the future if the opportunity should arise.

Lynne was very disappointed and shed a few tears after hearing the news that she was not chosen to be a manager. Steve offered her the A.M. assistant manager position at Smith Hall. She accepted the offer so that she could spend her evenings with her new husband.

The changes will happen immediately, with old managers training new managers during the next two weeks. The assistant manager hiring will take place after the new managers are trained.

Discussion Questions

1. If you were Steve, how would you have handled informing the unsuccessful candidates? Why?
2. What action, if any, should the student manager at Dinan Hall take upon hearing that Jim may not stay? Defend your answer.
3. If you were Jim, what would you do? Why?

Rocky Mountain University

Rocky Mountain University (RMU) is located in a progressive Colorado city at the base of the Rocky Mountains. The university has a population of 22,000 graduate and undergraduate students. Because the university is known for its high-quality education, its beautiful surroundings, and its close proximity to the Denver metro area, it attracts an extremely diverse student population from all over the country.

Freshman students at RMU are required to live in the residence halls during their first year. The residence life and dining service departments serve students living in the residence hall system and are organized under the division of student affairs. The dining services department consists of six self-operated units that provide three meals a day, seven days a week.

The director of dining services, **Ron Jackson,** is 59 and accepted his current position after a very successful career in university dining at a California college. He is well respected within the college and university hospitality segment and has the reputation of a fun-loving guy who likes to have a few drinks with "the boys" after work. Ron accepted the position at RMU under the premise that he would retire when he reached 63. At this time in his career, Ron has no desire to encounter any new, major projects, but instead plans to ease up as he approaches retirement. He has an open-door policy and feels it is his duty to develop younger professionals in the industry that has been part of his life since his army days in the 1960s.

Nichols Dining Center is one of six dining units on the RMU campus that is operated by the dining services department. Similar to the other five units, Nichols is operated by a three-member management team. **Dillon Schafer** is the senior manager and **Lisa Plath** and **Lynette Miskell** are his assistants. Dillon has just been diagnosed with HIV and is experiencing both physical and emotional problems. As a result, he has left most of the day-to-day operating decisions to Lisa and Lynnette. Lisa, who works the A.M. shift (6:30 A.M. to 2:30 P.M.) is an experienced manager who worked in the federal prison foodservice system. The P.M. manager, Lynette, is a recent college graduate with very little supervisory experience. She has an outgoing personality and is eager to learn. Her hours are from 11:30 A.M. to 7:30 P.M.

Three cooks, two dishwashers, two salad workers, and two floaters are employed at Nichols Dining Center to feed its 750 student customers. Each employee supervises student employees and is covered under the collective bargaining agreement negotiated by the American Federation of State, County, and Municipal Employees (AFSCME). Presently, the cooks are paid between $10 and $12 per hour, and dishwashers and service personnel earn about $7 per hour. At $7 per hour, employees can barely afford the standard of living necessary to live in this affluent city.

David McGrath is a dishroom supervisor employed during the A.M. shift. He is 35 years old, lives at home with his parents, and loves his job. He has worked for the university for the past ten years and takes his responsibilities very seriously. He is well aware of all policies and procedures of the operation and sometimes needs to be reminded by his co-workers that he is not the manager in charge.

David feels very at home in his job and has never worked in any other dining center. He has excellent technical knowledge and works well with his hands. His biggest weakness is that he has a learning disability and reads and writes at the second-grade level.

One afternoon, Lynette was in the office working when a student employee, **Kim Kuehl,** approached her. Kim awkwardly explained to Lynette that David had recently begun asking several female student employees to go to a movie after work. All had declined David's invitation, but he did not seem to understand that *no* meant *no,* meaning none of them wanted to go out with him. Kim then proceeded to show Lynette a typewritten note that David had given her the day before.

Clearly the note and two others Kim had already thrown away were a strong indication that David did not understand either the inappropriateness or the seriousness of his behavior. Because Dillon was in the hospital at the time, and Lynette was unsure of how to proceed with the situation, Lynette decided to seek advice from Ron.

Kim—

I love you. I want to mary you. If yes plese say yes. I love tosee yu in a dres I love tosea yu in yur shorts. I love to sea yu ina bukeni. Did you know I have a catWe culd go to the movies yuand me in my car. Wuld yu like that if yes plese say yes. I love you

Yur frind, DAVID

After Ron read the note, he told Lynette that he had been in this business for thirty-seven years, and it wasn't until recently that women began complaining about harassment. Ron felt that if a woman had a sexual harassment complaint, she probably was asking for it in the first place. After making a few phone calls, Ron discovered the procedure to follow in an informal harassment complaint. He then assisted Lynette in documenting the case as well as forwarding a copy to the affirmative action office on campus. The complaint was eventually forwarded to the ombudsman's office for clarification and mediation.

Discussion Questions

1. From a legal standpoint, would this case be considered sexual harassment? Why or why not?
2. Why is it important for an organization to have a written sexual harassment policy?
3. If a sexual harassment complaint is filed, what responsibilities do you as a manager have?
4. Some companies prohibit fraternization among employees. What are the pros and cons of such a policy?
5. How do you think this situation could be handled effectively? Support your answer.

Twin City Schools Food Service

Cindy Parker is the current school foodservice director (see job description) for a large public school system with an annual food service budget of $850,000. Cindy has been in this position for twelve years and plans to retire from her position within three. She would like to have the foodservice employment climate as stable and organized as possible before she leaves.

Cindy Parker does all the interviewing for foodservice positions and makes recommendations to the school board. She must have approval from the board for any hiring she does.

Organization

Cindy's office is in the high school building, where central kitchen employees prepare all food for the high school, the middle school, and nine elementary schools. Lunches are delivered in bulk to the satellite locations starting at 9:30 A.M. The central kitchen employees also prepare food for meetings, concerts, and receptions held at any school. This usually consists of three functions a week. Each satellite unit has a manager and several workers. Foodservice workers are scheduled during lunchtime, usually for a two-hour shift.

Salary and Selection

Salaries for the school foodservice system employees are based on a salary schedule with eleven grades. Each grade involves greater responsibilities over the one below it and has a corresponding salary increase. The foodservice director conducts annual evaluations. Currently there is no policy for job progression. Cindy

Job Description—Foodservice Director

Qualifications:
- Bachelor's or master's degree in hospitality management, food and nutrition, or related field.
- Foodservice management experience.
- ADA-registered dietitian desirable.

Job Goal: Coordinates production and serving of nutritious, quality lunches to students at the lowest possible cost in the most efficient manner.

Salary Range: Negotiable, dependent on qualifications, 230-day contract

Reports To: Executive Director of Human Resource and Management Support Services (Business Manager)

Performance Responsibilities:
1. Administer all aspects of the foodservice program.
2. Develop and implement departmental policies and procedures.
3. Determine food service personnel needs: interview, hire, train, supervise, direct, and evaluate each employee in coordination with unit managers.
4. Maintain an efficient, well-organized, and cost-controlled foodservice program.
5. Oversee the operation of the foodservice office computer management system, record keeping, payroll reporting, accounts payable and receivable, and processing of free and reduced lunch applications.
6. Plan menus and purchase all food, supplies, and equipment needed.
7. Administer all national school lunch program regulations.
8. Keep up to date on legislation pertaining to foodservice programs and make recommendations to the administration as appropriate.
9. Assist with the development of nutrition curriculum for grades K–12. Visit classrooms for nutrition education purposes, as invited and as time permits.
10. Cooperate with principals, faculty, students, and staff to make the foodservice program an integral part of the total school program.
11. Attend districtwide meetings concerning wellness and/or support staff as time allows.
12. Other duties as directed.

has considered implementing a procedure for employees to begin training for the next higher position within the department.

Food Production Manager

Next in line to Cindy is **John Lindstrom,** the food production manager (see job description). John grew up in a nearby suburb and received a degree in food and nutrition five years earlier from the state university. He enjoys the professional sports, climate, and culture the area has to offer. He and his family are content with this location.

The food production manager is a grade 11 (top grade) on the salary schedule. John heard of this foodservice position from his uncle, who is the school board president. Cindy has been very pleased with John's performance. He consistently has done well in supervising production employees at the high school and assisting with their evaluations. Orders and records always are completed as required. John has shown himself to be responsible in performance of his regular duties and related duties assigned to him by Cindy. He has been trained to assume Cindy's responsibilities during her absences.

Cindy feels that John would be the best person to assume her position when she retires. She has talked to him about how to improve his qualifications, and now John is planning to resume his education part-time while he continues to work. He has been accepted in the hospitality graduate program at the nearby university. John always did well in school and is looking forward to the challenge graduate school will offer him.

Recently some employees have complained to Cindy about John's performance. He has been coming to work late, leaving early, and getting behind in some of his responsibilities. These times have been followed by weeks when he seems very dedicated to his job and works long hours. Many hours, however, are spent trying to catch up. Cindy also has been aware of the recent change in John's behavior. Earlier she heard from some friends that John and his wife, Patti, are having marital problems. Cindy mentioned this to John, and his response was a quick denial along with a hasty exit. After another two-week period of slacking performance, Cindy again approached John. He became very emotional and told her his personal problems.

John and Patti have two children: Eric, who is 9 years old, and Anna, who is 6. Two months ago Patti filed for divorce. John moved out of the family home and into a nearby apartment. He and his wife have worked out a temporary physical custody arrangement in which each parent has the children for two-week periods. John has had a great deal of difficulty adjusting to the increased responsibilities that come with being a single working parent, but he wants to make the arrangement work. Both children are in elementary school, yet too young to be unsupervised in the morning before school. John wants to be a quality parent during the two-week period he has custody, but he is finding the responsibilities exhausting. He already is feeling the stress from divorce/separation, legal fees, and the increased demand of his children. John's attorney told him that Patti has stated, via her attorney, that she is very happy with the arrangement and would like to make it permanent.

Job Description—Food Production Manager

Qualifications:
B.S. degree in food and nutrition, hospitality management or related field or five years of food production management experience and demonstrated mathematics skills.

Supervisor: Foodservice Director

Supervises: Foodservice production employees at the high school kitchen.

Job Goal: Organize and direct food production in an efficient manner.

Terms of Employment: School days when lunch is served, plus hours as arranged; salary established by the board of education.

Performance Responsibilities:
1. Operate the department in the absence of director.
2. Bear primary responsibility for production of the total menu, including determining quantity of food to be produced, issuing recipes to each work center, and posting work schedules.
3. Work on standardization of department recipes.
4. Plan efficient use of leftovers, keeping freezer storage of leftover items to a minimum.
5. Complete daily storeroom orders for custodian.
6. Forecast weekly number of meals to prepare daily and keep records to aid in accuracy of future forecasts.
7. Understand objectives and philosophy of the organization and the federal meal regulations and be familiar with the overall program.
8. Assist in evaluation of production employees.
9. Arrange for substitutes in production, as needed.
10. Assume responsibility for security of food and supplies and maintain inventory.
11. Check supply deliveries against purchase orders.
12. Help students develop nutrition awareness.
13. Assist with menu planning.
14. Serve food to students and staff from cafeteria counter.
15. Supervise distribution of food from central kitchen.
16. Direct special food preparation for school-sponsored events.
17. Order food as authorized by foodservice director.
18. Perform related duties as assigned by foodservice director.

Evaluation: Annual evaluation by the food service director.

Grade 11 on Support Staff Salary Matrix

Foodservice Worker

The foodservice worker position (see job description) is a grade 1 and starts at an hourly wage of fifty cents above minimum. This position has always been hard to fill due to the community's low unemployment rate. There have been two openings for foodservice workers at the elementary school level for the entire year. They currently are being filled on a substitute basis. Two more openings are expected for next fall due to the relocation of some families. Occasionally, the manager at the elementary school has to cover this position.

Job Description—Foodservice Worker

Qualifications:
1. Read, write and follow instructions.
2. Perform simple mathematical functions (+ − × ÷).
3. Experience in residential or institutional food service.
4. Basic knowledge of food, products, and small equipment.
5. Ability to lift 50 pounds and withstand conditions of high temperature and humidity.

Supervisor: Foodservice unit head

Supervises: None

Job Goal: Assist in efficient foodservice operations.

Terms of Employment: School days when lunch is served, plus hours as arranged; salary established by the board of education.

Performance Responsibilities:
1. Assist in serving, cashiering, and cleaning as assigned.
2. Check supply deliveries against purchase orders.
3. Maintain standards of sanitation, health, and safety.
4. Help students develop nutrition awareness.
5. Maintain student conduct in cafeteria.
6. Wash and sanitize dishes, utensils, and production equipment.
7. Punch lunch tickets in serving line.
8. Count money.
9. Perform related duties as assigned.

Evaluation: Annual evaluation by the foodservice director.

Grade 1 on Support Staff Salary Matrix

Job Description—Middle School Foodservice Manager

Qualifications:
1. Completion of Food Service Short Courses I, II, III, or their equivalents.
2. Experience as a service worker.
3. Knowledge and skills in use of satellite equipment; knowledge of products and procedures.
4. Ability to lift 50 pounds and withstand conditions of high temperature and humidity.

Supervisor: Foodservice Director

Supervises: Foodservice workers

Job Goal: Efficiently manage school food service unit.

Terms of Employment: School days when lunch is served, plus hours as arranged; salary established by the board of education.

Performance Responsibilities:
1. Train employees to use approved work methods and evaluate their performance.
2. Develop daily service plan that maintains efficient service.
3. Adopt departmental guidelines and apply federal regulations to the school unit.
4. Maintain records and order supplies as authorized by director.
5. Report equipment malfunctions to the director.
6. Assume responsibility for the security of food, supplies, and/or money.
7. Check supply deliveries against purchase orders.
8. Monitor student conduct in cafeteria.
9. Monitor portion sizes.
10. Prepare food for school-sponsored events.
11. Maintain records of free meals and meals sold at full or reduced price.
12. Count money.
13. Supervise production.
14. Perform general cleanup.
15. Perform related duties as assigned.

Evaluation: Annual evaluation by the foodservice director.

Grade 6 on Support Staff Salary Matrix

Middle School Foodservice Manager

Doug Richards, the middle school foodservice manager (see job description), started as a foodservice worker seven years ago when he dropped out of high school. The promotion to middle school foodservice manager and the salary increase came when his wife was pregnant with their third child. He supervises five foodservice workers. They all enjoy working for him, and he is popular with the students.

Doug has trained his workers well, and his turnover rate is the lowest of all schools. The performance is always very high at this school. For the past several months, however, Doug has become increasingly bored with his job. He wants more responsibility. Cindy has heard that Doug has been applying for positions in many unrelated fields and has so far been unsuccessful. She would like to find ways to increase his job satisfaction so he will stay.

Plan of Action

As the foodservice director, Cindy sees some obstacles she wants to take care of before she retires. Some require her immediate attention and others are not as urgent. She wants to have some recommendations in mind for future school board meetings.

Discussion Questions

1. If you were Cindy Parker, what would you see as major employee problems? Explain.
2. What role should a supervisor take when an employee has personal problems? Defend your position. Should Cindy have approached John the way she did? Why or why not? What can be done for an employee in John's circumstances? Justify your response.
3. Is there a need for organizing job progression? Why or why not? What criteria are important? What are the advantages and disadvantages of doing this?
4. What are some suggestions for filling the foodservice worker positions? Defend your answer.
5. What can be done to increase Doug's job satisfaction? Should this be part of Cindy's responsibility? Why or why not?

University Memorial Center

From: Zack
To: Josh
Sent: 9/2
Subject: Settling in

Hi, Josh, how are you doing?

I miss you and the rest of the gang and I hope you guys are well. How's your day going? As for me, getting into a new school in the U.S. and starting my first job at the same time seems to be coursing adrenalin right up my veins. This is a big campus. People here are also very friendly toward foreigners. This morning, on the way home from class, almost everybody who passed me smiled as a gesture of friendliness, I guess. Besides, professors are also very nice.

Did I tell you that I got a 20-hour part-time assistantship from this university? Well, guess what, I will be an AA, which is short for administrative assistant. Never heard of that, huh? Me either. Anyway, I'll go and see my boss, **John Greene,** first thing tomorrow morning, and I figure he is going to walk me through all of this.

Are you still with the HR department at the Hilton? Last time I heard from you, you said you were slated to become the department manager. Congratulations! Way to go, Josh!

It's getting late. Drop me a line or two if you can. ☺

_____

From: Josh
To: Zack
Sent: 9/3
Subject: Hey, pal

I am doing fine. Thanks a bundle!

Well, I AM the manager now and boy, do I feel good about it! In your last letter, you said you were going to see your boss the next day. How was it? What kind of job are you going to take? Is it hard for you? Tell me about it. Maybe I can be of some help.

I bet you must feel somewhat lonely from time to time. Well, I know you are the kind of guy who always sees a glass of water half full. Keep up the good spirit. I know you are going to make it. I have faith in YOU!

_____

From: Zack
To: Josh
Sent: 9/4
Subject: Re: Hey, pal

As for my new job, I finally got a feel of it when I went to see my boss, Mr. Greene, this morning. He is a good guy. He reminded me of an uncle. I was a little bit nervous when I first met him though. But after several minutes of talking, I felt pretty much relieved. He told me that I would become a part-time night/weekend manager in the University Memorial Center (UMC) and my job was to supervise all of the general services (GS) people working in this multifunctional complex on campus.

I asked him to describe general services. He told me the job is to set up the rooms for all the events held in UMC, such as student meetings, society gatherings, wedding receptions, banquets, etc. He also said that unless there are lots of backlog setups and the GS really needs my help, my first order of business is to SUPERVISE the GS and make sure everything is in good shape on nights and weekends. That said, he gave me a big thick training manual, which I think would make perfect bedtime reading material.

Then **Victor Bahr,** a full-time co-worker, showed me around the building and walked me through some of the video-audio equipment and fire alarm and PA systems. I watched a training video for about an hour, with Victor by my side explaining everything I didn't understand. After I was done with the brief training session, Victor and I chatted for about 30 minutes. He told me that John was a pretty laid-back, easygoing boss. As long as everything is in order and nobody complains, Mr. Greene is happy. He also told me that this job is pretty easy. Just work with the guys and earn their respect, then everything is going be fine.

I thanked him and left UMC for my apartment, preparing to do my first shift tonight. To tell you the truth, I didn't quite follow many specific details of the videotape, but I think I will figure it out later. Nobody knows how to swim before he actually gets a chance to make a splash in the water. I am no exception. I will make it through. No problemo!!! ☺

From: Zack
To: Josh
Sent: 9/5
Subject: First night on the job

Last night I worked for the first time at the UMC. I've inherited a good team. Almost everybody was friendly to me. I introduced myself to them in English, and they seemed to understand what I was saying. Isn't it amazing? Even I sometimes have a hard time understanding my own English. I just wish I could have a third hand to give myself a pat on the back.

Before I came here, I thought only Americans worked here. Apparently I was wrong. No wonder they call America "the gigantic melting pot." The majority of employees in GS are Malaysians, Indonesians, and guys from Southeast Asia. They are all good people. Yet the biggest problem seems to be the language gap. Frankly speaking, I had a hard time understanding their English. Anyway, I think I'll get used to it pretty soon.

Let me introduce you to a partial cast of my team: Victor, the guy who gave me a brief training session this morning, has been here the longest; he is the only full-time employee in the GS and we hit it off instantly. He seems to be mature, pragmatic, and very good with people. From where I stand, I'd say he is the informal leader of the gang and the temporary mentor of mine. He is universally trusted.

Arif Komosito, an Indonesian, is the kind of guy you would have a couple of beers with after hours. Know what I mean? He knows his craft and he works hard too. **Danny Chung,** a Chinese Malaysian, chatted with me in broken Mandarin for a few minutes, which amazed me. He is a nice guy, a little bit quiet though. I haven't quite figured him out yet. I think he may be shy, just like me.

Then there's **Sue Wong,** the no-smile, no-nonsense, tough guy from Malaysia, who's got me slightly worried. Maybe because he intimidates me just a bit. Victor once told me Sue has been here for three years, which is second only to Victor. He's fast and meticulous, but he is like a cold fish just pulled out of a liquid nitrogen vat. He never talked to me all night. I tried to bring up a common topic, but he just gave me the "sound of silence." He'll bear watching though, I think.

I hate the Chinese food here, though. You'd know what I mean if you were here. ☺

———————————

From: Josh
To: Zack
Sent: 9/8
Subject: Hi there

Sorry for the delay—or should I bring your attention to the fact that my response is still much faster than most of the trans-Pacific snail mails? Anyway, it's good to hear from you. Things here in China are pretty slow for me—work, work and more work. Sometimes I just want to get out of this drudgery and see the world.

Speaking of the world, how is your new job? How's it going with this Sue guy? Tell me more about him. ☺

From: Zack
To: Josh
Sent: 9/12
Subject: Re: Hi there

There's nothing about Sue that I can put my finger on. Here's why. Tonight, when I was working with him and the rest of the gang, I flubbed a setup time. Victor told me once, but I didn't pay too much attention at that time. And Sue really lit into me. I know I made a mistake, but I made it up pretty soon. It's not like the end of the world. There's no need for HIM to dress me down as if he were the boss. He raised his voice like 100 decibels and went all ballistic. He could have gotten the point across more tactfully, not yelling at me in front of everyone else. Who does he think he is? Sultan of the Turkish Empire? Give me a break!

Any good advice for me? I know I can always count on you.

From: Josh
To: Zack
Sent: 9/13
Subject: wait and see

I totally understand how you feel about this Sue guy. I know you are no pushover. However, based on my own experience, I think your best plan of attack here is to tread lightly your first three or four weeks. It's not wise to mess up with the old birds because your boss may doubt your ability to manage these guys. Just lay low and grit your teeth. Remember, there is an old Chinese saying that every king has a big heart that is so wide that you can row a boat in it.

Maybe you need to talk to Sue and give him a piece of your mind. Maybe you guys can become good friends. Who knows?

From: Zack
To: Josh
Sent: 9/14
Subject: thanks for the advice

Thanks for the advice. I think I need to cool down and talk to Sue. I am sure I can turn him around and become friends with him. At least I'll try my best. Thanks a lot.

From: Zack
To: Josh
Sent: 9/25
Subject: tougher than you think

Thanks but no thanks for your advice. Tonight it's my shift again. After classes in the morning and afternoon, I went to UMC and started doing my job as a night manager. Did I tell you what a night manager's job is like? It is to supervise those GS guys and to make sure everything will be in place for tonight's and tomorrow morning's events. I am to lead the guys through tons of room setups each night. Every night, I will have nearly 30 rooms to turn over. I remember last Wednesday night. We turned over Lincoln Hall and the other big ballrooms twice during the night. We spent two hours setting up the required 1,000 chairs, thirty oval tables, and twenty covered and skirted six-inch tables. After the banquet was over, we had to the clear the rooms for custodial floor work scheduled at midnight. After the custodial guys mopped and waxed the floor, we had to set up another 800 chairs and thirty round tables (Note: why can't we just use ovals for both events?).

After we were done with all the work and called it a day, I looked at my watch. Guess what, it was already past 3 A.M. and I had an 8 A.M. class the next morning. Guess how many guys I had? Two. Only TWO guys, Danny and Sue. Remember what Mr. Greene said when I first met him? I don't have to work with the GS unless there are huge setups and the guys can't cope with that. That's not true. I have to work as a GS. There's simply no other way around. Don't ask me why. All I know is that recently, the U.S. economy has headed toward a recession, and the state government has handed down huge budget cuts several times. UMC, a state-subsidized nonprofit organization, also got a pretty deep cut this year. So the manager cut deeply into the GS workforce, and I ended up working like mad, so did the other two guys.

Danny is a good guy. But he is also a little bit too slow. Then there's Sue. He is fast and efficient. He knows all the setup maps by heart, and he has practically led us through the work during the past two weeks. I was on the learning curve, though. Know what I mean? Mr. Greene was way off base. I have to work with the guys. I will be held accountable for all the problems that transpire during my shifts. In other words, I will be regarded as the last line of defense against quality problems and customer complaints. I will be the last one to leave the building after everything is over and checked. To tell you the truth, I like this job, warts and all. Except . . . Well, here's a little incident.

Around dinnertime, I called Sue through the radio (the kind of big heavy walkie-talkie that cops use all the time) to get him and the other GS guys to set up some rooms for tonight's event—the President's Council. This is a major event, and the university president is going to be here to give a speech. Victor told me a couple of days back to pay special attention to this room's setup. Anyway, I called Sue through my radio, and he did not respond. He is not supposed to leave the building while still on the clock. So I went upstairs and checked the punch card. He was on the clock! I went to the GS office and was surprised and enraged by the scene—the TV was on (watching TV is definitely prohibited), and Danny was watching it with his feet on the table. He told me Sue had the schedule with him. I told Danny that the President's Council was starting in 45 minutes and the room was not set up yet. That said, I rolled up my sleeves and stormed into Lincoln Hall. When some guests arrived 20 minutes later, we were just halfway through the setup. The coordinator of the event, Miss Miller, asked me why the room was not done. She said perhaps it's better for her to see Mr. Greene about this. I explained and apologized profusely. Then Sue showed up. I pretended not to see him.

After we finished the room setup, we went back to the GS office. I asked Sue why he was not available when needed. He said that he went out to dinner with the radio set on the wrong channel. I warned him that leaving while on the clock is against the center's policy. You know what he said afterward? "Who cares! I've been here for three years and we always go out to dinner and watch TV in between setups. Nobody has ever said a thing about it. Not even Victor. Who do you think you are?" Then he kept complaining about the low wages and late hours.

Strangely enough, I noticed Danny nodding his head when Sue ranted about the low wages. I was pretty much confused. What's going on here?!

From: Josh
To: Zack
Sent: 9/26
Subject: talk to Victor

You might consider having a small chat with your amigo Victor and get some insider information about Sue. My own instinct tells me that there's more that you didn't see in this continuing Sue saga. Victor is the key here!

From: Zack
To: Josh
Sent: 9/28
Subject: Ha!

I talked with Victor, and he provided me with some valuable bits of information. Here's another facet of this "continuing Sue saga." Last semester Sue asked for a raise from Mr. Greene, but to no avail. He went right past Mr. Greene to the general manager, and still nothing happened. Enraged, he organized some of his old buddies in GS to ask for a raise, and Sue even threatened to go on strike if management would not give him a satisfactory response. **Paul Jan** and **Peter Rhyan,** the former night managers, opposed Sue's plan vigorously, citing the fact that GS employees have lots of free time on their hands in between setups. Thus, Sue and the gang now hold a grudge against all night managers, including me.

Do you have any suggestions, big boss? ☺

From: Josh
To: Zack
Sent: 9/30
Subject: bottom line?

I see. He is a pain in the neck. It's your first time on the job, and you are the boss. In China, nobody can treat a boss like that, certainly not on his turf. Two days ago a guy who has been with us for quite some time yelled at a new manager. The manager warned him to behave or . . . Well, the guy took it personally and went to the GM, Mr. Zhang. Mr. Zhang and I discussed the whole matter and in the end, you know what, this hot-tempered guy got fired the next day.

Don't be a softie; talk to him and tell him this kind of behavior will not be tolerated. I hate it when a guy chews me out in front of everybody else. Clearly, you have to establish your own authority with him, or he will set a very bad example and pretty soon some of the other guys will follow suit. Then what are you going to do? Kick him and kick him hard. Trust me. It's the only way out! Take this Sue guy out for a walk and teach him some manners, will you? Or go the quick and dirty way—give him the pink slip and let him go. You are going to feel much better after he is gone.

From: Zack
To: Josh
Sent: 9/30
Subject: Re: bottom line?

I don't think he'd have gotten away with his nastiness for so long if his performance weren't top flight. As Victor told me, "The guy won't get a very high score during any Emotional Quotient test, but you'll love him when he works for you." He is meticulous, efficient, and experienced—the best I've got (in terms of pure performance). I'd have to be crazy not to want him on the team. Besides, I don't have the authority to fire anybody. After all, I am just a part-time manager. I think I might keep him for a while and try to make friends with him. People can change, right?

From: Josh
To: Zack
Sent: 10/2
Subject: Re: bottom line?

Well, then, I see you are trapped between a rock and a hard place. Wish you luck!

PS: I don't think this arrangement will work out. If I were you, I would kick him out. Hee hee . . .

Discussion Questions

1. What options does Zack have? What are the pros and cons of these options? Explain.
2. As Zack, how would you remedy the problems concerning Sue? Discuss in detail.
3. Evaluate Zack and Josh's management styles. Identify which one is better for the university center in this case. Why?
4. Explain why Sue confronted Zack. Could Zack fire Sue? Why or why not?
5. What is Victor's role? Is he key to solving the problem, as Josh claims? Explain.
6. If you were Victor, explain how you would help the new manager.
7. How do you characterize Mr. Greene? Is there any way he could be of more help? Explain.
8. As a new manager, describe how would you earn the respect of the longtime workers. Was Zack too soft towards Sue and other co-workers? Explain. What would be your plan of attack? Why did you choose this plan?
9. If you were Mr. Greene, how would you train new managers? Explain why this would be a good tactic.
10. Have you ever met an employee like Sue? If yes, give an example and describe how you dealt with him or her.
11. What do you make of Josh's advice? Try to characterize his management philosophy. Do you agree with him? Why or why not?
12. Are language and cultural gaps probable contributing factors in this case? Support your answer.
13. How do you deal with the increasingly diversified workforce in the hospitality industry? How can you communicate with people who can't speak English well?

Wellman State University

Background

Stevens Hall is one of three dining halls managed by a contract foodservice organization on the grounds of Wellman State University. Each dining hall has the capacity to serve 600–1,000 students per meal period. Stevens Hall serves approximately 500 students during the two-hour, forty-five-minute breakfast period; 600 students during the two-hour, forty-five-minute lunch period; and 800 students during the two-hour, fifteen-minute dinner period.

Most students purchase meal plan packages by the semester allowing them to eat in only one dining hall. Students select from three five-day meal plans: A—breakfast, lunch, and dinner; B—breakfast and lunch; and C—lunch and dinner. Separate meals can also be purchased: breakfast, $3; lunch, $5; and dinner, $7. For any meals consumed outside the meal plan, the student is charged the per-meal plan price plus $2.

Meals are served cafeteria-style. At lunch and dinner meals, students select one entrée from a choice of three, with unlimited side dishes and a choice of fresh fruit or a dessert item. The student is entitled to unlimited self-service beverages and salad bar. At the breakfast meal, the student has unlimited selections of toast, breakfast rolls, hot cereal, a hot entrée, self-serve beverages, and a cold cereal, fresh fruit, and yogurt bar.

The Staff

Local residents are hired to work in foodservice through the contract organization's central office on campus. Stevens Hall has two shifts of employees whose work times overlap. The A.M. shift is responsible for breakfast and lunch meals and consists of four cooks, two salad workers, two bakers, twenty students (who participate in service, cleanup, and so on), one supervisor, and one assistant manager. The P.M. shift is responsible for the dinner meal and any special catering orders and consists of seven cooks, thirty students, two supervisors, and one assistant manager. The salad and bakery departments prepare food items needed for both shifts. The dining hall has one manager who oversees the entire operation (see the Wellman State University organization chart).

As in any organization, the styles of leaders and followers differ. The A.M. assistant manager, **Sue Hobbs,** believes that she practices a participatory management style. In an effort to make equitable decisions, Sue solicits information and opinions from employees involved in and/or affected by the decision. She has an open-door policy and is available to help out wherever she is needed. She feels that her flexible, laid-back approach to leading is the best way to manage an operation. Occasionally she feels frustrated when an employee does not respond positively to her leadership style.

Jerry Adams, P.M. assistant manager, practices a more inflexible, autocratic leadership style. He tends to keep to himself and prefers to make decisions on his own, without consulting his staff. He frequently finds himself in crises regarding his staff members.

The manager, **Jackie Smith,** feels frustrated by the lack of direct contact she has with staff members. She is a flexible leader who is willing to allow her assistant managers to make decisions on their own without consulting her. When Jackie is in the hall, she is willing to help the assistant managers make decisions if they ask for her assistance. Because much of her time is spent in meetings and finalizing reports, she appears not to notice the details of her operation, but she actually has a good command of what is happening. Perhaps Jackie's greatest fault is her method of problem solving, which is nonexistent.

Most of the A.M. shift responds positively to Sue's leadership style. The department heads appreciate the opportunities they have to express their opinions and help make decisions. Two new cooks on the A.M. shift require a great deal of instruction for each task and must be monitored continuously while working to ensure task completion and acceptable products. Other employees appreciate the independence that Sue allows them, knowing they can depend on her help in any way, if needed.

Shirley Marcus, the A.M. supervisor, is also an independent worker. For the most part, she is reliable and can be depended on to complete any assigned tasks. She tends to be somewhat inflexible, feeling frustrated when the management staff appears to bend the rules or change decisions or policies. Shirley feels threatened by Sue's leadership style. Although she appreciates Sue's open-door policy and the opportunity to offer suggestions, Shirley feels that Sue's presence throughout the cafeteria indicates that Shirley is incapable of good work performance.

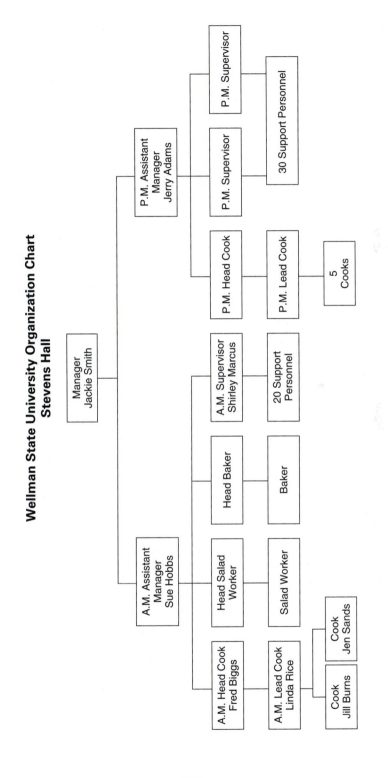

**Wellman State University Organization Chart
Stevens Hall**

A Discipline Problem

Jill Burns was thrilled six months ago when she was transferred from Brooks Hall, where she had worked for ten years as a salad worker, to Stevens Hall where she works as a cook on the A.M. shift. She received an hourly pay raise of $2.50. Jill is 38 years old, has never married, has no children, and has always approached any job in a responsible, conscientious manner. She has quiet mannerisms and is well liked by her co-workers. She wished she didn't need much job instruction, but knows that she has a lot to learn about being a cook and wants to be the best cook she can. Now, however, she feels she has been set up for failure.

Jen Sands also was thrilled six months ago when, after one year as a cook on the P.M. shift in Wells Hall, she received a transfer to cook on the A.M. shift in Stevens Hall. She needed to work the A.M. shift so she could be available to attend her children's after-school functions and maybe even get a part-time evening job to help make ends meet. Besides, she sensed that other employees on the P.M. shift didn't like working with her. She heard them talking about how she always seemed to make mistakes.

Jen is 40 years old and has two teenagers at home and a husband who has only seasonal work. She tends to approach any job as merely a means to make enough money to keep the bill collectors away. But she knows she must perform well at work in order to keep this job and its good pay and benefits. She resents the ongoing job instruction she receives from Sue, **Fred Biggs** (head cook), and **Linda Rice** (A.M. lead cook). She wished she could prove that she can do any task assigned to her.

Jen exhibits boisterous mannerisms and tends to ask questions or speak before thinking through her thoughts. She has a congenital disorder that causes her right eye to twitch constantly, giving her face a strange distortion.

Sue is wondering what went wrong in her working relationship with Jill and Jen. She knows that very few shift members seem to like Jen as a person and co-worker. In fact, the other cooks are quick to inform Sue of Jen's many failures. Sue has attempted to respond quickly and appropriately.

On Monday, October 11, Jen was assigned to make a coffee cake from scratch. The previous Friday, Linda had reviewed the ingredients and the procedure for the coffee cake with Jen. On Monday, Jen measured out all the required ingredients and mixed them according to the recipe. After the coffee cake was in the oven, Jen discovered that she had omitted the eggs in the recipe. Because she was cleaning up her work area, she simply threw the eggs away. The coffee cake failed. Sue and Fred reviewed with Jen the necessity of the eggs in the coffee cake in order to have a proper product. They discussed better ways to handle the situation. The incident was documented.

On Wednesday, October 27, Jen was assigned to prepare 300 hamburgers for the serving line. Ideally, no more than ten hamburgers should be held in the warmer at any one time. Hamburgers prepared this way take approximately twenty minutes to reach appropriate doneness. Fred reviewed with Jen the appropriate cooking method and timetable. However, within one hour of the lunch serving period, Sands had cooked all 300 hamburgers, although only 150 customers had been served. The other 150 hamburgers were held in a warmer for the remainder of the serving time. At the end of the serving period, the hamburgers were dry and inedible and had to be discarded. The incident was documented.

On Tuesday, November 9, Jen again was assigned to prepare the same coffee cake as earlier. This time Fred and Sue reviewed appropriate measuring and mixing methods for the coffee cake with Jen. Jen claimed that she followed the recipe correctly using all the ingredients, but she could not explain why the coffee cake never did rise. The incident was documented.

On Wednesday, November 17, Jen again was assigned to prepare 300 hamburgers for the serving line, with no more than ten held in the warmer at any one time. Sue and Fred reviewed the method with Jen and Sue helped her make up a timetable for preparation. Throughout the meal, Fred monitored Jen's progress. However, toward the end of the meal, Fred was called away to help another cook, and Jen soon had all the patties prepared. Again, they were held too long, and seventy-five hamburgers had to be discarded. Another documentation was placed in her file.

After consulting with Jackie, Sue wrote a letter of reprimand to Jen regarding the hamburger incident and Jen's failure to practice batch cooking. Jen was extremely upset. When she demanded an explanation, Sue stated that Jen's work performance was below average and very costly for the organization, based on the amount of product for which she was responsible that needed to be discarded. Jackie informed Fred about the letter. Jen felt misrepresented and betrayed by Sue as gossip spread throughout the kitchen.

Then, on Wednesday, November 24, Jen was instructed to lay up 450 corndogs (2 per serving) on 18-×-26-×-1-inch sheet pans. The pans were to be placed in a labeled, closed cart and put the cook's cooler so the frozen corndogs could temper at refrigerator temperature overnight.

The next day, Jill was assigned to fry the corndogs as needed on the service line. After only seventy-five customers had been served, Jill informed Fred that she was out of corndogs. They searched all the coolers and freezers for more corndogs. They informed Sue of the missing corndogs, and Sue repeated the search. After finding no more corndogs, Sue instructed Jill to prepare an alternate entrée for the remainder of the meal.

At the end of the meal, a large cart was found in the main cooler. It was boldly labeled "Corndogs" and filled with that product. Jen immediately took Sue aside and demanded that Jill also receive a letter of reprimand. Later, Jill took Sue aside and, tearfully, said that she felt set up.

Discussion Questions

1. Are there any forms of biases in this case? Explain your answer.
2. Did Sue handle the hamburger incident correctly? Is there a better way? Why or why not?
3. Should Jill receive a letter of reprimand? Why or why not?
4. Identify possible reasons for Jill to feel set up. Support your answer.
5. What action should Sue take? Why? What action should Jackie take? Why?
6. Are there better ways for Jen to deal with errors she made when preparing the coffee cake? Describe them. Why do you think she didn't do this?

A Conflict Problem

Sue Hobbs is feeling frustrated and confused. She transferred to this position in May after working as the P.M. assistant manager in Carter Hall. In November, during her informal oral six-month performance appraisal, Jackie gave her an excellent rating. Jackie stated that she enjoyed working with Sue and felt that her leadership style was a strong asset. Now, however, Sue is getting the "cold shoulder" treatment from the A.M. lead cook, Linda Rice.

On January 20, the full-time employees began their afternoon break twenty minutes early. Sue happened to be directing another employee in an area near the break room. Shortly after Sue left the area, Jackie entered the break room and directed the employees to return to work until the appointed break time. The next day, Linda left the break room whenever Sue joined the employees and, again, spoke to Sue only when it was absolutely necessary.

One month earlier, Linda had had her yearly formal written performance appraisal. Jackie conducted this appraisal using input from Sue. Linda received a generally acceptable performance review, with only a few areas needing improvement. These areas included abuse of break time limits and a need to increase supervision and "roaming/floating" aspects of her position. Prior to this performance review, Linda had seemed to work well with Sue.

In keeping with her open-door policy, Sue has offered, even pleaded, to discuss with Linda the cause of her sudden behavior change. Linda has refused, saying only that whatever the problem, it is something that Sue cannot change. Finally, on January 28, after three days of this behavior change, Sue discussed the situation with Jackie, who recommended that Sue allow Linda increased independence in her job. This recommendation is based on the work habits of the past assistant manager, **Teresa Holly.** Teresa would stay out of the day-to-day operation, allowing Linda to run the operation, intervening only when Linda came across a situation she could not handle. Jackie reminded Sue that Linda was not used to having a participative manager on her shift, suggesting that Linda felt threatened with Sue's continual presence. Jackie also told Sue that she had overheard Linda complaining that Sue is too aloof and does not want to be close friends with her staff.

Sue reluctantly agreed to try this leadership style. However, two weeks after allowing Linda independence, Sue feels that the operation is not functioning as smoothly as she expected. Indeed, in a quick sweep through the kitchen and dining room, she noted, on more than one occasion, flagrant disregard for the organization's policies by employees whom Linda supervises. Employees were observed serving portions that were larger than specified in the recipes, allowing customers to dine without paying, and eating and drinking while on duty. Sue feels that her hands are tied. How can she intervene when she is allowing Linda to be in charge?

Discussion Questions

1. Describe how Sue should deal with Linda. Support your answer.
2. What alternative courses of action are available? Which one would you choose and why?
3. What is the importance of being friends with employees? What are the dangers?
4. If you were Sue, what action would you take? Justify your response. How would you implement this action?
5. If you were Jackie, what would you do? Justify your response. How would you implement this action?

PART 7
Other Facilities

Buy-Lo Supermarket Bakery
Crystal Lake Resort
Department of International Relations and Tourism
Drake and Taylor
Vacation Time Resort

Buy-Lo Supermarket Bakery

The Dyersburg Buy-Lo Supermarket is part of a supermarket chain across the Midwest. Each store has a store manager and two assistant managers, and each department, such as the bakery department, has a manager. Although there are several full-time employees at Buy-Lo, mostly part-time high school and college students are employed. Recently two personnel issues have developed in the bakery department.

John Parker is the bakery department manager. About 150 assorted loaves of bread, 250 dozen hamburger buns, 200 dozen donuts and rolls, 50 dozen bagels, 100 dozen cookies, and 200 dozen wholesale items (items for delivery and pickup orders) are produced daily. There are two points of sale within the department: the display case and the shelves that hold bagged products.

There are four full-time bakers and one regular-time cake decorator (a regular time employee works thirty to thirty-nine hours a week and receives part of the benefits of full-time employees). In addition, eleven part-time employees work between ten and twenty-five hours a week.

There are three part-time shifts. Employees during the early morning shift, 3 A.M. to 9 A.M., ice donuts; place donuts on trays for the display case; box, wrap, label, and price donuts for the shelves; fill orders for delivery and pickup; and, as time allows, bag and label other bakery products for the shelves. The duties on the second shift, 9 A.M. to 2 P.M., consist primarily of bagging and labeling bakery items for the shelves. At times, employees are responsible for putting items on the shelves for sale. The other part-time shift begins in mid-afternoon and ends with closing, about 7 P.M. This employee is responsible for bagging and labeling remaining bakery items and boxing and wrapping items from the display case for the shelves. After this is completed, he or she washes trays that held products, sweeps the floor, wipes off counters, and cleans display case windows.

413

Bridgett

About two weeks ago, John hired **Bridgett Evans** because she seemed like she would be a good employee. However, with a problem that has developed lately, John is not sure he made a good decision in hiring her.

Bridgett is in her mid-thirties and a single mother of a teenage boy. To make ends meet, she also works at two other jobs. However, Bridgett cannot read or write. When John first realized this, he didn't see it as a major problem. There were jobs in the bakery that Bridgett could do without having these skills.

Lately, it has become clear that this situation could develop into a very large problem. He is afraid of losing Bridgett or other employees because of the friction occurring among everyone. Employees feel that they are doing Bridgett's work, which tends to result in a decrease in their efficiency. Service also has become slower.

John schedules only two or three part-time employees during a shift because he feels that that number is sufficient to complete the work. One employee takes care of filling orders and delivery, while the other two fill the display case with donuts, wrap bread products (depending on the shift), and help customers. Employees take turns answering the phone and taking orders for delivery and pickup, waiting on customers at the display case, and running the cash register. John also assigns special tasks as they arise.

John has realized that when Bridgett works, tasks don't get done as quickly or efficiently. There also are many complaints from employees about Bridgett not doing her share of work. John is concerned about losing customers and possibly employees.

John decided to watch closely the events that take place during Bridgett's shifts to determine the problem. He soon discovered that one employee ended up doing much of the work, while Bridgett usually bagged products for the shelves. Because she couldn't read, she never labeled or priced products. She also did not take orders over the telephone because she can't write. He also realized that she is having a hard time helping customers and is unable to run the cash register. This resulted in one employee trying to help customers, answer the phone, and label products for the shelves. During most of her shift, Bridgett was in the back bagging products.

John knows that something has to be done. His other employees dread coming to work when they are scheduled to work with Bridgett, and they talk about her when she isn't there. He realizes this is not a good working atmosphere. Also, production slows considerably during her shifts because other employees are covering for her lack of ability.

What should he do? He doesn't want to embarrass Bridgett or put her on the defense by calling attention to her illiteracy. Also, Bridgett is a good employee, is always on time, works hard, and always is willing to stay late if John asks her. She has shown an interest in learning new tasks, such as running the cash register, helping with baking products, and decorating cakes. However, John hasn't taken the time to determine what tasks she can do.

He knows she needs the job, and he needs good employees. But the problem seems to be getting out of hand and morale is decreasing. Something has to be done.

Mary

At the same time, John is working on another problem concerning **Mary Freeman,** who has been working at the Dyersburg Buy-Lo bakery for nearly a year. She is in her early forties and a single mother of a 17-year-old daughter. She is a very good worker and has never missed a day of work, is always on time, and is willing to stay late, if needed. The concern is that she is blind. When Mary first started, John knew it would take some time for his employees to adjust to working with someone who was blind, but he expected them to adjust after a few weeks. Unfortunately, this is not the case. Employees tolerated her at first, but they have become more and more resentful of the special things they have to do for her, such as getting labels and pricing them. Also, employees are complaining that they have to do all the work when Mary is scheduled. Tension is in the air.

John observed Mary at work for three weeks. He found that when she worked with some employees, she was more capable of doing her job than when she worked other employees. She bagged products and with some help, she could label them. He observed that she could tell the difference between types of products by shape as well as whether the product was wheat or white bread. She then asked for a specific label, and the employee working with her would get the labels and price them so Mary could put them on the bags. She then placed products on a rack so other employees could take them to the shelves. She worked very quickly and a lot of work got accomplished.

However, John observed that when Mary worked with a majority of employees, they essentially refused to work with her. They would not get labels and price them for her. They even told her she was in the way. On these days, productivity would drop considerably, and there was a lot of bickering among employees.

Although Mary has not complained directly to John, he knows she is unhappy. As a result, she has requested to work part of the week in the salad bar department. John is upset because he may lose a potentially valuable employee, but he doesn't know what he should do. He has tried to talk with the employees, but it hasn't seemed to do much good. Their actions improve for a few days, and then employees revert to their previous actions. He needs a way to help his employees understand the importance of working together as a team regardless of the employee's abilities.

Discussion Questions

1. How could John have prevented the problem with Bridgett? With Mary? Why would this work?
2. What options does John have in the situation with Bridgett? Which would you select? Why?
3. If he decides to keep Bridgett, what types of changes need to take place to remedy the situation? Defend your answer.
4. Describe how you would implement these changes.
5. What can John do now, if anything, to keep Mary in the bakery department? Justify your response.
6. Should John discipline employees for not working well with Mary? Why or why not?
7. As the store manager, how would you work with John to help him deal better with his employees? Why do you think your suggestions would work?

Crystal Lake Resort

The Johnson/Smith family reunion occurs every five years during the summer. The family spends a lot of time planning the reunion because they want it to be a special time for the eighteen families that attend. Family members take turns planning the reunion, and it usually is held in or near the city where the families who are planning the reunion live. **Steve** and **Ellen Johnson** and **Peter** and **Bonnie Smith** are responsible for organizing this summer reunion. They have decided to hold the reunion at the 150-room Crystal Lake Resort beginning the Sunday of the week in July in which July 4 falls. On July 4 and 5, there are firework shows over the lake for hotel guests.

They have a block of eighteen rooms held because even the families who live in the area stay at the hotel/resort. All rooms face the lake, so family members could watch the fireworks from their rooms. The resort is about ten miles from an international airport, which makes it convenient for the families who fly to the reunion.

Crystal Lake Resort was chosen because it has reasonable rates, a good reputation for quality service, and many amenities. One goal of each reunion is to spend time together as a family and not participate in other area activities. The resort has two restaurants, banquet rooms, and room service. In addition, there are tennis courts, lawn bowling, indoor and outdoor pools, an eighteen-hole golf course, a workout room, and a playground and indoor activity room for children. The resort is situated on Crystal Lake, with a beach for swimming and opportunities for water skiing. Three families have boats that will be accessible for the reunion, and Jet-Skis can be rented for a reasonable price.

The organizers were excited to get the reunion underway. Most family members would be arriving on the Saturday prior to the reunion. Because the reunion is in the Midwest, only three families would be arriving by air.

The Front Desk

Lindsey Kane, the front desk clerk on duty, was not excited about the weekend or the week to follow because she knew it would be very busy with the holiday. She is very frustrated because she seems to be scheduled for all holidays and evening shifts. Lindsey feels that she has no future because **Jeremy Liu,** the front desk manager, is a good friend of the manager. Jeremy has told her that he plans to stay at the Crystal Lake until he retires in ten years.

When several of the families who arrived in the late afternoon got together for cocktails, they commented that Lindsey was not very friendly or helpful. When **Mary Smith,** a mother of three small children, asked her what time the casual restaurant closed, Lindsey curtly said, "I don't know; you need to ask someone who works in the restaurant." Mary was not feeling too positive about the upcoming week if this was any indication of the friendliness of the staff. Her sister **Carolyn Ferris** commented that she hoped the whole staff was not rude, because she too felt that Lindsey had been short with her.

Mary and Carolyn had requested that their families have adjoining rooms so they could spend more time together. They were disappointed that this arrangement was not made, even though calls to the resort indicated that their rooms were next to each other. Because they were two of the earlier families to arrive, Lindsey begrudgingly moved their rooms.

Two families who were flying in also had requested adjoining rooms: **Jason Smith's** family from Arizona and **Nick Smith's** from Pennsylvania. Jason's flight was delayed due to mechanical failure, and he had notified Bonnie that they were not to be expected until close to midnight. Because rooms were guaranteed until 7 P.M., Bonnie notified the front desk of the delay. Lindsey said she would leave a note for **Pam Kruse,** who was to replace her at 11 P.M.

Bonnie stressed the importance of holding the room for them, but she was not aware of the plan for Jason and Nick to have their rooms next to each other. Nick had not arrived yet.

When Jason and his family arrived shortly after midnight, their reserved room was not available. Lindsey had not left a note for Pam because she was eager to get out of the hotel. Fortunately, there was room left, but it was not near any of the other family members' rooms. Jason and Nick were very disappointed.

The Banquet

A family banquet was scheduled for the last night, the same night as the second night of the fireworks. Many of the families did not stay up to watch the fireworks the first night, because the schedule for Saturday night included a banquet followed by fireworks. The banquet did not start as scheduled because an earlier banquet did not finish on time. The time delay was becoming a large inconvenience because it was getting later and later. Some of the family decided to eat in the restaurant instead of the banquet because their children were hungry. Steve asked **Al Jorhorst,** the banquet supervisor, to reduce the banquet charges because not all families ate at the banquet due to the delay.

Al could not make the decision. He had to ask **Jeannie Gillette,** the food and beverage director. Jeannie was out of town for the July 4 weekend, as was the general manager (GM) of the resort. Al was very apologetic, and said if he could do something to fix the problem, he would. The four-member planning team was extremely disappointed about the situation and Bonnie and Ellen didn't even enjoy the fireworks, nor did they sleep very well that evening. What was supposed to be a wonderful reunion at a resort with a fine reputation was becoming a nightmare. Al did contact Jeannie later that evening, and Jeannie approved reducing the banquet bill.

Training Programs

When Steve investigated, he found that nine months ago, the resort's GM had shifted the training responsibility from the human resources (HR) department to each department. He felt that the HR department was overworked with personnel issues, insurance, benefits, performance appraisals, recruiting and hiring activities, and public relations, so it would only assist with designing and implementing training. The training, however, would be left to each department. This meant that Jeremy would provide training for the front desk, **Helen Jaha** (the housekeeping manager), for housekeeping, and Jeannie for restaurant and banquet services.

Jeannie held frequent training sessions on meeting customer needs. Her intentions were good, but training videos were outdated, and she rarely took time to follow up on employees. She has never initiated a procedure for assessing customer satisfaction. On the other hand, she is very conscientious about keeping employees up to date on new policies and procedures, any major changes, and upcoming events. She holds monthly meetings to inform employees of these matters and encourages their input into any decisions that need to be made. However, she has the final authority and approves all decisions before they are implemented.

Jeannie and Helen have implemented a program to determine customer satisfaction. Customer satisfaction cards are left in each room with a notation that when the completed card is turned into the front desk, the customer will receive a 10 percent discount on one meal from the restaurant. Jeannie realizes the importance of meeting customer needs, but she lacks knowledge on what is required to attain this goal. She is learning a lot from Helen and some ideas she has implemented to get customer feedback.

The Housekeeping Staff

The Johnson/Smith family members were very pleased with the housekeeping staff. Bonnie especially noted that each morning when a housekeeper was cleaning her room, she took time to ask her if she was having a good time and enjoying seeing her family. However, on Wednesday when Bonnie asked the housekeeper how she could get a newspaper, the housekeeper told her about the free copies at the front desk and offered to get one for her. Bonnie wondered why she was not informed before asking. Even so, Bonnie was impressed with how the housekeepers seem to go beyond what was necessary. Their attitudes were positive compared to those of some of the front desk employees.

Helen provides a thorough training for the housekeeping staff. She realizes that her staff has limited interaction with guests, but knows that each encounter can make a difference. Helen wants customer feedback, so she has been instrumental in helping her staff take the comment card/10 percent discount offer seriously. The comment card is the size of a postcard and asks three questions: (1) How are we doing? (2)What can we do better? (3) How would you rate the friendliness of housekeepers, front desk, and food and beverage employees. She uses comments from these cards to reward her employees.

Helen empowers her staff to help guests in any way. Staff members recognize that Helen would prefer that they take time to make a guest happy, rather than ignore the guest to get their work done quickly. She also keeps an open line of communication with her staff, organizes monthly meetings with refreshments, and has a quality service committee that works on improvements and handles complaints and compliments.

The Smith/Johnson families had an average impression of the resort. They commented that front desk and banquet employees needed to take lessons from the housekeeping staff on customer service. It certainly would have left them with a more positive impression of the resort.

Discussion Questions

1. Did the employees have a negative or positive impact on the resort guests? Why or why not?
2. Suppose that you are Helen. You notice that many front desk employees are not providing quality service. In fact, you read that information on the comment cards. How would you convince Jeremy of the need to improve customer service?
3. Develop a quality service plan that Jeremy can implement. Explain how Jeremy should implement the plan.
4. What suggestions do you have for measuring customer satisfaction? Why do you think these suggestions would provide you with the information you need?
5. How can Jeannie improve her department's quality of service? What new ideas would you recommend? Support your ideas.
6. What barriers prevented the planning team from getting quality service? Were there barriers on the part of resort employees? Explain your responses. What would help eliminate these barriers? Why do you think that would work?

Department of International Relations and Tourism

Romania, a developing country in Eastern Europe (EE), wanted to become a member of the European Union (EU). Criteria required to obtain membership were related to economic and social development, having a strong economy and democratic institutions, and being capable of competing within the western markets. Because no EE countries met the criteria, the EU invented several tools to help EE countries reach Western European (WE) standards.

The EU provides a variety of grants (and sometimes long-term loans) to EE countries to help with economic development and investments. The grants are awarded according to strict guidelines in order to improve different areas of the economy (such as infrastructure development, transportation, social services, education, and tourism) and to help small businesses grow. Grants ranging from $15,000 to $150,000 per project are given two to three times a year based on the viability of the project and its potential to affect regional and national development. Once a grant is awarded, project implementation is supervised by EU officials to ensure that the EU money is spent according to the budget and that goals are accomplished. EU officials have the power to change the grant to a high-interest loan and deny future funding if they find inconsistencies. Therefore, it is important that the application and budget be prepared carefully and implementation be completed as specified.

Organization

The Regional State Administration (RSA) is located in a Romanian county and composed of different departments and offices that oversee the overall development of the region. One important activity in the region is tourism, and during the past years, the region has attracted many tourists, both international and national.

In the last fifteen years, the decrease in quality of services resulted in a lower number of tourists, so the RSA officials stated that tourism was one area to be developed in the region because it could be an important source of income in the local budget. Considering the shortage of money from Romania's central budget, the most important source of funding for implementation of the tourist development strategy was a grant from the EU. The Department of International Relations and Tourism (DIRT) was developed to do the following:

- Implement a strategy for tourist development in the region
- Submit a completed application for funding to the EU for tourist promotion
- Implement project, if funding is received
- Handle all international relations of the RSA
- Organize and accommodate visits of foreign delegations
- Escort foreign guests through the region; arrange accommodation, meals, and meetings throughout the territory; and provide interpretation services

DIRT falls under the direction of the president of the RSA (see the RSA organization chart), and seems to be the preferred department of the president. DIRT has good collaboration with the Department of Programs (DP), and has the following responsibilities:

- Submit completed application forms to EU for funding projects, other than tourism, and implement projects
- Keep contact with all local councils in the territory

A vice president of RSA oversees DP's direction. DIRT is composed of five people: Robert, head of DIRT, and Anna, John, Paul, and Andrew, all inspectors with different responsibilities within DIRT.

Robert Kostovich, the head of DIRT, has a degree in sociology and has taken several short-term courses in tourism promotion, eco-tourism, rural tourism, and European institutions and funding. At 55 years old, he has experience in tourism promotion and speaks French, German, and Russian. He is very friendly and acts as a link between other members of the department. He has a participatory leadership style and seems to get others to participate in the decision-making process. He is appreciated for his abilities and skills in working on important EU projects and has successfully coordinated the implementation of four major EU projects in the last two years. Periodically he goes to several international conferences, meetings and training sessions, and his absence affects regular department

Regional State Administration—Romania Organization Chart

The organization chart of RSA is represented in short. In reality it is more complex, but it is not relevant to the case.

activities. He puts people first and cares a lot about his employees. Everyone in the department is happy to work with him, as he is seen as a father or an older brother.

Anna Moranso is a 38-year-old inspector with a university degree in rural development and has participated in several short-term courses and training sessions in rural tourism, eco-tourism, mountain tourism, and European institutions. She has extensive experience in working with EU organizations and she was involved in communication with EU during implementation and evaluation of previous projects. She has good computer skills and the ability to write winning projects, of which she takes major leadership. She speaks English, French, and Italian. Anna is very friendly and helpful, but sometimes she seems hesitant in the decision-making process. However, she is a very good project team member.

John Molonavik, a 56-year-old inspector, is experienced in cross-border cooperation because he speaks all the Slavic languages. He lacks computer skills. Friendly but reserved, John is lazy and often late for work. He will retire soon and seems not to care about what is happening in the department. He is interested in earning money and welcoming Slavic guests. Other employees would describe John as a "laissez-faire" kind of leader.

Paul Natavik is a 24-year-old inspector with a university degree in tourism and several training sessions and short-term courses in eco-tourism, rural tourism, and European institutions and funding. Although young, he has good experience in working with EU organizations. Paul has good computer skills and is friendly and hardworking. He speaks English, French, and Italian. He is responsible for the proposal budget. He is considered a very good team member.

Andrew Narashki, a 26-year-old inspector, has a university degree in tourism but has no further training in tourism or EU funding. He has no experience in working with EU organizations, but he has good computer skills. He speaks only English. Although he is friendly, others feel sometimes he is selfish.

The Problem

On Monday, May 18, everyone was in the office except Robert. He is never late and often he comes to work early. Today, he was expected to come early because there was a lot of work to do:

- June 8 is the deadline for submitting a tourist project proposal to EU, which is vital for the implementation of the tourist strategy. In case of failure, the RSA would lose $150,000.
- On May 20, a French delegation is coming for two days.
- On May 24, a Ukrainian delegation is coming for seven days.

After several calls to Robert's home, two of his colleagues went there, where they found him drunk. It appeared that he had been drinking all night and was unable to go to the office. His colleagues found this strange, because he rarely drinks liquor, and he was drunk only once during the past three years. His colleagues decided to leave him at home to rest and went to the office to continue the daily duties without him. They informed the president, and he said he would talk privately to Robert about this issue.

The next day when Robert did not show up, his colleagues went to his home and found him drunk again. He incoherently explained his intention to retire to his colleagues. He insisted that they not call an ambulance because he would be okay. He promised to stop drinking. After a week of desperate calls and encouragement, they called an ambulance and Robert was transported to the hospital, where he stayed for a week.

In the meantime, problems accumulated in the department. Fortunately, everyone did their tasks very well, and the two delegations were handled fine, but because Robert was missing, accomplishing various tasks took longer than usual. Robert's absence caused a lot of disturbances with DIRT activities, especially with the tourism project work, because his role of linking all the information was essential.

On May 27, the president came to DIRT and insisted that Robert be replaced. This surprised Robert's colleagues because the president was a good family friend of Robert. The president had a short meeting with the inspectors in the department, saying that Robert would not be available, and Anna would take command for the next week. If she was not comfortable with that position, he would try to find another person. He told Anna that for the moment, she was the most appropriate person to take Robert's position until he found a solution. However, he informed her that she would remain in that position if she was able to do a good job. He also told Anna that the tourism project MUST be completed by the deadline, with or without Robert.

The president had two other possible candidates to replace Robert: John and **Peter Zympinski** (the head of DP). Other remote solutions would be Paul or Andrew, but they seemed to be too young to take that position.

Peter, with a degree in sociology and several short-term courses in European institutions and funding, has a lot of good experience. However, Peter does not speak any foreign languages and is computer illiterate. At 50 years old, Peter is a good manager who has a friendly relationship with the president. Moreover, Peter is an adviser to the president and has influence upon him. He has an authoritarian leadership style and tries to solve problems by himself. He usually does not give others a chance to use their abilities and skills. Peter seldom delegates and sometimes supervises his people so closely that they feel uncomfortable and are afraid to make mistakes. He is interested more in punishing a person for failing to do a task correctly than in explaining to him or her how to perform that task better. He knows almost nothing about tourism.

It is June 1 and Anna seems uncomfortable with the new position because she is not familiar with the daily routine discussions with the president and other important staff. She seems hesitant in making decisions. After one week, Anna refuses to be the department head and the position becomes vacant again. Because the deadline for submitting a EU proposal is approaching, the president wants to fill the position soon so that all the work during this very busy time can be coordinated. Mistakes are not permitted because RSA could lose the $150,000. An incorrect handling of foreign guests could have a negative impact on further international relations of the RSA. As DIRT is an important department, the president feels he needs to decide by the end of the day who should be the new head.

Discussion Questions

1. Why do you think Robert was so important for DIRT? Explain.
2. What should be done about Robert's drinking problem? Does this become a DIRT problem? Why or why not?
3. Why do you think Anna was chosen as the interim head? Support your answer. Would you have chosen her? Why or why not?

4. As the president, which of the possible options do you think would be best choice for the head of DIRT? Why?

5. If you were Anna, would you have taken the head position? Explain why or why not.

6. Do you think there is any way that Anna might be enticed into taking the head position? Why or why not? Would your reasoning work when Anna was first appointed as interim head? Why or why not?

7. What do you think the president's decision was by the end of the day? Justify your answer.

Drake and Taylor

Brian O'Riley eagerly opened the letter he had just received from his company headquarters. Drake and Taylor, a United Kingdom–based management consulting firm with 114 divisions throughout the world, had submitted a winning bid to assist the Armenian government in privatizing its industries, including a large tourism sector. Companies submitted project bids to the government agency, which then selected the winning project according to established criteria, such as low cost for high-quality services. This letter confirmed his new appointment as a project manager for the Eastern European country of Armenia, a newly independent state that had emerged from the former Soviet Union.

The European Union (EU) had provided the Armenian government with financing for privatization of state-owned enterprises, with a stipulation that European companies would do the project. Due to difficulties that Armenia had experienced in its transition to a market economy after the collapse of the Soviet Union, the Armenian government could no longer finance any industry sector. The tourism industry, once one of the country's largest sources of revenue, was no longer profitable. Thus, a major part of the project was preparation of the country's four largest hotels for international sale. The hotels' assets would be evaluated and an initial price established. Interested international investors would then compete to buy the hotels, which would be sold to the highest bidder. The Armenian government viewed these sales as the most viable solution to the hotels' many problems.

Brian intended to hire and train a team of local specialists who would assist international consultants and work with each hotel's management. In addition, the team also would serve to link each hotel manager to the government privatization agency.

Brian, who has an MBA degree from New York University, was a successful and highly respected executive manager in a large company for the past fifteen years. However, at age 56, he looks 65 years old, a result of extensive work hours and his recent divorce, initiated by his wife. Feeling that he needed a change and that this would be a pivotal year in his life, he had expressed a willingness to relocate and sent his résumé to headquarters, asking to be considered for the new project. He was longing to travel to the unknown country of Armenia for new opportunities and, he hoped, for more relaxed working conditions.

The four hotels that were to be prepared for the international tender were located in the country's capital, Yerevan. They had historical Armenian names: Ani, Dvin, Yerevan, and Armenia. In the past, the hotels had operated at full capacity throughout the year, with most tourists coming from the former Soviet states. At the time Brian arrived, the hotels were hardly covering maintenance costs because there were no tourists.

Launching the Project

Upon arrival, Brian was provided a one-room office on the same floor as the State Privatization Commission (SPC), which was working toward privatization of state-owned enterprises. The office building was located across from the Armenia hotel.

The Armenia was located on the Republic Square, the most popular public area in Yerevan, and was of particular interest to international investors because of its location, capacity, unique architecture, and well-maintained condition. The Yerevan and Ani hotels were located within walking distance, and the Dvin hotel was located within a few miles from the square.

As a first step, Brian's local team worked closely with management of each hotel, preparing important information about the hotel's assets and its business plan. The government would then be asked to approve the hotels for privatization and international sale. Brian soon learned that no existing educational institutions in Armenia trained hospitality specialists. Instead, there were two newly established Western-type universities, which were to produce their first MBA graduates in a few months. In Eastern Europe, "Western-type institution" implies an educational model found in North America or Western Europe (one of the new colleges was an affiliate of a university in California; the other was an affiliate of a university in Beirut, Lebanon).

Brian began by gathering current information about recruiting employees and understanding Armenians' work habits. Brian talked to the chief advisers of various EU-funded projects occurring in Armenia and to several government officials involved in the privatization process. By doing so, Brian thought he could gain valuable advice and would be able to choose the right people to work for him. In addition, he believed that finding qualified people would be easy because he would be paying in foreign currency, and would be offering three times the minimum salary paid in Armenia. Brian decided to hire the most essential staff members during the first months. Once he learned more about the country's culture, he planned to hire more people, if needed.

Finding qualified, educated employees in Armenia—where 98 percent of 3.5 million people have at least a high school education—was not going to represent any challenge for Brian. However, the challenge was in finding people with good computer and English-language skills. Thus, Brian initially set the following selection criteria:

- Excellent knowledge of English (for the translator)
- Basic understanding of English (for supporting staff)
- Knowledge of Word and Excel computer programs
- College degree (major not specified)

Soon after the job announcement was printed in a widely read, local newspaper, Brian had a pool of candidates to consider.

The Staff

Ann Dvionian, who was 36 years old, bright, and computer literate, was the first employee hired as an English translator based on her excellent communication skills and previous work experiences. Brian considered himself lucky to have hired her because she could explain the people's perceptions and expectations as well as the local business culture to him. Ann also would be responsible for translating all necessary documentation from Armenian into English.

Brian felt comfortable selecting **Diane Cholukian** as a computer operator from all candidates. She had excellent computer skills, spoke some English, and had a good recommendation from a foreign adviser with whom she had worked.

Because Brian did not speak Armenian and felt uncomfortable about driving in a foreign country, he needed someone to provide transportation and help him do his grocery shopping. **Nicholas Asatrayan,** introduced to Brian by a government official from the SPC, had a résumé stating a college degree in mathematics, but he had assured Brian that he was willing to do any job to support his extended family. Nicholas spoke little English, but because Brian had no other support-staff candidates who spoke English at all, he hired Nicholas on the spot. Brian had expected to allocate funding to provide English-language training for his employees.

Initially, Brian wanted to follow the recruitment and staffing procedures that were conventional in the United States, such as using newspaper announcements and interviews. However, he soon received calls from SPC officials mentioning their relatives as the best candidates. Although this hiring practice seemed unethical to Brian, he sensed that he would need the support of those officials, and therefore he promised that he would interview their relatives—Alex, Robert, and Natalie—among other candidates. **Alex Miroumian** and **Robert Arkovichian** had degrees in physics and economics, respectively, and had only basic knowledge of English. With the collapse of the Soviet Union, they both lost their jobs. **Natalie Asravian** was a senior in computer science at Yerevan State University. Brian was hesitant to hire them, but did so when he experienced increasing pressure from the government officials. Finally, after consulting with Ann, he decided to give all three of them a chance. Alex, 38, was hired as an office manager; Robert, 39, was hired to assist the managers of the hotels; and Natalie, 21, became a part-time secretary.

For the first month, Brian and his small team, while waiting for foreign consultants to arrive in a few weeks, were involved in routine discussion of various important privatization issues with the SPC. Additionally, Brian's team was preparing two privatization surveys. With the help of foreign professors who were teaching in the two newly established Western-type colleges in Yerevan, Brian hired second-year MBA students to conduct these privatization surveys for him. Having the MBA students conduct the surveys gave Brian an opportunity to select the best candidates as additional staff members, and thus make his own hiring decisions along with practicing more conventional ways of recruitment.

Brian became acquainted with **Mary Yervanian** through her participation in the surveys and preparing reports on the findings. Mary, who was expecting to graduate from an MBA program in a month, did not seem interested in the privatization project. Brian perceived that she had a "can-do mentality" as well as the skills needed for the project. Mary was intelligent, worked hard, and had a warm personality along with excellent communication and interpersonal skills. Initially, Brian hired her on a temporary basis, so that he could observe her performance and efficiency in various tasks and situations. Soon he noticed that his permanent staff, managers of the hotels, foreign consultants, and government officials enjoyed working with her. Within a few months, Mary became more involved and more interested in her job. Consequently, Brian hired her as a permanent consultant to work with the hotel managers and to assist foreign consultant groups.

As the numbers of tasks in the project increased, Brian added **Greg Ferlechian,** an MBA graduate, to assist him in preparing financial documentation on the hotels. **Angie Adamirian,** a recent graduate of Yerevan State University's English department, was hired as a part-time English translator. Thus, by late that year, Brian's office had nine team members. The tasks were shared fairly, and the office operations seemed to run smoothly. Groups of EU consultants frequently visited and worked with the team. Brian was satisfied that he had a good team and that all team members sensed that they shared the same goals. He therefore thought he could assign tasks and leave Armenia for a week or two at a time.

The Conflicts

Mary liked the people with whom she worked, but periodically she noticed increasing tension between Nicholas and Alex, or between Alex and Angie, Diane, or Natalie. When Brian was absent, Nicholas would try to convince his co-workers that Brian was very stingy. Nicholas assumed this based on information he got from people working on similar projects. He knew that Brian was underpaying him and probably underpaying the rest of the staff as well. Nicholas also would complain that Brian was checking the mileage on his car frequently to avoid paying more than a set amount for travel expenses. Nicholas felt he was overworked by being required to provide transportation for Brian and the foreign consultants as well as running all office errands. Nicholas eventually won Angie to his side. Mary and Ann, however, argued that all salaries were fair and that Brian had spent a considerable amount of money on English classes, office picnics, and help of one kind or another for all employees.

Alex was trying to take over Brian's role while Brian was out of the country, and frequently would direct the staff to do tasks other than the ones Brian had assigned because Alex considered them of higher priority. In Brian's absence, Nicholas usually showed up in the morning and soon disappeared for a few hours, which irritated the office staff, especially if they needed transportation to the hotels. Alex would complain that Nicholas was out of the office for several hours almost every day, and Alex also needed Nicholas to drive him on personal business. Nicholas would answer sharply that he was not Alex's personal driver.

Nicholas sometimes would disappear for the entire day, which irritated Alex even more. Alex would then put pressure on the rest of the staff, who thought he was treating them as his servants. For example, he would assign Angie to wash his tea or coffee cups, or he would use Diane to type his personal communication, which disrupted Diane's work. Angie and Diane would object to such behavior on Alex's part. Mary and Greg would be met with rude responses from Alex when they tried to intervene. They did not like Alex and Nicholas's behavior in the office, but agreed that it was Brian's responsibility to solve the problem.

When Brian returned from one of his trips, Angie told him how Alex had treated her. Natalie and Diane confirmed what Angie said and also told Brian about their work environment concerns. Brian expressed surprise and concern about what had happened, and he promised to talk to Alex about his behavior. In the next few weeks, the situation seemed to settle down, especially after Brian hired a part-time housekeeper for tasks such as washing dishes. Brian also talked to Alex in private, and at least for a few days, Alex seemed calmer and treated the staff politely.

However, Alex continued to create tension in other ways. He would try to alter most of Brian's decisions, and he objected to new ideas of the team members, doing so in a highly opinionated way. Brian would try to disagree or respond to Alex in a diplomatic manner, which obviously required a great deal of patience. These incidents were very stressful for everybody.

Robert, who appeared to have excellent communication skills and had shown commitment toward his work at first, also changed his behavior. He and Alex frequently left work for several hours without notifying anyone of their destination. Upon their return, they would state that they had needed to get some important information from a hotel manager. Brian sometimes appeared annoyed by this behavior, but he usually would remain patient and try to assign separate tasks to them in an attempt to keep them apart.

To condone their absences, Robert and Alex frequently told Mary and Greg (in Armenian) that they shouldn't take work so seriously. When Brian was not present, Alex and Nicholas often would engage in spats and exchanges of sharp words. Mary would try to avoid such displays and was glad that she could be out of the office much of the time, working with the management in the hotels. She kept very busy attempting to accomplish her tasks, which she enjoyed. But Greg, who was very quiet, increasingly expressed concerns about the office tension and once told Mary that he was looking for other job opportunities.

Despite a great deal of stress in the office, most hotel documentation, preparation of hotel business plans, and translation into English had been completed by the fall. This was accomplished primarily through the hard work of Brian, Greg, Ann, Mary, Diane, and Angie. The local team was expecting the last group of foreign consultants, who were to conduct an independent assessment of hotel assets as well as develop several scenarios of how the properties could be sold through international bids.

Brian was facing difficult times. He had developed health problems, including a cataract and a painful injury to his right foot. Consequently, he needed surgery and a six-week recovery period at the very time the consultant team was expected to arrive. Brian had never been absent from the office for so long. He wanted to assign Alex, as he had done before, to coordinate the work. However, Brian was apprehensive about the outcome of such an assignment, because the relationships among Alex, Nicholas, and the rest of the team were very poor. Additionally, his translator had told him that several team members planned to quit if Alex received such an assignment. Brian then considered Mary as another possible candidate to manage the office in his absence.

Brian consulted Ann about his concerns and asked for her opinion. Ann knew many SPC government officials, including Alex's brother. Ann told Brian that Alex and his brother would verbally harass Mary if Brian denied Alex the opportunity to coordinate the work. Also, Ann warned Brian that Alex and his brother (who had a very abrasive personality) would create obstacles to completion of the work. However, Ann told Brian that she along with Diane, Angie, and Natalie would quit, because they would find it impossible to work under Alex's management.

Brian was left with a very delicate and hard decision to make.

Discussion Questions

1. What problems did Brian face upon his arrival in Armenia? Could he have avoided any of them? If so, how? If not, why?
2. What would you have done when approached by SPC officials to hire their unemployed relatives? Explain how you would ensure that your actions were right.
3. Which problems became worse with the passage of time? What underlying reasons account for the worsening of the situation? Explain.
4. What could Brian have done to improve the quality of the work in his office? Why do you think these measures could have helped?
5. If you were Brian, what decisions would you make before you leave the office? What are your alternatives? What would you do? Why?
6. What problems may arise while Brian is gone? Explain why you think these might occur.

Vacation Time Resort

Vacation Time Resort (VTR) is a family-oriented resort located on a lake in the Midwest. It is open year-round but most of its business is between April and October. The resort includes front desk, reservations, sales and promotions, janitorial, maintenance, supply, grounds, security, recreation, shops, and food and beverage departments. There are two restaurants, a lounge, three gift shops, two pools, an exercise room, a game room, and a marina on premise. VTR serves as the reservation office for itself and three other properties.

VTR has 66 timeshare units and 106 rental units. These units consist of luxury townhouses, one-bedroom suites, studios, rustic cabins, standard rooms, an executive suite, and a bridal suite. Employees also are responsible for the Long Beach property, about a quarter-mile away. Long Beach has a restaurant and lounge, thirty-one apartment-like rooms, and fifteen condominium-like rooms that are rented seasonally.

Approximately 200 people are employed during the summer. A majority of employees are from the immediate area and are interested in part-time work.

Since July, occupancy has been below normal because of flood conditions in the area. Long Beach, except for the seasonally rented units, was closed on July 10 due to flooding. Several reservations were cancelled at the last minute. However, units at VTR were resold to several people from other areas who lost their homes in the flooding.

Steve Rettallick is the general manager of both properties. He has worked for VTR since it opened twenty years ago. For the most part, Steve is an easygoing manager who fits into the vacation scene. He is laid back and doesn't interfere too much with employee matters. However, he has been made aware of some personnel problems in the front desk department. It seems that most employees are unhappy with a new employee's lack of productivity and poor work habits.

The Staff

In March, **Dorothy Vallier,** the front desk manager, and **Liz Walker,** the human resources manager, hired **Kent Schlenker** and four other employees to work at the front desk during the summer months. Kent is a college graduate with no experience in the hospitality industry. The other four employees have moderate hospitality work experience, and two are hospitality management students at a local two-year college. In April, Dorothy was promoted to rooms manager, and **Eileen Payer** was promoted from front desk representative at another property to front desk manager at VTR. It was decided that Eileen would schedule employees, and Dorothy would overlook all operations at the front desk this summer because Eileen lacked training experience.

At the beginning of July, Dorothy told Steve that she would be leaving VTR because her husband had taken a new job in Texas. She would stay on until their house had sold, but didn't expect to be at VTR past the end of August.

At the beginning of summer, there were two night auditors plus one part-time night auditor/guest service representative, two switchboard operators, and five guest service representatives. Within three weeks, one night auditor and the part-time night auditor/guest service representative quit. Nobody else was hired, so a service representative was trained to do night audit part-time.

Temporary employees were introduced to the resort during a special summer orientation. Any other training was left to department heads. Eileen went through the front desk manual with all new employees, but other training was done in the work setting during normal hours of operation, basically training as the situation arose.

Kent started out with a really good attitude and seemed to try his hardest. He was easy to talk to and would often speak with guests, making them feel comfortable. It was obvious he had never worked in hospitality operations, but with proper training it appeared that he shouldn't have any problems.

Problems with Kent

Three weeks after Kent started working, his behavior changed. It seemed he could become a difficult employee if his habits were not corrected. He showed up late several times with no real excuse; he started to challenge leadership and his actions around other employees were not appreciated. Several times, employees cringed when he communicated to guests in a rude manner. By the end of June, Kent's conduct had been reported several times to Eileen and Dorothy.

Employees had few expectations from Dorothy, who was putting in minimal effort after she made it known she was leaving. Dorothy and Eileen talked about Kent and their options. Firing him was not one of them unless another employee could be hired, because the front desk was understaffed. Dorothy was not interested in confronting Kent with her concerns, so she decided to take all front desk employees through a refresher training session.

Dorothy and Eileen held a special meeting with the employees and went over the entire front desk manual. They thought that if they held the training session and told all employees about the complaints they were receiving, the employees would work together and work harder. Using this session would alleviate the need to single Kent out from the other employees. However, when the employees left the training session, they were upset. They did not feel responsible for the complaints that were being received, and they did not think it was fair that Kent's behavior was handled in this manner. Again, they blamed Dorothy's action on the facts that she was leaving soon and Eileen was too new to handle the situation.

About two weeks after the training session, Kent's negative attitude became more noticeable than ever. He hung up on guests and potential customers. He actually appeared a bit arrogant. Other employees felt that he had not gotten the message from the training session. His customer service continued to decline. For example, while he was running guest lists, three guests wanted to check in. He tried to check them all in at the same time as well as keep an eye on his guest listings that were printing. This disregard for guests upset several employees. The guests were becoming agitated as they waited, with the first guest in line commenting that service should be done on a first come, first served basis. In addition, tardiness continued. All desk employees worked one of three eight-hour shifts between 6 A.M. and 11 P.M. Kent often worked the 6 A.M. to 2 P.M. shift. The employee who was in charge of the shift and the cash drawer often noted the times Kent arrived. Documentation showed he almost always was late by five to fifteen minutes, and several times by thirty to sixty minutes. Dorothy met with Kent to discuss his behavior.

At this point in the summer, Steve began to sense that things at the desk were probably worse than they had been in past years. He was especially concerned because during the flood many victims were accommodated. He wanted these people to have the best treatment possible because of the hardship they were experiencing.

Guests, **Robert Garske** (the night manager), and other employees brought several complaints against Kent to Dorothy and Eileen. They finally decided to meet to discuss Kent. Dorothy wanted to fire him, but Eileen would not do so unless someone else was hired. This decision was followed by Dorothy telling Eileen that she could not have a day off without checking with Dorothy. Dorothy met with Kent again and told him he would be terminated if his attitude didn't improve. Kent left the meeting angry and vented his feelings with co-workers at the front desk. He told them he had been trying hard to do his job well, and he thought he was an asset to the company. He decided Dorothy didn't like him. His attitude became worse. He decided that if they wanted to fire him that was fine with him; he could easily find another job in the resort community. His behavior improved for the next two weeks, but then he regressed to his old ways of displaying a bad attitude, upsetting guests, and coming to work late.

Realizing that Eileen and Dorothy were not going to do anything about Kent, Robert spoke to Steve. Robert stressed the fact that something needed to be done.

Steve told Robert he was aware of the situation and agreed it was a problem. However, he had given Dorothy the responsibility of the front desk this summer and wanted her to handle it. Robert suggested that Dorothy might be part of the problem. Steve responded that he didn't want to overstep Dorothy because she had such little time left at VTR. He emphasized that there would be changes soon. Robert took this to mean that when Dorothy left, there would be opportunities for improvement at the front desk.

Eileen was sick of trying to deal with Kent and all the employee and guest complaints. She went to **Galen Yaeger,** the human resources employee, and asked him to start recruiting new employees. A week later, she went back to find out what Galen had done. He had done nothing. She gave him another week only to find out that he still had not done anything about advertising for new employees. By this time, Eileen was tired of trying to deal with everyone. She decided to try to make do with what she had. It seemed that she had no choice.

Discussion Questions

1. What options does Eileen have? Which would you choose? Why?
2. Could Kent's problem have been prevented during the hiring process? Support your answer.
3. How would you conduct the meeting with Kent? Why would your suggestions work? Would you have a third meeting? Why or why not?
4. If you were Kent's co-worker at the front desk, what actions would you take? Why?
5. Should Eileen overstep Dorothy's authority? Why or why not? What consequences might Eileen face if she did? Why do you think these will be consequences?
6. What problems can result when an employee has lost his or her commitment to the organization because the employee is leaving? Explain why each is a problem. What would you do with someone like Dorothy who is just waiting to leave? Why would you do this?

Contributors

Jean Anderson
Karina Belzilex
Erika Bierman
John Britto
Anthony Cawdron
M. Chang
Chi-Ting Chen
Yi Chen
Curtis Downs
Dawn Fiirh
Mary Harrington
Jane Heikenen
Yu-chen Hwang
Kent Johnson
Gwenda Kingland
Maria Kiswanto
David Knutson
Georgios Komodromas
John Kramer
Judith Lemish
Gina Lopezi
Katherine Lynott

Michael MacHatton
Vern Markey
Marina Miroumian
Cristian Morosan
Freeman Moser III
David Olds
Caroline Palmer
Don Paulson
Jiang Peng
Kevin Roberts
Dee Sandquist
Lynnly Schiebel
Marcus Scott
Jackie Steffens
Weiwen Sung
Justin Triebel
Bhanu Verma
Barbara Walline
Phillip Walters
Faith Washington
Heng Xu